Hit Me,
FRED

Hit Me, FRED

· · · · ·

Recollections of a Sideman

FRED WESLEY Jr.

Duke University Press

Durham and London

2002

© 2002 Duke University Press
All rights reserved
Printed in the United States of
America on acid-free paper ⊗
Designed by Amy Ruth Buchanan
Typeset in Melior by Tseng
Information Systems, Inc.
Library of Congress Cataloging-in-
Publication Data appear on the
last printed page of this book.

• • •

There are so many people who
have contributed to my being the
man, the musician, the human
being that I am and having the
happy life that I have today. I
hesitate to list them individually
for fear of leaving out someone
very special. Instead, I would
like to dedicate this book to my
brother, Ronald S. Wesley,
without whom I would not be
alive. Thanks Ron. I will never
be able to repay you or express
how important your support and
faith has been to me. I love you.

Contents

List of Illustrations ix

Foreword xi

1. A Musical Upbringing 1

2. Higher Education 31

3. Uncle Sam's Army 55

4. James Brown 84

5. California 115

6. James Brown Again 132

7. Bootsy's Rubber Band and
    Parliament/Funkadelic 190

8. Count Basie 211

9. Hollywood, Hollywood 228

10. Mile High in Denver 263

11. JB Horns 285

12. Star Time 301

Selected Discography 313

Index 317

Illustrations

Fred Wesley Sr. 2
Fred Wesley Sr., Mrs. Vetta S. Wesley, Mrs. Janie Wesley Panting 3
Fred Wesley Sr.'s Downtown "White Gig" 7
The Rhythmic Sensations, 1947 8
Thaddeus Williams and Fred Wesley Jr., age 14 16
Mobile Bandmasters 19
Joe Lewis 23
Funk Brass Pioneer, Mack Johnson 39
Sergeant "Pete" Petracco 62
CWO Bob Edmonds 62
Tom Zale 62
Esteban Romero-Sepulveda 62
John Klink 65
Ray Lamier 65
Perry Parks 65
Hurricane Alice, me, and Spot 70
Mastersound 76
Ms. Gertrude Sanders 86
James Brown Band on the Road 87
In Our New Black and Proud Outfits 108
Clifford Solomon 118
Sam and the Goodtimers 120
Clifford and Me 121
Phelps "Catfish" Collins 134
Dave Matthews 136
Me and Bob Both 153
Ladies of the James Brown show 173
Surrounded by Africans 174
James Brown and my Daughters 188

Maceo and Bootsy 193

Clarence "Fuzzy" Haskins 195

Horny Horns 204

Backstage 213

Count Basie Band Dressing Room 216

Count Basie Band at Disneyland 220

Basie at Home 224

S.O.S. Band 236

Ernie Fields 241

Studio 245

Rudy Copeland 253

Dr. Theodric Hendrix and Patience Dabany 254

Me, Steve Williams, Ernie Fields 256

Bad Days 261

Ron Wesley 264

Me and David Nelson 269

Bruno Carr 271

Andy Weyl and Me 272

Joe Bonner 274

Ken Walker 274

Joe Keel 278

Mr. Homer Bown 278

Teresa Carroll and me 278

Jim Payne 287

Bob Greenlee 287

The JB Horns 288

Maceo Parker Band, November 1994 297

I Can't Go No Further 311

Foreword

Rickey Vincent

• • •

Well, here it is, the definitive take on the life of a jazz musician who can play The Funk. But not just any jazz musician. Fred Wesley is easily the greatest trombonist alive today. If you judge him by his definitive swanging jazz-funk soloing style; his chart-topping recording accomplishments; the body of legendary music he has arranged, produced, and recorded; the depth, breadth, and range of his touring and performing background; or his pure longevity, Fred Wesley is one of the world's Master Musicians.

While Fred Wesley is a unique and uniquely enduring character in black music, his life encompasses the struggles and aspirations of generations of black musicians. What you hold in your hand is the archetypal story of every black musician of the past forty years. Yet these forty years have undergone wave after wave of revolutionary change, from the rhythmic foundations of funk to the changing racial composition of soul and jazz to the technological innovations of synthesizers and samplers, all of which make up the music we live with today—and Fred Wesley was there in the engine room making that revolution happen.

So much of black music has taken from the Fred Wesley sound. As bandleader for James Brown for most of 1970–75, Fred was responsible for some of the greatest funk tracks ever recorded: "The Payback," "Papa Don't Take No Mess," "Get on the Good Foot," "Pass the Peas," and "Doin' it to Death," among so many others.

In response to the brilliance of the JBs, in the early 1970s many other acts—such as Kool & the Gang, Tower of Power, the Average White Band,

War, and Earth, Wind & Fire—developed their own "big band" sound with jazzy horns and funky grooves. At its peak during the Mothership Connection days, George Clinton's P-Funk Empire was driven by the outrageous and undeniable sounds of Fred Wesley's horn arrangements. Nowadays everyone in hip-hop, from Dr Dre to D'Angelo, is looping or snooping around Fred Wesley's funky tones to get that "sweet and tangy" lick into their sound.

The career of Fred Wesley covers the entire revolution in music: from be-bop jazz to the high energy rhythm and blues of Ike and Tina Turner, two hellacious stints with the Godfather of Soul James Brown, an outrageous excursion on the P-Funk Mothership, a dreamy tour with the serendipitous Count Basie band, and all kinds of adventures as a session producer in and around the Los Angeles music scene.

But *Hit Me, Fred* is so much more than a musician's memoir. It is that story that has needed to be told ever since the myth of Motown in the 1960s manufactured for America that Horatio Alger rags-to-riches story of integration in popular music. As a black music memoir, *Hit Me, Fred* has more in common with Charles Mingus's outrageous *Beneath the Underdog* and Miles Davis's *The Autobiography* than with James Brown's comparatively polite autobiography *The Godfather of Soul.*

The life of a black musician in America is fraught with private glories and public disappointments. The tedium of practice and the seemingly unresolvable conflicts between personal growth and personal success with your instrument is vividly explained by Fred. Fred Wesley explores with style and sass the essential elements of life as a modern musician: the generosity and wisdom of musical elders that helped him to learn his craft and become the most recognizable trombone player in the world; those bitter yet necessary trials of starving on the road with act after sorry act in the 1960s, reliving those horror stories and folktales for a generation of soul brothas and sistas who have "paid their dues"; those fleeting moments of glory, whether on record, on stage, or, as occasionally happens, in contact with true respect and acknowledgment of a lifetime of work; and that ever-so-sad cycle of anonymity and humiliation afforded to great black musicians of this generation. Fred combines a gracious tolerance with a feisty bitterness that brings all these emotions into focus.

While it's bad enough for once-proud bandleaders to suffer the indignities of obscurity, the extremes tolerated by sidemen are truly dramatic, and Fred speaks volumes for *every* struggling musician, from those who have enjoyed moments of glory and fame to those who never will, yet who will never waver from their life's calling—to play. At the same time, Fred knows intimately what it takes to become a "star" in this business, and anyone with aspirations to success needs to bear witness to Fred's attitude, humor, and expertise.

Fred has been through it all in black music. The trials and tribulations he experienced during his early efforts as an Army Band performer, a rhythm and blues sideman, and a frustrated jazz musician reveal as much about our culture as does his tenure with superstars Ike and Tina Turner, James Brown, George Clinton, or Bootsy Collins. *Every* person he recounts is important to his narrative, for a great musician is the sum of all of his or her influences, and Fred Wesley's sound and style is a combination of all the characters and committed artists he has ever worked with and learned from.

Hit Me, Fred also explores the status of black musicians within black working- and middle-class family life. The precarious relationship between entertainment and art, and the difficult line between playing and making a living are universal torments that Fred brings to life ever so vividly in these pages.

Fred's passion for jazz is utterly delicious, the yin and yang of his commitment to The Funk is fascinating, and his love-hate relationship with James Brown is simply hysterical. The Godfather will never be seen in the same light again. Yet, as harsh as Fred's words for James Brown are, the greatness of Soul Brother Number One continues to resonate through Fred's book and through black music in general. It is essential to understand the incredible operation James Brown amassed—an operation that pulled Brown himself along with dozens of other obscure yet driven black artists to the pinnacle of success and global celebrity—surely, one of Black America's greatest achievements. However, to fully understand the power involved, one must delve beyond the myth-making and examine the often ruthless methods of a man known around the world as the "Hardest-Working Man in Show Business."

Fred Wesley is there in every way. He is a tagalong musician, learning from the masters, Alfred "Pee Wee" Ellis and Maceo Parker; he is a team player, finding his place among the luminaries in the James Brown band; he wins the confidence of Mr. Brown and becomes bandleader himself, participating in some of the most important black music ever recorded. All the while, Fred Wesley navigates his role as sideman to a superstar, often backing up Mr. Brown even when he doesn't think Brown deserves it.

This story goes far beyond the contrived accolades of outsiders. It is an inside story of life with James Brown that every fan of black music should know and understand. Fred Wesley exposes for all time the levels of pain and sacrifice needed to make "Star Time" sparkle worldwide. Of course as a card-carrying funkateer, I'm also thrilled to read about Fred's exploits with George Clinton, Bootsy Collins, and the P-Funk mob, where he characterizes himself as the only earthling among a band of funky spacemen who were just visiting from the "Chocolate Milky Way."

What black folks have needed for at least a generation is a bold, incisive discussion of our music, of what motivates us to generate such powerful sounds, and of what keeps us so maligned and "forever suffering." *Hit Me, Fred* is that window into the workings of a subculture that has taught the world to dance. Most importantly, this book tells the story of Fred Wesley Jr., son of a music teacher, who grew up in southern Alabama and made an indelible mark on the music of our era. With *Hit Me, Fred,* the world's greatest sideman finally gets his just desserts.

1

A Musical Upbringing

• • •

I was born into a musical family. My father was director of music at Mobile County Training School. Later, when Central High School was formed, he was part of the contingency selected to seed the new faculty. This was in 1948, so both schools were black.

As music director at Central, my father developed the most dynamic high school choirs in the state of Alabama. Now that I have traveled and had the opportunity to hear many good choirs, I'm convinced that the Central High School Concert Choir was probably the best high-school choir in the world. It performed everything from the "Hallelujah Chorus" to Charles Wesley's "I've Been 'Buked and I've been Scorned." The choir took on his personality, which has been described as swaggering, intense, cool, sporty, and sensual. You would have to have actually been in his presence to understand the kind of overwhelming and devastating person he was. I've seen Bernstein, Mehta, Mitch Miller, and many other great conductors, and not one of them was as dynamic, inspiring, and entertaining as Fred Wesley Sr. To this day, I encounter his former students around the world who attest to the positive effect he had on their lives.

His mother, Mrs. Janie Panting, is a little easier to describe. She was a no-nonsense piano teacher. Her method was simple. First, learn the basics. Then, the classics. Hymns and gospel. She never mentioned blues and jazz. I don't know if she disapproved or approved. She had to know about it. My father had a big band that rehearsed in her living room at least once a week. By age three even I knew who Duke Ellington and

Fred Wesley Sr. Courtesy of
Wesley Family Archives.

Count Basie were. I think my grandmother felt that by not pointing it
out she could delay students from jumping headlong into what was then
the popular music, giving them more time to develop basic skills. I know
now that once you get bitten by the jazz or blues or any popular music
bug, you tend to stop practicing scales and such.

I never knew where my grandmother got her training, but she was
an accomplished pianist and organist. She was organist and director of
the Metropolitan AME Church Choir. She was also on call for weddings,
parties, and other social functions around town. I remember hearing her
say, "Saturday evening I'm playing for a tea" or "I'm playing for Mrs. So-
and-so's daughter's wedding." She took great pride in doing these events.
It made her a part of an affluent society that she was not financially
privy to.

Her forte, however, was teaching. She was a very efficient person,
and her day was arranged around her teaching schedule. She would do
her cooking, cleaning, sewing, and other chores in the mornings and
afternoons. An excellent seamstress, she made most of her own clothes,
since fitting herself off the rack was almost an impossibility—she was
not much over four feet tall, and she was very narrow up top with a very,
very wide bottom.

Fred Wesley Sr., Mrs. Vetta S. Wesley (my mother), Mrs. Janie Wesley Panting (my grandmother). Courtesy of Wesley Family Archives.

She was also a great cook. I especially remember her gumbo, pecan pies, and fruitcakes. Her ancestors were from New Orleans, so all her food had sort of a Creole flavor with some straight-up Alabama country thrown in.

She was very particular about everything she did and was therefore very particular about what you did for her. To say that she was hard to please would be understating how hard it was to live with her. And we did live with her for a couple of years when my father first brought us from Georgia. He had met and married my mother while stationed at Fort Benning, Georgia.

When we moved to Mobile, the piano lessons for my sister and me started immediately. As far back as I can remember, I was hearing such commands as "practice your lesson," "mop the hall," "go to the store." It seemed as if I couldn't do any of these things right. I was always mopping the hall again or taking something back to the store or spending hours at the piano trying to get something that seemed impossible right. It was real miserable for a little kid. I guess it made me appreciate the value of doing things right. My kids say it made me mean. I know it made me hate the piano.

My sister, Janice, my brother, Ronald, and I spent a lot of time with my grandmother because my mother and father worked two jobs apiece during the early years in order for us to get our own house. The good thing was that by about age five, I had a very good understanding of the basics of music. And, although she was a severe taskmaster, I'm still approached regularly by her former students who remember her not only for cracking their knuckles when they played a wrong key but also for instilling in them a sense that hard work leads to excellence.

My father, between teaching school, working at Brookley Air Force Base, and playing for his church choir, still found time to have a big band. The highlight of my week was—I think it was Wednesday night—when the big band rehearsed. Right after my grandmother's last student, I would start moving furniture, setting up music stands, and putting out ashtrays, eagerly anticipating the arrival of the cats.

Charles Lott was usually the first to show up. He was a small man, dressed very well but relaxed. He was always business-like but still hip and regular. He worked full time at the Air Force base and was married to a schoolteacher. He also booked bands and shows on the side. I guess you could consider him upper middle class in Mobile black society. Drove a Cadillac. Lived in a nice house. Playing saxophone was mainly a hobby, although he loved it very much. Mr. Lott, as I still refer to him, has been a lifelong friend.

Eugene Fortune was the alto soloist. He had a raspy voice and a cheerful way of talking. He could be jovial, as was the case most of the time, but when explaining something he could suddenly speak very tutorially. He was a great soloist, unlike anyone I've ever heard before or since. Being mainly self-taught, he was not bound by any musical or technical rules. Thus, his style was very original. It seemed like he squeezed and twisted notes out of the horn. Fast or slow. He was funky and bluesy but could fly at you with a flurry like any good be-bopper. He often brought tears to my and everybody else's eyes with his interpretations of ballads like "The Nearness of You," "Moonlight in Vermont," and "September Song." It's a shame Fortune was never recorded. I don't remember what his real job was, probably something manual. He never wore a suit except on the gig. He had a wife and family. Drove a slick Pontiac. Drank Scotch but didn't get drunk. Smoked cigarettes and didn't cough. He always took time to help me when I was trying to learn to ad lib. Although it was impossible to teach the way he played, I'm sure that just listening to him and watching him and being in his company tremendously influenced the way I play.

The other alto sax player was Hubert "Hawk" Stanfield, a very good lead alto sax player, with a sound much like Bobby Plater or Marshall Royal. I later found out that he played as much piano as he did sax and was a great arranger. He, too, was a family man, and he earned his living as a mail carrier. Although he was a great musician, his demeanor was calm and unassuming, modest even. Just a great, solid, steady, confident, dependable human being.

Somewhere in the sax section was Hubert's brother, Edwin. I don't think he was really a musician. I don't remember anything about his playing. He might have been a lawyer or something, as he was always in a suit and spoke authoritatively. Everybody seemed to treat him a little different, like he wasn't one of the boys, yet he was all right. Anyway, he moved away while I was still young.

The tenor soloist in the band was Joe Morris. Joe was smooth. His manner and his playing were cool. He was an all-around soloist, who could honk on the blues like Red Prysock or Clifford Scott and could bebop like Stan Getz or David "Fathead" Newman, all in his own laid-back way. He wasn't great, but he was adequate and very entertaining. An extremely good-looking guy, very popular with the ladies, he always dressed in the latest styles, as his day job was salesman at Top Men's Store, a local haberdashery. He befriended me right away—I think because he saw potential he could use in his own small group. He was good at putting together bands of young musicians who had yet to be recognized as professional. He gave many of us our first combo and night-club gigs. To this day, he has a good young band working around the Mobile area.

The lead trumpet player was Melza "Chappie" Williams. I didn't know too much about Chappie, except that he, too, was a daytime mailman. He was also president of the Musician's Union. He was definitely from the Dixieland school. His claim to fame was that he actually knew Cootie Williams personally, maybe even was related. He always counseled me about the importance of education.

James Seals played second trumpet. A good trumpet player with a beautiful tone and a sufficient range, he also was a great sight reader and a fairly decent be-bopper. His day job was bandmaster at the aforementioned Mobile County Training School. It was he who introduced me to Miles Davis. I remember him pointing out to me that Miles "played a lot of shit" within the middle register of the instrument (which is a musician's way of saying that he ad libbed expertly on the changes without resorting to too many high notes). I was really impressed by the way Seals attacked his solos—he was never hesitant or timid. His professionalism would have made him a great studio musician. I learned a lot about good musicianship just watching him in rehearsals.

In the early '50s everything was segregated, including bands. It was rare to see a racially mixed band, but there was a white trumpet player in my father's band. His name was Al Bogosh. He was from New York or Chicago or someplace. Somehow I know he sold jewelry. He was a gregarious type of person who seemed to like everybody, and everybody seemed to like him. He drove a big, fancy Lincoln and dressed real flashy. I don't remember too much about his playing—I probably was too busy looking at a white man among all those black people. His playing must have been all right, because the band as a whole always sounded good to me. I never got to know him well, but he was a real oddity to me.

When I first saw a trombone, it didn't for a second occur to me to play one. Sure, it intrigued me with the way it looked. It was gold like a trumpet or a saxophone, but it had nothing to press or mash down to make notes. Pressing valves and mashing keys to make different notes was fascinating enough, but a slide, with no marks or frets, made no sense to me. And look at the guys who were playing this crazy instrument.

First there was Mr. Robert Petty, who always had something profound to say, usually about sex. He knew how to shock a young man and would talk as long as you would listen. He was, however, a good trombonist. Sweet, smooth tone and obviously very well trained, in the Army, I think. He played sort of a Dixieland bebop, but lead trombone was his strong suit.

The other trombone player was Henry Freeman—a true wild-and-crazy guy. The first story I heard about Freeman was that the first Father's Day he was married he had no children, but the next Father's Day he had three children. It happened that his new wife gave birth to their first child soon after Father's Day, then gave birth to twins less than a year later. His baby-making prowess continued through the years. Last count I know was twelve. I can't remember what his day job was, but it must have been rough trying to raise all those kids on whatever salary he had. He was always in good spirits, though, and made all the rehearsals fun for everyone. He had tremendous energy and his solos reflected this energy. He was every bone player from Tyree Glenn to J.J. Johnson, but not really. If you took his solos apart technically, most of the notes would be wrong,

Fred Wesley Sr.'s downtown "White Gig." Left to right: Eddie Bolden, Henry Freeman (on drums), Fred Wesley Sr. Courtesy of Wesley Family Archives.

but his energy made it sound like and feel like he was the baddest player ever. He was the spark of the band. Everyone, in the audiences and in the band, eagerly awaited Freeman's solos. I can't say for sure, but watching Freeman rear and buck and thrill people may have helped my decision to play the trombone.

The rhythm section consisted of Billy Holmes on bass, Daddy on piano, and, they tell me, Harold Broadus on drums. For some reason I do not remember Harold Broadus at all. I have heard Harold Broadus stories that include people I know very well, but I can't for the life of me put a face to the name, although the name does ring a small bell.

Billy Holmes, on the other hand, I remember very well. He was a quiet, well-mannered man who didn't drink or smoke or talk dirty or fool around in any way. All he did was play the hell out of the acoustic bass. If any musician was world-class in Mobile, it was Billy Holmes. Always in tune, always on time, in the right key, knew the changes. You got the feeling that he already knew the songs, even the originals. You felt like he was always waiting for everyone else to learn their parts. A true pro-

The Rhythmic Sensations, 1947. Left to right: Willie B. Ross, Henry Turner, Frank Ponquinette, Edwin Stanfield, Charles Lott, Bill Washington, Harold Broadus, Herman "Bo Bo" Simon, Mrs. Vetta Wesley, Fred Wesley Sr. Courtesy of Wesley Family Archives.

fessional who, like everyone else in this band, earned his living doing something else. He was also a fine tailor who worked both for individuals and for the best men's stores in Mobile.

And, of course, there was Daddy on piano. His forte was boogie-woogie and stride, but he also played a little jazz and blues à la Count Basie and Duke Ellington. He interpreted ballads beautifully and played vibes every now and then.

It was a good band with a good name—the Rhythmic Sensations. Daddy would copy records of Basie, Ellington, Buddy Johnson, and others. I think his favorite was Louis Jordan. The first songs I remember the band playing were "Open the Door, Richard" and "Caldonia." I was the band boy when I got big enough to set up stands, pass out music, load and unload the car for the gigs, empty ashtrays, and so on. The only time I got to go to a gig was if it were in the daytime. The band members wouldn't let me go to nightclubs or cabarets or any place where liquor was served. I longed for the day when I'd be old enough and big enough to play in the band.

All through elementary school I watched as the band played on. I continued my piano lessons, working through the blue book, the red book, and various solo pieces as I prepared for my grandmother's annual recitals. These were very good programs, and I dreaded them as much as my grandmother and her other students looked forward to them. All the other students were girls. Maybe that's why I wanted to play a horn so much. All the good piano players I knew of were girls or like a girl, except Daddy. He didn't play like a girl. He must have learned by himself, because my grandmother wasn't teaching me to play like he played. When I asked him to show me how he played, he'd tell me to learn the basics and the jazz would come later. I was sure that what he did was due to a special gift that only he had. Whatever he played was unique. Even when he played classical or gospel, it had a different thing to it.

I knew I could never play piano like he did, so I wanted a horn. Any horn. I kept asking him to get me a horn. There was a piano, an organ, and a xylophone in the house—but no horn. He would say, "Master the piano first, and then if you still want a horn I'll get you one." Now what did that mean? Master the piano? To what extent? I actually tried to get into the piano for a while. Really tried. But in the back of my mind I saw myself turning into Gwen Howard or Vivian Sheffield (students of my grandmother), playing stuff like "The Minute Waltz" or "Claire De Lune." I didn't see my training leading to "Blues After Hours." I managed to get through Rachmaninoff's "Prelude in C Minor," then hit a mental block. I simply could not go any further. I just didn't want to be Gwen Howard, who played the hell out of the piece at the last recital. I wanted to be Freeman and play the shit out of the trombone solo in Duke Ellington's arrangement of "Things Ain't What They Used to Be."

At some point, my grandmother, Daddy, and everyone else finally recognized that I was not ever going to play the piano. Daddy then started saying "If you can't learn the piano, what makes you think you can learn a horn?" I kept insisting I could.

Here's what happened. You remember Mobile County Training School? It was the main high school for blacks in Mobile until Central High School opened. Well, County was fed by Mattie T. Blunt Junior High in Mobile's Prichard and Whistler areas. Central was fed by Dunbar Junior High from downtown. All through elementary school we lived with my grandmother in Prichard, so I was all set to go to Blunt, but my family bought a house in Toulminville, which is halfway between Prichard and downtown Mobile. At the same time, a new junior high school opened in Toulminville. So I enrolled at the new school, which was named Booker T. Washington—and which had a *band.*

The bandmaster was E. B. Coleman. A native of Virginia, he was a graduate of Alabama State College, where Lott, both Stanfields, Henry Turner, and some of the other guys in my father's band had gone. In fact, he and Hawk were roommates at State. He had completed a tour of duty in the U.S. Army. Taught a couple of years in a small town nearby—Jackson, Alabama. Coincidentally, he had just married the most beautiful girl in town, Ann Owens, daughter of Reverend Owens, pastor of Hope Chapel AME Zion Church, where Daddy was choir director and organist. Since one of the Harold Broadus stories was that he drank too much and was a problem for the band, Coleman became the new drummer with the Rhythmic Sensations. So, when I got to junior high, I already knew the bandmaster from rehearsals at the house and the few times I'd seen him when I went to church with Daddy. At first all I thought of him was "big ol' ugly-ass country nigger, come in here, marry the prettiest girl in town (whom I secretly had a serious crush on)." But when I got to know him, I really liked him. He always took time to talk to me, not about anything really, but man to man, like a big brother.

Apparently, he and Daddy had been talking about my lack of piano skills and my desire to play a horn. So, during the summer before I started junior high, Daddy bought me a trumpet. It was the best day of my life.

I would ride my bicycle to Coleman's house two or three times a week for lessons, and I made amazing progress. By the end of the summer I was ready for the Booker T. Washington Band. Over that summer, Coleman and I developed a special relationship. Not only student-teacher but personally as well. My mother and father were getting a divorce during this time. I hardly ever saw my father, but I was with Coleman a lot. He knew our family situation, so he was there for me when I needed his fraternal guidance.

So now I'm playing trumpet in the Booker T. Washington Junior High Band. I remember marches like "Our Director" and concert pieces like "Light Cavalry Overture." The band rehearsed every day and played for assemblies, holiday programs, and other in-school and school-related events. But Coleman fancied himself a jazzman and was a very good arranger and composer. In addition to the standard stuff the school board recommended, he would write his own arrangements and even use his own compositions for the band to play. And, of course, being a jazzman, some of his pieces were jazz. This was quite controversial. There was an element in the school system that felt he should stick to the book. Maybe they were right, but it was great for me because jazz was all I wanted to play anyway.

I'm coming along pretty well on the trumpet, when one day I walk into the band room and see these two, brand new, absolutely beautiful baritone horns on Mr. Coleman's desk. When he came in he asked for volunteers to play these horns. Along with everyone else, I hesitated. I was just beginning to get comfortable with the trumpet and didn't know if I wanted to start all over on a new instrument. Since no one immediately volunteered, Coleman, with some wisdom unknown to us, chose me and Tommy Thompson. By my estimation, we were his two best trumpet players, although that may or may not have been the reason. I've learned since that the baritone was his favorite instrument. He said, "The baritone horn is to a band what salad dressing is to a ham sandwich." So maybe he wanted it played as correctly as possible. He did favor the baritone parts in his writings, and he insisted it ring out in marches and such. The fingering was the same as the trumpet, but the mouthpiece was bigger. T.T. had no problem switching from trumpet to baritone and back, but for some reason, I eventually lost my trumpet chops. So I stayed on baritone exclusively. This was all right with me, as I had grown to love the instrument. I was concerned, however, since I had never seen or heard of a baritone horn in a jazz band. I thought, "Maybe I won't play jazz," or "Maybe I'll be the first jazz baritonist." Actually, I didn't think a whole lot about it. I was just enjoying playing the instrument and was getting good at it.

I spent all of my free time in the band room fooling around with the drums, the string bass, and other instruments. Sometimes James McCall would let me mess around with his new Olds Ambassador trombone while he messed around with my King baritone. I discovered that, for some reason, anything I could play on baritone, I could play on trombone. I didn't know how or why, I just knew. I later learned the natural relationship between the different lengths of the slide and the lengths of tubing manipulated by valve combinations. Anyway, I could now play the trombone. I still didn't really know what I was doing, because I couldn't read trombone music, which is written in bass clef, as opposed to baritone music, which is in treble clef. So I'm playing trombone, but I don't know the notes I'm playing, because I'm thinking treble clef. I had to learn it first on baritone before I could play it on trombone. I don't think Coleman noticed me playing bone. If he did, he never said anything about it.

During my second year of junior high, Coleman put together an extra-curricular jazz combo, made up of T.T. and myself on baritones, Harvey Jones on tuba, Marvin Robinson, who Coleman was teaching to play trap drums, and Coleman himself on piano. He wasn't a helluva pianist, but he could chord. (Chord? Grandmother never said anything to me about chords. Daddy didn't either. Maybe I could have done that on piano. Oh well, maybe someday.) The group was called the Sounds. We did all E. B. Coleman arrangements of standards and Coleman originals. Everything was written out, including the walking bass lines and the solos. The sound of the Sounds was unique. Even though we were all first-time jazz players, the group managed to swing, mainly because of the strong vibe of Coleman on piano. Coleman had a strong natural groove or vibe—what we would now call funk or soul—in his body. It infected everyone he played with, even us novices. I first noticed this about him as he played drums with the big band. Playing with the Sounds was a great musical experience as well as a lot of fun. We rehearsed twice a week after school.

So now I'm learning a horn. Two horns, really—the baritone seriously and the trombone on the side. At the same time, Daddy is working with the big band less and less, and is also at home less and less. He's teaching school during the day, working part time at the Air Force base, and playing a gig with just himself, a drummer, and a horn player almost every night at a white club downtown. After finally deciding to give up the big band altogether, Daddy gave the music, the stands, and all the bookings to Coleman. The Rhythmic Sensations became the E. B. Coleman 16-Piece Orchestra.

The band remained mostly intact, but Edwin Stanfield had moved out of town, so the reed section was shaken up a bit. The altos were now Fortune and Conrad Bouchelion, a classmate of mine. Conrad was one of the kids who came to Booker T. Washington from Dunbar, as did T.T. Joe Morris was still solo tenor, and Marshall Ezell was now the other tenor. The word was that Marshall was Reverend Ezell's son who had just returned from the Air Force or something. He often talked about Florida A&M, where he had gone to school with Cannonball and Nat Adderley. He wasn't much of a soloist at that time but a great player on any woodwind instrument, including all flutes and double reeds. And Charles Lott was now on baritone sax.

Jimmy Seals anchored the trumpet section along with Chappie Williams, my classmate and baritone buddy; Tommy Thompson; and Conrad's older brother, Horace, who we called Toby and who had recently been admitted to Spring Hill College, thus single-handedly integrating the previously all-white school. (During that time in the South, there were in fact many steps toward integration being taken without fanfare or trouble.)

The trombones were Petty and Freeman, as usual. To my surprise, Hawk Stanfield was now the piano player, and he was every bit as good as Daddy and way more modern. Coleman added Dewey Long on guitar.

Now let's see, four trumpets, five saxes, four rhythm, two trombones —that's only fifteen pieces. Coleman came to me with an old Olds Ambassador trombone and an Arban's method book. Said, "If you learn to read and play trombone music by the time school opens in September, *you got the gig.*" I could pay him for the horn and the book out of the money I'd be making.

That summer it was me and that trombone. The big band, under its new director, began rehearsing in the Booker T. Washington band room. Daddy's book was pushed aside almost immediately. Of course, we kept Kenton's "Intermission Riff" and . . . that's the only one I can remember. Everything else was arranged or written by Coleman. I scuffled along at first but finally got the hang of reading trombone music, somewhat. (The real story is that I still have trouble reading any kind of music. I can write better than I can read. I just learned how to fake it real good.) I even got to try my hand at the ad lib solo. I was really pitiful at first, but all the guys were supportive, especially Freeman, whose opinion really mattered to me. He helped me a lot, mostly with encouraging words: "Get on out there," "Don't be scared," "Make 'em listen to you." His words have stayed with me to this day.

I don't remember my very first gig, but I do remember having to deal with my mother. She was a religious lady and very concerned about her oldest son's morals being corrupted by the musician's lifestyle. Daddy's consent didn't mean much to her, for she more or less blamed his lifestyle for the break-up of her marriage. But she had great trust in Mr. Coleman. He was the kind of person everybody seemed to automatically trust to do the right thing. He could charm the paint off the wall. So although there were guys in the band who she knew had reputations for womanizing and drinking and other things, Coleman convinced her that I'd be safe and that he would be personally responsible. Ha!

The band played mostly cabarets, balls, and parties. The Mardi Gras season and Christmas seasons were very busy. Usually, the band worked just two or three times a week. Not only was the big band interesting musically for me, Conrad, and Tommy, but we got to see our parents and their friends in a party atmosphere. In a small town like Mobile, people who went to cabarets and balls were the middle- to upper-class members of the black community. So we got to see our teachers, postal and other civil service workers, business owners, doctors, lawyers, and other hoop-tee-doo people let their hair down, get drunk, mess with each other's husbands and wives, and generally act complete fools. We learned what to do, how to do, what not to do, how not to do, and what you can do and get away with if you do the right thing most of the time. At any rate, I'm sure that at an early age I formed some lifelong attitudes about life that caused me to bypass a lot of childhood. Maybe that's good. Maybe it's bad.

But I was there mostly for the music. I just loved being a part of this great music-making machine. I would get so excited when one of my solos approached that I would almost faint. I longed for the day when I could stand up there and calmly blow a solo like Fortune, Joe Morris, or James Seals. I wondered if I could ever have the nerve to rear and buck, gyrate, and walk up and down like Freeman. Or run through chord changes, making perfect sense, the way Seals did. I was improving, but I still had a long way to go to feel comfortable.

At ages thirteen, fourteen, and fifteen, my life was about going to school, playing in the school band, rehearsing with the Sounds, rehearsing with the big band, and playing a few gigs a week. I was making good progress as a jazz player; I was beginning to feel what I was doing. It's hard to explain, but somehow I knew some things instinctively. The band guys and the audiences were beginning to recognize that I had something special. Being a young guy playing at clubs and cabarets and balls, I became somewhat of a celebrity. Not many kids my age got to stay out all night with older guys and earn eight to ten dollars to boot.

Of course, I did all the kid things, too. I was a bicycle fanatic. A fairly decent fullback and pretty good baseball catcher. I hung out with the boys in the neighborhood. My best friend was Thaddeus E. Williams, the son of Reverend and Mrs. T. E. Williams Sr. His mother was a local radio personality. A grade ahead of me in school, Thad was already playing the trombone when I met him—before I even had a trumpet—but his playing trombone had nothing to do with me playing trombone. He was a helluva person. An "A" student. A gifted athlete. I'm sure he could have been a world-class baseball pitcher. He had actually played some with Hank Aaron and his brother Tommy at Carver Park in Toulminville. He taught me a lot of things. How to ride a bike. How to catch a baseball, because he needed someone to catch for him as he practiced his fast ball and his curve ball. My left hand still hurts from hours of stopping his 90 mph fast ball. He and our other friend and neighbor, Costello White, were into tennis, so I learned that game, too.

Thad and Costello were intellectuals. Both their parents were black activists before it was popular and while it was still real dangerous. Their conversation was about integration and civil rights, democracy versus other political systems. Things like that. They were also into collecting and listening to jazz. Before my first year of high school, all the music I got came from my grandmother's music books, Daddy's band book, and the stuff Coleman wrote. I never thought much about records. Sure, I'd heard records. Our bedroom at my grandmother's house was no more than ten feet from the jukebox in the Blue Diamond Cafe. I heard blues all night long from the age of three. Daddy had always had 78s of Nat King Cole and Count Basie, and we would listen while he transcribed records for the band. But this was 1954–55, when the LP first hit the scene, and Costello already had quite a few. He would come over, bringing his "sides," and we would sit for hours listening to Basie, Ellington, Clark Terry, Gerry Mulligan, and many others. The guys in the big band would now and then mention different players. As I said before, Seals was into Miles, and Ezell claimed to know the Adderley brothers. I didn't really know who these people were, but I knew they were held in high regard.

I don't know if it was Freeman or someone else who first said the name J.J. Johnson to me, but I knew that he was held to be "the cat" on trombone. So I put my pennies together and bought my first LP—Johnson's "'J' is for Jazz" (Columbia, 1956). I was impressed by the album jacket alone, which showed J.J. sitting at a table with a cigarette in his fingers and a half-full shot glass and a black bell trombone sitting on the table. J.J. looked so cool. And it was without a doubt the most beautiful horn I'd ever seen. Then I heard the music. I was wrecked. Never before had I heard such a big, full, smooth sound come out of a trombone. I couldn't believe how clear and articulate he was. His lines made so much sense. It was complicated, yet easy to understand. Freeman was basically a Dixieland player. While his solos were mostly an act that paid little attention to notes, chord changes, melody, and harmony, he played notes

Thaddeus Williams and Fred Wesley Jr., age 14. Courtesy of Wesley Family Archives.

clearly, distinctly, cleverly moving from one chord to another with dynamics and articulations. This was where I wanted to go. This was the type of music I wanted to play. This album changed my life. It opened my eyes to what it is possible with a trombone.

At that time I knew very little about chord changes. I only knew my parts and could play what my ear dictated. I started questioning Coleman, Stanfield, and anyone else who could help me progress to play like J.J. My next album was by Jay and Kai (J.J. Johnson and Kai Winding). The sound of two trombones fascinated me. Thad, too. We would copy things from the Jay and Kai albums and impress our friends in the band. We even called ourselves F and T. We never copied a whole tune. Just little phrases we could manage. The point is I'm now listening to records big time. I get my own stereo. I discover Horace Silver, the Jazztet with Curtis Fuller, Bird, Stitt, and a host of others. All this listening I'm doing, I still don't have a clue as to how these cats play all this jazz on these instruments. I guess I thought it was some kind of magic. I would have been happy to get the Freeman thing down. At that point, most of the solos I was playing were written by Coleman. Deep down, I found it hard to believe that all of the melodies and phrases that these people were playing were being made up on the spot.

It's 1957 and I graduate to Central High School. Tommy Thompson, Conrad Bouchelion, Harvey Jones, and many others from Booker T. join the band. The bandmaster is Mr. John Irons, reputed to be a Dixieland trumpet player from New Orleans. A real regular guy, with a volatile temper that he occasionally lost. Not the teacher Coleman was, but a great organizer. He had to rehearse hundreds of kids, prepare them for parades, football game half-time shows, and school concerts. I learned about organizing and people handling from watching "Chief," as he was called. There wasn't any jazz in the Central High band program except what happened to come up in half-time shows.

I'm taking algebra, world history, physics, French, social studies, and music theory. At the insistence of my father, I also sing in the choir. My father also happens to be my social studies and music theory teacher. This was just great. A band with no jazz, and I get to look in my own father's face three times a day. But I did enjoy marching in parades. And the half-time shows gave us all a sense of pride and accomplishment. The Negro spirituals and classical works the concert choir performed were very challenging and pleasurable. What I learned in music theory class has benefited me to this day. I still had the big band. And I spent most of my free time listening to records and imitating what I could. High school wasn't that bad at all.

One day the high-school band played for the opening of Hillsdale Heights, a new black housing development in west Mobile that was supposed to be an area for upper-income blacks. The opening was a pretty big to-do. All of the black high-school bands in town participated, along with a couple of local club bands, including Ed Pratt and his players. Ms. Dinah Washington was the special guest attraction. She used Pratt's band as backup but brought her own piano player, Wynton Kelly. (I didn't know who he was at the time, but Thad hipped me later.) Kelly was less than spectacular playing the sultry ballads and low-down blues of Dinah's performance. But she was so sexy, I hardly noticed anything else while she was singing. When she passed by our band, one of our bass drummers yelled out, "Make Me a Present of You," a title from one of her albums. She stopped and turned, gave him a look that could melt steel, and said, "You wouldn't know what to do with it, honey."

What really impressed me was Pratt's band. I had heard about Pratt's band. Freeman played with him sometime. Coleman and some of the other guys in the big band knew him from Alabama State, and it was rumored that Pratt was as good as Joe Henderson or Benny Golson, who I'd heard on record. Pratt's father had been bandmaster at Central until his untimely death, which I remember as a great tragedy in town. (Mr. Irons was imported from New Orleans to take his place.) My father, who had studied with Pratt Sr., spoke of him as if he were a great music genius.

Pratt played tenor sax along with Artee "Duke" Payne. James "Noon" Matthews played bass. Leonard Horton played piano. Booker (as far as I know, that's all the name he had) played drums. Pratt approached the microphone and said in a real hip, husky voice, "We gonna do a tune entitled 'Farmer's Market.'" I'm thinking "farmer's market"? My uncle in Georgia was a farmer, and I went with him to take some pigs to market one time. So maybe it's a hillbilly song like we hear on the radio in the country in Georgia. Or maybe its blues like what I'd hear when I went to the fish market with Grandmother.

What I heard was totally unexpected. Pratt counts off a fast 1–2–1234, stomping his foot at the same time. They went, bop ba doo ba–bop ba doo ba–doo bi doo bop–baaa ba ba doop ba doo ba doo bi doo bop, and so on. I'd heard fast before on record, but we didn't do anything fast in the big band or the Sounds. I'd never seen an entire band play that fast and that together before. They all seemed to know what they were

Mobile Bandmasters. Left to right: James Seals, John Irons, E.B. Coleman, Edward Pratt. Courtesy of Pratt Family Archives.

doing. It was like they were all collectively possessed by something. After they finished the head, Pratt jumped off into his solo. Jumped off into it was exactly what it sounded and looked like. For someone to play that many notes that many different ways was completely unbelievable to me. His eyes were tightly closed. He was sweating. Yet, he was actually saying something musically. This was much more exciting and entertaining than just singing or playing a written part. After he finished, he calmly stepped back and leaned on the piano, horn still hanging around his neck. Lit a cigarette as Duke lit into his solo. Duke did the same kind of thing Pratt did, only he added squeaks and barks, honks and squeals, less musical but just as exciting, maybe more. They went through the piano and bass solos, traded fours with the drummer—all spectacular— and played the head out. Impressed is not the word. I was wrecked. I'm thinking it must be some kind of magic, a trick. These couldn't be normal humans. Maybe some kind of machine attached to their instruments or something, or the mikes were hooked up to a record. Me being able to do that never occurred to me.

I would have liked to have met Pratt and Duke that day to try to get some first-hand knowledge about bebop. But to me they seemed unapproachable. They probably spoke some language I wouldn't understand or were busy discussing and meditating on things far above my head. I realized later that Myrna Pratt, an upper-class girl in my father's theory class and pianist for the concert choir, was his sister. She was nice and, although extremely talented, a normal person. Pratt's mother was head dietitian at Central. So this short, prematurely bald guy from a normal but talented family became the focus of my attention. Most of the musicians I knew knew him, but they seemed to view him as being as aloof and unapproachable as I did. The word was that he was sort of a rebel who drank a lot and "smokes them reefers."

My friends from downtown, Tommy and Conrad, either knew Duke or knew of him. He had gone through Dunbar ahead of them and was reported to be a kid whose mama got him anything he wanted. He was a natty dresser. His shoe wardrobe was legend. He drove a Cadillac in high school. He was an "A" student. He was, at the time I first saw him, attending Tennessee A&I State University, majoring in chemistry, and playing music on the side. It seemed to me that playing saxophone the way he did would be a full-time endeavor.

Thoughts of Pratt and Duke and that band completely consumed my mind. I couldn't sleep. I couldn't think about school—I was too busy thinking about chord changes, tunes, and bebop. I got to be friends with an alto player in the school band who they called "School Boy" but whose actual name was Emmett Salisbury. He turned me on to some Charlie Parker books he had gotten hip to in Detroit. These books had tunes and solos of Parker's written out. They seemed to work for him but weren't what I was looking for. Most of my days were spent sitting in the band room, horn in hand, trying to play some of the things I heard J.J. or Curtis play. Yes, all day. Yes, I cut a lot of classes. Yes, I stayed in trouble. I didn't care. I wanted to play jazz.

Because the big band didn't work very much, a lot of the guys played in smaller combos around town, in clubs and for occasions whose organizers couldn't afford the price of the big band. Coleman himself led a combo called the Moderns, composed of the big-band rhythm section (Hawk, Billy, and Coleman), alto (Fortune), and trumpet (Seals). He added the beautiful Ellen Daffin, who was also the singer with the big band. The Moderns played some ultrahip compositions and arrangements of Coleman's. Sort of the Sounds with conventional instrumentation and professional musicians. By now, I felt I could handle the Moderns gig, as it was so closely related to the Sounds. It was within my realm of comprehension. At that time, Charles Lott, the bari saxist in the big band, was reorganizing his own band, the Charles Lott Allstars, and he invited me to play with them. They played blues and other *stuff* you hear on the radio. I consulted with Coleman, and he thought it would be good experience.

Lott had a few written arrangements, but most of the tunes were put together by listening to records. What we call head arrangements. You made up the arrangement in yo head and kept it in yo head. (The recycle bin of my brain is *full* of head arrangements.) I quickly learned to take advantage of my God-given super ear. This was good for me. I got to play some other kinds of music, like blues and R&B. Most of the time I was the only horn, which meant that I had to play all of the saxophone solos and in some situations I would even play the guitar part. In a small band like that, everyone had to do whatever it took—even sing—to help the music sound as close to the record as possible. Most of the Allstar's gigs were in nightclubs, which meant exposure to people who were different from the normal school and church people I was used to. I got to be friends with hustlers, prostitutes, gamblers, drunks, addicts, and all types of fun people who hung out in nightclubs. Most thought I was cute. Some teased me or tried to tempt me with the debauchery they were into, but I was protected; most of the guys in the band were my father's friends or knew who he was and what he was about, so I was treated like a younger brother or a son or a nephew.

I was also invited to join the Excelsior Marching Band. This was a New Orleans–style street band. All you needed to play in this band was a bus-driver cap, a dark suit, and the ability to play Dixieland music, which, with my great ear and a little coaching from Petty, Chappie, and Freeman, I caught onto real quick. Most of the Excelsior's work came during Mardi Gras season. Yes, we have Mardi Gras in Mobile. In fact, the first Mardi Gras carnival in the United States was held in Mobile, Alabama. (I don't know what year. What am I—a historian? Ask Tommy Thompson. He knows those kinds of things.) New Orleans is more famous for Mardi Gras, I guess because of the larger population, but there is still a big and important Mardi Gras tradition in Mobile, with clubs and other organizations much like in New Orleans and even Rio.

By my junior year of high school, I'm playing with a big band, an R&B band, a jazz combo, and a Dixieland band. At age fifteen, I'm depended on to hold down my part in each of these bands. I'm accepted as an equal member, not as Fred's son with potential or some cute added attraction. I feel like and get treated and paid like a professional. I can hardly stand myself. I'm still playing written solos in the big band and, in Lott's band, imitating solos off of records. I'm now beginning to understand the blues form and blowing some pretty good rock gut solos on slow blues. The Excelsior band, which is all about going for it with your ear, is giving me a chance to experiment with the Dixieland genre—"When the Saints Go Marching In," "Back Home in Indiana," "Dream, Dream, Dream"—and other traditional jazz forms. My ear is developing, and my confidence is growing. I'm given the chance to solo on Coleman's arrangement of Blakey's "Moanin'." We do a head arrangement on "Watermelon Man" in Lott's band, and I get to do a solo on it. And I'm still blowing my ass off every day in the band room, in between getting yelled at by my mother and my father. I still don't care. Chief lets me come in after lunch in my free period, and I just cannot stop and go to algebra, which is the next period. So I just stay on through social studies (Daddy's class) and French. Somehow, I make it to the theory class, the last class of the day. I can't help it. Because I'm getting to where I can play blues choruses and rhythm choruses. I don't know exactly when it happens, but it feels so good, I just can't stop.

Just about this time news got around that Joe Lewis was back in town. He had recently been discharged from the Air Force and was looking to start a new band. He made a few big-band rehearsals, just for fun. A helluva jazz player, he was not quite as fiery as Pratt or Duke, but amazingly lyrical and smooth. And he was such a beautiful person. Friendly, intelligent, clean-cut family man with a wife named Gwen, who was also beautiful and nice. He was a good friend of Joe Morris and Ezell. I liked him right away. We talked at length about my efforts to get comfortable with bebop. He sympathized with what I was going through as he'd gone through the same thing while in the Air Force. He emphasized the importance of studying chords and chord progressions.

When he formed his band, it consisted of me on trombone; Joe Morris on tenor; Toby Bouchelion on trumpet; James "Noon" Matthews, who was playing with Pratt, on bass; a kid even younger than me, George Weaver, one of Coleman's students, on drums; Marshall Ezell on bari and flute; and Joe Lewis as leader and arranger, playing piano and alto and tenor saxes.

At first it was an experimental band. A workshop, so to speak. The mix of veterans and novices made for a very good learning situation. Joe was sharpening his arranging skills as Weaver was learning to swing. It

Joe Lewis. Photograph by
Fred Wesley Jr.

was an opportunity for Toby, Ezell, and I to practice playing bebop as
much and as long as we wanted to with a high-energy bass player, a correct piano player, and an eager-to-please drummer. Noon was learning
to read music, and Joe Morris increased his repertoire with some jazz
tunes. Veterans like Morris and Noon kept us grounded and realistic. For
months we rehearsed Joe's arrangements on tunes like "Doxy," "Bernie's
Tune," and "Yesterday," to name a few. I learned so much at those rehearsals. Joe had written out the changes to all the tunes, and I would practice
and study all the week, eager for Sunday to show the fellows what I'd
learned.

The rehearsals were at Joe Lewis's house every Sunday afternoon.
One of the guys would pick me up, at least until the following summer,
when I turned sixteen and immediately applied for and got my drivers
license. At sixteen years of age, I had an income, a career, and freedom
to move about like an adult.

My Sundays were pretty much filled up. I had become a Sunday-
school teacher, so I was at Samuel Chapel AME Church every Sunday morning at 9:30. And, of course, I stayed for morning services,
which lasted until about one. Then I'd take my mother home, change my
clothes, and head to Joe's house for rehearsal, which was usually over
by 5:00. I'd head back home, change clothes again, and return to church
for A.C.E. League, a young people's Methodist Christian organization, of
which I had been the president every year since Thomas Jackson (T.J.),

one of my early heroes, left for the Air Force. From 6 to 7:30, Willie Nobles and I, along with a few other morally conscious kids between the ages of twelve and eighteen, discussed the problems facing teenagers.

My church involvement greatly pleased my mother. I was happy to please her, but that wasn't the only reason I embraced Christianity—I also had a strong admiration for our pastor. He made me really believe in obeying the Gospel. I saw him as a clean-living, moral man whose words were strong and convincing. I bought wholeheartedly into his teachings. I prided myself on my ability to resist the temptations that confronted me all the time, being as how I was in decadent situations in my work. I really was in it just for the music. The other stuff didn't interest me at all. Anyway, I resisted. I wouldn't smoke or drink and had actually decided to keep my virginity until I married. I was serious. I even, at one time, thought about becoming a minister.

Two things happened. First, Noon's van broke down. I had a raggedy but functional station wagon, so I added to my Sunday schedule, picking up Noon and dropping him off at the Kings Club after rehearsal, with his bass and amplifier. Pratt's band hosted a jam session there every Sunday at 5:00. I'd just drop Noon off, but he always asked me to come in and play some. I'd made great progress, but I didn't think I was ready to play with Pratt. Plus, I had to be at A.C.E. League at 6:00. This went on for a couple of months.

Then, a friend of mine, an older girl who had finished Central a year earlier and was attending the Mobile Branch of Alabama State College, had gotten pregnant out of wedlock. I was shocked. She was one of the girls in the A.C.E. League. This was the sort of thing that we of the league were united against. How could this happen? It really hurt me personally because, deep down, I had a secret crush on her. She was older, but I had felt that if I didn't marry her it would be someone very much like her. I was shocked, hurt, and sad, all at the same time. She didn't come to church at all during her pregnancy, but after the baby was born, she began to bring him to church. I didn't know what to say to her. I was all set to deal with the situation without acting ugly or giving her any grief. I was going to say what a cute baby and go on about my business. But when I saw the boy, it was like in the movies. Zoom in on the baby. Zoom in on the pastor. Zoom in on my horrified face. The baby looked just like the pastor. He was, without a doubt, his son. I was shocked, hurt, sad, disillusioned, and now angry and sick to my stomach, for real. I know everybody else also saw the resemblance. But they acted like they didn't notice anything. Maybe everyone but me knew all the time. My mother was saying things to me like, "He's only a man," "He's only human," "These things happen." I had always thought your religion strengthened you against this kind of temptation. If not, what good was it? Why read all the words? Why go through all the rituals? Why deny yourself if the person you look to for guidance and strength turns out to be "just a man," "only human"? From then on, I only went to church to please my mother. Slowly, I weaned myself away from the A.C.E. League, and one Sunday I took Noon to the Kings Club, parked the wagon, got my horn, and walked right on into the jam session.

We were early. Only Booker, the drummer was there. Noon introduced me. Booker gave me what came to be his usual, short "Hey, man." Then Freeman came in, loud and laughing. "Fred Jr. Come to kick my ass, take my gig." I insisted, "Naw man, just came to learn." Which remained my way of diplomatically dealing with Freeman. Although he was my first inspiration, I was all the way into the J.J.–Curtis style now. I felt that I had cheated on Freeman somehow. And I did want his gig with Pratt, although I knew I wasn't ready. I never told anyone how I felt nor openly campaigned for the gig. I think it was evident, and everyone knew I wanted it.

Leonard Horton, the piano player, came in next, struggling with his newly acquired Fender Rhodes piano, which he proceeded to set up. He referred to me as Fred's son or little Fred or something and quietly said, "Glad to have you" or something like that. He was short spoken like Booker but not nearly as sinister. Now everything is ready, and we're waiting for Pratt. Them, anxious to play. Me, apprehensive about how I'll be received. Will he let me play? If I play, will he laugh at me? I was scared to death, although Noon and Freeman both assured me I would do all right.

Finally, Pratt burst though the door carrying a plethora of instruments. A tenor, an alto, a soprano, and a flute. He proceeded immediately to the side of the bandstand and began uncasing his horns. The guys headed for their positions on the bandstand, ready to play. I still hadn't taken my horn out. I didn't want to seem like I knew he was going to let me play. Plus, I didn't know what the procedure was. I just didn't want to appear presumptuous.

I hope I wasn't trembling outside, but I was surely trembling inside as I approached the unapproachable Mr. Pratt, flanked by Freeman and Noon. I think it was Freeman who said something like, "Pratt, this is Fred

Wesley Jr., wants to play some." We shook hands as he looked at me and chuckled and said something like, "Well, what are you waiting for—an engraved invitation? Get your horn out and let's play."

I hadn't expected that. I thought they would play a few tunes, and maybe later, after we discussed and agreed on something, I would play. But NO. It was right now. Hit it. Get on up there. I had no idea what tune we were going to play. But I got right on up there like I knew what I was doing. God was with me. The first tune he called was "Bye, Bye, Blackbird." Although I'd never played this tune in public, I did, for the most part, know it from playing along with the Miles Davis recording over and over and over. But would we do the same arrangement? Would it be in the same key? I was so relieved when Leonard hit the familiar Red Garland intro, bip beeeeee bop be doo be doo be doop beep. . . . Pratt played the head pretty much like Miles on tenor. After the intro, when the rhythm section came in, I can't explain how good it felt. This was better than the Miles Davis record. This was real. It felt so good, I almost cried. You see, to me, bebop is like what religion is to most people. It is all consuming, completely thrilling, deeply emotional—the most pleasant feeling, on par with and sometimes better than sex. To be right there in it is a joy I can't explain. And this was my first time going all the way. The big band, the Sounds, Lott's band, Excelsior, and even the Esquires were like foreplay compared to this.

Pratt went through his solo, completely intimidating me as if I wasn't intimidated already. Then Freeman roughhoused an otherwise mellow groove, yet still produced an entertaining solo. Then it was my time. My mouth was so dry it's a miracle I got any sound out of the horn at all. I'm sure my knees knocking interfered with the groove. As I started to play, it seemed like—and now I know for sure—that the rhythm section literally led me through the first chords until I settled down enough to get through about three choruses. After I finished (I think I finished in the right place), the audience, which I became aware of for the first time, erupted into applause. I looked at Pratt right away for, I hoped, approval. He kinda smiled and said, "Yeah." Freeman and Noon had broad grins on their faces, satisfied that their predictions of my success had come true. I wanted to kiss Leonard for leading with the melody practically throughout the entire solo. He kept a straight face like he hadn't done anything, but I knew and he knew that without his subtle guidance, I probably would've gotten lost and made a complete fool of myself. God only knows what Booker was thinking. He always looked totally unconcerned as he laid down the hardest heartstopping grooves I've ever felt before or since. I was just happy I hadn't had a heart attack and died or gotten weak in the knees and fallen down. I *was* kind of pleased with the audience's acceptance, now that I think about it.

I made it through the rest of that first jam session playing some blues I didn't know the head to but could blow on the changes. I had the blues form down pretty well. The tunes I didn't know, I worked on during the week. That was practically all I was doing those days. I'd work on tunes I'd gotten from Joe Lewis and tunes I wanted to learn for the sessions. School became less and less important to me, as did church and everything else. My entire life focused on Sunday. The Joe Lewis rehearsals. The Pratt jam session.

Now that I know I can somewhat hang, I want to really get it together. I'm trying to increase my repertoire by all means available. I'm listening to all the records recommended to me by Thad, Costello, and the guys I meet at the session. I'm taking advice from everybody, and everybody is giving it freely. It's like they all want to see me get better. A trumpet player, Bobby Sharpe, comes to mind. I kinda knew him. His mother was a member of our church and a friend of my mother. I'd seen him come to church with his mother sometimes, although we never met until we met at the session. I found out he was an Alabama State graduate and was teaching somewhere "up the country," as we say in Mobile. He took me to his house a couple of times, and sat and taught me some tunes. I don't remember exactly which ones. I do remember he wrote the music, chords and all, to Horace Silver's "Tippin'" and Miles's "Four" for me. He was a very good bebop trumpet player, and although he obviously had other things to do, he took the time to help me out. I'll always love him for that.

Lott added another tenor player, named Theodore Arthur. We called him Tha Do (pronounced thay-dough). He was about my age and was at Mattie T. Blunt High School, where Pratt was bandmaster. He was real good at playing the blues style of tenor, much like Clifford Scott or Syl Austin. Together with Lott, we made a pretty good "head" horn section. We performed a lot of Ray Charles material, and those Hank Crawford arrangements were kind of difficult to hear in your head. So I took it on myself to copy down on paper some of Hank's more complicated arrangements. "Drown in My Own Tears," "Them That Got," and a few tunes from the *Fathead* album were some of the first that I copied. Tha Do was as into Ray Charles and the guys in Ray's band as I was into J.J. Johnson. He also turned me on to Bobby Bland. The band and individuals in the band more so than Bobby himself.

So now I'm getting hip to Hank Crawford, David "Fathead" Newman, Don Wilkerson, James Clay and Leroy "Hog" Cooper of the Ray Charles band, and Don Myrick of the Bland band. I'm also beginning to appreciate the arranging of Joe Scott for the Bland band. I wasn't really that interested in arranging, but I did love it when the music came together and sounded like the record. Tha Do, like me, had heard and was equally enthralled by both Pratt and Duke. He was also into learning tunes and increasing his repertoire, so he taught me tunes he knew and I taught him tunes I knew and we, together, sharpened up the tunes we both knew. We became great friends and remain so to this day. It seems he started out on the blues side and moved toward bebop, and I started out on the bebop side and moved toward blues, and we met somewhere in the middle. We definitely influenced each other. He became a world-class tenor player, and, of course, I became Funky Fred. Seriously, when you consider my emulating Tha Do, who had been influenced by so many great players, it's easier to understand why my style of trombone playing is unique. Other than J.J. and Curtis, all my influences, especially people I played with, were bad-ass tenor players. I adopted tenor licks, tenor approaches, and tenor attitudes.

Along with playing trombone and dabbling with arranging, I soon began fooling around with drums. I would go to the big-band rehearsal early to set up Coleman's drums for him. I couldn't resist banging around on them until it was time to start the rehearsal. Eventually, I got to where I could hold a groove on some simple things. On gigs, I sometimes would give Coleman a rest, usually on some easy rock-and-roll tune or a slow blues. The point is, I got to be a fairly adequate drummer.

A friend and neighbor of mine who played drums in the Central High band graduated and enlisted in the Army. He was also a really good funk drummer with bands around town. I don't know how he came to have possession of an upright acoustic bass, but he did, and he asked me to keep it for him. Not "until he came back." Not "for a while." Just "keep it." So I did. And there was no way a bass was going to sit in my house and not get played. Of course, it needed a little maintenance. A string. A bridge. A little polish. Being me, I didn't think to get a book or some instruction. I'd seen the best in the world, Billy Holmes, play this thing, so I'd just do what it looked like Billy was doing. Easy, right? *Wrong.* One night, after I had thumped around with the bass for a few months, I felt confident enough to show Billy that I could play a little bass. He reluctantly let me touch his bass. I started walking some blues, but before I got going good he stopped me. Said I was doing a few basic things wrong. "First, your hands are backwards. You finger with your left hand and pluck with right hand." Then he asked, "How do you play with the low string on top and high string on the bottom?" He and the whole band laughed. That was the joke of the band for almost a year. Billy then proceeded to show me little things here and there. The point is, I became somewhat proficient on bass.

One of the things Daddy left in the house when he and my mother split was a xylophone. I wasn't interested in it at all for some reason, but Thad became fascinated by it. Maybe because we had just heard Lionel Hampton's rendition of "Stardust." We set it up, and he would come over and practice diligently until he got pretty good. I joined in with him on the bass, and together we developed sort of a sound. We got Marvin Robinson to come in and rehearse with us on drums. Thad was tall and slim and struck a confident pose as he played, which made him look like he was playing more than he was. Me, with my short, dumpy self, looked like the bass I was playing, which made me believable. And Marvin, even shorter than me, was mostly buried by the drums but very animated. We were as much a sight as a sound. Together, we managed to be quite entertaining with our five or six tunes. We did a few gigs, mostly for our own pleasure and the pleasure of our friends. We didn't last long because Thad was getting ready to graduate. Plus, he had loftier goals than playing jazz the rest of his life. He enrolled at Tuskegee University. (I told you he was smart.)

It was about time for all of us to start thinking about college. Conrad, who was an extremely good athlete as well as a musician, got a football scholarship to the University of Wyoming. Tommy, who was as academically astute as he was musically inclined, went to Tuskegee to study veterinary medicine. Many of our classmates went to Tennessee State, Florida A&M, North Carolina A&T, Jackson State, and other black colleges. Costello, who was the real brain, attended the University of Wisconsin. We even had one girl in our class, Vivian Malone, who was one of the first two blacks to study at the University of Alabama.

Tha Do and I had decided to follow a career in music. We had narrowed the choices of colleges down to Florida A&M and Tennessee State, mainly because of their great marching bands, music departments, and the people we knew or had heard of who had attended these colleges. We both applied to both colleges. Tha Do got accepted to Florida A&M and went with some kind of a work and ROTC scholarship and his family's help. I got accepted to both, but my mother and father couldn't help me. However, I was invited to attend pre-band drill at Tennessee State, with the possibility of obtaining a scholarship if I did well. I was very excited and apprehensive about being away from home on my own for the first time. It would be great to make it at Tennessee State and be a part of a great and famous band and study music with some great musicians. So I put my pennies together, got a little help from Mom and Dad, and boarded a bus to Nashville.

2

Higher Education

• • •

When I got to pre-band drill, I discovered that although I could play bebop, certain aspects of my trombone training had been totally overlooked. Things like diaphragmatic breathing, double and triple tonguing, and lip slurring I knew nothing about. Some basic musicianship practices had also been neglected. I could read, but I was accustomed to Coleman and Joe Lewis taking time with me to work the music out until it sounded right. The people at Tennessee State were putting music in front of us and expecting us to read and play it correctly on the spot.

Other kids there, competing for the same scholarships, were cutting it with no problem. I felt like I didn't know anything. The only thing I took solace in was my belief that probably none of them could play bebop like I did. But not once did I get a chance to play any jazz at all. It was all about the marching band. Physical training with the football team in the mornings, marching 100 steps a minute in the afternoons, and sight reading music the rest of the day. The word was that if you did happen to make the marching band, a process called "shaking the tree" would eliminate 60 percent of the marchers for concert season.

Needless to say, I didn't make it, although I did manage to stick it out for the entire two weeks. I returned home in utter disgrace. I was mortified. This was how I had thought I might feel had I failed at the jam session. I don't know what I thought Tennessee State was going to be like, but the whole thing was unexpected. The one positive thing was getting to meet Louis "Smitty" Smith, the marching band director. I only had one personal encounter with Smitty, and it was when he was basically telling me I hadn't made it. But he also took time to point out my faults and told me what to work on. Although I didn't immediately take his advice, his words—"push from here," "look ahead," "warm up," "lip slurs," and so on—stay with me to this day.

On the way home from Nashville, I pondered my future. I realize now that all my teachers up to that point had basically been interested in their particular band sounding good, not in preparing an individual to further his or her musical career. It didn't matter to most of my contemporaries who went on to other careers, but to a person like me, whose only goal was to play music professionally, the lack of basic musicianship training was detrimental. My having been lauded for my ability to play not only bebop but any kind of blues or R&B gig around town had caused me to ignore the need to prepare for the possibility of a broader career in music. So now I, like so many other good, potentially great, musicians, was stuck in a maze of local gigs. I was making as much as it was possible to make playing gigs locally and still just barely supporting myself. If I were to take a wife I would have to get a job at the post office or something. Like everybody else. My only hope of not becoming Fortune or Freeman was the far-fetched possibility of getting a road gig with B. B. King or Bobby Bland or Ray Charles or one of the many other bands that came through town. My success with bebop had severely limited my options as a total musician.

I knew I had to get some kind of an education. My father pointed out my poor study habits in high school and suggested I join the Army and develop some discipline before spending a whole lot of money on college. My alternative and the alternative for many others who couldn't afford to go away to college or hadn't been accepted to a desirable college was the Mobile Branch of Alabama State College—a two-year junior college barely a step above high school. I enrolled because it was what I could afford on what I made gigging, and I needed to do something to occupy my time while I waited for that far-fetched road gig that would get me to New York, where I would be discovered as the next J.J. Johnson, record big-time albums, and live happily ever after.

I majored in music, of course, and minored in history. There was no band. The music course consisted of mandatory choir, music theory, and concentration on an instrument. There was only one music teacher, Mr. Carter. He directed the choir and played piano, so your instrument concentration had to be voice or piano. Back to piano again. I still didn't want to end up Gwen Howard, but I *really* didn't want to end up Alice Bumpers, who was Mr. Carter's star vocal student. In the two years I took music theory in college, we covered the exact same material we had covered in high school. I was hoping to get to counterpoint and arranging-composition, which I'd heard about. In my entire college career, however, I never got past four-part writing. (This explains a lot about my subsequent horn arrangements and compositions, doesn't it?)

There were required courses. Physical science I hardly ever went to. When I did go, I didn't know what the hell Mr. Lee was mumbling about. Something about elements and valences. Luckily, this was one of those classes where if you showed up enough for him to know your face with your name, you got a C.

My history teacher was Frank Miller, the consummate college professor. He dressed like, looked like, acted like, and talked like a professor. To pass his class, you simply had to listen to his colorful lectures and write a number of essays, all of which had to begin the same way. For example, if we were studying the Magna Carta, the essay would have to begin, "The Magna Carta is significant in that. . . ." I thought that was so cool. If you listened, did a minimum of reading, and could put your memory into words, you could pass this class easily. I may not remember much history, but I did learn to listen attentively, take appropriate notes, and organize ideas so that they could be easily understood.

The teacher for the humanities course was a very odd person named Ms. Evans. She was a fair-skinned black woman of indeterminate age. She wore glasses. Had long nappy gray hair that she wore in a ponytail that looked more like one gigantic dreadlock. Her teeth were gapped and uneven, though healthy and clean. She wore long dresses like a pioneer woman and an enormous diamond ring. I never knew where she came from or what her story was. She was different, but she seemed to have only one purpose in life, and she pursued it constantly and vigorously. That purpose was to impart some appreciation of culture to us country boys and girls. Most of us didn't understand the importance of her course at the time, but I now see that she gave us a starting point to learn about the finer things in life. The course was varied. Some days we learned about art by looking at paintings or studying color and texture, different periods, and great artists such as Renoir, Van Gogh, and Picasso. Other days we found ourselves in a dance class, doing what she called "stunts and tumbling." Hygiene was an important part of the course. Almost every day we had some discussion on V.D. or pregnancy-related subjects. And any time you saw her outside of her class, whether it was on campus or downtown in church, she had some kind of pertinent lecture or information for you. I will always love and appreciate her for her dedication and diligence.

My favorite class and the one I'm sure I got the most out of was English Literature. Ms. Harris, who was passionate about literature, exposed us to the great English masters like Shakespeare, Kipling, and Keats. At the same time we learned the mechanics of writing. Surprisingly, I really enjoyed the challenge of putting ideas into poetry or prose. To this day, one of my greatest pleasures comes from putting words into music and music into words. It all started in Ms. Harris's English Lit class.

Although "the Branch" wasn't a world-class university and we all looked at it as just something to do until we could get into a real college, Mr. Bishop (the dean) had put together a faculty that really cared about exposing youngsters to a variety of ideas that would have eluded them had the Branch not existed. At the time, my classmates and I viewed Dean Bishop as someone you feared would put you out of school for bad behavior or low grades or for failing to pay your tuition. But now I realize that the work he did was a labor of love born of his concern for the survival of his people.

During my two years at the Branch, I continued to play gigs in and around Mobile. I was juggling bookings with Coleman's big band, Lott's band, Joe Lewis's band (now called the Esquires), and any- and everything else that came along. Since these gigs were my sole support, the type of music I played was secondary to how much a gig paid. I still loved jazz and wanted to advance my bebop skills, but I had fallen into that syndrome of playing with whoever paid the most. So, in order to work a lot, I took a lot of R&B gigs and blues gigs with bands that worked regularly. I still managed to make the jam session most Sundays, and by then I did a gig or two with Pratt whenever Freeman couldn't make it. My jazz chops suffered because playing loud and long on R&B and blues gigs did a job on my flexibility and articulation. However, I was picking up some phrasings and dynamics that the strict bebop player doesn't encounter. Along with being influenced by bad-ass tenor players, I was then being influenced by bad-ass guitar players. On some gigs, with bands that didn't have tenor players, I would be the one to play the tenor solo if one came up or the guitar solo if we didn't have a guitar. That's how I learned Bill Doggett's "Honky Tonk"—by playing the tenor and guitar solos. In many situations, I was the only horn or the only one in the band who could solo.

This was the early '60s, with Jim Crow still in effect, and whenever an

R&B show came to town, the place for the band to stay was the Le Grand Motel, across the street from Clayton's Baby Grand Lounge. Usually, after each show Ms. Clayton McCord, the proprietress of the lounge, would have Pratt's band host a jam session where, it was hoped, the stars or at least the guys in the band would come and hang out, maybe even perform. I saw this as an excellent opportunity to play with and be heard by some top-notch musicians. I did get to meet people like Johnny Coles and Marcus Belgrave and James Horbert and most all of Ray Charles's band. I met and am still friends with June Gardner, the drummer with Sam Cooke. I knew all the guys in Bobby Bland's band—Melvin (Runt) Jackson, Pluma Davis, Mel Brown, Wayne Bennett, and so on—as well as musicians from every blues and R&B band on the road, from B.B. King to Earl Bostic. I even got the chance to play behind Arthur Prysock, Jerry Butler, and Curtis Mayfield when, for whatever reason, they came to town without their bands.

Once, a bass player friend of mine, Marshall York, who had played with B.B., put together a band to go to Gulfport, Mississippi, about fifty miles away, to do a show with B.B., whose band was stranded somewhere out on the road on a broken-down bus. It was great to be in the company of a big star like B.B. I discovered, even though I'm sure B.B. didn't do his regular show, that I was able to hang with a professional artist. I didn't get to do a solo, but I was sure that if one had come up I would have been able to handle it. B.B. was a big star at that time, but he related to everyone— including me, who was obviously very young—like he was a regular person. After the show he had a drink of Scotch with everybody and paid me $29. (I don't know what everybody else made.) That was three times as much as I had ever made in one night locally. I couldn't believe it. I was scared something was going to happen before I made it the fifty miles back home.

Another time, I was just hanging around the Ebony Club watching the Five Royales set up for a show, when they realized that their drummer was somehow incapacitated and couldn't make the gig. They asked me if I knew a drummer. I tried calling every drummer I could think of, to no avail, then finally admitted I could play a little drums and made the gig.

I would let all the road musicians I met know that I was looking for a gig. They all acknowledged that I was good enough, but said I was too young for the rigors of the road and was doing the right thing by going to school. Still, I always made sure everyone had my number in hopes that someday I'd get that call. I did get one call, but it came to Clayton, the lady who ran the Baby Grand. She told me that somebody from Ray Charles's band had called for the young trombone player. She told him that I had the same name as my father who was a teacher at Central High School and should be easy to find in the phone book. Only thing, she thought my father was Freeman Jones, who was indeed a teacher at Central and did have a son named Freeman Jr., but he didn't play an instrument at all. I later found out that someone had called Mr. Jones from Ray's band, and he had no idea what they were talking about. I guess the words, teacher, Freeman, trombone, and son got mixed up in Clayton's mind, and as a result, I missed my big chance to go out with the Ray Charles band. My quest for a road gig continued.

In the meantime, I completed my two years at the Branch and received a junior college degree. Even though I had gone there just to pass time, I was proud of my degree, and I had actually learned a lot.

In order to get a B.A., I would have to go to the main college in Montgomery. So, still with nothing better to do, I enrolled at Alabama State College. Besides, I had fallen madly in love with Alice Bumpers, and she was going to be there, so how bad could it be? My close friend Kerwin Ridgeway, also a music major at the Branch, and I took his car to Montgomery. Mine probably would not have made the almost 200-mile trip. We got a room in a rooming house near the campus where other students also boarded.

The band at Alabama State was a mess. The only thing I remember is rehearsing "Stardust" over and over again. I think we wore the same uniforms that Coleman and Pratt had worn when they were there. I kinda jived my way through some history classes, some more of the same music theory, and a physical science class that was really serious this time. I met a tenor saxophone player named Willie Gresham, who got me an every-night gig with the Al Stringer Band. So my first year at Alabama State was spent going to school every now and then, running behind Alice Bumpers, doing the Al Stringer gig at the Afro Club, and eating pig ears and practicing with Willie Gresham.

Eating pig ears and practicing with Willie Gresham took up most of my time. Most days, we would start out early in the morning, go to the store, pick up a couple pounds of ears, go to his place, put the ears on to cook, and start practicing some Coltrane solos that he had transcribed. He would suffer along with me for a while, then tell me to continue to work while he went into the other room and worked out of some weird scale book he had. I would get frustrated and say, "Er . . . Willie, I'm gonna call it a day" or "I've got a class" or "I've got to meet Alice." He'd get real mad and yell at me. "No! Hell no! You need this. You can make up your schoolwork anytime. Alice, if she really loves you, she'll wait. Get back in there and practice!" I don't know if I was scared he was going to jump on me, or if I knew he was right, or if I just wanted to be there when the pig ears got done, but I stayed and worked harder than I ever had before on runs and scales and things that should have been for tenor players. Whenever I could duck Willie, I would try to find Alice, who I was sure was cheating on me. But if I spent too much time with Alice, I felt like I was cheating on Willie.

By then school was incidental. I was torn between love and sex with Alice and the serious progress I was making with Willie. But there was nowhere to play up to the proficiency I had achieved. The Stringer gig was mostly R&B and blues, although Willie and I managed to throw in a little jazz. Also, the money I was making at the Afro Club wasn't nearly enough to pay my rent and tuition. I was getting farther and farther behind in both. My diet consisted of pig ears (of course), whatever Alice could sneak out of the cafeteria, the pot of beans and rice Ridgeway and I cooked once a week, and the occasional fried chicken dinner, usually on a Sunday, that Alice and Rosetta, Ridgeway's girlfriend, would cook for us. I was surviving, but I could see the end of the rope approaching.

I had passed the first year by some hook or crook and had passed all my exams for the second quarter of the second year except one. Physical science. The professor had allowed us to take the final exam either in the morning at eight o'clock or in the afternoon at one o'clock. It was a Monday morning after a busy Sunday night with Alice and the gig. I woke up at nine o'clock. "No problem," I thought. "I'll just take the exam at one o'clock." I went back to sleep and woke up at two o'clock. I went to the professor and told him what happened. He was very unsympathetic, mainly because he didn't know who I was because he hadn't seen me very much. He said I would have to see the dean of the science department. He was the dean of the science department. I felt myself being jerked around, and I never could stand that. I said fuck it. Of course, this meant that in order to graduate I would have to, at some point, take physical science again. That reality, along with being three weeks behind in my rent and not knowing how I was going to pay my next quarter's tuition, brought the end of the rope into full view.

Ridgeway was in similar dire straits. So we loaded up his car in the middle of the night and got the hell out of Dodge. The car had a busted engine block, but someone had told us that adding cornmeal to the radiator would seal the block temporarily. So carrying a bag of corn meal and making frequent stops for oil and water, we limped back to Mobile and arrived spewing smoke all over the place and smelling like corn bread.

Back home, I tried to hook back up with my old gigs. But I found that everyone had successfully adjusted to me being gone. I was squeezed in wherever Lott or Coleman or Pratt or Joe Lewis could manage, but the reality was that I had no income. Everyone was impressed with the progress I'd made, but business is business and there was no place for me right away.

But, as it has been throughout my career, when my chops are up, good things happen. I got a call from Tom Koch, owner of Club Harlem. He said that Ike and Tina Turner had played there the night before and needed a baritone saxophone player, but he had talked Ike into hiring me on trombone instead. He had convinced Ike that I was the greatest thing since salt and could handle anything.

This was not the kind of gig I had hoped for. At the time, Ike and Tina were not on par with Ray Charles and Bobby Bland. Sam Cooke and Jackie Wilson were the real hot artists during this time. A gig with a jazz group like Horace Silver's or Art Blakey's would have been most desirable. But I was broke and had to give it a try. I rushed down to the Le Grand Motel and had a brief meeting with Ike, who seemed very business-like, and I was hired without being heard. I was expecting to have to audition. But, on the word of Tom Koch, I got the gig at $25 a night, from which I had to pay my own room and board.

Their next gig was in Gulfport, Mississippi, the same place I had played with B.B. King. I met the bus in the morning. The first of the musicians to greet me was Mack Johnson, the trumpet player. He didn't talk much, although I was trying to get as much advance information about the show as possible. He just kept saying, "Wait, you'll see, it's not hard, you'll be all right." I had a lot of questions. "Was there any music? What do I wear? Will I get to rehearse?" He just said, "Be cool. You'll find out."

Then the rest of the band boarded the bus. First was saxophonist Rashi Ashima, a short man, solidly built, who walked with a slight limp and wore a white turban. Right off, I assumed he was in some sort of religion, but when I talked to him he didn't come off religious at all. Then came a happy-go-lucky type named Junior. He was part bass player, part roadie, part valet, part bodyguard, and part anything else needed to make

Funk Brass Pioneer, Mack
Johnson. Promotional photo.

things happen. The bus driver was a big, strong, healthy dude named
Duke. Looked like a bodybuilder. About 6' 2". Carried a briefcase. Obviously country but tried to talk proper.

Everybody else came in twos. Sam Rhodes and Jesse Knight. Sam
was the actual bass player. Everybody called him Skillet, maybe because
of his dark complexion. He turned out to be a real great guy—friendly,
helpful, and the first truly funky bass player I ever played with. Jesse
Knight was actually Jessica Knight, one of the Ikettes nicknamed Mucho,
for good and obvious reasons. She was muuuuucho.

Next came Jimmy Thomas and Vanetta Fields. Jimmy was one of the
featured singers, and Vanetta was another one of the Ikettes. Looked like
my cousin Marva.

Ernest Lane and my favorite Ikette, Robbie Montgomery, came next.
Lane was the piano player. A well-built, good-looking, neat guy who
played pretty good blues and rock-and-roll piano. Robbie was so cute,
with a sorta sleepy smile, smooth yellow skin, long legs, and a beautiful
slim body. Plus, she was nice to me. Said I was cute. Gave me the nickname Hog Jaws, because of my cute little fat jaws. I should have been
insulted, but because it was coming from her, I was honored to have
the name.

The strangest couple in the group was Thomas "Nose" Norwood and
Bobby John. Nose was the drummer. About my age. Skinny, light-skinned

guy from Chapel Hill, North Carolina. The first truly funky drummer I played with. Bobby was another featured singer with the show. Did a Marvin Gaye imitation. Acted like he was Nose's mother. "C'mon on this bus, Nose." "Where yo' clean socks, Nose?" "You better leave that girl alone, Nose." Stuff like that. And Nose went along with it like a little kid. I don't know what that was about.

Then came Ike and Tina Turner. Ike was real talkative now. Laughing and joking with everybody. Whatever he was saying wasn't that funny, but everybody was laughing anyway, so I laughed, too. Tina didn't impress me much at that first meeting. She was a nice-looking girl. Not much stuff to speak of. Kinda quiet. Nothing special. Her sister, Alean, who apparently served as her valet, was more noticeable, with her big butt, flashing eyes, and flirty demeanor. She was darker skinned than Tina. I learned later that she was also part of a couple; the somehow incapacitated baritone saxophonist, whom I was replacing, was her boyfriend. I wondered if she came with the gig.

On the way to Gulfport, they all made themselves known to me, calling me young blood, country boy, and the like. It seemed they were all from St. Louis but now lived in Los Angeles. They made Los Angeles sound real interesting. I couldn't wait until we played there. When we arrived in Gulfport, some of us went to get some food, while Junior and Nose set up the stage. When we got back, we had a short rehearsal to get me acquainted with some of the show. I think it was that day that I began hating that type of rehearsal. The kind of rehearsal in which the leader— in this case, Ike—tries not so much to better the show or learn a particular song but to impress someone—in this case, me—as to how much he knows or what a great musician he is. Ike was a fairly decent blues-type guitar player. I expected more of a performance from him, being as how the show was called Ike and Tina Turner. Ike's band was sorta like Mr. Lott's R&B band with extremely bad motherfuckers at every position.

I had to forget being cool. Every tune had an accompanying dance step or "routine." The steps were pretty simple for the horns but the rhythm section—Ike, Sam, Junior, and Lane—did somersaults and other fantastic stuff. But I was most impressed with Mack Johnson. He played with so much energy at all times, it was unbelievable. Whether he was soloing or just playing parts, he was all into it. The only other time I'd heard a funky trumpet soloist was on a recording by Phillip Upchurch called "Can't Sit Down." It turned out that Mack was that same trumpet player. Well, now I'm a Mack Johnson fan. I'm listening to everything he does. What notes he plays. How he approaches a solo. Ever since I had started with Lott's band I had halfheartedly tried to play funky, but I felt funny playing that kind of stuff on a brass instrument. Mack, in a way, freed me up—gave me permission to be funky as I wanna be.

The show was much like any other R&B gig I'd done, although on a higher level, of course. The band was tight. Each player was perfect. The groove was consistently strong. It wasn't jazz, but it was good. Real good. The band did a couple of numbers. Jimmy Thomas sang a couple. Bobby John did two Marvin Gaye songs. All the while, Ike was onstage, sort of directing the band.

And then Tina came on. The girl I had been so unimpressed with as she boarded the bus was now a flaming beauty. When I had seen her on the bus, she had had on some pants, a sweater, and a scarf on her head. Now, she was in high heels, a short shoestring-strap dress, and a long wig. I was speechless. I didn't believe it was the same woman. Plus, now she had an attitude. She strutted up on the stage, grabbed the mike, and went crazy. Screaming and hollering like a Baptist preacher. Dancing and slinging her hair and acting all sexy. She was, without a doubt, the star of the show. And the Ikettes looked even more appealing than they had on the bus. That first show was so thrilling to me, I should have bought a ticket.

By the time we played Pensacola, Florida, and Montgomery, Alabama, I pretty much had my part down, although I was still having a little trouble with the routines. The next stop was Memphis. But, by then, the baritone sax player, Marvin Warrick, had recovered, so I was set to go back home. However, Rashi, the tenor player, was scheduled for some kind of hernia operation. Since I had learned the show so fast and so well, Ike decided to keep me rather than try to break in another tenor player, especially since Rashi was planning to come back.

Over the next few weeks, I settled in and became the trombone player with the Ike and Tina Turner Revue. Between me, Mack, and Marvin, nobody ever missed the tenor player. It wasn't jazz, but it was fun.

This was what I wanted. Life on the Road. Town to town. Motel to motel. Or so I thought. This was 1962, and some cities didn't have motels for blacks. We either didn't stay in those towns or stayed in rooming houses, which could be very interesting. Rooming houses were usually someone's residence or a place where they rented rooms by the hour. We would try to double up in order to save money. (This was before I had ever heard of "plus room and board" or "plus per diem.")

I ended up rooming with Junior, who was a good person to show a new guy the ropes. He knew all the towns. He was proud of and enjoyed sharing his expertise about the clubs, girls, and other things you needed to know to get along on the road.

When we got to Memphis, we stayed at the now famous Lorraine Motel. I also got my first experience in a recording studio there. Somehow, it had gotten around that I could write music. So Ike got me to write down some ideas he had for horn parts. We recorded at the famous Sun Recording Studio, and although I don't remember it, we met Isaac Hayes, who was doing odd jobs there at that time. We must not have recorded a hit, because I don't remember the tune, but I do remember that I enjoyed it, hearing myself played back for the first time. Ike seemed happy that it went well and that I did a good job playing and writing. There was one point at which he wanted me to play some kind of gliss or slide. He implied that only he knew what he was talking about, trying to make it seem like I was so young or so inexperienced that I couldn't pick up on what a great and experienced recording artist like Ike Turner was trying to say, although he had probably never seen a trombone up close before. But it ended up being that he had taught Fred Wesley Jr. to do what has always and will always be known as "the smear." (There's a hand gesture that goes along with the smear.) Sam Rhodes does it best, to this day.

The Ike and Tina Turner Revue was a dynamic, well-organized, hard-driving show. I had seen Ray Charles's, Bobby Bland's, and B.B. King's shows, and they didn't come close to being as entertaining as Ike and Tina. Ike's show didn't compare musically, but overall it was far more exciting.

But there was serious dissension within the band, caused mainly by Ike's personality. He was basically an abusive person who seemed to feel like he was doing you a favor by having you in his band. No matter how well we played, he would find something to bitch about. At first, I thought there was really some problem, but I soon realized that he would find a problem no matter what. If not with the band, then with the Ikettes or one of the singers. If not about the music, then about the uniforms or hair. I came to the conclusion that all his ranting and raving was his way of justifying his position as boss. I think he thought that if he didn't point out our shortcomings, he couldn't justify his existence to us, the public, or himself. And maybe the show wouldn't have been as tight if he didn't keep everyone on their toes. But I didn't like the disrespectful way he spoke to people, especially the women, calling them bitches and whores and the like. He would impose fines, which came to be known as Turner Tax, seemingly just when you could least afford it, like in a big city where hotel bills were high or in a week during which you only worked two or three days. We usually worked every night and at $25 a night, less hotels, which averaged about $4 a night, I was doing pretty well. But a couple of $20 fines could really mess up your week.

Ike would also threaten violence. I actually saw him pull a gun on one of the guys in the band. And, although I never actually witnessed him hitting Tina, I did see her face all beat up. Some people in the group would take his insults and abuse and go on as usual, but some would grumble and talk about quitting as soon as we get to this place or that place, or as soon as I get paid, or as soon as something. Because I was new, I didn't get too much abuse. I guess you had to be eased into a position where you would have to take his insults and humiliations. You see, with just two days in the band, there's nothing to lose. You could just walk away. But get comfortable with your salary and make a few commitments. Suddenly, you think that being called a dumb motherfucker ain't so bad "as long as I get paid and he don't put his hands on me."

By the time we got to St. Louis, Mack Johnson had quit for a gig with James Brown, Marvin Warrick decided not to leave St. Louis, which was his home, and Rashi was still recovering from his operation. That left me as the only horn. So, like it or not, I became pretty important to the Ike and Tina Turner Revue. There was no actual horn music, and nobody else in the band, including Ike, knew enough about horns to put another horn section together. So Ike hired three players from St. Louis: Vern Harrell on baritone sax, Buggs Harris on tenor sax, and a guy named David on trumpet. We spent a couple of weeks playing around St. Louis. I was in and out of Ike's house in East St. Louis, rehearsing the horns, and spending the rest of my time at the Washington Hotel on Delmar Street.

I learned a lot about putting shows together during that time. I also learned a lot about life in general around Ike's house and around the Washington Hotel. Suddenly, I'm no longer an innocent kid from Mobile, Alabama. I'm now another one of those road musicians that people warn their daughters about. I learn how to drink Ol' Grand Dad and throw up. I smoke pot with a policeman friend of the band, in the police car. Learn all about sex from a tall, beautiful black girl named Stella at about $20 a lesson. I do a recording session, in which I write the arrangements, for

Fontella Bass. And, most important, I gain the respect of the great musicians of the Ike Turner Band. I'm in the big city of St. Louis, making money as a professional musician. Was this the big time or what?

It wasn't long before I got real comfortable with my new life. But, as it has been throughout my career, when I get comfortable, I get bored, or at least restless. I was happy with where I was, but my goal to be the next great jazz trombonist had been put aside. This came back to my attention once when we were in Columbus, Ohio, and I got the opportunity to sit in with Johnny "Hammond Organ" Smith. They called some tunes that I didn't know, and the ones that I knew were more difficult to play than I remembered. It was clear that the music I was playing every night wasn't doing my jazz chops any good. I seemed to be losing speed and flexibility, although gaining strength. I could play louder and longer but not nearly as smooth and lyrical. This concerned me greatly. I didn't intend to play with Ike and Tina Turner or any other R&B band for the rest of my life. Indeed, this was just a way out of Alabama. A stepping-stone to hooking up with a jazz band. The reality was that very seldom did R&B bands and jazz bands cross paths. So I decided to discipline myself to practice during the day and on off days. This was hard to do, because usually we traveled during the day and on off days. I started making plans to save up enough money to leave the revue and just move to New York or L.A., where I could get back to studying jazz and actively seeking a jazz gig.

About a year into the Ike and Tina Turner gig, we ended up in Atlanta at the Forrest Arms Hotel. This was the early sixties and even in a large city like Atlanta, there weren't many places for black people to stay. So most bands stayed at the Forrest Arms. It was conveniently located, close to the Royal Peacock, a popular nightclub/showroom on the "chitlin circuit," where we had just played and where most of the top blues and R&B artists played regularly. The hotel was also close to Ford and Mae's soul-food restaurant. Best food I ever ate. We had a few days off after the Royal Peacock gig, so I got a chance to see a little of Atlanta. Every day, at least twice a day, I would be at Ford and Mae's. I met *a lot* of people as I ate. Most were just local people who loved the food, but some were other music professionals who stayed at the hotel either temporarily or permanently.

Among them was Gorgeous George, a famous emcee, comedian, and tailor. We mostly talked about the possibility of him making me some clothes so I could look more like an R&B musician. But I was still Alabama conservative and wasn't about to wear the kind of clothes he had on. He took a liking to me and showed me around, introduced me to some people, mostly beautiful girls. Somehow, we got to talking about how I really wanted to play jazz and how my gig with Ike and Tina was just a means to hook up with a jazz band. He informed me that Hank Ballard and his band were permanent residents of the Forrest Arms, as was he. And that Hank's band often jammed in one of the rooms when they weren't working. He introduced me to Pat Patterson, Hank's bandleader and trumpet player, who invited me to come by and jam with them. He said they were doing it in the saxophone player's room. So I told Vern, our baritone sax player.

When Vern and I knocked on the door, I was shocked to see my old friend, classmate, and teacher, Willie Gresham, open the door. I hadn't seen Willie since I'd left Alabama State and had wondered what had happened to him. I couldn't believe that a die-hard jazzman like Willie Gresham would take a gig with Hank "Thrill on the Hill"/"Work with Me Annie"/"Do the Twist" Ballard. I would've felt like I had to justify playing with Ike and Tina Turner, but as we talked, I realized we were both doing the same thing—biding our time until we could get a better gig. So jam we did. Until we could jam no mo'. There were just the two horns with Hank's band, and Willie and Pat bragged about how Hank gave them freedom to do anything they wanted with the band, including hiring musicians and choosing songs the band played. Vern and I were disgruntled with Ike for not letting us play anything "too jazzy" on the show, even during the band set. Willie and Pat said that their band set was almost completely jazz and that Willie had even done some jazzy horn parts for "Work with Me Annie" and "Thrill on The Hill." They started talking about adding two horns, and Vern and I started talking about leaving Ike and Tina. The kicker came when we got to the money part. We were both making $25 a gig with Ike. They said they could pay us $35 a gig. Well, that did it for me, and for Vern, too.

The only thing left to do was the hard part of telling Ike I was leaving the band. Ike was so unpredictable, you never knew what his reaction would be. Both of us leaving would definitely disrupt the Ike and Tina show. We didn't know if he'd jump on us or shoot us or what. We had seen him go crazy when somebody put him in some kind of difficulty. When I finally got up the nerve to face him, I called myself trying to do the right thing by giving a two-week notice. He simply said, "That won't be necessary. Bye." However, Tina came to me later and said that I shouldn't leave, because Ike really liked me and was thinking about making me band leader. It was not his way to tell me something like this after I had told him I was leaving—it would sound too much like begging, and Ike was a very proud man. Well, it wasn't my way to change my mind after receiving this new information—it would look like I was politicking or something. I, too, God help me, am a very proud man.

For the first time in a long time, "The Gong Gong," which is what the Ike and Tina Turner bus was called, pulled off without me. I was left with sort of an empty feeling. After all, that bus had been home to me for almost a year. I would really miss Duke, Junior, Robbie, Mack, Buggs, Vanetta, Mucho, Sam, Bobby John, Nose, Lane, Jimmy, Ike, and especially Tina—watching her prance back and forth across the stage, slinging her hair and singing so passionately until she made herself cry. It was a pleasure to have shared the stage with that most exciting performer. I shudda bought a ticket every night. So once again I'd left a comfortable situation to embark on what I was sure at the time would be a better road to lead me to my ultimate goal.

I thought I'd covered all the important questions about the Hank Ballard gig, but there were a few areas I failed to get straight. Like, how many gigs did Hank do a week? This came up after we'd been around Atlanta almost a week, rehearsing. This was fun, hanging out with Gorgeous George and rehearsing jazz licks for such songs as "The Twist" and "Annie Had a Baby." But it was all with no gigs and no money. And I still hadn't seen Hank Ballard's face. Whenever I'd ask about the gigs or Hank, Pat would tell us that Hank had gone to New York to meet with his manager, Ben Bart, and would return soon with the new itinerary and money. "Don't worry. We'll be rolling in a little while." So I relaxed and had fun, even though I was running out of the little money I had managed to save (you remember, to go to New York). I had almost forgotten. I was so excited about playing jazz regularly with my main man Willie and behind big stars like Hank Ballard and the Midnighters. Why should I worry? The Midnighters had many more hit records than Ike and Tina. This was a step up. This was really the big time.

After about two weeks of hanging out, rehearsing, and becoming a regular fixture around the Forrest Arms Hotel, I was down to my last few dollars, sustaining myself on Ford and Mae's fifty-cent bowl of Lima beans and rice once a day. Hank finally showed up. He was a very friendly, hip-talking, real nice guy. Not at all what you'd expect a big star to be like. He seemed to be happy about the idea of having a bigger band. He said that we were going to be doing the theater circuit soon and making the real big money. But first, we were going to do a few small gigs on the East Coast and around the South. We were getting ready to go to the first gig, somewhere down in Alabama, when I realized that I also had neglected to ask about the bus. Where was the bus? There was no bus. There were two station wagons. A very nice, brown Oldsmobile station wagon, known as the brown one, and a very nice, blue Pontiac station wagon, known as the blue one. The no-bus revelation made the reality of the Midnighters important. Let's count up. There were me and Willie, P.P. and Vern, bass player Evins, guitar player Melvin, drummer Gasden, a piano player I can't remember, Norman, Box, bald-headed Henry, and Hank. That's twelve people. And their instruments. And their luggage. Plus, we were to take turns driving. I had wondered why they kept asking me if I could drive.

Big time? What had I gotten myself into? Being the new person and the youngest, of course I got to ride in the middle, in the back of the brown one, on the hump. At that time, the Ike and Tina Turner gig, playing rock and roll all night, wasn't looking too bad. But I was young and looking forward to playing more jazz and things being much better when we started the theater circuit. It *was* kinda fun driving up and down the road, footloose and fancy free. We worked out of Atlanta, mostly weekends, usually leaving on Thursday or Friday, depending on how far we had to go. We went through Mississippi, Louisiana, all the way to Oklahoma and Kansas City. Whenever it came time to get paid, we'd hear that "We got a check" or "The deposit is in the office in New York" or "You'll get it at the end of the week, or when we get back to Atlanta." Along the way, I would be handed out $20 or $30 draws and promises of more soon. But I held on to the promises of going to New York and theaters and more money and all that.

Things got to be so bad that people began to leave. At one time, we were playing shows with just a bass for rhythm. I even played drums for a while. We finally picked up a drummer from Columbia, Missouri. He couldn't play, but he was a nice person and very eager to travel and learn. He traveled, but we never did go back to Missouri and he never did learn.

For a while, we worked a few gigs out of Washington, D.C. We stayed at a rooming house across from the famous Howard Theater. Hank disappeared again. Went to New York to get money from his manager. Ma Buford let us have the rooms by the week. I especially remember having a very small room on the top floor, in the attic really, for $15 a week. After Hank was gone a week, Mrs. Buford demanded the rent for the second week, which we didn't have. She was a very nice lady, but she needed her money to play the numbers every day. Plus, she had a bad case of arthritis and had to have her medicine. She would bug us every day but let us stay on, as we promised Hank would be back any day now. It was rough, but due to her kindness and the restaurant next to the Howard Theater giving us credit, we survived. One night, I was in the restaurant trying to convince the owner to let me have one more bowl of beans on credit and was overheard by a short guy who turned out to be the pianist Erroll Garner. He said he understood the plight of struggling musicians, and he bought me a full meal. We talked. I made a friend.

The people at the Howard Theater knew that we were with Hank Ballard and would let us watch the shows on slow days. The Howard was one of the main stops on the theater circuit that was being dangled in my face. I got to see Ray Charles and reacquaint myself with some of his band members. Of course, the spot they had called me for had been taken by a great player named James Horbert, from Memphis. I felt good seeing them in another city with me having a professional gig of my own. I tried my best not to let Hogg Copper, Marcus Belgrave, and Fathead Newman know what kind of fix I was really in. Although I think they knew. We would go out and jam around as there were a few hot jazz spots in the neighborhood. The real famous place was the Bohemian Caverns. I got to hear Shirley Horn and Betty Gray. I met and got to know Mickey Bass, who showed me around and gave me the opportunity to be on some very good sessions with some great musicians. I particularly remember meeting and playing with Leo Morris, who is now named Idris Muhammad. He was Jerry Butler's drummer at that time. I guess I shouldn't have been, but I was surprised at what a fine jazz drummer he was. I also met this old man who walked with a limp and played tenor sax like nobody I'd ever heard. His name was Johnny Brown. He took a liking to me and would come to my room and help me with tunes like "All the Things You Are" and "Night in Tunisia." He never told me, but I found out later that he had once been lead alto player with Dizzy Gillespie. That explained why he was so lyrical on tenor. All I know is that he was very patient with me and that I learned *a lot* from him. To this day, I can hear his voice saying "learn the changes."

James Brown played the Howard for a week while we were there. I found out then that Mack Johnson was in the band. He said it was a good gig, paying a salary, which was unheard of for R&B bands at that time. He was making $225 a week, work or no work. He also said that they might be interested in hiring a trombone player and that he would recommend me if I wanted it. Being a little more cautious, I told him to wait and I would think about it first.

One of J.B.'s saxophone players, Brisco, had the room next to mine at Ma Buford's. He was a heavy drinker. It seemed like he would start drinking before the first show at ten o'clock in the morning and get drunker and drunker as the day went on until after the fifth show at midnight he'd be so drunk he couldn't stand up. So he would get to talking. He told me horror stories about fines and marathon rehearsals, threats of violence, and other stuff. He must have gotten fired ten times during that week. One day I went over and caught a show. It was unbelievable. Not only was the singing and dancing that James Brown was doing fantastic, but the band was working and dancing almost as hard and blowing horns at the same time. But there were not nearly enough chances to play jazz. I thanked Mack but declined. I was still hoping to hook up with a jazz gig.

Hank finally showed up, late and with barely enough money to pay for the rooms and the restaurant bill. My reasons for taking this gig and staying on this gig were becoming fewer and fewer. That the gig was about sex and drugs became clearer and clearer to me, starting with the time we were scheduled to play Erie, Pennsylvania, on a Friday night.

Erie is about 900 miles from Atlanta. We pack up on Thursday morning, ready to go. Hank is in his room with a girl. He says he'll be right down. We wait. One hour. Two hours. We send someone up there again. He's coming. We wait. Now it's noon. We're getting worried now. Has something happened to him? No. He has done this before. Don't worry. He's coming. Now it's night, and I'm really concerned. Nobody else seems to care, because everyone except me and Evins are grooving on cough syrup.

We finally left early Friday morning, driving like bats out of hell, and got to Erie just in time to start the gig late. I was really fed up, but I was stuck. I also started grooving on the syrup and participating in the orgies, and I got used to trying to make the gig with whoever showed up in whatever condition.

Many things became more important than the music. On the way to the East Coast from the Erie area, we made a detour through Pittsburgh, where P.P. knew a doctor who would get us five gallons of Robitussin AC. We got it. It took all the money everybody had. And we had to leave some luggage to get that five-gallon jug into the station wagon.

We finally made it to New York City. We kinda limped into town and checked in at the famous Cecil Hotel in Harlem. This was another favorite hotel of road bands, centrally located in beautiful downtown Harlem, one block from the legendary Apollo Theater. Was this it? Are we here to play the Apollo? I certainly hoped not. We were all ragged and dirty, half out of our minds from drugs. Here I was, at last in the Big Apple, and all I wanted to do was sleep in a bed. We had been hitting and running for the last few days. Hank had once again gone to meet with his manager and get us some money. I did get some sleep and cleaned up as best I could and started thinking about getting out and playing. That's when I realized that my chops were probably way down because I had all but abandoned my practice discipline.

Again, Hank's meeting with his manager lasted for days, so I got a chance to look around New York as much as I could with no money. Evins had run into some friends of his from Texas. A band called Garnell Cooper and the Kinfolk. They were Etta James's backup band. The drummer, a young phenom named Richard Waters, and Evins were good friends, and we set up a jam session right in the room at the Cecil Hotel. This was my first killer session. I never knew just how much bass Evins played. They kicked off a tune—I think it was Charlie Parker's "Tune Up"—at a breakneck tempo and played it all day. It was the kind of personal thing between bass and drums where a horn solo was incidental. I played as long as I could, then gave it up to Willie, went out and had lunch, and came back. P.P. and some other cats had come by, and Richard and Evins were still playing. I think the tempo had picked up. This went on literally all day. I would play a little while, give it up to other horn players, then come back and play some more. Evins and Richard were still playing. I think the only thing that stopped them was that Richard had to pee.

One night P.P. said he was going to take me to Birdland. We had heard that Art Blakey and the Jazz Messengers were playing there. This was the night we were supposed to get paid. As soon as the eagle flew, we were ready to go check out Art Blakey, Freddie Hubbard, Curtis Fuller, and the rest of the Jazz Messengers. But in the meantime, we were waiting for Hank. By then "waiting for Hank" had become an art form. Even I expected him to be at least two or three hours later than the appointed time. He was to pay off at seven o'clock. We were to leave for Birdland at nine o'clock. Ten o'clock would have been okay. We would still see most of the Messengers set. Hank finally showed at 11:30. Not with money. With another piddlin' draw and a story about getting uniforms, a bus, stuff like that. I didn't care. I had really made up my mind to quit this gig anyway. At that moment, I just wanted to hurry up and get to Birdland.

By the time we got there, Freddie was deep into his "Skylark" solo. It ended, and the Messengers went into the theme. Something on rhythm changed. I was at the front door, trying to explain to the lady why I didn't want to check my hat while Curtis was playing his eight bars. By the time I got in, they were taking it out and the set was over. That was okay, because we were going to get to see the entire second set. We settled in, ordered drinks. I noticed people moving equipment around on the stage, like they were packing up. Indeed, they were. The waitress informed us that the Gerry Mulligan eleven-piece orchestra was doing the second set. Just great. I went there to hear my favorite band and end up hearing a band headed by my least-favorite player on my least-favorite instrument. They did what you call "modern jazz." E.B. Coleman and the Moderns in Mobile were way more exciting than these eleven guys. Plus, I didn't get to meet anyone and nobody heard me play.

Only once did I get to play during the week or so that I was in New York, at the club at the hotel called Minton's Playhouse. The house group there was fronted by a wonderful organist named Trudy Pitts, who let me play a couple of tunes. However, neither Norman Grantz nor Creed Taylor came up to me to offer a big recording contract. I couldn't understand it. Then again, I could understand it. I wasn't as good as I had thought I was, I didn't play as well as I could have, and I had other things on my mind. And Norman Grantz and Creed Taylor certainly weren't coming into Richard Water's room, where we were smoking dope, or into my room, where I was telling that girl with the boots how good I could play and how good she looked in just those boots.

I started to realize that I'd made a mistake. In fact, I had made a lot of mistakes. Leaving a very stable job with Ike and Tina Turner without properly checking out the Hank Ballard job was a case of seeing only what I wanted to see rather than seeing what was real. I really never bothered to consider the facts. The fact was that the Ike and Tina Turner Revue was on the way up, as history bore out, and I, at a very young age, could have been in a command position. Who knows how far I could have gone? Tina really liked me—for my musical ability, of course—and she did finally go all the way to the top. But NOOOO. I just had to go with my buddies and Hank Ballard and the Midnighters, who turned out to be a bunch of drug addicts and sex fiends and nearly ruined my life. It's a wonder I didn't get killed or seriously injured, driving up and down the highway all doped up and tired night after night, day after day.

But I did get an education. I learned that a sure $25 a night, six or seven nights a week, was way better than a promised $35 a night. Particularly when the person who promised it wasn't even the one who was to pay it. And when the one who was to pay it didn't really care about anything but sex and dope. I also learned not to take a gig until I found out the answers to certain questions, such as how often do we work? When, how, and by whom do I get paid? How do we travel? I also learned that everyone has his own agenda and you should stick to your own.

I didn't want to leave New York, but I had no money, no place to stay, and no choice but to follow the Midnighters. We headed to upstate New York. I don't remember exactly what cities. I know we ended up in Rochester at a real nice Menger Hotel. I never knew how that happened. We usually stayed at cheap motels or, down South, in rooming houses. Somebody had some money, and it wasn't me. After the gig, we went back to the hotel with a lot of girls and a lot of dope. There was a party that night and the following few days like I've never seen before or since.

After two or three days of almost nonstop partying, I was sick as a dog. I was coughing, feverish, and sore all over. I was so weak I could hardly load my gear in the wagon, and nobody else was in any shape to help me. That money that somebody had had was all gone. We had to use green stamps to buy gas to get back to Atlanta. Somehow, we managed to drag our dead asses back to Atlanta. All I wanted to do was go home. None of us had money, so I got Gorgeous George to loan me bus fare to Mobile. I'll never forget him for giving the $10 or so to get me home. I'm sure I would have died if I hadn't gotten home. Somehow, I made the two-day trip. My mother took me straight to the doctor. I had pneumonia. I was ashamed and disgusted with myself. But I was alive and glad to be home.

By now, I don't know what to do. I'm about twenty years old. Half an education. No job. Living with my grandmother. Driving her car. I lived with my grandmother because she, for some reason, didn't bother me about going back to school or getting a job or joining the Army as my mother and father did. I guess my grandmother enjoyed the company and didn't want to run me away. I also had the freedom to practice all day if I wanted to, and I had her music room in which to write music and rehearse with my band. She just loved to hear us practice, so it was a good arrangement all around.

My friend Theodore Arthur was back home from Florida A&M, and we would practice tunes and scales and the like. Somewhere along the way, we got with Bernard Odum, Marion "Mole Man" Payne, Ozzie Portis, and Randolph Odom and formed a band. It was sort of a strange instrumentation. Bernard Odum, an electric bass player, was at home off the road with the James Brown band. Mole Man played piano and organ and had just left the Bobby Bland band. Ozzie Portis, who had recently graduated from Florida A&M's music department, where he was a standout reed man, played baritone sax with us. Randolph was without a doubt the funkiest drummer I ever played with. He had just come home from years with Little Junior Parker.

We spent hours in my grandmother's music room copying tunes off of records. We developed quite a repertoire, and soon we were looking for gigs. We found quite a few in and around the Mobile area. The gigs didn't pay much, as most of the clubs were locked in to a fixed amount that they paid bands. One particularly colorful club owner, Tom Koch of Club Harlem, was accustomed to four- or five-piece bands that he paid a total of $50 a night. After we told him we had six pieces and would have to have more money, he said, "I don't givadam if y'all have a hundred motherfuckers up there, I ain't paying you no mo' than $50."

We ran into similar problems throughout the area, but we didn't really care. Most of us were at home, living with our people, waiting for the next real gig to come along. The New Sounds, as we called the band, was basically an experiment, a practice tool, a means to further and keep sharp our craft.

During that period, our working together depended on who was in town and not working on a real gig. Many of the guys also had day jobs. Ozzie's real job, for example, was as an instrument repairman in a local music store. After I didn't get a gig for a long time, I ended up working as a delivery person for an office supply company. For the next couple of years, my life consisted of gigging around town with whomever, playing with the New Sounds whenever we could get together, and delivering file cabinets, paper, and other office supplies for Power's Company. I was making a living but generally getting nowhere at a moderate tempo. I knew in my heart that there was more somewhere for me. The people in Ike's band spoke so highly of the music scene in California that I wanted to go there. I knew a few people in D.C. and thought about going there. And, of course, there was New York. I just wanted to try some deeper waters, but I was afraid of starving to death or having to sleep in the street. I never could save up enough money to have a stake, so to speak.

One idea was always in the back of my mind. I tried to ignore it because it was put there by my father. That was the possibility of joining the military. I finally swallowed my pride and talked to my father. He knew a lot about the Army because he had taught basic education when he was enlisted. He convinced me that it would be a good way to get training since I hadn't finished college. He mentioned skills like electronics, welding, and key punching, and, finally, brought up the possibility of getting into the Armed Forces School of Music.

So I went downtown to the recruiting office and signed up to audition for the U.S. Army Band. They sent me to Ft. Rucker near Ozark, Alabama, about two hundred miles away. Again, my lack of basic musicianship came into play. I didn't do well at all. I didn't qualify for any of the Army bands, but I was guaranteed to go to the School of Music at Little Creek, Virginia, after basic training, provided I enlist for a three-year hitch. If I did well at the music school, I would be able to choose a permanent duty station either within the United States or overseas. This would give me a chance to be stationed in California or even Germany or Japan. Sounded like a good deal to me. However, if I didn't do well at the music school, I would be sent straight to the infantry. I wasn't worried.

I was worried about basic training. I'd heard stories. Push-ups, running, war games. I wasn't exactly in shape, but I wasn't all the way out of shape. Pushing those file cabinets up and down stairs and loading stacks of paper in and out of my cute little red van took a little bit of physical endurance. So on July 16, 1964, I enlisted in the U.S. Army.

3

Uncle Sam's Army

• • •

I was sent to Fort Jackson, South Carolina, for basic training. The things I'd heard about push-ups and running and stuff was true. What no one told me about was the drill sergeants and how they would get in your face and yell at you.

My sergeant was a white guy from Maine. Sergeant Lee. Right off, I didn't like him. First thing he said to me was that he was going to run that weight off me. Looked like he just had to say something about fat every day. And you know I hate fat jokes. I wanted to kick his ass. However, he was bad. He could do a million push-ups, and I'd seen him demolish the other drill sergeants in hand-to-hand combat demonstrations. So I had to live with my dislike of him and the whole Army system.

Total disrespect. These people obviously didn't know who I thought I was. They made me stand in line to eat. Stand in line to go to the bathroom. Stand in line for haircuts. Stand in line for my mail. And this was in the hot sun or rain, anytime, anywhere.

No-let-up physical training. The first mile-long run I tried made me tired and out of breath, so after about halfway I stopped running. That was the best I could do. But NOOO. Sergeant Lee wouldn't accept that. For the rest of that day, he made me run. Up the hill. Down the hill. The next day and every day thereafter, I had no trouble finishing what had become a little, short mile compared to the all-day running I had to do if I didn't finish.

By the time we ran, pushed up, swung on monkey bars, practiced hand-to-hand combat, and sat in boring classes about everything from military conduct to VD, there was very little time left for sleep. We were up in the morning at four o'clock, marching around and doing meaningless chores like cleaning the grease pit and picking up every little bit of trash off the ground. And that dumb rifle. That stupid gun became like a part of my body. Everywhere I went I had to not only run but also carry that thing, and carry it in a certain position. It was like being in hell.

I got a break around the third week. The first sergeant found out that I was a musician and ordered me and a fellow recruit named Lattimer to play drums to march the troops back and forth. This meant that we were exempt from certain daily chores. No KP (kitchen patrol) or latrine duty, for example. I played the bass drum, which meant that I had to strap that heavy thing onto my chest and march with it—along with my backpack and rifle—sometimes for very long distances. It wasn't the trombone, but it was music. Lattimer had a natural funky feel for the snare drum, and together we came up with some real slick and interesting cadences. It was hard, but I actually came to love it. Our platoon enjoyed it, too, and it kinda made the drudgery of basic training easier to bear for everybody. We were the only platoon in the battalion with a rhythm section. At times, we would hire out to the company or the battalion or to other platoons. Noowww they know who I think I am. I'm somebody. Not just another troop. I'm recognized in the mess hall and in the PX. I finished my basic training as sort of a celebrity. Sergeant Lee had bet us that we would like him by the end of the training cycle. He was wrong about me. After graduation, most of the guys were running up to have him autograph their cycle books. Not me. I was busy signing autographs myself. But maybe I did get to admire Sergeant Lee a little bit. He was a great soldier. I never told him so. Maybe I should have.

After a short furlough at home (showing off the uniform, making my mother, father, and grandmother real proud), I was off to the Armed Forces School of Music at Little Creek, Virginia. This was in the Tidewater area of Virginia. Little Creek was essentially a Navy base. The Army element was billeted in a section of the second floor of a Navy barracks, which we shared with Navy musicians. Downstairs was the barracks for the Navy SEALS trainees. This was a training paradox that manifested itself during mealtimes, since we all shared the same mess hall; the SEALS would gobble down what looked like practically raw meat and potatoes, while we, the musicians, would sip our soup and munch on stir-fried this or that.

The SEALS and the musicians made a point of staying out of each other's way. This wasn't a problem, because the musicians spent the day in concert and jazz band rehearsals, taking lessons on individual instruments, and in theory classes. We had a little bit of military activity, like reveille, occasional barracks inspections, mild physical training, and the like. We rarely saw the SEALS unless they came running through the parade ground with boats on their heads or carrying telephone poles. Sometimes they would get drunk and trash their barracks. Usually just the downstairs. We heard they spent most of their time swimming forty or fifty miles a day and learning how to kill people. The only time the musicians almost had a problem with the SEALS was after what they called "hell week." They went completely crazy when that was over. We managed to avoid them successfully, as they tore up everything they got their hands on, which was mostly each other.

The school didn't do much for me in the theory department. We covered material I had been through in high school, then again in college. In fact, with my practical experience with Ike and Tina, Hank Ballard, and the bands at home, I was way ahead of most people in the theory classes.

I benefited most from the lessons on my instrument. I had a great trombone teacher in CPO Joe Phillips. He was a fairly decent jazz player in the mode of Carl Fontana or Frank Rosolino. But the things I learned under his patient tutelage about basic trombone playing have been invaluable to me through the years. My tone became much more rounded. My range increased. My articulation became much faster.

The school also gave me a chance to become a real musician. We had big-band rehearsals and concert band rehearsals. Both gave me a chance to develop my sight-reading skills and other basic musicianship skills. I was able to see a wide range of music by a plethora of composers and arrangers, whereas all the music I had read before had been written by Coleman, Joe Lewis, or myself. I also got to meet and play with some great musicians, most notably Cecil Bridgewater, the great trumpeter with the Max Roach band. I also met many other lesser-known but as great musicians, like pianist Clarence Cybren, drummer Jim Zimmerman of the Shirley Bassey Band, trombonist-arranger Don Cooke, and many others whose names I can't remember but whose skill and musicianship stay in my mind and guide my efforts to this day.

On off days, the army musicians would venture into the big town in the area, Norfolk, and seek out places to play, although it was prohibited by military rules. The word on that particular rule was that it was hardly ever enforced. So we found a place with a jam session on Sunday evenings, just like in Mobile. A very fine organist named Willie Burnette led the house band. He knew all the tunes, and we had great times there on the weekends. I met other local musicians, most memorably Hamiet Bluiett, the great baritone saxophonist, who was at the time stationed at one of the nearby Naval bases.

I made friends with a tenor player named Earl Swanson. He was what you call a honky-tonk tenor player, sort of a star around Norfolk. He had once been married to Ruth Brown, the great songstress, and had also led her band. After that, he had had a band in the Tidewater area. He lived in Portsmouth. When he found out that I'd played with Ike and Tina and Hank Ballard, he took a liking to me and let me play with his band whenever I could. This went on for three or four weeks. He would pick me up after duty hours, and we would go to the gigs or just hang out around the area. He was a pretty slick hustler-type dude. He wore that processed pompadour I told you about. Mohair suits and those new polyester, big-collared paisley shirts. He gave me a couple of shirts. Come to find out he sold shirts out of the trunk of his Cadillac. I don't know where he got them. I didn't ask.

Remember that hardly-ever-enforced rule I told you about? Well, one morning I got called into the first sergeant's office. It had been reported that I had been seen playing at a club in Newport News. I couldn't imagine who could have turned me in. Best I could figure out was a sergeant at a nearby Army base, whose girlfriend I'd seen a couple of times. Maybe he turned me in. I never knew for sure. I was given an Article 15 and confined to the base for the rest of my time at the school. It was bearable; I only had four weeks left. I didn't make the little extra money. I didn't see the girl again. But I got to do a lot of practicing. A few of us even formed a little band and played each other's arrangements. But I never saw Earl again. I miss him. He was a great guy. I'm glad I knew him for the short time I did.

The next four weeks I concentrated on my instrument with Chief Joe Phillips. Played jazz with Cecil, Jim, and Clarence. Watched Don Cooke write amazing music and dreamed about where I might be stationed after school.

In the second or third week at the school, we received a list of all the U.S. Army bases in the world and were supposed to choose two stateside and two overseas bases that we would like to be sent to after graduation for permanent duty station. I remembered that if I didn't graduate,

I would be sent to whatever duty they needed me to go to, probably infantry, but I also knew I would most likely graduate. The music school had been very interesting, and I had enjoyed almost every minute of it. I chose Germany or Japan for my overseas station, and California or Seattle for stateside station. On graduation day, in typical Army fashion, they lined us up and one-by-one called our names and one-by-one we went up and received our certificates and duty stations. When my named was finally called, I marched up proudly, shook the commander's hand, took my certificate and my orders, and marched smartly back to my place in formation. By then all the other guys had opened their orders and most were happy to be going to Europe, exotic places in the Far East, California, Texas. Bridgewater was going to Hawaii.

I was so anxious. I opened my envelope and couldn't believe my eyes. It must have been a mistake. I was going to Redstone Arsenal, Alabama. Where the hell was that? I was from Alabama, and I'd never heard of Redstone Arsenal. Why, it didn't even sound right. I was looking for Fort something or other. I thought an arsenal was a place where the Army stored weapons. Did my orders get mixed up with one of those Navy Seals or something? Nope. It said Fifty-fifth Army Band, Redstone Arsenal, Alabama. What did they need with a band at an ammunition dump? I had no idea what I was in for. I only thought the worst. I pictured this dreary place where everybody lived in tents and played reveille in the mornings and walked around with guns and guarded weapons all night. And in Alabama? I had just left Alabama. I didn't want to go anywhere near Alabama. I was trying to travel as far away from Alabama as possible. All I could figure was that it must have been some kind of punishment for the Article 15 I had gotten earlier. My bus ticket was to Huntsville, Alabama. All I knew about Huntsville was that it was where Alabama A&M College was located. Alabama A&M College was where people went to study farming and animal husbandry. I just knew it was a one-horse country town full of unhip, non-jazz-loving people. There was nothing I could do about it. The closest large city was Nashville, and you know what the music scene there is about. I was doomed.

I arrived in Huntsville at about nine o'clock on a Sunday night. I noticed signs about Marshall Space Flight Center. I wondered if this had anything to do with Redstone Arsenal. I was right about it being a small town. It kinda reminded me of Selma or Tuskegee, both small towns in Alabama. At the bus station, they seemed to expect soldiers. Fares to the arsenal were posted all around. "Directions to the United States Army

Missile Command." I at least felt like I was in the right place. I got a cab to my barracks. I found the charge of quarters (CQ) office empty. This was very unusual. CQ duty was sort of like guard duty. This office had to be manned at all times. If the officer of the day came by and caught this post unmanned, the CQ would be in big trouble. I hoped he'd just gone to the bathroom or something. I waited. Nobody else was around. That wasn't so unusual. It was Sunday night. Everyone was probably still out in the town—although I couldn't imagine where, the town was so small. I decided to look around. I heard a TV going down the hall. I cautiously approached an open door, looked in, and saw a half-uniformed soldier dozing in front of the TV. I knew he couldn't be the CQ. The CQ had to be in full uniform of the day at all times. I gently woke him up, introduced myself, and asked where the CQ was. He said he was the CQ and to come on, he'd check me in. I followed him back down the hall ready to go through my "report in" procedure.

As he went into the office and behind the desk, I snapped to attention, saluted, and shouted out "PFC Wesley reporting for duty, sir!" He looked up kinda startled and said, "Yeah, yeah, sign here and relax all that Army stuff with me." He took my papers, proceeded to show me my bunk, the latrine, and the like, and told me to relax. "Reveille will be at 7 A.M. You can come watch TV with me if you want." I unpacked my bags, made my bunk, and was getting settled when the door opened. In walked the CQ with an older guy dressed in civilian clothes. The CQ introduced him as the first sergeant. Again, I snapped to attention. Again, it was waved off as not necessary. He welcomed me to the outfit and said how glad he was that I had finally arrived. At the time, I didn't know what all he was saying meant. I figured he was just a nice guy being nice. He said he had to go. He was late for a gig. I guessed it was some kind of Army thing. As he left the room, he turned to me and asked, "By the way, do you have a gig yet?" Remembering my Article 15 and thinking maybe he had heard about it and was trying to trick me or was joking with me about it, I said, "No." He said, "Don't worry. We'll get you one. There are a lot of gigs around here." I didn't know what to think. I spent the rest of the night settling in and watching TV with the CQ.

Monday morning the place was buzzing. I met my three roommates (all of whom had spent the night somewhere else), my squad leader, and began meeting the rest of the guys. They all seemed extra friendly and unusually happy to see me. We did the reveille thing led by Duty Sergeant Petracco. The head count was three people short. Nobody seemed angry, just a little concerned about whether the three guys were in some kind of trouble or just being their usual irresponsible selves. They all eventually showed up in good shape—all except Nicky Caste, who had hit a deer on the way back from his gig in Chattanooga. Gig in Chattanooga? How could he talk about that so casually? It was strictly against Army regulations to earn money outside of the Army doing the same thing your job was in the Army. He was okay, but his car was messed up. It was just funny now.

I couldn't believe how relaxed everybody was. I was just out of basic training and the music school where Army protocol meant a lot. Here, after a quick cleanup of the barracks, everybody went to have coffee across the street at the little PX. I still hadn't seen the commanding officer (CO). The word was he'd be in at nine for band rehearsal. Even though I didn't drink coffee, I went along with the program, expecting to soon be playing some stale ol' marches and Army stuff in the up-and-coming rehearsal. But the talk was about jazz. I was repeatedly questioned about whom I'd played with, tunes, changes, and things like that. The other trombone players seemed to be interested in my jazz playing also. All the talk at coffee was about jazz playing and big-band music. Now I'm wondering, what is this band really about?

When we got back from coffee, there was a drum trap set up, an upright acoustic bass, a grand piano, and a big-band seating arrangement. Could it be? Are we about to play some big-band music? Could this be heaven, not hell? The music was passed out. I was handed the first trombone book, and a thick book it was. Thumbing through it, I saw some Sammy Nestico charts, some I was familiar with from the music school. There were Pete Rugolo charts, Frank Foster, Stan Kenton. This was going to be all right. Only thing, I had never played first before. At the school, I mostly played second or third. Second was my favorite because it had the most solos. As everyone warmed up and got settled, I could tell right away that these guys could play. Mr. Edmonds, the chief warrant officer, finally arrived. He, too, welcomed me in a special way and expressed how happy he was that I had finally arrived. It seemed like my arrival was an eagerly anticipated event.

Mr. Edmonds started calling tunes by numbers. I noticed that every chart he called had a first trombone solo on it, and if it didn't, one of the other bone players would exchange parts with me to make sure I had all the solos. As we played the first few tunes, I picked up that the bone player sitting in the second chair was really the lead bone player. He kept

(above) Sergeant "Pete" Petracco. Courtesy of Gordon La Vere.

(left) CWO Bob Edmonds ("The Old Man"). Courtesy of Gordon La Vere.

(below left) Tom Zale. Courtesy of Gordon La Vere.

(below right) Esteban Romero-Sepulveda. Courtesy of Gordon La Vere.

showing me little marks he had made on the music and alerting me to things in the music. He also passed me all the charts with jazz solos from the second book, and he played lead on the ones that had jazz solos in them. This didn't make sense to me, so I suggested he keep playing lead and I'd be perfectly happy playing the second part, with which I was more comfortable anyway. Mr. Edmonds agreed. He said he had gotten the impression that I was a lead player. I wondered where he had gotten any impression at all about me, as we had just met. Everybody in the band seemed to know something I didn't know. After every solo I played, not only did I get applause but there would also be sort of a discussion about the solo and the chart in general between everyone in the band except me. I didn't know what was going on. All I knew was that I was having fun.

The band was kicking. Without a doubt, the best big band I'd ever played in. This was what I dreamed it would be like to play in Count Basie's band. The drummer was world class. His name was Henry Okstel. A health fanatic. He had chops, could swing real hard, and kicked a big band like Buddy Rich or Louis Bellson. Tom Zale, from Cleveland, was the piano player. Classically trained. Good comper, good soloist. The bass player was a converted clarinet player, still learning the bass, but adequate for the job.

The reed section consisted of: Bob Hedman, a hippie-type and serious be-bopper from San Francisco, on second tenor. Esteban Romero-Sepulveda, a cool Puerto Rican, on fourth tenor. An adequate section player. Not much of a soloist. Nick Castiglia—a.k.a. Nicky Cass—a Philadelphia Italian, on third alto. A real showman. Although short in stature, looked and talked like a gangster. He was the nicest guy in the world. He did all the house-rocking stuff. The baritone sax player was Charles Everett Heinz, a self-proclaimed redneck coon-ass from Covington, Louisiana. Not a soloist but a good musician with a tone as big as his ass. The CO, the old man himself, Mr. Edmonds, played the sweetest lead alto I'd ever heard.

The trumpet section was a powerhouse. Roy Fox was the lead and soloist. He played lead like Cat Anderson and solos like Lee Morgan. He was the perfect player to lead this band. Dyron Rauk played second. A great, strong player. Floyd Cotton played third. Another strong, good musician. The fourth chair was held by an older sergeant, Ray Lamier, who also was a good musician. After shuffling the music around so I had all the solos, the bone section turned out to be, John Klink, a former paratrooper from the special forces on lead; me on second; Clyde Seiler, an outdoors-man who played the trombone in the army in order to finance his hunt-ing and fishing expeditions, on third; and Staff Sergeant Alf Pedersen on bass trombone. Pedersen was also band librarian. It seems that he was responsible for most of the book. Somehow the music had followed him and ended up in his possession throughout his sixteen years in Army bands. He never admitted actually stealing music. If he didn't have it and it couldn't be ordered legally and you knew the title and/or the writer or arranger of a particular chart, he could get it from his network of chart collectors all over the world. This accounted for the extensive library of the Fifty-fifth Army Band. One French horn played by Perry Parks com-pleted the brass section. Perry was a decent player who talked as much about flying airplanes and helicopters and jumping out of airplanes and such aeronautical stuff as he did about music. Once, he invited me to go skydiving with him, and for some reason I accepted. I did, however, come to my senses and fail to show up on the day I was supposed to jump. Perry left the band for, I think, helicopter school, and I understand he became a decorated combat pilot in the Vietnam war.

Mr. Edmonds called me into his office after that first rehearsal—I thought to orient me to the policies and inner workings of the band. But he just wanted to again welcome me and explain how such a great group of musicians had gotten together. Not by chance, it turned out. He told me how he and a few other noncommissioned officers had stumbled on this great book that Alf had scrounged and how they'd gotten the idea to put this great big band together at the Army's expense. Redstone Arse-nal was the perfect post to do it. The duty was easy. We only had to play once a week for the missile school graduations. The whole arsenal was simply support for the missile school and the Marshall Space Flight Cen-ter, which provided many opportunities for classy dances and banquets and the like. So, over the previous few months, the band's musicians had more or less been handpicked. I was the fulfillment of a request to the music school for a lead trombone player who could play jazz solos.

That finally explained what I was doing in Huntsville, Alabama. It turned out to be a good thing. The post as a whole was not really regular Army. We had very few infantrymen. We were issued rifles, but we didn't really remember where they were kept. I know I didn't. Most soldiers at Redstone were teachers at the missile school, students of the missile school, or some type of general logistical support for the school or the

(left) John Klink.
Courtesy of Gordon
La Vere.

(below left) Ray
Lamier. Courtesy of
Gordon La Vere.

(below right)
Perry Parks.
Courtesy of Gordon
La Vere.

Space Flight Center. Medics and cooks lived in the barracks above the band. Every unit was responsible for some aspect of defense in case of emergency. The band was the chemical, biological, and radiology (CBR) team for the post. Once a year, we went to Fort McClellan, Alabama, near Anniston, for CBR training. Even that turned out to be fun. After dressing up in gas masks and measuring radioactivity during the days, we got to fool around with the Women's Army Corps band at night. We, and they, looked forward to these yearly encounters.

Of course we had to undergo periodic GI (I still don't know what GI stands for) inspections, but overall being in the Fifty-fifth Army Band was not like being in the Army at all. Duty for me was reveille, cleanup, coffee, big-band rehearsal (!), and that was it. We were finished by about 1 P.M. most days, except Fridays. On Friday, we had to play for the missile school graduations. There were military people from countries all over the world studying at the school. Each week or so, a cycle would complete, and we would have to be there to play ruffles and flourishes for the general and the national anthems of the countries of the students graduating. Sometimes there would be maybe four or five different countries represented. And we were supposed to play something—I forget what you call it—to lower the flag at sundown on Fridays, but we, including the CO, did everything and anything to get out of doing it. If it rained, we didn't do it. If the temperature went too high or too low, we didn't do it. There were a lot of legal loopholes that allowed us not to do whatever it was called. If we couldn't find a loophole, we made up one or just didn't do it.

Most people had full-time jobs off post to which they would go after band rehearsals. I'm serious. Full-time jobs. Sergeant Parzek managed an auto tire store. Sergeant Pedersen and a couple other guys worked there for him. Almost everyone who wanted a job had a job. These kinds of jobs were technically legal as far as the Army was concerned. But everybody who wanted a gig had a gig, too. This, as you and I know full well, is not legal. But not only was it condoned, it was encouraged by everyone from the band CO and first sergeant to the commanding general, who was a close friend of Mr. Edmonds. We would play gigs at the general's house and get paid as if we were a civilian band. Not just once or twice but regularly. Every time the general had to entertain a visiting dignitary or have any kind of party, we'd play. And get paid well. We looked forward to these gigs, because we knew we would get paid one or two hundred dollars and have a really good time. We also had to do some functions around town as the Army Band for local goodwill. We called these nonpay GI gigs. We had to wear our uniforms and be spit-shined and all that.

We also did some civilian pay gigs. These didn't pay as much as the general's, and they did sometime present other problems, especially for me personally. Did I mention that Floyd Cotton and I were the only two black people in the big band? There were two other black saxophone players in the unit, James Ransom and Maurice Richardson, but they only did the Army gigs. After I was there six months, Cotton joined the FBI or something, and I was left the only black in the big band. This was northern Alabama in 1964 and 1965. Racial tensions were high, to say the least. I didn't notice any bigotry as long as I was on post, but just beyond the gates, it was there and there big time in Huntsville, Alabama. Most of the civilian gigs were cool in that we played for upscale, affluent society types, who, if they were prejudiced, kept it under wraps as long as I didn't piss on the floor or hit on one of their daughters. Although it wasn't something we discussed much, everyone in the big band was aware of the potential for a racial incident and was on guard at times. I wasn't exactly a quiet member of the band, either. With me playing many of the solos and being featured on many more tunes, sometimes it looked like Fred Wesley and his band. I definitely stood out for more than one reason.

We never had a real problem, but there was that one time we played a party after the famous Guntersville boat races. The party was at the plantation of a wealthy person in the town of Arab, Alabama. Arab (pronounced *ay'-rab*) was renowned for not having any black residents or even allowing blacks to pass through. There was said to be a sign that read something like, "Nigger read, nigger run. Nigger can't read, nigger run anyway." We all knew about this town, but none of us ever expected to have to play a gig in Arab. My first thought was not to go. That was dismissed as out of the question. Mr. Edmonds and everyone else agreed that either we all did it or none of us did it. Since we were a diverse band anyway, consisting of Rebels, Yankees, Jews, Italians, Germans, Puerto Ricans, me and Floyd, and plain ol' white people, some with wives of equally diverse ethnicity, we could not believe that Arab could be as bad as reported. We decided to do the gig.

When we got there I did get some funny looks. I had planned to not make any waves. Just play the gig and come home. Stay near the bandstand on breaks. Not try to mingle or socialize with anyone and basically stay out of sight as much as possible. After all, I was breaking a rule that had been upheld in Arab for years. The locals were proud to say that no blacks had ever spent any time in their little white Mecca. We didn't know if they would give it up quietly. After the first set, I prepared to settle in behind the bandstand and wait until the next set started. The guys didn't want to leave me alone, and, frankly, I didn't want to be left alone. So everyone sat behind the bandstand with me. It looked ridiculous and was inconvenient for the guys who wanted drinks. So a few would go get drinks for the rest of them who stayed to guard me. I felt very silly but somewhat safe.

After the second set, there was a hot food buffet. The band was invited—no stipulation mentioned. Now the question was, how do you keep a band, any band, away from free food and still stand guard over an endangered buddy? The answer was, take the endangered buddy with you. That's exactly what we did. We formed a bunch with me in the middle and, all together, made our way through the crowd to the buffet table. We stayed in that formation for the rest of the intermission. We finished the gig without incident. Apparently, preservation of Arab's lily whiteness took a back seat to the big-band sounds we were blasting out. I know my eyes were opened to the fact that music creates strong bonds of friendship among peoples of all races, religions, and ethnic backgrounds. We had all kinds represented in that band, and not one let me out of their sight throughout that whole evening. It was a love and togetherness I hadn't experienced before. Some say that war brings people together like that, but music brought the potential enemy and us together that night, and music had done it before and will do it again. If there is someone you don't like or someone who doesn't like you, take them to hear a big band. You'll like each other better afterward.

What I had thought was going to be a terrible experience became a very enjoyable and educational one, both musically and socially. I had never had a friend who wasn't black like me before. Don't get me wrong. I didn't turn white or anything. I just learned that you have to get to know a person—black, white, blue or green, old, young, or in between—before you determine whether you like him or not.

At Redstone, I was also filling in the gaps of my musical education. I still had the need to play bebop. The drummer in the big band, Henry Okstel, told me about a gig he was playing at a club in town where I would be welcome to sit in sometime. One night, I took him up on the offer. The club was a quiet, intimate place, and the band was a piano trio that featured a singer. The piano player was Earnest Vantrees from Nashville. A fine jazz pianist in the mode of Red Garland or Wynton Kelly. The bass player was Earl Williams from Atlanta. A good, straight-ahead jazz bassist. Of course, Henry was on drums; I discovered he could play bebop as well as he could kick a big band. The singer was a tall, handsome, impeccably dressed, regal-mannered, gregarious young man named Cortez Greer. And he could sing good, too. A jazz singer much like Lou Rawls or Joe Williams. He also did the Top Forty thing well. I would go with Henry whenever the gig was appropriate and when they played in, or close to, town. Most times, they went far out of town for weekends, and it wasn't convenient for me to sit in.

I did get to meet other local musicians. I met a band called The Hi Fi's. The saxophone player, Carl Jackson, was from Mobile, attending school at Alabama A&M. I hadn't known him in Mobile although he'd attended Central High, as he was younger than I was and had finished four or five years behind me. Naturally, he knew my reputation—good jazz player, traveled with Ike and Tina and Hank Ballard and all that—and spread it around through the town. The Hi Fi's was a good band, playing everything from jazz like the Crusaders and Art Blakey, to R&B like Sam & Dave, to blues like Jimmy Reed. The rest of the band consisted of Frank McCray on sax, Lloyd Jones on piano and vocals, Sam Davis on bass, Ted Walton on drums, and Danny Pollock on guitar. They were all local Huntsvillians, except for Danny, who was from Oxnard, California, doing time in the Army at Redstone Arsenal. I would sit in with them, but there was not really a spot in the band for me. It was just great to hang out with guys with whom I shared a similar background and experiences and with whom I could use "the N word" and other ethnic and regional vernacular with the love and respect that only people who grew up expressing themselves with such language can understand. In other words, I could speak without considering whether or not I would offend or be misunderstood. Although I loved my buddies in the Army Band, it was difficult to call a spade a spade or a nigger a nigger or a motherfucker a motherfucker or a bitch a bitch around them without being misunderstood.

The word came around that the regular band at the Hi Fi Club needed a tenor player. I still didn't have a gig other than the occasional big-band shows. So I went by the Hi Fi Club with my horn one night. The band was "Poonanny and the Stormers, featuring Hurricane Alice." The band had Poonanny on drums, Bo Dollar on Hammond organ, Spot on guitar, and, of course, Hurricane Alice singing. They were strictly a Top Forty/R&B band. The musicians were adequate for the task of playing what the

Hurricane Alice, me, and Spot.

young adult, white audience that frequented the club wanted. In fact, they got over big time.

Without a doubt, Alice was the most visible member of the band. First of all, she was fine. Not just fine, but superfine. With skin just a little darker than pecan tan, her face was sort of Italian with high cheekbones, big beautiful eyes, big beautiful lips, about 5'-8", a teeny-weeny waist, titties just big enough to be big and small enough to be absolutely perfect. She had long, perfectly shaped legs that flowed upward to form magnificent thighs topped off by the most beautifully rounded ass anyone had ever seen. Her attire and make-up were carefully designed to accentuate all of her natural attributes. Tight, short skirts, high heels, various wigs, false eyelashes, heavy eyeliner, red lipstick and fingernails, plunging necklines. And she could sing. And she could dance. Her act was mesmerizing, approaching lewd, every bit as provocative as Tina Turner. She was a great entertainer.

I watched their first set. When they took a break, I righted myself after having been devastated by Hurricane Alice, then went up to Poonanny, introduced myself, and told him I wanted to audition for the gig. He said he wanted a tenor player and that looked like a trombone I had. I said I understood that but I could do all that tenor stuff with no problem. He kinda chuckled and said in a condescending way, "I'd just as soon hire a violin player or clarinet player as a trombone player. We like to do stuff like 'Honky Tonk' and you need a tenor for that." I said, "I can do 'Honky Tonk.'" He laughed again and said in a plain, southern, black, country drawl, "If you play 'Honky Tonk' and make me like it, I'll give you the gig." I knew "Honky Tonk" really well, because I had done it many times with Charles Lott's band in Mobile. Poonanny jumped right on "Honky Tonk" when the next set started, as if he were anxious to see me embarrass myself so he could have himself a real good laugh. I wish I could have seen his face when I did the Clifford Scott solo practically note for note. He was behind me on drums, and I could hear him laughing—with me not at me like he had expected. Not only did he like it, everybody in the club loved it.

After a thunderous round of applause, I headed off the bandstand. Poonanny stopped me by saying, "Don't go nowhere, you got the gig." Well, you know me by now. After the Hank Ballard experience, I don't really feel like I have the gig until a few particulars are discussed. But I finished out the set to the delight of the band and the audience. When the gig was over, Poonanny and I agreed to fifty dollars a week until he could get the club owner to come up with more money. I knew that was some bull. He was, for sure, paying the other tenor player more than that. He still couldn't see paying a trombone player the real salary. I figured I'd let the audience get used to me and then go for the correct money after a couple of weeks or so. Anyway, I didn't have anything else to do, and he agreed that if I had anything with the Army I could take off. Plus, I would get to see Hurricane Alice every night.

Poonanny and the Stormers were all from Birmingham, Alabama, which is about a hundred miles south of Huntsville, so rather than commute every day or stay in a hotel, they had rented a house in the neighborhood. Sometimes they would go home on Monday, their one day off. I would go over to the house when I got off work at the Army and rehearse or just hang out. They were all nice people, and I enjoyed their company. Alice and Bo Dollar had a thing going, but it was obvious that she was hanging with him for the convenience of it. He was an older gentleman who drank too much and gave the twenty-four-year-old Alice anything she wanted. She didn't seem to mind giving him a thrill every now and then, and he didn't seem to mind paying for the privilege. Although it literally ran Bo Dollar crazy, she also kept her datebook open so she could pick and choose from her many suitors as it benefited her the most. She was the first woman I ever got to know personally who knew how to use what she had to get what she wanted and still maintain a modicum of self-respect. I was lucky she didn't see me as anything but a friend. She could have used me up and thrown me away like I saw her do so many others. I grew to like her and respect her because she was a good person and a helluva performer. Poonanny, who was actually named Joe Burns, got his nickname because he had the dubious talent of being able to pass gas—or poot—on cue. Anytime, anyplace.

I must have played the gig at the Hi Fi Club for five or six months. Poonanny never had any intention of paying me any more money, and the gig was getting to be so boring, even Hurricane Alice couldn't keep me awake. I was actually playing the last set in my sleep most of the time. I told Poonanny I had to have a hundred dollars a week or I quit. I was re-lieved when he refused. It was a shame, because we had developed quite a thing. I really got my only-horn-in-the-band thing together. I was still without a gig but glad to move on. Funny thing happened. When I left the band, Poonanny hired a longhaired white boy on tenor and paid him a hundred and fifty dollars a week according to Alice. Two weeks later, Poonanny was fired after two years at the club, and the white boy had his band in there. Good for his jive, funky ass.

At this time, the Hi Fi's (the band) was going through some changes. Frank had gone to California and gotten a gig with Little Richard. Sonny (Sam Davis) had caught Ted in the back seat of his car with his wife, so they weren't speaking to each other. Danny was out of the Army and gone back to California so the band was more or less broken up. By this time I had gotten to be pretty good friends with Jack (Carl Jackson) and Sonny Davis. We did some put-together gigs at the Amvet club and some of the other clubs in the neighborhood, using some of the other local musicians. People like Horace (Pap) Rice, a real good drummer around town and also a student at A&M. Burley Marshall and his brother Curtis played guitars and used either both of us or one of us on gigs here and there. I was begin-ning to be a fixture in different bands all over town. Sort of the freelance, designated horn player. Jack and I would try to book ourselves together, but due to the low-pay policies of the clubs, this wasn't always possible. I was doing all right financially in not committing to any particular band. I kinda enjoyed not being locked in to any schedule other than the Army's easy one. I was the toast of Huntsville. I'd gone and got my 1956 two-tone, green Pontiac Catalina two-door hard top. Had a good base salary thanks to Uncle Sam. Extra money for clothes, so that most of the locals didn't even know I was in the Army. I more or less played a gig when and if I felt like it. I never expected the Army to be like this. Life was good.

I don't know what came over me. I certainly wasn't lonely. I had many friends, male and female. I think living in the barracks or not having any place in which to really be alone or that I could call home was unacceptable to me. I had gotten used to having my own room when I was on the road, and I enjoyed having my own space at my grandmother's house. Even if I did spend some of my nights off post, it was on somebody's couch or in the bed with somebody with whom I couldn't relax because I was afraid some boyfriend or husband would come in. My Cancerian, homebody tendencies were taking over. I needed a home. I saw the guys who were married come in every morning and go home after work and, for some reason, this appealed to me. Plus, the Army gave you extra money to live in military housing on post or civilian housing off post. So, on June 28, 1965, I married my lifelong friend and neighbor, Gertie Lee Young. We had been writing to each other all the time I was in basic training and at the music school, and she was finishing her last year at Southern University in Baton Rouge, Louisiana. We moved into one of the nice little apartments that the Army provided for its married personnel in an area aptly named Redstone Park. It didn't take long for Gertie to get a teaching job, and with our combined incomes, we were able to move to a luxury apartment in town. We needed more room because on July 22, 1966 our first child, Joya Lynne, was born. Life was still good, only in a different way.

My new wife and new baby were the joys of my life. But with them came new responsibility. The first year after the baby was born, Gertie didn't work. Trying to pay the rent in Valley Garden on what the Army was paying me wasn't making it. The few freelance gigs and Army bigband gigs became absolutely necessary. As luck would have it, they were now coming few and far between. It was time to take charge and make something happen.

I approached Jack and Sonny about putting together a serious band. We needed a drummer, a keyboard player, a trumpet player, and a guitar player. The trumpet player was easy. There was an engineer, a petroleum engineer I think, who was around the clubs wanting to sit in with the bands all the time. He wasn't that good a soloist or even that good a trumpet player for that matter, but he was willing and available. His name was Carl Gholston. He was from San Antonio, Texas, and living in Huntsville, working for the government in some capacity. He was one of these guys who made a good living at what he was doing but loved the glamour and excitement of the musician's life and jumped at the chance to be a part of it. There was a youngster named Teddy Caldwell who had just flunked out of or quit school at A&M. I don't remember what he was or was not doing in school, but he could sure play the drums. He was a little rare for the times in that he was equally fantastic at playing jazz and straight-ahead as he was at playing funk and R&B. His only problem was that at times he would get excited and get carried away and overplay sometimes. Of course, we not only approved of but also actually encouraged that sort of thing.

There wasn't much of a choice for guitar. The best players in town were the Marshall brothers. Curtis was really the best, but by being the best he was in big demand around the area and wasn't available to re-hearse the way we wanted to in order to create the sound we were look-ing for. Burley was the younger of the two and just beginning to play and was anxious to learn. This was attractive because we wanted to do some new and different things. So Burley Marshall became the guitar player. No piano player presented himself to us, so we went without one. We concluded that the absence of a keyboard would contribute to the unique sound.

The Amvets club had once been a popular spot, but for some reason it had lost all its business to the Nite Lite, the VFW, and the Elks Club. The Amvets owner, Charlie Ray, let us use the club to rehearse, and we let the audience in on weekends. He sold beer and drinks, and we kept whatever one dollar a head brought through the door. I began writing. I did an ar-rangement on "Love For Sale," the Beatles's "Yesterday," the Crusaders's "Young Rabbits." I also did some composing, writing "Sweet Loneliness" and "Le Fete," among others. Jack did some arrangements and some origi-nals, too. We also played R&B favorites like "The Horse," "Tighten Up," and "Can't Sit Down." We really hadn't thought about a singer, but the guy Jack lived with, Pete Lou, kept telling us that he could sing. We didn't pay any attention until we realized that in order to compete with other bands in town and make some money, we would have to do some vocals.

By now our crowd at Charlie Ray's was getting to be a thing on week-ends. The place held about 300 people, back-to-back, toe-to-toe, and that's the way they came in there every Friday, Saturday, and Sunday night. Pete Lou had been rehearsing a "Sam & Dave" type of thing with a friend named Bill Brandon, so we incorporated their act into our repertoire and developed a very dynamic show. We had clearly outgrown the Amvet both physically, logistically, and artistically. There were too many of us to fit on the stage. Pete Lou and Bill had to perform on the floor where everyone was dancing. We had only one mike and that came out of a taxicab—you had to hold the button down for it to work. The singers had no problems, but Jack had to hold the button down for me to play my solos, and I had to hold the button down for him to play his solos. This was okay, but I got a lot of spit on my hand when he played a flute solo. It got so hot in that little place that after the first set everyone was soaking wet. Wearing clothes that looked good was out of the question. In the words of Shaka Zulu, "This was ridiculous." We had to make a move.

The move came to us. The Elks Club had just been completely renovated after being closed down for months because of a fire. They wanted to start new with a new band and everything. Even though we were in this little small club, word of our great show had spread throughout the area. The Elks Club wanted us. This presented us with a loyalty problem. Charlie Ray had opened his doors to us and allowed us to get our thing together, and the crowd and our fans had supported us all through the times when we didn't sound good. It would be using the club and its clientele to develop, then turning our backs and moving on to greener pastures.

You see, the Amvets and the Elks catered to two different classes of people. I used to check out the girls at the Amvets. They would work all the week at some minimum-wage job. Buy a new outfit. Wear different versions of that outfit and party the whole weekend, spending all of their money, then start the process all over again. There must have been two or three hundred girls who followed this pattern week after week. We were the beneficiaries of the practice, because the Amvets club was the place these girls came to lay their traps for guys who basically were doing the exact same thing they were doing. We had the catch crowd. People who had steady boyfriends and girlfriends would go to other places like the Nite Lite Club or the VFW. On the other hand, the Elks Club was geared to the more affluent members of the black society in Huntsville. Professional people like doctors, lawyers, teachers, and scientists and engineers who worked at Redstone or the Marshall Space Flight Center. Of course, there also was the crossover element. Girls who went to the Elks to trap bigger fish, and guys who went to the Amvets in search of fresh young meat—and vice versa.

Although we felt like we were deserting our loyal constituency, we

Mastersound. Standing, left to right: Sonny Davis, Teddy Caldwell, Burley Marshall. Kneeling, left to right: Carl Jackson, me, Carl Gholston. Mastersound Promotional Photo.

opted to go for the step up. The Elks had a nice big stage, a sound system, somewhat of a dressing room, and a ready-made audience full of beautiful people. We named the band the Mastersound because of the fact that we grew out of a variety of sounds—jazz, blues, R&B, Latin, gospel—and created one dynamic, master sound.

As part of the Elks grand opening, they booked the Ike and Tina Turner Revue, with us being introduced as the new house band and playing during the intermission. I had often mentioned the Ike and Tina show as a model of how to play with confidence and energy. I was so happy that my band would get to see what I was talking about in person. It turned out to be quite a night. Seeing all my friends with Ike and Tina was great. Many personnel changes had been made, but there were still some people in the group that I knew. I was greeted cordially but not overly enthusiastically by Ike, warmly by Tina and the other guys and girls. My band was really impressed that I actually knew big-time performers. It instantly gave me more credibility. Ike and Tina did their first set with us watching and marveling at every move they made. Seeing the Ike and Tina show again at an objective distance made me re-realize what a great and devastatingly entertaining show it was. The looks on the faces in my band concerned me. I hoped they hadn't been scared out of their wits and wouldn't be unable to play.

To the contrary, they hit—and I do mean hit—the stage like a band possessed. During the half hour we played, Teddy broke sticks, Burley busted a speaker, Sonny pulled blood blisters on fingers he'd been playing on every day. Both Pete Lou and Bill sang themselves hoarse. We jammed a whole gig's worth of energy into thirty minutes. Experiencing the Ike and Tina Turner Revue firsthand was the best thing that could have happened to the Mastersound. We played at a new level from then on. No band in the area could touch us. We started thinking about bigger and better things.

Now, the Mastersound was rolling. We were doing about as well as a local band could do in Huntsville, Alabama. We had Friday, Saturday, and Sunday at the Elks. We later added a Wednesday night at the Nite Lite Club. I personally lucked up on an afternoon gig at the local Quality Court Motel Lounge. A young private who had just transferred into the Fifty-fifth Army Band on clarinet got the gig playing organ and singing standard tunes for happy hour in the bar. From five o'clock until eight o'clock Monday through Friday, I made forty dollars a day accompanying him on drums. It was the easiest forty dollars I ever made. Everyone in the Fifty-fifth Army Band made good money, but I think I was the only one making this kind of money doing nothing but playing music. By now Gertie was working again. I was buying cars from people who were transferring out and selling them to people who were transferring in. I made Specialist Five. The Mastersound was thriving. My beautiful daughter was getting prettier and prettier. Life, once again, was beautiful.

Things were going so well in Huntsville that it crossed my mind to re-enlist. The Army had a plan wherein you got $5,000 and a choice of duty station if you signed up for another three years. It also was proposed to me by Mr. Edmonds that I apply for warrant officer school. This would more or less lead to a career in the Army. These options probably would have been more attractive if it hadn't been for the Mastersound and the fact of the Vietnam War. The Mastersound was such a good band, I was thinking of touring, recording, and getting out there and competing in the real world. The problem was I didn't know how to connect with booking agents and record companies and managers in the music business. We had been approached by a man who came through town talking about booking us in some clubs in other cities around the South. Of course, this wasn't possible as long as I was still in the Army, but I was approaching the end of my enlistment and was thinking more and more about taking Pete Tyler up on his offer to book the band in some other places. Pete did a lot of talking about how rich he was and how he owned a big ranch in Oklahoma. However, he drove an old beat-up Chrysler Imperial and didn't look at all rich. Jack and Sonny wanted to jump out there into that deep water, too, but there was certain equipment we had to have that we hadn't needed while playing locally. Pete said his money was tied up in some kind of tax problem and he couldn't help us. We were seriously suspicious of this guy, but he was all we had. Although Pete Tyler had crook written all over him, we turned him loose to book us. At least he could get us out there, and we weren't about to sign anything with him.

We borrowed $9,000 dollars from Sonny's dad, bought a used Corvair nine-passenger van, a trailer for the equipment, three sets of uniforms, and painted "Wesley–Davis Mastersound" on the trailer. Sonny became my partner and business manager when his daddy loaned us the money to get started. I was music director, he was business manager. Pete Tyler was whatever. The agreement was, Pete got 10 percent plus expenses, and we took care of the band and our own expenses. Pete talked us into having a girl singer. He said we needed a girl to give us that sex appeal. We agreed, and we knew just the girl. Hurricane Alice. We had to replace Carl Gholston on trumpet, because although he was fascinated by the music business and was holding down his part unexpectedly well, he didn't want to leave his secure engineering career to take a chance on making it as a trumpet player. If anything went wrong with this band, he didn't have the training or experience and probably not the talent to pursue music as anything but a sideline. He was a good person, and we all loved him, but I think he made the right decision. We replaced him with a friend of Jack and mine from Mobile named Robert Rice. He was a professional trumpet player and a very entertaining blues singer and comedian to boot. He had no problem fitting in, and we built some of the show around his singing and comedy.

I got honorably discharged from the Army just in time. They had begun extending people's enlistments for six months and sending them to Vietnam. Without warning, orders would come down, and a person who had never seen combat or had any combat training would be gone to Vietnam. I'll never forget how it hit us when the always-jovial Sergeant Petracco—who had been in the Army for twelve years, always in bands, never in combat—was suddenly shipped out to Vietnam. There was panic throughout the band. If he could go, anybody could go. At the same time, Mr. Edmonds got transferred out and we got a new CO. I forget his name. All I remember is that he was a real old man who didn't give a hoot about jazz, the big band, or even music if it didn't directly apply to the Army and military concerns. The party was definitely over. Guys had to give up jobs. We had to keep our gigs secret. It was back to the "Brown Shoe Army," as the older guys called it. My last six months at Redstone was like I had expected it to be when I first heard I was being sent there. I managed to survive with only one Article 15 for missing a parade. By the grace of God, I was discharged on July 17, 1967. My career in the Army was over. I left behind many good friends and took with me many lessons and memories, mostly good.

With no Army to report to, I was now free to pursue a career as leader of a regional band, with intentions of creating a vast following, cutting a record, and going big time. First I had to learn how to drive a van with nine people on board, pulling a trailer that weighed more than it did. We couldn't afford the insurance that covered everyone. Only Sonny and I were covered. Cautiously, we headed toward Montgomery, my old stomping ground. We had Sunday night at the Elks Club there. If we drew a big enough crowd, we were promised a regular engagement every Sunday. At about 40 mph, we made it to Montgomery. Checked into a nice motel. Put on our pretty new uniforms. Set up on the very comfortable stage upstairs in the Elks Club. Waited for Benjamin Wright and his band to complete their Sunday afternoon gig downstairs, then proceeded to tear the roof off the place. It was full, thanks to a lot of people who re-membered me from Al Stringer's band five years earlier and to my deejay friends Al Dixon (Dickie Doo) and Stinson Holmes, who gave us radio advertising. Also, some of the people from downstairs stayed around just to see who we were and how we would do. How did we do? We turned it out. We were an instant hit in Montgomery.

We soon extended our territory to include Dothan, Alabama (another Elks Club), on Mondays. A VFW in Columbus, Georgia, on Tuesdays. Another Elks in Selma, Alabama, on Wednesdays. Thursdays, Fridays, and Saturdays, we played wherever we could get a good price or a good deal for the door. We played Montgomery, Birmingham, Mobile, Tusca-loosa, Pensacola, and even as far as away as Nashville if we could there overnight at 40 mph from the previous job.

Wherever and whenever we performed, we were spectacular. Pete Lou and Bill had really come together as a duo and as individual performers. It's funny how audience acceptance dispels shyness and fosters self-confidence. Everyone in the band, from the inexperienced Burley and Teddy to Jack and Sonny who had definitely done it before, were elevated to being "out-front" performers. Alice, already a great performer, was the perfect icing on what had developed into quite a delicious cake. Of course, I continued my role as organizer and part player, taking pride in the fact that I had put together such an outstanding band and show. I was especially proud of the fact that we were pleasing what were ordinarily blues, R&B, and Top Forty audiences while playing mostly jazz. Funky jazz, of course, but only about 50 percent Top Forty stuff. Not even all the vocals were R&B. One of our biggest hits was "Tobacco Road."

Things were going very well for the first couple of months, although we never were satisfied with the count Pete Tyler came up with off the door. Plus, he always came up with some unexpected expense like placards or repairs on his car. Things we hadn't allowed for in our planning. Still, we managed to pay everybody and still eke out a fairly decent profit. Sonny and I were planning to get rid of Pete just as soon as we could find a way to operate without him. But at the time, all the gigs were his.

Aside from the continuing strife with Pete, there was beginning to be dissension within the band. As leader, music director, and founder, I was calling all the shots, musical shots anyway. All of a sudden, these musical geniuses and show producers got together and decided that the show needed to be changed. They had heard that the Commodores, another band that shared our area, were playing more of the latest hits than we were. A few people had requested some of these songs, such as "Cold Sweat" by James Brown. I had heard "Cold Sweat" and was very unimpressed with it. It was not on par with the material we were playing. It only had one change, the words made no sense at all, and the bridge was musically incorrect. I wasn't about to abandon our upscale style and selection of music and sink to the level of a little honky-tonk sissy singer and sound like every other band up and down the pike. Our uniqueness was what made us. We had a different sound, and that sound was what I was counting on to take us to the top. I felt that the Commodores were going nowhere, trying to sound like everything you hear on the radio. This was my concept, and nobody was going to tell me how to run this band. What did this bunch of amateurs know anyway?

The rift got serious. We almost came to blows after a show in Tuscaloosa. Somebody in the audience asked if we knew "Cold Sweat" and was very disappointed that we didn't. Well, everybody in the band jumped on me. I knew it was a very hot tune, but I stuck to my guns. The song was out of our thing, and I wasn't going to do it. They rebelled and said they were going to do it anyway. I was drinking that night, and by that time I was good and drunk, and it was raining. All the while we were loading up after the show the argument continued. Finally, as they were pulling off (I was in my own car that night), I ran alongside the van, stepping in mud up to my ankles, screaming, "You're all fired! Plus, I quit!" They paid me no attention. I followed them all the way down the driveway of this club, still yelling and cursing as they disappeared into the night, leaving me to find my way back down the driveway in pitch darkness, stepping in mud and God knows what else, all wet, drunk, and scared of getting lost or bumping into a snake or some other animal, and so mad that I was crying. After about an hour of fumbling around in the dark, I finally felt my way back to my car.

Along with my refusal to compromise the Mastersound concept, there was some jealousy beginning to simmer between the two male singers. Seemed like every day there was some discussion about who should get the most time on stage or what song they would do or who the girls liked the best. I got real tired of this silliness. It got so bad with Pete Lou and Bill that finally Bill quit. He felt that since Jack and Pete Lou were so close, he got the short end of the stick all the time. Maybe he was right. But what it did was force us, mainly me, to revamp the show to compensate for his absence. It was rough at first, but with the blues singing of Robert and Jack, we overcame the loss. Although we adjusted, the show wasn't the same. The sound wasn't the same. It was still good, but that sparkling sound and vibe had been seriously compromised.

I was very unhappy. I started thinking about giving it up. The fire I had felt for the group was beginning to cool, but I hung in there because we still had that bill to pay and I had a family to support.

A crushing blow came when I discovered that Teddy and Alice were rooming together. At first nobody thought anything about it. The rooming arrangement was this: Me and Sonny, Jack and Pete Lou, Robert and Burley, Bill and Teddy, and Alice in her own room. After Bill left, Teddy was all alone. We thought nothing about Alice letting Teddy room with her, because she was a grown lady and Teddy was a little boy—well, not really a little boy, but a very young man. We thought she was just doing the kid a favor and helping him save some money. It turned out she was doing him more of a favor than we thought. I noticed them sitting very close to each other in the van and generally being together a lot of—no—

all the time. I mentioned this to Sonny. He had noticed it, too, but we all passed it off. Surely she wouldn't give any of that stuff of hers to that young boy. He was definitely not her type, and we had seen her run some full-grown, really tough men stone crazy with it.

The situation got more and more serious, and finally Teddy confessed to me that he was in love with Alice. I went to Alice to chastise her for messing with this fine young man's mind. To my surprise, she confessed her love for him, too. We were all shocked. It didn't make sense. I could understand Teddy falling for Alice, but Alice falling for Teddy was mind-boggling. And that ain't all. One day in Montgomery, they showed up, married, ring and all. Things changed after that. No longer could we treat Alice like one of the boys. I don't know why that was important, but it was. Alice was now Mrs. Caldwell. I felt funny calling certain tunes for her to sing. It wasn't long before Alice got pregnant, and she and Teddy decided to quit the band, go home to Birmingham, and start a family. This was devastating to the Mastersound. Not only had we lost our star singer, but she had taken with her our drummer, who was the backbone, the "feel," the heart of our sound. It was Teddy's unorthodox style that inspired a lot of the original tunes.

We were lucky to find a very good replacement right away. There was a drummer in Montgomery who was also a terrific singer looking for a gig. His name was Walter "Clyde" Orange, and he had star written all over him. I thought I would have to play drums while he sang or something like that, but it turned out he could play real funky drums and sing, making all the accents and fills at the same time. He was incredible. However, we still couldn't quite do a few things that were our trademark. That sound that was the Mastersound was gone forever. Completely dead. We were now that good R&B/Top Forty band that sounded like every other band up and down the pike. I continued to do it, but my heart was not in it. I stuck with it as long as I could, but eventually I just couldn't bear to do a show that was so completely different from my original concept.

I squared it with Sonny by agreeing to continue making payments on the loan his father had given us. The band continued to play for a while but eventually dispersed. Clyde later joined the Commodores, who instead of Pete Tyler for a manager had Bennie Ashburn, who turned out to be — needless to say — a great manager who got them astronomical results.

I went back to Huntsville, gathered my wife and baby, and moved into Gertie's mother's house back in Mobile. Although the rent was cheap in Mobile, I knew from past experience that there was no way to support a family on what I could earn playing music in Mobile. I had done the maximum before, and it took working every night and doing all kinds of odd and sometimes silly gigs. So I went about looking for a J-O-B. I was working whatever gigs I could get at night and putting in applications for real jobs in the daytime. I found it hard to believe, but after all I had been through, I was about to turn into Freeman—working an ordinary job in the daytime and playing gigs at night.

I applied for everything from the post office to the sanitation department to the recreation department. I was hoping to get that recreation department job, because it involved teaching music to kids and maybe directing a community band. It didn't pay much, but it would have been interesting work. I got a call back from Barber's Milk Company to take their test. I didn't know what the job was, maybe milking cows, but I took the test. I was called a week later and asked to come in for an interview. I was told that the job was for a milk packaging and dock loading, and that I had passed the test. In fact, I had made the highest score anyone had ever made on this test. The interviewer told me I had the job if I wanted it. The salary wasn't great, but pretty good. I surmised that with the milk salary and what I was making gigging, I could continue to support my wife and child in the manner to which they had become accustomed.

But this was 1967, and many companies and public facilities were integrating their work forces. Because of the high score I had made on the laborer test, I was invited to take the test for milk delivery. If I passed this test, I would have my own route—be the milkman, for real. This would make me the first black milkman in Mobile. I took the test and passed it, too, with flying colors. I was all set to get my white suit, white truck, and settle down to a quiet family life in Mobile, playing gigs on the side just like all my friends I had grown up with. How bad could it be? It wasn't what was expected of me, and it wasn't what I had planned for myself, but I had given the big-time musician thing a try and ended up here. At least I was breaking new ground in helping to integrate the work force. Life was tolerable.

James Brown

• • •

I was all prepared to start my milk route when I got a call from Freeman. He had been in Pensacola and gone to the James Brown Show, mainly to see Waymon, who we all knew was now playing with the James Brown band. Waymon had introduced Freeman to some of the guys in the band including bandleader Pee Wee Ellis and Levi Rasbury, the trombone player and road manager. It seemed like Mr. Rasbury's dual duties were becoming too much for him to handle efficiently. Being as how he was leaning toward the road manager job, which paid more, offered more opportunity, and, frankly, was a job for which he was better suited, Mr. Ellis was looking for another trombone player. The job was offered to Freeman, but he had to turn it down because of all his kids and his tenure on his good day job. Starting a new career on the road would not have been a good idea for him at that time. I was the next choice. Freeman told me all I had to do was call Pee Wee in Ocala, Florida, and the job was mine.

It wasn't quite that simple for me. I was committed to the milkman job. Although I hadn't started yet or signed any kind of contract, a lot of people were counting on me to take that job. But I reasoned that I was first and foremost a musician. It wasn't like I was faced with the choice between a jazz gig and a funk gig—the choice was between music and milk.

Sure enough, when I talked to Pee Wee, I got the gig. I took my first airplane flight and joined the show in Tampa, Florida, getting there just in time to board the bus for the next show, which was in Orlando. Boarding the bus was no small matter. Nobody I knew was on the bus. Bernard and Jabo, my homeboys, were with the truck that hauled the stage equipment. Waymon and Pee Wee had apparently made other arrangements for transportation. After a serious confrontation about where to put my suitcase and horn with a guy who I thought was the bus driver but who turned out to be a roadie, I attempted to board the bus. It turned out that everybody had assigned seats and every time I sat in what appeared to be a vacant seat, this lady would yell at me and make me get up. "That's Pee Wee's seat." "That's Waymon's seat." "That's Maceo's seat." The bus was an old-style Trailways with two seats on each side of the aisle and just enough seats down the aisle for everyone in the show to have a side of the aisle to him- or herself. I noticed two ladies sitting together, but everyone else sat in one seat and had their stuff in the other. It was obvious that I would have to share a seat with someone. No one volunteered.

The lady who seemed to be in charge, Ms. Sanders, was the one who had to make the decision. She took her time, making sure that I and everyone else knew that she and she alone was about to pass judgment as to who was low man on the importance list. She went on and on about how she had to consider "that man's clothes"—apparently meaning Mr. Brown's wardrobe—which were hung and placed in the racks above the seats and in the bins beneath the bus. Everything and everybody else came secondary. After much yack from her and a few arguments with various people who, to me, seemed to be temporary on the bus, one of the violinists, Richard Jones, reluctantly and disgustedly volunteered to let me sit with him for the time being. The seating altercation was so traumatic that I was *that* close to telling them all to kiss my ass and catching a bus back to Mobile.

By the time we got to Orlando, Richard Jones had filled me in on who was who and what was what on the bus.

The lady with all the rap was Gertrude Sanders, a career groupie whose main claim to fame was that she was an Etta James look-alike. She made her living as Mr. Brown's wardrobe mistress.

The muscular dude who made sure I didn't put my horn and suitcase on top of "that man's clothes" was Kenny Hull, a street thug turned roadie-bodyguard. Both of these people, I was warned, were the eyes and ears of the Boss and would tell it in a minute if you did anything that violated the James Brown rules, which were renowned to be many.

The two ladies sitting together were the second and third parts of the violin section, Mr. Jones being the first. There was another young lady sitting alone, who Mr. Jones described as the last remaining JB Dancer, Ann Norman. There had been, at one time, as many as five, I understand. I

Ms. Gertrude
Sanders. Standing
by "the bus."
Photograph by
Fred Wesley Jr.

recognized the gentleman with a gray streak in his hair from having seen the James Brown Show in Washington, D.C., at the Howard Theater, and in Huntsville, as well as from photographs of the show. Although he was very recognizable, I had never known his name. It turned out to be just as memorable—St. Clair Pinckney. The word was he was playing tenor with the show even before James Brown was singing with the band.

Mr. Jones pointed out Clyde Stubblefield, the "give the drummer some" drummer; Jimmy Nolen, the lead guitar player; Alphonso "Country" Kellum, the rhythm guitarist; and Joe Dupars, the other trumpet player. As I remember, the other people on the bus were Junior Gunther, light man and stage manager; Joe Ginyard, a promoter of some sort; and Danny Ray, the renowned voice of the James Brown Show. He was much smaller than his voice would indicate. He looked remarkably like Sammy Davis Jr.

We arrived at the Sports Arena in Orlando, and I finally got to see some familiar faces. Jabo and Buddy (Bernard Odum) were there with the truck that transported most of the stage equipment. I had met Jabo but mostly knew him by reputation and through other people. Buddy, on the other hand, was a good friend. We had played together in Mr. Lott's band when I was still a kid. He was like a big brother. While I was still in high school, he would come and pick me up at lunchtime, and we would hang out on the beach, in some clubs, and he had let me drive his cars. I particularly remember some outstanding vehicles of his. A green and white '57 Pontiac that was beautiful, and a red and white '56 Oldsmobile that was unbelievably fast and powerful. I hadn't seen him in a long time, as I'd been in the Army when he had rejoined James Brown three years earlier. It was good to see him again, although our relationship had changed somewhat. I was no longer that green kid he had befriended in the late '50s. I was a grown man now, with two road gigs, the U.S. Army, and a family under my belt. It had been almost ten years.

We were sitting on the bus talking when I saw a blue '68 Ford sedan pull up alongside the bus. Out stepped two men Buddy identified as *Maceo* and *Pee Wee* with the finest little bowlegged sister I'd ever seen and a skinny white woman. The bowlegged sister was identified as Maceo's fiancée and former JB Dancer, Bunny. The skinny white woman was Pee Wee's wife, Barbara. Between Buddy and Richard Jones, I was cautiously introduced and cordially received by both Maceo and Pee Wee. I was careful, because I didn't know how the reputed star of the band and the bandleader who was supposed to be some kind of genius would treat a new guy who Waymon had held up to be a bad mother-

James Brown Band on the road. Left to right: Maceo, Pee Wee, Clyde, me, St. Clair, and new drummer Nate Jones. Courtesy of Barbara Ellis.

fucker also. So I was careful not to be too cocky or too humble. It turned out that, as usual, a person is a person and a musician is a musician. Although Pee Wee was the musical genius everybody said he was, he was a regular guy with certain unique weirdities that we all have. And Maceo was just as affable and jovial as his solos would lead you to think he was. He and I had similar black college backgrounds. He had attended, but not graduated from, North Carolina A&T. Like me, he had been on the road before. He had spent a year or so with James Brown before he was drafted into the Army. He had just recently been discharged and had returned to the show.

Maceo, Pee Wee, and I became and have remained close friends, with Waymon being the connection and catalyst between us. Joe Dupars and St. Clair Pinckney completed the horn section at that time. The other James Brown horn players, who I had known before, Brisco Clark and Mack Johnson, were long gone. For reasons that became clear to me later, there was high turnover in the James Brown horn section. As we sat around between the dressing room and the bus, Waymon, Pee Wee, and the other guys told stories of Brisco's drinking, Mack's insubordination, and other confrontations with the Boss. Jabo, Bernard (who for some reason was known as "Dog" in this band), Junior Gunther, Kenny Hull, and the local stage crew went about setting up the stage.

At about six or seven o'clock, Mr. Brown and an entourage of about four people arrived in what looked to be a rental car. Mr. Brown didn't ride the bus. He would station himself at a central point, in this case Miami, and fly in his private Lear jet back and forth to gigs in the area. Mr. Brown exited the driver's seat, went straight to the stage, and began fooling around with the Hammond B-3 organ that had been the first thing to be set up. He was much shorter than I had imagined him to be from seeing him on stage. Ms. Sanders and the people who were busy on the stage greeted him respectfully. I and the other guys were out of sight on the bus and just kind of observed the arrival.

A beautiful, well-built, light-skinned girl got out of the car and went directly into Mr. Brown's dressing room without saying anything to anyone. The guys told me that she was Marva Whitney, the featured singer on the show, and hinted that she also had a more personal relationship with Mr. Brown. A stockily built guy with what looked like a hairdryer in his hand followed closely behind Ms. Whitney. This, I was told, was Henry Stallings, the hairdresser. Although he sported a nice "do," he looked like anything but a hairdresser. His demeanor also wasn't what you'd expect of a hairdresser. He had the loud, gruff, profane way of speaking you would more likely attribute to a gangster. A big, tall, black, rough-looking dude got out of the car last. He was scuffling with getting the luggage out of the car. This was Baby James, who *was* a gangster. His job was body-guard, general enforcer, and whatever else Mr. Brown needed done that required brute strength and not a lot of brainpower. Actually, all of the nonmusical employees of the James Brown show sort of fit that description, except for Mr. Bell, the fourth person in the entourage, who was a middle-aged white man who piloted the James Brown Lear Jet.

After an afternoon of meeting people, reacquainting myself with old friends, and generally getting to know my new gig, it was finally time for the show. Unlike the Ike and Tina Turner show and the Hank Ballard show, I didn't go right onstage. I was told that I had to watch, go through a few rehearsals, and be fitted with some uniforms before I could go on-stage.

I didn't know what kind of show to expect. I had only seen a small part of the show back in 1962 at the Howard Theater. The Orlando Sports Arena was hardly a theater. This place was more suited for rodeos and stock shows. (There were actually some live animals corralled in the back of the place.) However, the stage was set up with a somewhat elaborate sound system. All of the backline amplifiers were by vox, as were the drums and guitars. In fact, I think the entire sound system was by vox. Conspicuously missing, though, was a monitor system. When I had visited the show in Huntsville, I had seen the four sets of drums onstage, but I still hadn't seen how more than one drummer at a time operated during a show. The multiple-drummer concept was the subject of much discussion and speculation among musicians throughout the world. I was anxious to see firsthand what it was all about.

The horns were positioned on the left of the stage (from the audience's point of view) and in front of the organ. Jabo's drums were positioned upstage, left of center. Clyde's drums were also positioned upstage, but right of center. The bass player—Bernard or Buddy or Dog, whatever you want to call him—was parallel to and between Jabo and Clyde. A little to the right and behind Jabo was Country Kellum on rhythm, and I do mean *rhythm,* guitar. A little to the right and behind Clyde was Jimmy Nolen, the lead guitar player. On an elevated platform, stage left, angled to face center stage, were the three violins, each plugged into their own sound-enhancing amplifier, also by vox. There were two mikes for the horns—one for the saxes and one for the trumpets and trombone. A single mike was at center stage. On a high riser in the center of the stage behind the band was the lone JB Dancer. Although this was a rodeo arena, the James Brown stage had a big-time, professional, showbiz theater look about it.

It was finally show time. The place was packed. There were chairs set up on a portable floor over the ground, which was the real floor of the arena, but most of the crowd was standing all around the arena. The house lights went down and the band took the stage. After an involved musical introduction that included some really hip jazz licks, some funky rhythms, and some real hard bebop-type runs by the horns that melted into a dramatic drumroll, an offstage voice announced, "L-A-DIES AND GENTLEMEN, THE JAMES BROWN ORCHESTRA." Under the direction of Mr. Alfred "Pee Wee" Ellis, the band did a set, about six tunes. The only ones I remember are "Hip Hug-Her," a then-current hit by Booker T. and the MGs, and "Why Am I Treated So Bad," a current hit by the Staple Singers. All the tunes were very interestingly arranged by Pee Wee, immediately convincing me of his musical genius. Maceo and Waymon played most of the solos, with a couple by St. Clair on tenor sax and Pee Wee himself on alto sax.

I was very impressed with the band. Although it wasn't a jazz band, they played jazz very well. It wasn't the Jazztet, but it was far more musical than I had expected. So far, I was happy about being on this gig. The people seemed to be people I could deal with. Some I already liked a lot. And the music seemed to be reasonably challenging. I would be happy if I had to play straight-up blues all night after the band's opening set. I was sure that associating with musicians like Pee Wee and Waymon would make the whole thing worthwhile.

But wait. There was more to come. Suddenly, the stage went black. The band played a grandiose, almost symphonic intro/fanfare type of thing, complete with strings and what I swear sounded like timpani and French horns. When this bodacious introduction decrescendoed, the lights hit center stage and there was James Brown. There he was. Sitting on a stool. Not just an ordinary stool, but a stool of carved, highly polished oak, with a padded leather back, more like a big high chair. He was dressed in a beige, mohair, three-piece suit, with a three-quarter-length coat, a turtleneck shirt, and the baddest burgundy alligator boots I have ever seen. He calmly sang Tony Bennett's "If I Ruled the World." Bear in mind, I'm expecting a screaming and hollering, fast-dancing little sissy to come out and sweat all over the place. Instead, I'm seeing a real cool man, milking one of my favorite ballads dry. The band went out of "If I Ruled the World" into a smooth swing version of Sinatra's "That's Life." The arrangements were absolutely fantastic. Sinatra and Nelson Riddle couldn't have performed the songs any better. I was totally surprised and amazed.

But that's not all. At the end of "That's Life," James Brown pushed the mike forward in a military-rifle-salute type move, accented by a rim shot from Jabo, and the band hit a descending drag triplet riff and went directly into a heartstopping Mobile, Alabama, blues type shuffle. Before I could get straight from the shock, James Brown was deep into "Going to Kansas City." The band was clicking like a funk machine, everything hitting in the right place. Jimmy Nolen, Country, Dog, and—leading the pack—Jabo, doing what nobody in the world can do like him. A hard-driving shuffle. They did several verses and choruses, increasing the intensity of the groove until it spilled over into a vamp that had the rhythm driving wide open, horns screaming in a frenzy, and James Brown, still basically cool, giving us a glimpse of the fury that was to come, with a little mash here and a split there, suddenly leaving the stage as abruptly as he had appeared. Danny Ray, still offstage, promised, "JAMES BROWN WILL BE BACK."

The audience went crazy. I went with them. I don't even remember exactly how it happened, but when I looked up again the lovely Ms. Marva Whitney was onstage singing some song I'd never heard before. It must have been an original. The highlight of her set was a beautiful arrangement of "People." Obviously, the genius of Pee Wee Ellis had struck again.

As she left the stage, the lights went out again, and the spotlight that followed her off followed James Brown back on, as the band hit the intro to "Man's World." This time James was wearing a pantsuit with a form-fitting shirt that had bloused sleeves and alternating navy-blue and white pleats. The pants were navy-blue velvet bell-bottoms. This time a pair of navy-blue lizard boots adorned his little fast feet. He was center stage by the time the violins finished their famous run. There was a pause. He sang, in his familiar voice, the familiar line, "*This is a man's world.*" The audience and I went berserk again. Even I, a jazz person, was familiar with that hit song. I can't say that I had liked it before. It made so little sense to me. He did the song all the way through. "Man made the car," "Man made money, to buy from other man," and all that. The words were usually silly to me, but seeing it performed, in person, now, was thrilling.

He went straight into a ten-minute vamp in which he did a complete production number that included everything from horn "hits"—one, two, three, and four times—to tricks with the mike and drops to his knees, all held together by a steady "motion of the ocean" groove by Jabo and the rhythm section. He finally turned us loose—just before everybody died from ecstasy—and left the stage again. Once again, Danny Ray, offstage, assured us: "JAMES BROWN WILL BE BACK."

The band left the stage, and Danny Ray made himself visible for the first time and made a few announcements about souvenir items on sale in the front of the arena. I had noticed a big fat man set up at a table, selling merchandise. This was the intermission. The band went into the stalls that served as dressing rooms and proceeded to change clothes. The place was littered with clothes bags, hangers, irons, shoes, shoetrees, socks, bow ties, belts, and accessories. After about fifteen minutes of furious activity, the band emerged, dressed in lime-green suits with white satin lapels, bow ties, and patent-leather shoes. The look was absolutely stunning. A startling contrast to the ordinary black tuxedos in which they had opened the show. Each band member looked as if he had just left home in fresh clothes straight out of the laundry. The Army would have been proud of the spit and polish of this band. They stood around, ready, waiting, I guessed, for Mr. Brown to come out of his dressing room.

After a while, Henry Stallings came out of the man's dressing room and in a gruff voice said, "He's ready." Everyone moved out immediately and took their positions on stage. I'm standing on the side of the stage now. The band started a quiet, bluesy-jazz vamp that went on until Danny Ray took center stage. The groove was cut off abruptly, and Ray went into his legendary introduction of James Brown. "The hardest working man in show business," "The man who made 'Try Me,' 'Out Of Sight'. . . ." Each of his phrases was accented by hits and riffs from the band. He continued: "The amazing Mr. 'Please, Please, Please' himself . . . JAAAAAAMES BROWN." With that, James—whom I could see framed in his dressing-room door, prancing and bucking like a race horse in the starting gate—stormed onto the stage and proceeded to do an hour-and-a-half medley of his repertoire. He did songs like "I Got the Feeling," "I Got You," and "I'll Go Crazy," going from tune to tune via clever segues and intros. The groove remained intense, even through all the tempo changes. Most of the things were fast and funky, with the exception of "Try Me" and another long production performance of "Lost Someone."

Mr. Brown was exactly as advertised. His dancing was unbelievable.

He did things that seemed impossible for the human body to do. How he could sing with that much energy and dance at the same time was amazing. His rhythm and soulful attitude and demeanor epitomized what black music was all about. The band was now literally a funk machine. Overpowering and relentless. I got the sense that James was plugged into the band, and it was generating energy directly to his body. At times, the band was totally musical, with beautiful chords and melodies mixing with the constant funky grooves. But, at other times, things happened that totally defied musical explanation. There were chords that were just sounds for effect and rhythms that started and ended wherever they started or ended, not in accord with any time signature or form. Through it all, the band was tight, doing all the complicated dance routines and the music at the same time. Everything conspired in exactly the right way to make for an extraordinarily entertaining show that was sometimes directed by Pee Wee, but mostly signaled by the same man who was also doing all the singing and dancing. The sounds, the sights, and the relentlessly intense feeling of that funky groove were completely thrilling and mesmerizing.

By the time the show climaxed with "Please, Please, Please" and the famous act in which James Brown collapses to his knees and is covered sympathetically with a cape by Danny Ray, the audience was completely fucked up, responding to any- and everything that James or the band did. After his third drop to his knees and covering by a third, spectacularly designed cape, James Brown left the stage as the band opened up and went all the way crazy. We were all thoroughly entertained, all funked up, wanting more but satisfied, when all of a sudden he was back and giving us what we had forgotten was missing: Mr. Brown's then-current hit, "I Can't Stand Myself." This encore was like a climax on top of an already all-consuming climax. The encore must have lasted another thirty minutes. The crowd—and that included me—was completely satiated. I felt guilty for not having bought a ticket. This was the most completely thrilling, spectacular, hypnotizing, soulful, incredible, unbelievable, entertaining, and satisfying show I had ever seen or heard of.

After the show was over and I had caught my breath, I could barely keep myself from raving to the guys in the band about how thrilled I was with the show. I was very anxious to get onstage and be a part of what had to be the greatest show on earth. It was clear now why they needed another trombone player. All during the show Rasbury was going back and forth between the box office and James's dressing room, and every now and then he would grab his horn, which was a valve trombone, and go onstage for a little while. I didn't miss his part, but it would definitely become a fuller brass sound with me onstage. When they cooled down and changed out of their suits, which were soaking wet with sweat, Waymon and Pee Wee took me to meet "The Man."

We went to the dressing room door and waited and waited until finally Ms. Sanders told us we could come in. As we entered the dressing room, I was amazed that what was probably supposed to be a storeroom had been transformed into a very comfortable dressing room, complete with a rug on the floor, racks of clothes hanging around, shoes lined up in a very orderly manner, an ironing board, a table with a large mirror and make-up on it, and, indeed, a professional looking hairdryer. This room had all the comforts of home. Ms. Sanders even offered us a soda from the cooler that was there.

Mr. Brown was sitting at the table in a robe, rubbing his face with a make-up sponge. He was still dripping sweat from his hair, which Henry was carefully rolling up as Brown talked in his fast, assured way to Rasbury—not leaving any space for Rasbury to get a word in edgewise— about how good the show was and how much the people enjoyed it. Brown seemed amazed and even relieved that the audience had accepted and enjoyed the show as much as they had. This surprised me. At that time, I didn't know if this was a new show that had not been audience tested or if the great James Brown was so insecure that he never took pleasing the audience for granted. I learned later that most true stars are never sure or confident about their performances. Mr. Brown was a glaring example of this insecurity, although he put up a self-confident and cocky, if paper-thin, façade.

After a long time of listening to him rant and rave about how big he was, how well his records were selling, and how much the people loved him, he finally allowed Waymon to say, "Mr. Brown, I'd like you to meet the new trombone player, Fred Wesley." He seemed unimpressed. He didn't turn around from the mirror. Instead, he kept on fussing with his make-up and wiping sweat, then glared at me through the mirror and asked, "Can you dance?" Taken aback, I paused and collected myself, then said, "Yeah." Then I realized that he had probably noticed that I was a little chubby and thought that dancing might be a problem for me. At the same time, I realized that I'd said "Yeah," not "Yes, sir," as everyone else was saying. So I quickly got myself together and started assuring him that dancing was not a problem for me. I said, "Yes, sir, I can dance. I can dance very well." I might have even given him a little step or two. I didn't want anything to keep me from getting this gig. He told me that I was on probation and would be watched and evaluated over the next few days to see if I would fit in. I assured him that I was the right man for the job and that he would not have a problem with me. He still seemed unconvinced but said, "Okay. We'll see."

The next few days found me adjusting to the day-to-day routine of the James Brown system. We worked almost every night, making that $225-a-week, work-or-no-work salary, not so great when you considered that the "work-or-no-work" clause was in favor of management. The salary covered anything that came up. Sometimes we did more than one show in the same place, two cities in the same day, recording sessions, and TV shows—all covered by the same weekly salary. I found out that what I had thought was security for a musician was really just a guarantee of cheap labor for James Brown. Most road musicians get paid by the show, making off days detrimental to their income. With bands like Hank Ballard or Bobby Bland or even a jazz group like Art Blakey, a guaranteed weekly salary was a good thing, because you were covered for those off days, and hardly any big stars worked seven days a week, three hundred days a year like James Brown did.

I figured out that James could make anywhere from $350,000 to $500,000 a week, but his payroll remained at about a paltry $6,000 a week. And he acted like he didn't want to give you that. I had to almost beg for a draw during that first week I was out there. It soon became clear that there was no set payday. It was supposed to be Sunday, but it never happened on time. You knew the money was there. You could plainly see bags and even cardboard boxes full of money being loaded into the rented car every night. It was now clear why there was such a high turnover rate in the band.

After my probation period, my salary shot up to $350 a week, so even with paying my own hotel and food out of that, I was able to get enough money home to support my family at least as well as that milkman job would have. Also, although there was a serious discrepancy between the money you were helping to generate and the percentage you were being paid, the salary was still just a little above what you could make in a year with most of the other bands working regularly. Still, like me, most of the guys must have had ulterior motives for staying on the gig; it was clear that none of the James Brown sidemen would ever get rich.

I'm sure that some of the old-timers felt that they were lucky to have a gig on this level and weren't about to take a chance on trying to get another gig even this good somewhere else. Others saw the James Brown show as a stepping-stone to bigger and better things. I'm sure that was the case with guys like Pee Wee and Waymon. And some were there simply because of the glamour and the opportunity to have fun and score exotic and beautiful women, who were always around big-time shows like this.

Whatever their reasons were, Mr. Brown took full advantage of them all and ruled his empire with an iron hand, using all they had to offer for his own benefit, giving back as little as possible in return. He had a knack for knowing how much to take and how much to give to keep his show operating. He knew who he could yell at without getting the hell knocked out of him. He knew how much to pay each individual to keep him hanging on. He also knew who and how to humiliate and insult in order to demonstrate his power and keep everyone on their toes. He would chastise and counsel his employees in front of certain disc jockeys, reporters, and local politicians to make himself look benevolent and merciful, so many people actually thought him to be a leader and father figure. He was a master of manipulation. I more than once saw him talk his musicians into getting into big debt with a house or a car only to fire them, watch them suffer for a while, then hire them back at a lower salary and at his complete mercy. Some of these people actually loved and respected him, no matter how horribly he treated them. It didn't take me long to realize that I was involved with a man unique among performers and among human beings in general. James Brown was a great performer, probably the greatest to ever live, but I had to be careful—this was a man with the power and will and, it seemed, the need to control not only the career but the whole life of every person who worked for him.

It wasn't long before I was onstage, playing and dancing right along with everyone else. I was onstage before my uniforms arrived. I did the gig at the Regal Theater wearing Jimmy Nolen's coat, standing behind the organ speaker to hide my pants. The Regal Theater in Chicago was the site of my first "James Brown Horror Rehearsal." This was a punishment rehearsal. A rehearsal that James called when he felt his grip on somebody or everybody slipping. This type of rehearsal was generally called at the most inopportune time. This particular one was called right after we had done three shows to sold-out Regal Theater audiences. The weather was abominable—there was a Chicago blizzard. Everyone was exhausted. James came out of his dressing room, still in his robe and slippers, and said that we had to get "Please, Please, Please" right. According to him, what we had been doing for weeks was, all of a sudden, all wrong. Of course, that was just his way of keeping us away from what we wanted to be doing after the show. This was the last day of a three-day stint in Chicago, and there was much to be done, like pack after being in the same place for three days. Also, when we stayed in one place for any length of time, many of the guys brought in their wives and loved ones. Brown knew that. He really seemed to hate any distraction or diversion from the show. At the time, I took the rehearsal as his way of letting me know, personally, because I was new, how he could control my life if and when he wanted to. But I now realize that his absolute commitment to the show drove him to want everyone else to have that same commitment.

This type of rehearsal was completely unnecessary musically. "Please, Please, Please" or "Try Me" were always the songs rehearsed because they were the only songs that he could almost make anyone believe he really knew. And it became clear to me right off that he didn't know those two songs either. I know it's hard to believe, but it would have been impossible for James Brown to put his show together without the assistance of someone like Pee Wee, who understood chord changes, time signatures, scales, notes, and basic music theory. Simple things like knowing the key would be a big problem for James. So, when James would mouth out some guitar part, which might or might not have had anything to do with the actual song being played, Jimmy or Country would have to attempt to play it simply because James was still in charge. We all had to pretend that we knew what James was talking about. Nobody ever said, "That's ridiculous" or "You don't know what you're talking about." The whole James Brown Show depended on having someone with musical knowledge remember the show, the individual parts, and the individual songs, then relay these verbally or in print to the other musicians. James Brown could not do it himself. He spoke in grunts, groans, and la-di-das, and he needed musicians to translate that language into music and actual songs in order to create an actual show.

So we just stood and took it while he went through changing little things that didn't need changing, adding things that didn't need adding, going over and over some little phrase and never being satisfied with it. He would tell the horns "It's not ladaladadida, it's ladalada*di*da." We would go ladalada*di*da, and he would say, "No, I said ladala*la*dadida." Over and over it continued, until you wanted to just scream. He would get mad and chew out certain individuals (the ones he knew he could get away with chewing out) and do anything else to take up time. After a few hours of this misery or after he finally got tired, he would appear to be pleased and say things like, "Nooooow, we finally got it right. Nooooow, we have an arrangement." The truth of the matter was that nooooow the stuff was so confused that Pee Wee would have to have a real rehearsal to bring the songs back to any semblance of recognizability. That's why, even today, it's hard to recognize some of the songs during the James Brown live performances.

The Chicago rehearsal lasted right up until almost time to get on the bus and go to the next gig. No time to spend with your loved one. Hardly enough time to pack or get some breakfast. Any chance to take care of any business in a large city was gone. All you had time to do now was get on the bus.

Another time in Hollywood, California, at Modern Music Rehearsal Studios, he called one of those rehearsals. Here we are in beautiful Hollywood, full of distractions and diversions, and we have a horror rehearsal. This one was especially memorable because not only did we go through the ladaladadidas and the usual random humiliations, but Brown also created a new and very time-consuming wrinkle. The premise was that if you really knew the show you could recite the song titles really fast. So he had someone write the order of songs down, including the segues, interludes, and introductions. He would then go around the band and have each person recite the order as fast as they could from memory. In the first place, everyone had his own way of remembering the show. I, for one, didn't think of titles. I went more by my part. This is where I play the high B, or this is the song in which I play this rhythm or do this routine, for example. I had many different ways of cueing myself. It was very interesting, the different cues people made for themselves. And the fact is that they all worked, and the show went on. Having to identify each tune by title was automatically confusing and, the real point of the exercise, time-consuming. To an outside observer, it must have been hilarious. Here were people standing around holding instruments and saying rapidly: "There Was a Time Try Me Got the Feeling Cold Sweat Lost Someone Brand New Bag Intro Brand New Bag Please Please Please Can't Stand Myself. . . ."

At first he went around the band in order for a few hours until most everybody got it, but he wasn't satisfied. He then sprang on people at random and actually timed us with a stopwatch, just draaaging the thing out. If you hesitated, you didn't know the show. If you missed something, you didn't know the show. If you didn't do it fast enough, you didn't know the show. We were in agony, but Brown never tired over hours and hours. I've seen people like Ike Turner and Ray Charles try stuff like this, but after a while they would get physically tired and stop. You, me, Ike, Ray, and any other normal human being would eventually grow weary or at least have something else to do. But, in Hollywood, California, James Brown, world-famous entertainer, with all the money in the world, could find nothing better to do than torment his band. I heard him say one time, "That's what makes me *me.*"

When you were in the midst of one of those horror rehearsals or recording sessions or self-proclaiming conversations with James Brown, you felt pain, excruciating fatigue, and intense boredom, which led to suppressed anger and hate. I wonder to this day why nobody ever bolted, telling him to his face how ridiculous those rehearsals were and just walking out. And to my knowledge, nobody ever did. I came close many times, but there was always some reason—economic, political, or psychological—that I didn't. Sometimes, oddly, I think that I simply didn't want to risk hurting his feelings. He was so definite in the way he spoke to you that you got the feeling that he really believed the ridiculous stuff he was saying and you didn't want to embarrass him. Also, the few times I did challenge what he had said, he got so loud and so much farther away from reality that I gave up, because I knew he would never admit to seeing my point. It was like being held hostage by real strong, loud, un-beatable ignorance. The kind of ignorance that can make you look crazy if you continue to confront it. To my mind, I am intelligent enough to know that such manipulation and torture is unnecessary to the creation of an act as exciting as the James Brown Show. But, on the real side, there has never been a show that exciting, that tight, that completely entertaining. There also has never been a man so dedicated, so determined, so focused. I reluctantly have to admit that the things he did that seemed so stupid to me were, indeed, what made him *him,* the greatest entertainer in the world. Conversely, the intelligent things that I do are what make me *me,* the greatest sideman in the world.

After my first horror rehearsal, the glamour of the gig began to wear off. I was now clinging to the aspects of the gig that made it worth the con-stant threat of a horror rehearsal or a fine or some other humiliation. I was still happy to be working with the likes of Pee Wee, Waymon, and Maceo, for instance. We did a lot of jamming whenever we could. Many of my bandleading, music arranging, and composing skills I learned by pay-ing attention to Pee Wee in rehearsals without James Brown. The shows themselves were fun—doing the routines, feeling the grooves. The "Cold Sweat" groove, which Clyde called "that washing-machine thang," was something I looked forward to every night. I became good friends with all of the guys, especially Richard Jones, who was my roommate most of the time.

During that first year, the personnel continued to change. Joe Dupars was gone. I never knew exactly why. It was probably about money. We weren't together long enough to get to know each other well. He was replaced by a young man from Louisville, Kentucky, named Richard Griffith, whose father was a bartender at the famous Louvillian nightclub in Louisville (an important stop on the chitlin circuit) and who had somehow gotten word that we needed a trumpet player. So he brought Kush, which is what everyone called his son, to the Freedom Hall to audition for the band. Kush didn't have much experience playing jazz and funk, but he was an excellent trumpet player in every other respect. He had just come out of college and had real strong chops. Kush had no problems adjusting to the show and to the fellows, and we kind of looked at him as a little brother (he was about the same age as my younger brother). We have been lifelong friends.

One reason for the fast turnover in the horn section was that after a while the show got boring, especially to a player like Waymon Reed, who was a world-class jazz improviser. Waymon didn't have an alternative jazz gig that would continue to support his family in the way that they were living at that time, and I could see he was getting more and more frustrated as time went by. Then, there was the legendary soda-bottle incident. On a particular payday at a theater in Gary, Indiana, James came to the gig early and brazenly announced to us that our pay would be a little late because he had invested the money in some Hawaiian airline stock. I guess we were supposed to be impressed because, for the first time in his life, he had done something with his money other than stash it in a safe deposit box or bury it in the ground somewhere. We were not impressed. But, once again, we all sucked it up for whatever reason and didn't jump on him or stage a mass walkout. Waymon, however, was so mad that he went out behind the theater and threw a case of soda bottles, one by one, up against the wall, until he felt better. Nobody tried to stop him. He was expressing what we all felt.

Much of the time the people in the show were in a state of depression for one reason or another. Riding the bus gives a person plenty of time to contemplate his or her situation. The catch-22 is that it doesn't give you much time to do anything about it. If there are problems with your family at home, you have to try to deal with them on the telephone, and you can only do that if and when the bus stops. Trying to deal with kids or bills or a wife or girlfriend who might be sleeping around is very difficult when you can only communicate every now and then, and only by long distance. So you tried to anesthetize yourself as often as possible. An attitude of "don't give a damn" prevailed in the organization, causing a hardening of the spirit and the soul. I imagine prison to be somewhat akin to that particular "on the road" situation. Sex and drugs become the main diversions, causing further deterioration of the spirit. There wasn't much opportunity to pursue hobbies like gardening or stamp collecting or golf. (Pee Wee and St. Clair did, for a time, have sets of golf clubs on the bus. When Mr. Brown found out, he went ballistic, saying that a black man didn't have any business trying to play a white man's game. Plus, the clubs took up too much space on the bus.).

There also was always the possibility of having to participate in one of those long, drawn-out teaching sessions with James, in which he would recount his achievements and generally put down the achievements of everyone else. When you have ridden the bus all night and all day, you don't feel like hearing stuff about how we're the only ones making it in showbiz and how lucky we are to have a job with James Brown and how he only went to the sixth grade. These talks would happen every day, right up to time to go onstage, unless you were lucky and he didn't show up until late, or very unlucky and he showed up early and had one of the dreaded HORROR REHEARSALS.

Brown felt threatened by other entertainers and would constantly minimize the importance of a current hit and would point out how the artist had copied him or wouldn't get another or how he or she was controlled by his or her record company. For the most part, all of what he said was true. He was the probably the only entertainer, especially the only black entertainer, who basically controlled his recordings and live performances.

He was in a great position to do unprecedented things for the talented people who supported him. Simply raising salaries to industry standards would have made life easier for everyone, including himself. His insistence on keeping salaries so low caused him innumerable problems. Just think. Paying decent salaries probably would have kept James Brown's show on top of the live-performance charts for four decades. He could have had an empire to rival Motown in the recording field. There would more than likely be two or three generations of well-educated, affluent black families contributing positively to American society. Everyone connected with the James Brown Show would have been fruitful and multiplied and have become positive vehicles for untold numbers of black people to prosper.

Instead, Mr. Brown was a man who lived by two paranoid creeds, the first being (and I quote): "You can't do nothing for someone else if you ain't nothing yourself." Once, after he fired my favorite guitar player, I was so upset that I went to Brown and told how I had spent a lot of time training this man and didn't want to have to go through that with another guitar player. I also mentioned that he was a good person and a good friend and needed the job. I gave Brown an ultimatum: If you fire this guy, I quit. Brown replied, "Look, son, if you love this guy so much, keep your job and send him some of your money. Don't quit and be a bum with him."

The other James Brown creed was: "I will use a fool as long as he will let me." Mr. Brown would use you, but he also showed respect, in his own way, to people who stood their ground. But you had to be careful, because he became like a wild animal, devoid of all reason and humanity if backed into a corner or if he *felt* like he was backed into a corner. He *would* win. Or die trying. Or make excuses forever about why he didn't.

The generally unpleasant atmosphere made all of us susceptible to drugs, alcohol, and sex. Even those of us who were married fell prey to the easily accessible girls who were seeking wild and adventurous sex with experienced men they didn't necessarily have to see again. There were also the women who were enamored with the glamour of entertainers and would do anything, including anything, to hook up with anyone associated with a big-time act like the James Brown Show—no matter if the person was married or not. Many homes and families were severely compromised and even destroyed by what was supposed to be a one-time fling. These encounters often started out innocently enough, but I've seen them turn into tangled webs that a spider couldn't figure out.

Drugs were another pitfall. A little pot here and there couldn't hurt, you would think. But when you start saying things like, "This is a two-joint show" or "This is a dime-bag bus ride," you realize that you have to have your weed to face certain situations. If you run out of your drug of choice, you tend to turn to whatever is available to ease the pain and the boredom. Before you know it, you've tried just about every kind of drug there is and like the way most of them make you feel. You have pot-smokers drinking and drinkers using cocaine and, if the real drought is on (drought is what you call it when everyone is out of everything), you might shoot up or drop acid to get through whatever situation might present itself. Droughts usually occurred when we played one-nighters, long distances apart, with no chance to check into a hotel over a period of days. These were called "gigs on the fly" or "hit-and-run gigs." When you do a few weeks of hit-and-run gigs in a remote part of the country with no big cities, you are subject to depleting your stash. I've seen proud men resort to begging his fellow musician for just a sprinkle of his weed or just a sip of his wine. It could get real pitiful. Fights would break out and people would stop speaking to each other. Otherwise honest people would steal. However, most of the time, we had no problem getting drugs. There were always people who hung around just to deal drugs. We had a dealer in most urban areas whom we could depend on to show up every time. There, too, were always fans or groupies who would have it just to be able to hang out with the fellows. Just as sure as the promoters knew they would have a crowd in certain places, we knew what places in which we were sure to get drugs.

Every now and then the bus would become like a pressure cooker. With all the loneliness, the feelings of being trapped, the drugs, the relationship you were forced to maintain with the Boss, and the constant threat of being confronted by him, pressure built up and, inevitably, someone would explode. In one particular instance, it was Waymon Reed, again. We were in an unusually long drought when we got to a small town in South Carolina. Somebody's friend, I think Kenny Hull's, showed up with a gallon Clorox bottle full of some illegally brewed corn liquor, locally known as splo (pronounced *splo*). It was a particularly smooth, clear, yet very strong brew. It must have been about 200 proof. However, once you got past the fumes and managed to swallow a few sips, it gave you a very pleasant high. Being devoid of all weed, which was the drug of choice for most of us, we welcomed a little alcohol to smooth out the bumps we all had on our personalities by then. Of course, the drinkers were right in their thing. All over the hotel you could hear laughing and talking. All beefs and misunderstandings had been forgiven, or at least forgotten.

I was with Mr. Jones, an experienced and regular drinker, in Waymon's room. Waymon, like me, hardly ever drank as long as there was plenty of weed around. After a few drinks, I felt really good and retired to my room to enjoy a peaceful splo-induced sleep, expecting Mr. Jones, my roommate, to follow soon. When I woke up, however, it was time to leave, and Mr. Jones's bed still hadn't been slept in. I called Waymon's room to see what was wrong. Mr. Jones asked me to come and help him get Waymon on the bus. When I got to Waymon's room, I found that Waymon was passed out on the floor. We scuffled and got his gear together and, with the help of the other fellows, loaded Waymon and his stuff onto the bus. When Mr. Jones and I got our things together and got to our seats and the bus pulled out, he told me what had happened.

We had started out with about a glassfull of that firewater, which we had poured out of Kenny's jug. It seems that Mr. Jones and Waymon had finished what was left in the glass at my departure and had then gone back to Kenny to get another glassfull *apiece.* This was no problem for Mr. Jones, who had a cast-iron stomach and a head to match. (I found that out one night in Little Rock, when I bet him I could drink as much vodka as he could. He still laughs about that night, and I still have headaches every time I think about it.) Apparently Waymon, too, thought he could hang with Mr. Jones. I should have warned him. Waymon was sprawled in his seat, out cold, sleeping like a baby. We only hoped that he wouldn't die.

Mr. Jones and I talked for a little while as the bus headed for the next gig in Fredericksburg, Virginia. After a few miles, we both fell asleep but were rudely awakened by Waymon standing over us, asking Mr. Jones, "got any more of that splo?" We were surprised to see Waymon awake. We were more surprised to see him standing under his own power. We were even more surprised that he was asking for more of what I was convinced by now was poison. The little bit I had had was killing me. Even Mr. Jones was looking forward to sleeping all the way to the gig in order to somewhat get himself straight. But here was Waymon, ranting and raving, pacing up and down the aisle of the bus quoting from the Reverend C. L. Franklin's famous "Eye on the Sparrow" sermon. He preached, at the top of his voice, about the way good musicians were treated by people like James Brown who didn't know a note from a goat. He made references to the rumor about a witch lady who had helped James sell his soul to the devil. He kept it up, yelling and screaming at times, for five or six hours until we got to the gig. Pee Wee managed to get most of it on tape. It was a complete outpouring of the frustrations that we all felt. We knew what had induced the explosion, but we had no idea where he got the strength to carry it on for so long. Somewhere in the world, there is a cassette recording of the infamous Waymon Reed "Eye on the Sparrow" sermon.

Even when we got to Virginia, Waymon was not finished. In the dressing room, he took out his horn and for hours and more hours played parts of Count Basie's "Shiny Stockings," pausing between licks to laugh real loud and say stuff like, "That's real music," not the honky-tonk stuff we have to play on this gig. He kept it up until hit time. The Boss had come in and heard what was happening but chose not to get into it. In fact, he didn't bother anyone about anything that day. We managed to get Waymon dressed for the gig. We knew that he probably would get fired or worse if he didn't straighten up and do the gig. He made it to the stage, but he was still acting crazy, playing "Shiny Stocking" and other Basie stuff through the first part of the show. I know the Boss must have noticed, but he still didn't say or do a thing—to everyone's surprise. About halfway through the show, Waymon couldn't take it anymore and kind of did a dance step off the stage, waving his hand vaudeville-style, still playing "Shiny Stockings." When the show was over, we found Waymon finally asleep in his seat on the bus, where he slept, this time, all the way to the next gig in Syracuse, New York.

The next day Waymon came to the gig and humbly apologized to James. James, in his benevolent, merciful mode, said that he understood how sometimes the pressure gets to a man, but next time, he said, Waymon should come to him for help and advice. With some of the pressure relieved and everyone having a good laugh and a great story to tell, things got back to normal. And the beat went on.

Back to normal meant some firsts for me. Among them, my first time in California. After hearing so much about Los Angeles from the people in the Ike and Tina Turner band, I finally got there six years later with the James Brown Show. We were flown into L.A. to do the Joey Bishop Show on TV. After we got to L.A., Mr. Brown decided not to use his band but to use the Joey Bishop house band. This meant that Pee Wee had to prepare music for the show. By that time, my ability to somewhat write music had been discovered, and I was unofficially Pee Wee's assistant. When we got to L.A. and discovered that we were not playing the TV show, I was looking forward to a few days off to spend time with my cousin, C.P., who was like a big brother to me. I hadn't seen him since he had left home fifteen years earlier to join the Marine Corps, so I was looking forward to spending time with him and his wife, Hazel, who was renowned throughout the family as a great cook. I had spent about a day with my family when I got a call from Pee Wee to come immediately to help him finish the music for the TV show.

My assistance was more logistical than musical. Picking up scores, dropping off parts, driving Pee Wee here and there was most of what I did. I did get to copy some parts and observe the process of writing music for a big-time TV show. I even got to go with Pee Wee and Mr. Brown and the lovely Miss Marva Whitney (whom Mr. Brown had bogarted onto the show) to the rehearsal and the actual taping. Although my job was simply to drive and pass out music, I was happy just to be in the entourage. I got to see, up close, Joey Bishop, Regis Philbin, and Jerry Lewis, who turned out to be a complete idiot for real, horsing around and humiliating his arranger, the great Marty Paich. Marty was trying to be serious about the music, but Jerry kept insulting him about his bald head, even biting him on the head at one point. Mr. Paich was obviously devastated by Jerry's high jinks, but took it with a forced smile, I guess because it was *Jerry Lewis* making fun of him. Again I wondered why such a great musician took this kind of abuse from such an obnoxious person, just because he was a star. I'll probably understand it better by and by. Overall, though, the experience was very educational, enlightening, and enjoyable for me.

My first recording session with Mr. Brown was also during that trip to L.A. The whole band was loaded into some station wagons and transported to the vox recording studios somewhere in the Los Angeles area. We set up and Pee Wee proceeded to put together a song—with no written music. He started by giving Clyde a simple drumbeat. Clyde started the beat and held it steady while Pee Wee hummed a bass line to Charles Sherrell, a bass player from Nashville recently hired onto the show. When the bass line had become clear to Charles and locked with the drumbeat, Pee Wee moved to Country, the rhythm guitar player, and began to choose a chord that would fit with the bass notes. A B-flat 9 was finally settled on and a chunky rhythm was matched up with the bass line and the drumbeat. I was, so far, amazed at how this song was coming together. Jimmy Nolen was allowed to find his own thing to fit the developing groove. He came up with sort of a womp-womp sounding, single-string thing that seemed to really pull all of the other parts together. At this point, we, once again, have that washing-machine thang going. That was the best way to describe the various sounds and rhythms, each in its own space, each in its own time, occurring in just the right places, to make for a funky groove. With the rhythm section solidly in place, Pee Wee proceeded to hum out horn parts. We were given some strategic hits with carefully voiced chords and a melodic line that happened whenever it was signaled. Of course, the reeds played a version of the James Brown horns' signature ladidadidat. With this groove firmly in place, Pee Wee started putting together a bridge.

Before he got started on it good, the Boss walked in. Everything went silent. He walked to Pee Wee and said, "Let me hear it." Pee Wee counted it off, and we played what we had been rehearsing for the last two hours. James listened intently, walked over to Clyde and said something to him as we all kept playing. Clyde then started playing a pop-pop every now and then. Brown made similar adjustments to all the parts and, sporting a little grin, started to dance a little bit and kind of winked at us and said "Nooooow *that's* a groove." James and Pee Wee continued to make up a bridge. The whole band did sort of an ensemble stop rhythm on an E-flat major chord, with Jimmy Nolen doing a little doodit solo lick on top. After James was satisfied that everything was in place, he pulled some scraps of paper out of his pocket and started reading what sounded like grunting and groaning, mostly to himself, as the band played on. We had been playing now for about fours hours straight, and I, for one, was getting tired. I mean, how many times can you go da daaaa da dot da dot da da without getting a cramp in your lip? I was young, all right, but I wanted to live to get old.

Just then, Mr. Bobbit, the road manager, and a bunch of people, mostly kids, walked into the studio. We stopped playing, and Mr. Brown went over and greeted them like he had expected them. I had no idea what they had to do with this recording. James was over on one side of the studio, talking and waving his hands with the kids. After this went on for a while, he came back to us and counted the tune off again. When the groove settled, he yelled to the kids, "Say it loud!" The kids responded, "I'm black and I'm proud!" He instructed the kids to say their line on cue and gave us cues to do the bridge and other things. With all the cues and signals in place, we were ready to record. All the time we were getting the groove together, engineers were in and out of the control room, setting mikes, adjusting amplifiers, placing baffles, and the like. They were ready, and we were ready. Mr. Brown was in control now. Pee Wee took his place in the reed section, and James counted it off. The groove was already strong, but when James counted it off and began to dance and direct, it took on a new power. All of a sudden, the fatigue I had been feeling was gone. The kids were doing their chant with a new energy. In fact, the energy level in the whole studio was lifted. James went straight through the whole tune and that was it. After about four hours of preparation, "Say It Loud, I'm Black and I'm Proud" went down in one take.

In our new black and proud outfits. Left to right: St. Clair Pinckney, Waymon Reed, me. Courtesy of Greta Reed.

After the recording session, we had a few days off. I got to spend a little time with some other friends of mine who lived in L.A., Frank McCrary and E.W. Waynewright, a sax player and drummer I knew from Huntsville who now lived in L.A. They came to the motel where we were staying and picked me up in a Mercedes. They took me out and showed me some of the more interesting parts of L.A. We left the motel to go someplace to play some jazz but ended up going from apartment to apartment meeting girls, with Frank and E.W. changing clothes everywhere we stopped. I never figured out what that was about. They showed me the Jungle, Crenshaw Boulevard, and South Central L.A. We ended up at Frank's place, smoking and drinking and watching Frank's lady come in and go out all night. I think I know what that was about. We never played any jazz that night.

The gig in L.A. was at the famous Shrine Auditorium. That night the James Brown Show was a part of some large fund-raiser. I remember Pam Grier presenting James with some sort of award. I helped her onto the stage. There was also a house band, and I spent some time talking to the bandleader, Preston Love. In the course of the conversation, I found out that Preston was a very busy contractor in L.A. I expressed to him my desire to one day relocate to L.A. He assured me that if I did, he would get me work. I felt like I had just drawn an ace and put it safely in the hole. I wasn't really thinking of leaving yet, but I also didn't plan to stay with James Brown forever. L.A., with a busy contractor on my side, was a comforting alternative if I ever did decide to change jobs.

By now, the bus had made it to L.A., and life on the road got back to normal. The difference was we were doing it on the West Coast. We played one-nighters from San Diego to Vancouver. In between were cities like Bakersfield, Fresno, San Jose, San Francisco, Portland, Seattle, and some towns whose names I can't remember. I was surprised, I don't know why, to see so many black people in the West. Maybe it's because, being a big fan of western movies, I hardly ever saw any black folk in the movies. Only big white people and Mexicans. There were plenty of white people and Mexicans all right, but mostly black people who looked and acted just like people from Alabama. As we headed back east through cities like Phoenix and Albuquerque, I met people named Manuel, Juanita, Andy, and Slim, but I also met people named Leon, Alice, Marvin, and Bubba. Except for the smell and the look of the terrain, the East and West Coasts were the same. Certainly, the people were the same.

Music, from my point of view, is the great common denominator. Be ye black, white, blue, or green, young, old, or in between, everybody shakes their booties to the same beat. I was observing, firsthand, the power of James Brown's music to unite people of all persuasions. I was also observing James Brown's power to promote and sell records. Two weeks after we left L.A., we had made it along the West Coast and worked ourselves all the way back to Houston. I had no idea why, but James decided to put "Say It Loud, I'm Black and I'm Proud" into the show. We rehearsed it in El Paso, or maybe San Antonio, and had it ready to perform in Houston. I thought it was too soon—nobody would have heard it yet. I didn't think it was even on the radio yet. But, to my amazement, when James hit the stage and yelled out, "Say it loud," there must have been 15,000 people who answered back, "I'm black and I'm proud!"

This meant that in less than two weeks the record had been recorded, promoted to disc jockeys, pressed, shipped, and sold to a lot of people. I thought the process of getting records in stores took much longer than that. But this record *was* very special. The message echoed the feelings of black people at that time. With the new civil rights bill and the new voting rights amendment now firmly in place, black people were ready for a theme song that inspired and inflamed that newfound spirit of pride and freedom. I was especially proud to be part of a recording that moved so many people. Whatever negatives that we, the people of the James Brown band, suffered among ourselves were offset by the positive image we portrayed to the public. James Brown was and continues to be an inspiration and a positive influence to untold numbers of people of all races.

We crisscrossed the country year round, making stops in most cities twice a year. We only slowed down long enough to record or play theaters. Most theaters were on the East Coast. The Royal in Baltimore, the Howard in Washington, D.C., the Regal in Chicago, the Uptown in Philadelphia, and the Apollo in New York City. Theater stints were three-to-five day stops. All other gigs were one-nighters. The only other time the bus stopped was to record. The "Black and Proud" session in California was one of the few James Brown sessions not done in Cincinnati at King Records recording studio.

The theater stops and the studio stops were welcomed in a way and dreaded in a way. The stops were welcomed in that they gave us a chance to take care of personal things like getting clothes cleaned, sending money home, spending time with loved ones, and generally catching our breath. On the other hand, these stops had you in close proximity to the Boss at all times. This gave him a chance to be in your face and on your case about everything from your nappy hair (one of his favorite things to harp on was the few of us who didn't have some type of hairdo) to trying to get you to spend your money on something you couldn't afford, like new suits or a car or a house in Augusta, Georgia. (He was always trying to get somebody to buy a house in Augusta.) All of his admonitions came with offers to help. He could get you credit in some clothing stores and would loan you money for down payments on a house or car. His "help," of course, had gotten several people in big trouble and thus inescapably locked to the gig, where they bore the brunt of most of his abuse.

Brown was like the devil, constantly laying traps for you to fall into so he could really use and abuse you. On one-nighters, you got a break from his taunting and teasing, at least for a little while, unless you were unfortunate enough to have to fly on the plane with him. Clyde had to do so very often under Brown's justification that Clyde worked so hard that he needed extra rest. I know he didn't get any rest having to listen to all that rap about how bad he had played the show. But even on one-nighters, Mr. Brown would sometimes come to the gig early and have what we call a "jam," where we would have to join in with his fooling around on the organ. This was painful for anyone who had ever thought of playing jazz. James Brown's organ playing was just good enough to fool the un-trained ear, and so bad that it made real musicians sick on the stomach. The really painful "jams" were when Pee Wee played organ and James played drums. I never saw anybody play so bad with so much confidence and determination. The look on Brown's face when he played drums was the funniest thing I ever saw. After we got accustomed to the jams and saw the looks on his face when he played, the real pain got to be trying to keep from busting out in uncontrollable laughter.

The studio in Cincinnati was run by a man named Ron Lenhoff, whom I had first met in L.A. at the vox studio, where I had thought he was a part of the staff. He was a master at getting the sounds together as the band got the music together. Many hours of drudgery were spent in King Studio. The first cousin to the horror rehearsal was the *drudgeri-ous* recording session, the difference being that at the end of the session there would be a great new record to point to with pride. I was on "Lickin' Stick" and many other James Brown songs recorded at King Studio. (The first commercial I was on was also recorded at King. A local young bass player named Booty or Bootsy used to hang around the studio, I guess waiting for Bernard or Charles to drop dead or come down sick or some-thing so he could get a chance to show us how baaad he was. The word was out about how another local white bass player named Tim Drum-mond had managed to get a solo on "Can't Help Myself." Bootsy was sure he was at least that good and if he hung long enough he would get his chance. And he did get his chance on that Coke commercial. He was, it turned out, truly amazing and blew everybody's mind. However, for some reason, Tim got the gig, starting at $500 a week, as I found out later. I never understood why a marginal bass player like Tim got the gig over a phenomenal bass player like Bootsy and at a starting salary more than twice mine. Maybe it was because he was white.)

Pee Wee was becoming more and more disgruntled with the James Brown gig. He was making his own way to the gig instead of riding the bus. Showing up right at hit time, sometimes barely making it, was not the way to stay in good favor with the Boss. A couple of times he actually showed up after the band set had started. We covered for him as much as we could, but we knew that James knew, what with all the snitches he had on duty at all times. It was not Mr. Brown's way to confront obvious, deliberate insubordination head on. It troubled him when someone he was supposed to have under control suddenly balked and became bold enough to fly in the face of his authority without apparent fear or remorse. I and the other guys in the band didn't know what to think either. When we would mention to Pee Wee that James had been asking about what he was doing and where he was, he would say things like, "Man, fuck him" or "As long as I get the job done, where I am and what I'm doing is none of his or y'all's business." Well, having total respect for Pee Wee and admiring him for taking a stand like that, we let him alone and backed way off the subject, at least when he was around. When he wasn't there, of course, the subject was number one on the gossip hit parade.

More and more, when things came up that required bandleader action, I was pressed into duty because Pee Wee wasn't there. I had to do things like voice chords for the horns and write things down whenever James had one of those impromptu songwriting sessions or one of those rehearsals during which we changed certain things around. I was the one who translated Mr. Brown's creative grunts and groans into musical terms that the band could understand. I had been Pee Wee's unofficial assistant over the previous few months anyway, so it was only natural that the band and Mr. Brown looked to me in Pee Wee's absence. Everyone even assumed that I knew what was up with Pee Wee. In fact, I was just as baffled as everyone else and was really kind of upset with Pee Wee for leaving me holding the bag, so to speak. I felt funny a few times when it happened that James had gotten me to rehearse something with the band and Pee Wee walked in during the rehearsal. It did James good to let Pee Wee know that things went on without him, but it was sort of embarrassing to me to have Pee Wee see me do his job. If he cared, he never said so or showed it in anyway.

One day when we were deep into our daily pre-gig jam session, Pee Wee walked in, late again. James couldn't take it any more. He asked Pee Wee why he hadn't ridden the bus. Pee Wee looked him dead in the eye and said, "I flew. When I don't feel like riding the bus, I use my own money and fly." James told him that from now on he wanted Pee Wee to ride the bus with everyone else and that if he flew again he was fired. Pee Wee grumbled something under his breath and turned and walked into the dressing room, leaving us to hear a long speech about how a guy gets too big on the James Brown name and starts to think independently, and how none of us were anything without him. It wasn't fair that the person who instigated this dissertation wasn't there to endure its length and pain. James spoke as if he were talking behind Pee Wee's back, kind of whispering and peering out of the corner of his eye. We could hear Pee Wee in the dressing room practicing some real hard scales and stuff.

When the verbal grilling was over, we confronted Pee Wee. "Why you put us through this, man?" Pee Wee gave us his famous high-pitched chuckle and said, "Y'all got me confused with someone who gives a damn." Sure enough, the very next day Pee Wee shows up in a rent-a-car from the airport. That's how and when I became the official bandleader.

I think Mr. Brown made a snap decision to make me bandleader in order to make Pee Wee think that his leaving was no big deal. Had he thought about it a little longer, I'm sure that he would have realized that Fred Wesley Jr. was not quite ready for all ramifications of the James Brown bandleader job. He had no particular hold on me other than that my salary was increased from $350 to a whopping $400. I was still basically independent of his domination. If I decided to up and walk away I would still have a life. (This is what happened with Pee Wee. Pee Wee had nothing to lose and, as it turned out, gained a great deal by getting fired.) Brown didn't know for sure that I wouldn't fly in his face and challenge him if confronted. He had not tested me on how I would react to a direct confrontation, so I was handled with kid gloves for the first three months. Learning to direct the band at certain points in the show was the most difficult thing. Directing the band while playing the trombone required some almost impossible body moves. James wanted me to direct some things with my foot. I felt like I looked silly doing this but went ahead and did it anyway. This was difficult for me, so as time went by I modified the moves that James had given me and developed my own style, which he finally accepted. (Funny thing, I now see NFL quarterbacks directing their offenses by doing some of the same things James had me doing with my foot.) All of my other duties kinda fell into place.

Our first confrontation came one day when the band was rehearsing an arrangement of Sly Stone's "Sing a Simple Song" that Pee Wee had left with us. I was going over some of the chord voicing with the horns when Mr. Brown walked in. He immediately stopped me and told me that what I was working was not important and that I should be working on the rhythm parts first. I said, "I'll get to that. I just want to hear these horn parts first." He said, "No son. That's not the way to do it." He then took over the rehearsal and preceded to downplay what I was doing, generally making me sound like an idiot, which pissed me off. I said, "Mr. Brown, if you don't like the way I'm doing the job, get somebody else to do it." He said, "Okay, you're fired as bandleader." Then, he asked the band, "Who wants to be bandleader?" Maceo said, "Mr. Brown, I think Fred is doing a great job as bandleader." This surprised me, because it was the first time that I had ever seen anyone stick up for anyone else in this organization. It was an unwritten rule that you were on your own when dealing with the Boss. This took some real guts, especially since Maceo and I were not real close friends or anything at that time. He was putting himself and his job in jeopardy in favor of me keeping my job. I looked at him with different eyes from then on. It was never settled at that time who would be bandleader, but it was settled that it was over for me. Mr. Brown told me that my salary would go back down. His exact words were: "You know your pay will be reduced, don't you?" I responded, "You know I can't work for any less that what I've gotten used to, don't you?" We looked at each other for a long moment and said simultaneously, "Two weeks," meaning that I was on two weeks notice.

5

California

• • •

I had no intention of returning home to Mobile after leaving the James Brown Show—in 1970 all roads led to L.A. Gertie and I had managed to save up a little moving money. The friends I had made with the Ike and Tina Turner band and Mr. Preston Love, the contractor I met when the James Brown Show played L.A., had all assured me that I would be able to work regularly if I ever decided to move to L.A. Ever since I had been with Ike and Tina, listening to the way the guys talked about L.A., I knew that it was the place for me. I had hoped that the Army would send me to the West Coast, but, of course, it had only landed me back in Alabama. I felt that in knowing people in L.A and in having Gertie's mother there to help with the children, this was the best chance I was going to get to live in a major city where I could advance my career in music.

At the same time that I was starting to get tired of the James Brown experience, my idol, mentor, and, during the previous few years, friend, Mr. Edward Pratt, had finally decided that being the baddest saxophonist in the South wasn't enough for him anymore. He, too, had chosen L.A. as the place to showcase his talents. He, too, had friends and relatives in L.A. Pratt had already secured a bandmaster job at Pomona High School, about sixty miles east of Los Angeles. His problem was that he had to report to the job by a certain date and didn't have the means to get there. My problem was getting my car to L.A. I didn't want to drive that long distance with two very young babies. (Did I mention that we had had another beautiful daughter, Lya, about a year earlier?) Pratt and I solved each other's problems. Gertie, Joya, and Lya flew to L.A., and Pratt drove my car and everything we could load into it to L.A., while I finished my last week with James Brown at the Apollo Theater in New York.

My family and I moved into an area of Los Angeles known as "the Jungle," a maze of apartment buildings on randomly arranged streets and alleys that made it difficult to find a specific place unless you were familiar with the territory. The Jungle was largely inhabited by middle-class, predominantly black entertainers and musicians. Mable John lived in the same building that I did. O. C. Smith was also a close neighbor. The apartments in the Jungle were very nice and not that expensive. We were told that the Jungle was originally an affluent Jewish neighborhood that had gradually been infiltrated by blacks who couldn't afford to live in Baldwin Hills, a nearby affluent black neighborhood with expensive homes. As the black population went up, the white population and the rent went down.

Pratt had a good friend in the neighborhood, Jim Sheldon, a native of Mobile, who was also a good friend of my father's. In my early L.A. days, Pratt and I spent a lot of time with Jim learning who was who and what was what—not only in the Jungle but in L.A. in general. Jim was a big jazz fan, and he took us out regularly to the hot jazz spots so that we could sit in, become known, and, hopefully, get a gig. We met and played with Leon Haywood at the Caribbean Room, Red Holloway at the Parisian Room, Gene Harris at the Tiki Lounge, and scores of other musicians at many other clubs in L.A. and the surrounding areas. We played a lot of good jazz and had a lot of fun, but neither of us landed a regular gig. I met a great trombone player named Thurman Green, who let me sub for him in Gerald Wilson's big band at Shelly's Manne Hole in Hollywood. I played three Sunday afternoons with pianist Rose Gales, wife of the famous bassist Larry Gales of the Thelonious Monk band. Other than that, no paying jazz gig came my way, but I didn't even consider anything other than a jazz gig.

Early one morning, I got a call from Art Blakey. Waymon had given him my name and number. After a short conversation about how thrilled I was that he had called me and how much I would love to play with the Jazz Messengers, we got to how much the gig paid, where the gig was, and how I would get to New York. Blakey, in his barely audible, raspy voice, told me that he worked close around New York as much as possible. In his words, "I don't like to get too far away from the 'Thang.'" I didn't know exactly what that meant, except that in order for me to do the gig I would have to commute back and forth to New York. It would have been wonderful to take the Art Blakey gig had I lived in New York, but living in Los Angeles with a family to support made it impossible. How ironic. I move to L.A. and get a call for what was probably the best New York jazz gig around. Life is not fair.

But life goes on. I had been trying to locate my friends from the Ike and Tina Turner band ever since I'd arrived in L.A. Phone numbers had changed. People were out of town. I had kinda set aside getting in touch with them while I explored the possibility of a jazz gig. But now I was getting desperate, and I needed all the help I could get. I contacted Preston Love, the contractor who promised me lots of studio work. He said things were slow, but he was glad I was in town and would call me if and when something came up. My friends Frank and Wayne from Huntsville were glad to hear from me, too, but they, too, had nothing to offer me. Frank did, however, know someone who knew someone who knew Bobby John. After a few phone calls, I got Bobby John's phone number. It turned out that Bobby John lived one block from me in the Jungle. Nose lived with him. This was a great stroke of luck, because Bobby John was always like the mother hen of the Ike Turner band, genuinely concerned about everyone's welfare and therefore up on and into everybody's business at all times. He gave me the run-down on everybody and everything of interest to me, as well as on many things I either already knew or cared little about.

Sam Rhodes, Ernest Lane, Mack Johnson, and Thomas "Nose" Norwood had, some years before, formed a band called Sam and the Goodtimers. It included guitar player Willie "Jitterbug" Webb, another veteran of the Ike Turner band, and the much-talked-about saxophone player Clifford Solomon, who had been away in prison during my stay with the band. They were playing a club in Hollywood named the Soul'd Out Club. I couldn't wait to see my old friends again and to meet the famous Clifford Solomon, who was spoken of as some kind of god. Not only did they laud him as an excellent tenor player, but he was their leader, and everyone agreed that he was really a great guy.

The Soul'd Out was on Sunset Boulevard in the heart of Hollywood. When Pratt and I got there, the band was on a break. The club was much like any other nightclub in the world—it smelled of smoke and beer and perfume and was crowded with sweaty people laughing and chatting— but this club was in Hollywood. The women were all extremely beautiful model types, and the guys were all the TV-type hip dudes. Everyone was dressed in the latest fashions. It was obvious that the guys were on

Clifford Solomon.
Courtesy of
Clifford Solomon.

the prowl for the girls and the girls were definitely setting traps for the guys. My head looked like it was on a swivel. People were drinking and smoking and making frequent trips in and out of the front door and in and out of the bathrooms, giving away the drug action that also was happening. The jukebox was playing classic R&B, and everybody was dancing. The black people were dancing very well, as usual, and the white people, as usual, were enthusiastically doing the best that they could. Actually, I did notice that the white people were dancing unusually well. Everybody seemed to know everybody. To my surprise, there wasn't even a hint of racial recognition. Everybody was everybody and everything was everything. It was a fun, relaxed, homey atmosphere.

I found Nose, and he showed me to Sam and Lane and Mack. We were very happy to see each other and caused somewhat of a disturbance in the already festive atmosphere of the club when we greeted each other. They introduced me to Jitterbug. He seemed to be a nice, quiet, cool guy. Then I finally got to meet the much-touted Clifford Solomon, who did have a kinda regal aura about him. He reminded me and everyone else of the nickname Robbie Montgomery had given me: "So, this is the infamous Hog Jaws." Apparently, there had been some talk about me, too.

We agreed that Pratt and I would play some after they did a couple of requests.

After the break, the first tune they did was Otis Redding's "Can't Turn You Loose." I had never heard Sam sing before. He did a real good imitation of Otis. In fact, he did Otis, and then took it somewhere else. The groove really got going after what we all knew from the record ended. The vamp was strictly a Sam and the Goodtimers original. I had forgotten what a strong, solid, steady, funky drummer Nose was. You know how fast "Can't Turn You Loose" is. Well, Nose took that straight, fast beat from the record, accented it here and there, and started a whole new thing. Sam jumped right in, bumping and thumping the bass in unusual but very effective places. The groove was set for Lane to come in jingling a ragtime-type riff on the Fender Rhodes. Jitter jumped in next with that Memphis twang sound combined with some kind of Texas stroke that sounded like Jimmy Nolen and Country playing together. There was something incomplete about the horns when they came in, but their hits and accents put the perfect icing on an already hard-driving cake. When this funky recipe was fully baked, Sam came back to the mike, squalling and preaching like a Baptist minister, and ate the whole thing up. Pratt, me, and the whole crowd were still reeling from the fast and funky ride that the Goodtimers had taken us on, when they eased us into "Going in Circles." Mr. Willie Webb from San Antonio, Texas, known to everyone there as Jitterbug, sang the lead on this one. His voice was as smooth and soulful as my initial perception of his persona indicated. Somehow, Sam, Clifford, Lane, and Mack did a beautiful job singing the background parts.

This was an unusually funky band with a special something I had never experienced before. It wasn't rigid and controlled like that "washing-machine thang" that Clyde, Jimmy, Country, and Bernard had been instrumental in creating. That type of funk depended on everyone paying close attention to whoever was directing and making military-type executions to excite the audiences. On the other hand, the Goodtimers were linked together spiritually by some intangible energy that flowed among the players and out to the audience. They hardly ever looked at one another. They played directly to the audience. Wooing and seducing and tantalizing each individual in a way that made you feel at times that each member of the band was playing just for you. In other words, there was a very personal connection between the band and the audience. Both methods are effective ways to entertain, but I had had my

Sam and the Goodtimers. Left to right: Ernest Lane, Clifford Solomon, Willie "Jitterbug" Webb, substitute drummer Ed Mosley, Mack Johnson, Sam Rhodes. Courtesy of Goodtimer's management.

fill of the strict, regimented funk. I wanted to see how it was to feel my way through a groove.

The Goodtimers knew about Pratt. Any musician who had ever passed through Mobile had at least heard about the baaddest sax man in the South. It seemed that Pratt and Clifford had crossed paths somewhere. I'm not sure. Maybe it was simply that they had so many things in common. Pratt was somewhat of a musical monarch in his home territory, as was Clifford. So, to accommodate Pratt, the first tune they played was Herbie Hancock's "Watermelon Man," the closest thing to real jazz that they had in their book. It went very well, with the band trying to play jazzy and Pratt trying to play funky. I just laid in the cut, more or less, enjoying the mutual respect these two entities were showing for one another, but also realizing that we were jerking the crowd around, because they had come to hear what Sam and the Goodtimers did best—classic R&B. Sensing that the applause was only polite, they jumped immediately back to the real program, with songs that included "Hold On, I'm Coming," "It's Your Thing," "My Girl," "Respect," and "Mustang Sally."

I was right at home, drawing on my experience all the way back to Poonanny. Pratt, who wasn't as comfortable as he would have been with Red Holloway or even Rose Gales, hung in there with us all the way to the end. It was the most fun I'd had since coming to California, and I had been in on some great jazz sessions. After the set was over, we all realized what was missing from the Goodtimers. They needed a third horn to complete the horn section. A trombone. Me. I informed them right then and there that they now had a trombone player whether they paid me or not. They agreed and kicked in twenty dollars apiece. The club owner, who also agreed, matched the amount, and I had a gig. We split the door receipts from a Saturday night after-hours gig at Club De La Soul on Slauson Avenue in the hood and from a Sunday morning breakfast jam session back at the Soul'd Out—bringing my weekly take to about $300. Eight gigs a week for $300 wasn't good, but it kept the chops up, it was big fun, and it almost paid the bills.

The Soul'd Out gig was supposed to be permanent. Sam and the Goodtimers had been there for four years. So I felt somewhat secure and went about trying to hook up some recording and/or arranging jobs. Clifford booked me on some sessions with Maxwell Davis, who was famous for doing horn overdubs real fast. We would go into the studio and do five or six horn overdubs in one hour at a rate of about $30 a tune. It was good supplemental income but very unsatisfying musically in that it didn't seem to matter to him how it sounded. He would keep whatever went down on the first take, mistakes and all. I got used to it.

I continued to contact my friend Preston Love, the man who was so instrumental in convincing me to move to L.A., but to no avail. The only time I saw him was on a session that Mack Johnson booked. There were a

Clifford and me. Courtesy of Bess Solomon.

few minor performers and producers who had heard that I had been with James Brown and therefore thought I had some kind of magic. They hired me more for window dressing than anything else. Most of these stars and star-makers couldn't understand how I had let the James Brown gig get away from me. It was like I had made it to where they were trying to get and somehow blew it. The more I tried to explain that a big-time gig like that was not all that it appeared to be, the sillier I looked and sounded to them.

The Soul'd Out Club was a good place to meet people who were in L.A. trying to make it in the entertainment business. Unfortunately, the ones I met either had little talent or were, like me, trying to find that right management or recording deal. The work I did for these struggling artists and producers was good practice and allowed me to experiment without the danger of my pitiful efforts getting out to the general public. In most cases, I had no idea what I was doing, but I played the role of an expert, having arranged and produced for James Brown.

My first big music-writing job in L.A. was for Canyon Records. The head of the company's publishing department, Dee Irvin, brought me about fifty songs—some on tape, some on vinyl—written by one of their artists, Jerry Williams (a.k.a. Swamp Dogg). Jerry Weaver was infamous among L.A. session musicians for having pulled off one of the biggest scams in L.A. non-union recording history. Mr. Weaver had booked the session to overdub horns on ten tunes at $30 a tune. (It is strictly against union rules to work "per tune.") There were about six horn players involved, most very prominent, so I won't mention their names for fear of jeopardizing their union status. At the end of the session, ten overdubs complete, Mr. Weaver informed the musicians that the bank had closed and that he didn't have the cash to pay everybody, but if they would all take checks he would increase the rate to $35 a tune. The musicians, smelling a rat but having no choice (other than to kick his ass right there), took a chance on the checks. Of course, the checks bounced, and Mr. Weaver was last heard of living in Europe somewhere. Anyway, my big job was to do lead sheets on all of Swamp Dogg's songs. Dee Irvin didn't give me a time limit, but he paid me, on the spot, $25 for every one I completed. This was like money in the bank. The only thing was, doing lead sheets is tedious work, especially with blues and R&B, as it's hard to exactly determine the melody. But whenever I needed money, I would churn out three or four Swamp Dogg songs. I don't think I ever finished all of them.

I remember doing arrangements for Jonelle Allen and Kathleen Bradley during that time. Neither made it as a singer, but both found success in other areas of the business. Ms. Allen has become a big TV celebrity, as one of the stars of the series "Dr. Quinn, Medicine Woman." Always a world-class beauty, Ms. Bradley has had a very successful modeling and acting career and is now the only black woman regular on "The Price is Right."

I became friends with and did some work for a guy named Leon Silvers Sr., who had a bunch of kids he was trying to get started in the business. One group I got involved with as a record producer consisted of four very young girls and was called Stage One. Their manager, Dee Blunt, who also functioned as the fifth performer, approached me. Although none of the girls was super-talented and Ms. Blunt's own musical ability was somewhat lacking, they all made up for what was missing with drive and determination. Plus, they were all extremely beautiful and didn't mind working very hard. With almost no money, we recorded two songs that were written by the group and arranged and produced by me. The final result was horrible. But we all gained valuable experience and knowledge about exactly where we stood in respect to the music business. Ms. Blunt has gone on to manage a successful acting career for her son, Erin Blunt, and is now operating a wonderful alternative school for underprivileged yet gifted children in South Central L.A. One of the other girls, Janice Marie Johnson, has had success as half of the hit duo Taste of Honey. And I learned what producing a record is all about. That good stage musicians don't always make good recording musicians. That a good stage arrangement is not necessarily a good recording arrangement. And basically that recording is a vastly different endeavor from performing onstage.

After about three months at the Soul'd Out, a rift developed between the management of the club and the management of the Goodtimers, whoever that was. All I knew for sure was that it was not me. Sometimes Sam paid me, sometimes Clifford, and sometimes I just went to the club manager and got it myself. All I know is that one night I got to the club and found out that we had quit. I never found out why. It didn't matter very much, because it was getting close to the time when the Goodtimers did their annual tour with the Monkees. Every since I'd been in the band, the talk had been about the Monkees tour. I was going to be able to make $1,500 a week on tour in the States and a whopping $2,500 a week when the tour went overseas. So leaving the Soul'd Out a little early wasn't exactly devastating, although it did make life difficult. Gertie had started substitute teaching, and we were doing all right, but the sudden loss of my income did present a problem. Especially when, after about three weeks of not worrying too much, we found out that the Monkees had decided not to do a tour that year. We were all devastated, having gone from holding a good job and looking forward to a better one, to no job at all.

L.A. can be a scary place when you don't have a job. But it's also a place of great possibilities and endless opportunities if you are forced to search them out. For a while there, I was thinking about a day job or maybe even some illegal enterprise to sustain myself during that unexpected dry period. But I was fortunate in that my association with Dee Irvin and his association with Wally Roker, who owned Canyon Records, as well as their mutual admiration for the Goodtimers, led to another very good gig. At least, it started out good. Wally, in the process of fulfilling a lifelong dream of his to open a top-notch, first-class nightclub, wanted Sam and the Goodtimers to be the house band. The club was fabulous. It was in the freshly renovated building that had formerly housed the Black Fox Club. (The story about the Black Fox is that it closed when the owner, a woman, chased everyone out one night with a gun. I don't know why, but it had been closed ever since.) Wally named his club Wally Roker's Showcase. Located in the affluent Baldwin Hills Area, close to where most of us in the band lived, the new club's only problem was parking. It was adjacent to a motel that rented rooms by the hour and right at the top of a hill where three big thoroughfares—La Brea Avenue, Overhill Drive, and Stocker Street—come together.

Opening night was a gala affair. We had the great jazz singer Dakota Staton as a special guest. Part of our job as the house band was to play behind all guest artists. Ms. Staton's music was not exactly our style, but we felt we could pull it off if she wasn't too particular. At the rehearsal, we immediately discovered that she was extremely—even maniacally— particular. So we canceled that rehearsal and went about calling a suitable rhythm section for her set. We got Larry Gales on bass, Jimmy Bunn on piano, and Paul Humphrey on drums. After they went over the first tune, Ms. Staton seemed satisfied with Larry and Jimmy, but she kept messing with Paul, and Paul was not a person to be messed with. We had felt lucky to get him to come anywhere south of Wilshire Boulevard for a club gig. He was one of the first-call studio drummers in L.A and had just broken the color barrier on the *Lawrence Welk Show*. Plus, he was really a great drummer and sounded superb to all of us. We had no idea what she was looking for.

Well, it didn't take long for her to piss Paul off, and he loaded his gear into his Ferrari (I don't know how he got a complete drum set into that little car, but he did), bade all of us some farewell expletives, and roared off toward Wilshire. So we called Frank Butler, a jazz specialist. Frank was famous around town for having once played with Miles Davis, and he was, without a doubt, a fine, world-class jazz drummer. If anyone could please this woman, Frank Butler could. She expelled him after the first chorus, even though he begged and pleaded for a second chance. She kept indicating that the tempo was dragging, or if it didn't drag it wasn't strong enough.

Finally, Clifford thought of a drummer who for the past five years had been playing a gig at a restaurant in Orange County called Charlie Brown's and who was dying to do something else, anything else. He said that he had once played with James Brown for a short time. I didn't know if having played with James Brown was a recommendation or a strike against him. And did the short time indicate that he wouldn't take the bullshit, which I could take as a recommendation of his good sense, or did the short time indicate that he couldn't keep time or could only play jazz or what? Two things we knew: that Clifford said he could play and that he should be strong after playing every night for five years. Eddie Williams showed up real fast—too fast to have come all the way from Orange County—but he was the one. And he did make a difference. He put that tempo on her and held it as long and as strong as she could stand it. I kept thinking, I'd hate to have to make love to that bitch.

Opening night was a complete success. All the jazz people were completely satisfied with the jazz legend. Notables in attendance included actress-singer Abbey Lincoln and trombonist-arranger Melba Liston. And, of course, the Goodtimers' crowd was pleased to see us back in action. In fact, that whole first week was a tremendous success. All the major players showed up at least once, along with many stars from the movie and TV industry. And almost every entertainer who had ever been anywhere and done anything or was trying to go somewhere and do something was there to see and be seen at the hottest new club in town.

After that first week, things began to calm down a bit. The crowd leveled off to where the club was full on weekends and maybe three-fourths full during the week. We played behind artists including Casheres, a Las Vegas-type lounge singer who emulated Neil Diamond. I pray to God that I never hear the song "Sweet Caroline" again. I promise I'll never play it again. There also were the Sweet Souls, three ghetto-looking girls who could really sing their amply endowed asses off. One night, the biggest girl was really getting down on some gospel tune when Clifford whispered in my ear, "I bet that bitch can bake some biscuits." I don't know what singing has to do with cooking, but at that time it was so funny to me that I laughed until I almost fainted. There were other artists that we looked forward to playing behind; repeat appearances by Gloria Lynn and Percy Mayfield, for instance, were highlights of what became known as the Wally Roker Showcase gig.

The crowd got so small during the week that we only had guest artists on weekends. Eventually the weekend crowd got so sparse that we stopped having guest artists at all. It got so bad that after a while the only people in the audience were our personal friends, usually girls waiting for one or another of us to finish playing and go do the wild thing with them. Since there was no crowd, some secret cross-relationships became apparent, and guys in the band got to arguing and fighting with each other over girls they thought were exclusively their own. And some girls who probably hadn't noticed each other before now realized that they were sharing the same member of the band. On top of all this, the club was way behind with our salaries, which had abruptly stopped when the IRS confiscated all of the door money one Saturday night.

We hung with the gig until one night when we were all standing on the stage, ready to play but waiting for someone, anyone, to come in. The place was empty except for the club manager, the IRS man standing at the door, the barmaid, and the two remaining waitresses. We were all angry about everything, including the fact that whatever money, if any, came through the door was going to the IRS. We were arguing about whether or not to play at all. Plus, there were a lot of little personal rifts going on between guys in the band about whose fault it was that we were in this fix, about what to do next, about why we weren't on the Monkees tour, and about just plain ol' messing with one another's girls. It was not a good time to rub anybody the wrong way. Everyone was at the end of his rope. Just then, in walked a tall black dude with a bleached-blond white girl on his arm. He was wearing platform boots; a big-brimmed hat with a long feather in it; a quarter-length plaid coat with big, wide lapels; and big, gold-framed sunglasses. He was smoking a cigarette at the end of a long holder and flashing jewelry all over the place. He whispered something in Wally's ear and took a seat at the front table.

Wally came to the bandstand and told us that the tall dude had a club somewhere in the ghetto and wanted us to audition for him. Audition? This dude wants us to "audition" for him? He must not know who we think we are! We wouldn't audition for the president. We don't do auditions. Who is this guy anyway?

Suddenly we were united by a common insult. Audition?! We all just stared off into space, collectively thinking, "Has it come to this?" "Do we have to audition for some ghetto pimp?" Suddenly, Sam broke into the intro of "Can't Turn You Loose." In an instant, the entire band joined in. With a vengeance we finished that song and went immediately into another. We did "Hold On, I'm Coming," "Dock of the Bay," "Funky Way to Treat Somebody," "Do the Dog"—a whole set, including exaggerated dance routines and background vocals. For forty-five minutes, we showed that pimp, his girlfriend, Wally, the taxman, the waitresses, and each other who we were and why we don't do auditions. Huffing and puffing and sweating, we finished, stomped angrily off the stage, packed our stuff, and left the club, never to return.

Once again in my short history with the Goodtimers, we had come to an almost standstill. Although the Soul'd Out gig and the Wally Roker's Showcase gig ended, we managed to keep the Saturday night after-hours gig at Club De La Soul. When the Wally Roker's Showcase gig ended, we were looking for anything to give us any kind of income, so we attempted to relocate our Sunday morning breakfast jam session. We found a club deep in the ghetto that was not doing so well and was looking for something to jump-start its business. This was Club La Rue, also on Slauson Avenue. The jam session at Club La Rue never got to be the crowded, bustling, fun-filled affair that it had been at the Soul'd Out, but it was okay, and we could depend on a little money from it. So we went our separate ways during the week and only got together for the two weekend gigs.

The after-hours gig was very interesting. Although we were the band and the featured act, we also played for other acts on the show. Skillet and Leroy was a comedy act that featured La Wanda Page, who went on to star as Aunt Esther in the sitcom "Sanford and Son." Skillet and Leroy were so raunchy they would make comedians like Richard Pryor and Eddie Murphy sound like Sunday-school teachers by comparison. There also was a female impersonator named Sir Lady Java, who was so beautiful and looked so much like a woman that you would have to actually see "it" to believe that that person was really a man. I never saw "it" myself, but I take the word of a player friend of mine who was fooled all the way to the bedroom and actually saw "it." My friend never really recovered from the shock. These after-hours shows got to be really wild and crazy sometimes. I don't how we got away with it, but some of everything, and I do mean everything, went on in the wee hours of those Sunday mornings.

At some point, organ player Doug Carn, who I had met during my early L.A. jazz ventures, began rehearsing for an album he was putting together and asked me to be a part of it. He was doing the project on his own, so there was no money, but the music was challenging, and I enjoyed the jazz experience very much. I learned a lot from Doug, who was a real student of music, especially jazz, much like my old friend Willie Gresham back in Alabama. We rehearsed as many times a week as we could get everyone together. Most of the other guys had other things happening and were all very good musicians. Doug's wife, Jean, was just beginning to develop her now-famous style during the rehearsals for this album. The same Doug Carn band did a few gigs behind singer-actor-stunt man Lee Duncan, gigs that were enjoyable and paid a little money. The diversion from the Goodtimers was welcomed as well as pleasant, but I remained loyal to them even though it looked like it was pretty much over. We continued to cling to the two gigs we had and to search for that regular gig again.

Our desperation for work led us to take a California Club gig, backing the great Solomon Burke. The California Club had once been very popular in L.A. When I had been a kid in the Ike Turner band, for instance, the guys had mentioned it along with the 54 Ballroom as a hot spot in which they had played with Ike and Tina when they first came to L.A. Now it was just another joint on Santa Barbara Ave., struggling to keep any crowd it could get. Yet another change of management trying to get a club restored to its former popularity. Solomon Burke was a pretty big star, and we still had a smattering of followers. We were able to gather everyone except Lane for the rehearsal. Lane had gotten really fed up with the situation and was working a day gig and wasn't available for this gig. Plus, there was only enough money for six people to make seventy-five dollars for the week. We were prepared to make do with what was there, but King Solomon, as he was calling himself at that time, insisted that we needed a piano player. He needed a piano so bad that he offered to pay the extra seventy-five dollars. So we called Lane, and he agreed to make the gig.

The rehearsal and the first night went well. Lane, for some reason, had the foresight to draw his entire week's salary directly from the club's manager after that first night. We didn't think anything of it. I, personally, preferred to wait and draw my complete salary at the end of the week. Through the week different people would get a few dollars here and there. Of course, we kept good records of each draw. We didn't attract a great audience, but the week was a minimal success, and we were getting set to do it again next week. At the end of the last show, we were settling up the money and our calculations came up seventy-five short. Then we remembered that Lane, who had gone home, already had his money and that Reverend Burke (he also claimed to be an ordained minister) had promised to cover the piano player's salary, which would make everything even board. When we reminded him of his promise, this great performer, the self proclaimed "King of Soul," this purveyor of the word of God, flatly denied that he had ever made such a promise. After an hour of admonishing and reminding and finally yelling and screaming and pleading with him and the club manager, we gave up in disbelief, somehow resisting violence as a last resort. We did, however, recite a few choice Bible verses to the good reverend and inviting him to kiss our collective ass. Then we left, each of us twelve dollars and fifty cents short.

The bad part about it was that the next week he had some other poor, unsuspecting band in the club and drew an even bigger crowd. For years, this Solomon Burke incident "stuck in my craw," so to speak. I found it hard to believe that such a great singer, a wonderful performer, so affable and thoughtful with his audience, could also be such an unconscionable liar. I kept thinking that maybe we all might have heard him wrong and it all might have been a big mistake. But once I was talking to a European man who had managed a Solomon Burke tour, and he told me that Solomon would have his valet gather the catered food from the dressing rooms, pack it in a bag, and sell sandwiches and drinks to the people in his band after the gigs and during the bus ride to the next gig. This, along with my own experience and some other stories I've heard about Solomon Burke, has convinced me that being a good entertainer does not make you a good person or exempt you from being a low-life motherfucker.

Our Sunday morning jam session at Club La Rue was doing well enough to lead us to believe that maybe we could do some business on the weekends at regular club hours. But the club owner wouldn't have anything to do with it. He had had just about as much as he could stand trying to run a nightclub and was attempting to unload it on someone else. He jokingly said that we could have the club and run it ourselves until he could find someone to buy it outright. And that if we turned it into a success before he found a buyer, he would let us continue to run it and pay him a percentage. This was a good offer if you were a person who really didn't want to work at delivering mail or loading trucks. We didn't have to invest anything but our time and our musical talents, which at the time were paying zero dividends.

So we cut the bartender in for an equal share in return for his expertise at managing a club, and we opened the doors on Friday, Saturday, and Sunday nights in addition to the Sunday mornings. We announced the weekend shows at the Club De La Soul after-hours gig, as well as at the jam session. That and an intense word-of-mouth campaign were the only advertisements we could afford. We were counting on the approaching Christmas season to bring us some spin-off business from both the extra tourists and the people who didn't ordinarily frequent the nightclubs getting out for the holidays. The first weekend, I think we got all twenty of those people. We sold enough beer and collected enough money on the door to pay the waitress and buy some beer for the next weekend. We were pretty discouraged, but our new expert partner assured us that it would get better, so we decided to try it another week.

The next week *was* a little better, and we felt we should continue to the next weekend, because it was Halloween and we were sure to have a big crowd on that week. It *was* a big crowd, but we ran out of beer, and our one waitress was so overworked that she threatened to quit if we didn't get her some help. Somewhat encouraged, we stocked up an extra supply of beer and hired two other waitresses, anticipating another big crowd. I guess those spin-off people spinned right back to wherever it is they had spun from, because that next week we had even fewer people than we had had the first week.

Now we are stuck with a lot of beer and three waitresses that take all the money from the jam session and everything from the weekend door and beer sales. So far, we have profited nothing from Club La Rue and are getting farther and farther in debt with these waitresses, who are threatening to get some big ghetto dudes to take their money out of our hides. Plus, we are discovering some other perks that go along with running a nightclub, like cleaning the bathrooms and vacuuming the floors, sweeping the sidewalks and bouncing neighborhood drunks who threaten to come back and blow up the place.

But we hung in there until Thanksgiving night, when we had the biggest crowd we had ever had. The place was packed. We had a very successful and enjoyable night, selling all the beer without actually selling out. Made what looked like a killing on the door. The waitresses were happy, and we were all happy, until we gathered all the partners after the gig to settle up, expecting to go home with a pocket full of money. That was not to be. After hours of adding and subtracting and dividing, mostly subtracting, my share came to seven dollars and forty cents. The waitresses were the only ones happy now. They had all made big tips, and we paid them for about three weeks that we owed them. They left with fat pockets. We contemplated robbin' dem ho's. Not only was I discouraged, I was actually afraid of what was ahead of me, what with Christmas was coming and the now-obvious fact that Club La Rue was not going to pay the bills, let alone buy Christmas gifts for the family that had recently increased by one more darling little girl named Shana.

James Brown Again

• • •

When I got home that night, I was dreading having to tell my wife that after all we had been through with the club, we ended up with nothing. I hoped that she would be asleep and I wouldn't have to deal with it until the morning. But no. She was wide awake. She had waited up to give me an urgent message from James Brown. The message was that he was having trouble with the guys in Bootsy's band and was putting the old band back together and needed me to help. Three months after I had left the James Brown band, there had been some sort of general walkout, and the band I had left with James was now doing it's own thing as Maceo and All the King's Men. Mr. Brown had replaced them with a band led by Bootsy Collins, that fine young bass player we had met at the studio in Cincinnati. Jabo and St. Clair had not participated in the walkout. When I spoke to Mr. Brown on the phone, he told me that he was getting Clyde, who had left the band before I had, and that Pee Wee and Waymon also were coming back. I found all that hard to believe, but I was easy to convince of anything, given my position. Plus, he was offering me a salary that far exceeded my previous salary. I asked for a small advance and got it. In less than two days, on December 3, 1970, I bought a new coat and was on my way to New York City and the Apollo Theater.

I returned to the James Brown band with a new attitude. My experiences in L.A. had taught me that being a good musician was only incidental to becoming a success and making the big bucks in the music business. There had to be something to set you apart from the ordinary good musician. Mr. Brown convinced me that if I took the job as his music director, I could go a long way. Although I still had my dream of one day becoming known as a great jazz player, it didn't seem to be anywhere in my future. What I had in my favor was James Brown. He needed me, and I surely did need him. The only hard part would be enduring the humiliation that he was sure to inflict on me as I had seen him do to all the people who worked closely with him. The question was whether I could subject my ego and self-respect to a man I didn't really like or respect— as a person or as a musician. I did, however, have a healthy respect for him as a performer, and he was a person who got done things that were all but impossible for black performers to do at that time.

He had just signed a monumental recording deal with Polydor Records. This was a new door opening for James Brown. Although he was the undisputed king of the single recording, this deal with Polydor required delivery of a certain number of albums a year. I never knew the exact details of the deal, but I know it called for J.B. to conceptualize and record a number of albums of himself and a few other artists. Mr. Brown was accustomed to getting an idea for a song—one song at a time—then rushing the band into a studio. If the band was near Cincinnati, he chose King Recording Studio. If not, the band would go to any studio in the area of the current gig and throw down the one or maybe two or three songs that he had on his mind at the time. His previous experiences with albums were limited to live recordings of Apollo Theater shows and compilations of singles that usually included at least one big hit and other singles that hadn't been released or hadn't done well. J.B. had had numerous gold singles but never a gold album. In fact, he had only released maybe three or four albums altogether in his entire recording career. He obviously needed help.

When I arrived at the Apollo, I found not only the James Brown band that featured the great Bootsy Collins on bass, but also eight additional musicians—four trumpets and four trombones—seated behind the amplifiers playing augmentation arrangements written by Dave Matthews, a transplanted Cincinnatian then living and working in New York.

The regular band had changed a lot from the way I had left it. Most of the names were new, and the musicianship was woefully substandard. The showmanship *was* somewhat updated, and even—to a point—elevated. Bootsy and his brother, Phelps "Catfish" Collins, who was on guitar, were excellent musicians and added some serious foot-stomping to the bass and guitar parts they had inherited from Jimmy Nolen, Country, and Bernard. The other guitar player was named Hearlon Martin

Phelps "Catfish" Collins.
Photograph by Fred
Wesley Jr.

but known to everyone as "Cheese"—so dubbed by the nickname king, Bootsy.

I was surprised to see that J.B. had added a hand drummer to the band. Johnny Griggs was not one of the Bootsy boys but a dyed-in-the-wool New Yorker, a veteran of the New York Afro-Latin and jazz scene, an excellent musician who had played with Mongo Santamaria, Freddie Hubbard, and many other Latin and jazz greats. He gave the J.B. funk an unexpected lift without compromising the sound—somehow, he made it sound not more Latin but more funky. This hand drumming—along with Cheese's manic "chanking," which sort of emulated the famous Jimmy Nolen chank, combined with Catfish's unique, twanging stroke and the relentless thump of the Bootsy bass—gave the audience a great simulation of the James Brown sound of the '60s, arriving at it from a different direction. When I had first joined the band, Jimmy, Country, Bernard, and Clyde and/or Jabo had that original thang. This wasn't that, but it was as good. Well, almost. The horns were a complete disaster. Although the players did some fantastic, athletic dancing, that tight, fat voicing that Pee Wee had established was replaced with a thin, atonal sound that Maceo described as "that Salvation Army Band thing."

I understood now why J.B. had added the brass ensemble, however sterile it came across. Although the Apollo crowd seemed to be satisfied, it must have been driving St. Clair, Jabo, and Mr. Brown crazy. They were the only people in the band that I recognized. Mr. Brown was literally dancing to Bootsy's version of his music. J.B. had substituted the flash of the dancing trumpets and the glitter of the tuxedo-clad brass section to compensate for the lack of that old gut-wrenching, heart-stopping, hard-driving band that soul audiences were used to seeing and hearing. The sad part was that the fans didn't seem to miss the real thing as much as J.B. did.

Also, the young guys in the Bootsy band didn't give Mr. Brown the respect that the old guys did. They were, for the most part, footloose and fancy-free and had nothing to lose if they lost favor with the man. These wild and crazy guys were not the kind of family-oriented, job-dependent people J.B. was used to having under his control. There was nothing he could threaten them with. They didn't care. In fact, they had actually become bored with the gig and were looking for something else to do. No wonder he tried to kiss me when he first saw me.

There wasn't much I could do right away. After the Apollo, we played the Howard Theater in Washington, D.C. I was installed immediately as the new bandleader but did little at first. I changed a few chord voicings to fit my trombone and played a couple of solos that delighted and amazed the young guys, and added a modicum of respect for the reputation that had preceded me. It was difficult to really take over as leader, because Bootsy was clearly the leader of the majority of the band. Mr. Brown exercised his control as well as he could by manipulating the money and individual egos. These youngsters were not going for the mental bullshit. They were very close for the most part and saw straight through Mr. Brown's efforts to divide and conquer. It was evident, however, that he had gotten into the heads of two trumpet players, Jasaan and Hasaan, who had bought the idea that they were not going to get this kind of limelight and feminine attention anywhere else.

Bootsy and his brother Catfish were on the verge of leaving from the time I arrived, and I really do believe that curiosity about me kept them around as long as they ended up staying. Everyone knew that Bootsy was ultimately destined for stardom. Mr. Brown had no idea how to capture and control this wild, young Jimi Hendrix look-a-like. It was interesting to observe Bootsy trying his best to give Mr. Brown the respect that he obviously had for him while avoiding the many pitfalls and traps Mr. Brown was constantly setting out for him. Nothing worked on Bootsy. He was his own man with his own plan, on his way to somewhere, somehow, some way. The only thing that was certain was that James Brown was not the way.

I think Mr. Brown gave up on him and turned his attention to me. I think he saw in me a person he could control, as well as the one per-

Dave Matthews.
Courtesy of
Dave Matthews.

son who could do for him what Dave Matthews was doing musically *and* give him a star soloist to take up the slack that Bootsy would leave on stage. I believe that Dave had come to a point in his career at which his James Brown credit had been well established, so he was ready to move on to bigger and better things in the New York area. The time was exactly right, and the door was wide open for me to step in. I didn't have to step on any toes—everyone could move on smoothly. All I had to do was take care of business. I knew that I was not nearly qualified for the task, but I was cocky enough to believe that I could fake my way through it until my program locked in.

During the Howard Theater show the audience spontaneously began chanting "SOUL POWER! SOUL POWER!" Naturally, the Boss, who always had his ear in tune with what was happening in the street (remember "Brand New Bag," "Out of Sight," "Cold Sweat," and "Black and Proud"?), picked up on the phrase right away. The night before the last night at the Howard, he called me to his dressing room and told me to get a groove together. He told me to use the lick that Bootsy and Catfish played at the end of "Get Up, Get Into It, Get Involved" and add a horn part, a bridge, and a turn-back. He gave me ideas on what each part and section should be like but left the actual construction of the groove to me. After the last show at the Howard, we boarded the bus and went to a studio in the D.C.

area. After a few minor adjustments by the Boss and some input from Bobby Byrd, we recorded a tune called "Soul Power."

I was very uptight about my first session as leader with James Brown. I didn't think about what I was doing business-wise. I would just be happy if everything turned out okay. In fact, it was the funkiest session I had ever been a part of. After we listened to the playback about a thousand times and finished slapping each other in the hand and on the back, Mr. Brown and I sat down to have a little talk. I reminded him of what he had said to me when I first returned. That he would let me make as much money as I could from his deal with Polydor. He said that for this session he was giving me a choice of getting $125 for the arrangement or 25 percent of the song. I, still trying to right myself from my poverty-stricken California experience, opted for the $125 cash. He told me that I had made the wrong choice because 25 percent of any song by James Brown—especially one this funky and this sure to hit—was worth waaaaaaay more than $125. But he was so happy with the session that he gave me the $125 *and* 25 percent of the song. It was a deal that remained in place and applied, more or less, to all the songs I recorded with James Brown.

My first few months back with the J.B. Show were spent watching what Dave Matthews did and reacclimating myself to the James Brown system. Conducting the augmented brass sections was not a problem. The James Brown music director tag gave me instant credibility with the brass players we hired through the union all across the country. The music for the brass was, for the most part, complete. I had to add an arrangement here and there, not that we needed them, but Mr. Brown was just testing my ability to do the unnecessary for the simple reason that he asked for it. This ability came in handy as my career with J.B. progressed. He would not only ask for the unnecessary but very often the impossible as well.

After we finished at the Apollo and Howard theaters, we played the Latin Casino, where Mr. Brown had picked a group of sassy young girls from Philadelphia. The group was called Honey and the Bees. They were managed by Mr. Jimmy Bishop, a prominent disc jockey in the Philadelphia area. Although they were an exceptionally good group, I could not see why we needed them on the James Brown Show. It probably was a favor for Jimmy Bishop, who made sure that all of J.B.'s records were on fast rotation in radio stations in the City of Brotherly Love. Frankly, these girls were so good they should have had their own show. As it was, they only presented me with new things to worry about, in addition to all the problems I already had with my responsibilities. These girls seemed determined to distract me from my duties, one way or another. I soon got rid of them. Most of them anyway. The show was exciting enough with Bobby Byrd and his wife Vickie Anderson doing featured spots.

The tour continued and carried me back to familiar places down South and through the Midwest until we finally ended up back in New York, preparing to go to Europe.

The European tour was quite an experience. The first stop was Brussels. This was my first time in Europe, so I had to rely on my high school study of geography and world history to inform me about where I was and what the people were about. Most of the people we encountered were into R&B music and welcomed us with open arms, so we didn't have to deal with many of the social and cultural differences that ordinary tourists faced. We basically went from the gig to the hotel, escorted all the way.

After the shows, we were usually taken out to a club or restaurant for some additional entertainment. The people who took us and the people at the places they took us to were into American music, especially black American music. We were scrutinized and emulated and generally catered to at all times. The Black and White Club of Brussels, run by a nattily dressed and very suave gentleman named Roger, was a Mecca of black music and black culture in Europe. After the Brussels show, Roger—escorting two fabulously beautiful young ladies, one black, one white—personally came backstage and invited us all to his club for an after-hours party. We were astounded to see all of the beautiful fur and leather coats the girls at the club were wearing. We were even more shocked when they pulled the coats off. We expected to see dresses, skirts, even mini-skirts, but what we saw were shorts. Not knee-length shorts, but short shorts. Very stylish shorts of every fabric from mohair to polyester, wool knit to satin, all decorated and ornamented in every way thinkable, from sequins to rhinestones. We had heard of "hotpants" and had even seen certain out-front, adventurous American women in them, but here, hotpants were the order of the day. The Black and White Club was filled with beautiful women of every color, from platinum blondes to deep-chocolate sisters with every shade in between. The sight of all those asses in so many different sizes and shapes dancing around inspired the James Brown smash hit "Hot Pants." The hotpants craze was evident as we continued the tour through Amsterdam and other cities in Holland. European audiences were unexpectedly knowledgeable about and appreciative of R&B music and responded to it as enthusiastically as American audiences.

In England, we played the famous Prince Albert Hall in London and did shows in Manchester, Liverpool, and Birmingham. The English didn't pronounce it "Burmingham" the way we say it in Alabama. After about a week of English food and no bowel movements, I developed a severe pain in my lower abdomen. A doctor in Manchester examined me and informed me that I had impacted feces. When I didn't seem to understand what he meant, he, having studied medicine in New York, translated the diagnosis to be "full of shit." He gave me a strong, yellow syrup laxative that finally relieved the problem. We went on to France, where we played three nights at the famous Olympia Theater in Paris and did shows in a few other French cities.

Most memorable was Lyon, where I was attacked by some type of ghost in the hotel. I had a funny feeling about this hotel even when we first checked in, although it was still daytime at that point. We had to use the one tiny elevator—or lift, as they called it—one at a time. When I got to my floor, the lift door opened to an almost completely dark hallway with only little lights along the wall to indicate where the timed light-switches were. After you pressed the switch, the lights came on and you had about thirty seconds to make it into your room or to the next light switch, or you'd be draped again in total darkness. The first press of a light-switch gave me just enough time to unload my considerable amount of luggage from the elevator. I then scrambled to the next light-switch as fast as I could, because I felt that I wasn't alone there in the dark. At least in the light I could see that there was nothing in the hall but me. In the dark, it felt like something was with me. After three moves of my bags and four mad dashes for the light switches, I finally got into my room, which was lighted, but very dimly. I didn't stay in the room. I washed up a bit and headed out to find something to eat with some of the other fellows. I then hung out in St. Clair's room until time to go to the gig. I couldn't explain it and didn't try to, but I just didn't want to be in my room alone in that hotel.

After the gig, I still refused to go to my room. I continued to hang in other people's rooms until finally everyone went to bed, and I was forced to go to my room. I went in, pulled my clothes off, and took a shower— all the time feeling like I was being watched. I kept turning around expecting to see someone or something. I never saw anything but continued to feel a presence. I finally got a hold of myself and dismissed all these funny feelings as a reaction to fatigue and the severe constipation I was recovering from. I got in the bed, turned out the lights, and tried my best to go to sleep. But I kept hearing some noises in the hall. Some strange thumping. Not like footsteps, but bumping and then scratching on the walls. At first, the sounds were way down the hall, but they were getting closer. I reasoned that I was not the only one in the hotel and of course there would be some sounds other than the sounds I made. Then it got dead quiet. I heard nothing but still felt a presence. I tried to ignore the feeling and go to sleep. But sleep didn't come. It seemed like hours that I lay there in darkness and silence, wide-awake and scared to death.

All of a sudden, something crashed through the door and jumped on me, pinning me to the bed. I can't say it was a person, but it was strong and heavy, and I tussled with it, trying to get it off me. I managed to flip it off of me, and it went under the bed. I don't know if it was shaking the bed or if my shaking was shaking the bed. But the bed was shaking, vibrating if you will. I was so scared I didn't know what to do. I was too scared to get out of the bed for fear that it would get me again, so I just lay there shaking. I finally prayed this simple prayer: "GOD, PLEASE GET THIS GODDAMNED THING OUT OF MY ROOM!" The next thing I knew I was waking up to the bright sun shining through a window that I had not even noticed before. There was even a bird outside singing. I was totally rested and felt very good. There wasn't even a hint of the presence or funny feeling I had experienced when I first entered the hotel. I had put an impossible situation in the hands of God, and everything came out perfect.

I found it strange that an artist of James Brown's caliber did not have his band treated better, at least in Europe. Most of the hotels we stayed in were of the two- or three-star variety. We didn't travel in luxury coaches with bunks and other amenities. We were lucky to get a bus of any sort. Most of the ground travel was by van. The one time we did fly, it was in a plane so small that we couldn't fit all of the equipment into its bins. Amplifiers and other pieces of sound equipment were tied to the seats with ropes, and we all had to move to the front of the aircraft in order to achieve take-off. It was very dangerous, and I wondered if playing with James Brown was worth this kind of risk. J.B., of course, flew on Air France. I guess the reasoning was that the band and the equipment were replaceable. James Brown, being one of a kind, was not. But the pilots assured us that we had a 90 percent chance of arriving alive, and we did. The tiny aircraft landed in Marseille on the same runway on which they were testing the new supersonic Concorde. The unbelievably loud noise from the Concorde engines only added to the tension and anxiety we were feeling from what had felt like a kite ride over the French countryside.

For some reason, we played the best show of the tour that night. After the show, we were invited—or, as it turned out, ordered—to a dinner with a group of tough-looking dudes who were, as it was whispered to us, bigwigs in the French Mafia. The meal was beefsteak—very rare beefsteak. I was getting ready to send mine back for a third time—trying to at least get it hot—when I looked over at the chiseled-faced, slick-haired, Tony Bennett-with-a-broken-nose-looking, deeply tanned, muscle-necked dude next to me, licking blood off his plate, asking for another one. I gave him mine. I didn't want him to get mad, and I wasn't about to eat any raw French meat.

The tour ended up with a swing through Italy. We encountered the same type of audiences as we had in France—loud, energetic, and determined to show us that they could dance and that they were hip to the music, the dress, and the lifestyle. The European tour opened my eyes to the fact that black music was spreading throughout the world and that, although these foreigners still hadn't mastered the dance, their ears were definitely in tune with the sounds that I had grown up with in Mobile, Alabama. They didn't seem to feel it in their bodies, but they were able to hear the sounds with their ears, see the musicians' movements with their eyes, and, with the part of the brain that perceives pleasure, pick up on the fun and enjoyment the performers were having. They connected it to the part of the brain that could cause them to imitate what their eyes, ears, and endorphins were perceiving, giving an observer the illusion of people partying just like at Club Harlem in Mobile.

When we returned to New York, I had a better understanding of how all black music—R&B, jazz, blues, and gospel—had the power to unite people of many racial, national, and religious persuasions, if only for the purpose of having fun. It's difficult to have issues with or dislike, let alone hate, persons with whom you're having fun. World peace must start somewhere. Funky music is as good a place as any.

Soon after we returned to New York, Bootsy, Catfish, Frank, Tiger, and all the Bootsy boys left abruptly—giving a very, very short, verbal, barely audible "See ya" as the only notice. I was left with Jabo, Cheese, St. Clair, Johnny Griggs, and Bobby Byrd, who would and was able to play the Hammond B-3 organ as necessary. I had two weeks to put together a band that was equal to the great James Brown bands of the past or that would at least appear to be as dynamic as those former bands. And, to make it more difficult, the first show was to be at the Apollo Theater, probably the toughest R&B audience in the world and the most knowledgeable about James Brown's music and musicians. Mr. Brown left the solution of this problem solely up to me. He went home to Augusta. He did help me out a little bit by sending me Augusta trumpet player Ike Oakley, as well as guitarist Robert Coleman and drummer John Morgan, both from Macon, Georgia. Thanks a lot, Mr. Brown.

Ordinarily, New York City would be the ideal place to put together a great band, but James Brown's musicians had to possess certain unique qualifications. Just being a good musician wasn't good enough. A musician also had to be willing to leave home for very long periods of time. And he had to have the disposition to deal with the unusual personality of a superstar like James Brown, which means he had to be able to take a lot of musical and personal shit without quitting and/or jumping on and/or trying to kill the bandleader and/or the star of the show. So I had to find musicians who played well enough to learn the show in two weeks and who would be impressed enough with the gig in the first place to stick through the grueling rehearsals I was about to put them through *and* through the final two or three days of rehearsals with J.B. himself— all for the meager salary that James Brown was willing to pay. It would have been easy to hire someone to write out the existing show on paper, hire some top studio musicians and rehearse three or four hours a day at union scale, and come up with a decent but not very exciting show. What I was about to do was start with what I, Jabo, Cheese, St. Clair, Johnny Griggs, and Bobby Byrd knew of the existing show, then teach all the notes, chords, and rhythms for every tune, as well as all the dance routines, cues, and cut-offs, to totally green people, and make it seem to an Apollo Theater audience like all the great James Brown shows of the past.

Needless to say, the musicians that I ended up with were not the cream of the New York crop. There were plenty of musicians willing and anxious to play with the great James Brown, but they were either astounded by the low salaries and the long periods on the road or had heard stories about fines and strict rules and humiliations. So, as usual, I had to rely on people already in the band to suggest players who might fit the unique profile we needed. Cheese was originally from La Grange, N.C., but had been living in Brooklyn for most of his adult life. The band he had previously played with was still gigging in Brooklyn, under the direction of bandleader Fred Thomas, a vocalist and bass player. Cheese felt sure that Thomas was right for the bass player job. While I now had a complete rhythm section, the question was how fast I could get Fred Thomas and Robert Coleman to learn the show.

To the horn section—which then consisted of me, St. Clair, Ike Oakley (whom we had never heard), and Jasaan, the trumpet player, who had changed his mind and decided not to go with the Bootsy boys—we added Fred Thomas's and Cheese's saxophone player, Jimmy Parker, who they said played alto because we said we needed an alto player. It turned out that he really played tenor sax; he didn't even own an alto sax and had never played one. I also called on a young trumpet player, Russell Crimes, who I knew from Huntsville and was certain would be enamored enough of the glamour of a big-time act like the James Brown Show to do whatever it took to keep the gig. This gave us the makings of a brass section and a reed section. I alternated between the brass and the reeds as needed. So, with Bobby Byrd, St. Clair, and Jabo by my side, I got a chair, a whip, and a gun and proceeded to do the impossible: construct a show that would first be acceptable to the Boss, then ultimately be acceptable to the great audience of the Apollo Theater of New York City. I didn't really have a gun, of course, but I did know where to get one fast if I needed it, maybe to use on myself.

The rehearsals went well. It was much easier than I had anticipated. The music of James Brown is very simple, musically. The main thing is to play the simple parts with enthusiasm and to have the endurance to hold those parts in a groove for long periods of time. Having a core of musicians who were experienced at doing this gave the new guys something by which to gauge their performance. Fred was a pretty good bass player but had never had to play as hard as he now had to play with Jabo relentlessly sticking that groove up his ass. John Morgan brought a different style of funk to the band. More complicated than the straight hard beat of Jabo. I was sure Mr. Brown had big plans for him in the future. For the time, though, because he basically knew how to play all the songs, he was a good relief for Jabo when Jabo needed it, and he needed it a lot. The only way to really learn how to play drums with James Brown was to play drums with James Brown. The best thing about Robert Coleman was his ability to play the blues. In fact that was what attracted J.B. to him, and it turned out to be the total extent of his ability. So I gave him all of the single string parts but still had to stay on him to keep the rhythm strong. He had no sense of funk or time. He had to just do it intellectually.

I don't think he ever felt it. Cheese was forced to become the mainstay of the groove with what has become that classic scratch stroke, which was originated by Catfish on the "I Got Soul" part of James Brown's hit record *Super Bad.* The strong hand-drumming of Johnny Griggs was the glue that connected the manic Cheese stroke, the unconscious Fred Thomas bass line, and the Robert Coleman single-string twang to the jazzy funk of the Jabo drums, all of which came together to create what now is the much-sampled JBs sound. This sound is most glaringly apparent on the James Brown hit record *Get on the Good Foot.*

Having locked down a formula for the rhythm section, the next thing was to get the new guys accustomed to watching the director, whether it be me or James. I was easy. I would position myself where everyone could see me and give precise signals in a crisp, sharp, military manner, in a place in the music that led smoothly to the next cue. If possible. In most cases. Unless the Boss made me do it differently. On the other hand, the Boss would give a signal or cue anytime, anyplace, from anywhere on the stage, in mid-split or coming out of a spin or jumping up in the air, and he would get real mad if you missed it. All I could do was alert the new guys that this was what to expect when the Boss showed up for rehearsal.

The horns were a different challenge. Remembering was a big part of the gig for everyone, especially the horns. Once the members of the rhythm section learned a particular groove, all they had to do was hold it, so remembering those parts was relatively easy. The horns, on the other hand, were what kept the groove from becoming boring. The horns gave the groove its flavor, moving things from here to there and keeping the stage from being all gray and colorless. This required remembering many different *things* both musical and physical. We soon discerned that St. Clair and I were the only great soloists, so we placed the three trumpets on one side of the stage, where they developed a fantastic, acrobatic dance show. Most of the playing was done by me, St. Clair, and Jimmy Parker, who finally figured how to play the alto sax. Of course, the trumpets played a lot, too, but their main claim to fame was their unbelievable dance routines.

By the time the Boss came to rehearsal, I had everything all together. Little tricks to keep Coleman on the beat. Little tricks and cues to help everyone remember the when and where and what and how of their parts. I had constantly urged everybody, especially Morgan and Fred Thomas, to play hard and keep the groove strong and threatened everyone with fines and verbal abuse by the Boss if they didn't do everything exactly right. When the Boss showed up, I felt that we were ready. I didn't expect everything to be perfect, but at least we had a good place to start from. We did the opening and brought on the Man, and what happened next was the most amazing thing I had ever seen. This ragtag group of mostly unrelated, half-ass musicians that I had strung together with spit, chicken wire, and chewing gum latched onto James Brown's vibe and became a group of BAAD MOTHERFUCKERS. It was like they drew energy from the Man. Coleman suddenly locked his part as tight as Country ever did. Fred Thomas played so hard he pulled a blood blister on his finger. Morgan broke sticks, and I finally actually heard Jimmy Parker's alto sax. The routines that the trumpets were doing made them look like they actually left the floor at times. The sound was full and powerful, even without the extra horns. The band generally lit up—everyone, everything was raised to a higher level. It didn't take long to develop either. Lightning struck as soon as he hit the stage. This made me realize that what everyone says about James Brown being nothing without his band might be true, but the real truth is that any band James Brown performs in front of instantly becomes a great band.

We had yet another successful stint at the great Apollo Theater. We left the James Brown legend intact. A few people asked about the whereabouts of Jimmy, Clyde, Bootsy, and some of the other old guys, but in general the audience focused on James Brown and enjoyed the show as usual. The individual players in the band were incidental and of no consequence to the success of the show.

Having been tried, convicted, and sentenced under the Apollo fire, the James Brown band hit the road again. The old guys had a new confidence that I hadn't seen since the Pee Wee days. The new guys took on an arrogance deserved only by the top musicians in the world. I guess they deserved it, because they were backing the greatest entertainer in the world. I was just proud and felt empowered because the Man depended on me to relate to the band and the band depended on me to relate to the Man. In a way, I was in control. Control of the hottest show on the road.

I had led bands before, but at this level every aspect of leadership was very important. My main handicap was the fact that I didn't have the final say. Everything had to be ultimately approved by James Brown. So I had to make him think what I wanted him to think and make the band think what I wanted them to think in the name of getting things done. For example, as we went along the road doing shows, we would stop and record whenever we had days off. Usually, after the show, I would have to meet with the Boss in his dressing room and discuss the show, making changes or correcting mistakes or adding things or deleting things. These after-the-show dressing-room meetings were also the times when Mr. Brown would hum stuff to me to put together for the next session. He would hum, sing, or beat out bass lines or drum licks or horn parts, and I would write this stuff down and translate it to the band either the next day at rehearsal or on the bus as we traveled or in the hotel rooms. I would have to have the band ready to record whenever we found a studio.

This system worked very well as it gave me a chance to pre-rehearse the band before he came and put the final arrangement together with his vocal or chant. Many of the arrangements happened on the spot—solos, breaks, and even some vocals and raps often came on the Boss's whim—but the basic music had to be in place. Chords, bass lines, some type of form had to be ready in advance. I don't think Mr. Brown could have worked with this particular group of musicians from scratch, because they were not as good as I led him to believe they were, and he was not as patient as I led them to think he was. The few times we tried to do it from scratch came out pretty good but took a lot of time and some serious intervening on my part to try to keep the Boss from looking stupid and to make sure it seemed that all the really good ideas were his. Mr. Brown had the most fragile ego, and I had to be constantly careful not to injure it. I often had to take over without it looking like I was taking over. I became real good at kissing the Boss's ass and being a yes-man while maintaining the respect of the guys under me. It was tricky, but I thought it necessary to keep peace and to produce good records and good shows.

And it was working really well. During this period, instead of doing shows every night as in the past, we spent a lot of time recording and preparing to record. In 1971 and 1972, we recorded "Pass the Peas," "Gimme Some Mo'," "Get on the Good Foot," "Make It Funky," "Hot Pants," and many others using the system: James gives it to me, I give it to the band, James comes in with vocals, solos, and final arrangement. We were rolling. I was getting a paid education. Everybody loved me. The Boss loved me because I agreed with whatever he said, and the band loved me because they were part of a big-time band and big-time records and were free to enjoy the amenities that came with that while I shielded them from the wrath of the Boss. I did feel like I was balancing a house of cards that could come crashing down on me with one wrong move. But, for the time being, I had it all under control.

My real education started when Mr. Brown ordered me to go into the studio with Dave Matthews and record some of my original tunes. Bootsy and the guys had started an album for the JBs. The JBs was the name given to the James Brown road band at that time. We were to use the tunes Bootsy had cut, some of the songs we had recorded on the road, and my originals to make the first JBs album. But Brown didn't want to use the road band on my tunes. He wanted to use some New York jazz musicians. He knew my desire to play jazz, and I guess this was like a reward for being such a good fellow and doing his bidding.

I didn't know how or where to start. The first thing I thought was to call Pee Wee or Waymon. But Pee Wee was off doing his music-directing thing with Esther Phillips, and Waymon was now playing regularly with Max Roach. But Dave told me not to worry because he could take care of everything. The first thing he did was introduce me to Emile Charlap.

Emile Charlap was and is to this day the top music contractor in the city of New York. I don't know how he and Dave hooked up, but they have more of a father and son relationship than a professional one, although the professional relationship was solid and seemed to greatly benefit them both. Emile was familiar with the James Brown situation, since Dave had done quite a bit of work for James before. Getting used to me was the only adjustment that had to be made. It wasn't like I was taking the work away from Dave. The James Brown/Polydor account stayed with the Emile Charlap office for contracting musicians, booking studios, and copying music, and Dave still got on most of the union contracts in one capacity or another. Besides, Dave was a really good and fast arranger and was in demand for a number of different types of musical arranging and composing. Dave did everything from classical music to low-down, dirty blues. Plus, the mainstay of the Emile Charlap office was the jingle business. The jingle work kept Emile a busy and rich man even if he never did a James Brown session. However, the extra business was welcomed. So I was welcomed as the new man on the James Brown hot seat.

Emile was a no-nonsense businessman. He was also an excellent music copyist. He played a little trumpet and was a very nice and sensitive man, although he tried to hide the nice guy under a gruff old man exterior. But that was just to keep everyone on his or her toes and things moving on schedule. I started that first session completely ignorant of how to conduct a recording session. So Dave and Emile took me by the hand and led me through it. The first thing Emile did was to tell me a joke about a man who died and stayed dead for about ten minutes before the doctors could revive him. When he regained consciousness, the doctors and nurses informed him that he had indeed been dead for ten minutes. They then questioned him about what it was like to be dead. He said it was just like it had been reported by others who had died and been revived: passing through a dark tunnel and being drawn closer and closer to this beautiful, warm, all-consuming light, then coming face-to-face with a loving presence. The doctors and nurses anxiously urged him on, asking about God. Did you see God? Tell us about God? What is God like? The man replied, "Well, first of all, she's black." I guess he told me the joke to let me know that he knew I was black and was about to em-bark on a venture of unexpected experiences and that he was the loving presence that would lead me through all the dark tunnels into the light. Or just to loosen up the situation. I was scared to death. Maybe he was letting me know that if I did die, he and Dave would bring me back and I could tell them about God.

Dave gave me a score pad and some pencils and a room with a piano, in which to write in private. He showed me how to notate for each in-strument on the score and told me that Emile or one of the other copyists would copy the individual parts. I knew nothing, and I made numerous mistakes and wrote a lot of stuff that wasn't necessary to write, but be-tween Emile and Dave, I was set straight right away. After a little while, I got fairly proficient at writing scores. Anything I needed to know, I just asked, was told, then did it. I learned by doing. My education was prac-tically applied immediately. My exams were hearing the music played back on studio speakers. The final grade came from James Brown. If he liked it, I got an A, got paid, and moved on to the next lesson. If he didn't like it, I got paid and was sent back to do it over again, then got paid again. This was great, except for the fact that James Brown almost never completely approved of what was done, and I always had to en-dure long lectures and humiliating criticisms, usually in front of people. Doing takes over and over—adding this and subtracting that—became a matter of routine. As long as I didn't blow my top or lose my cool, I con-tinued to learn and to make money. At first, the songs were my original compositions. But, before long, Mr. Brown said, "You don't know what you're doing, son. Have the bass do this and the guitar do that," and so on. More and more, I began taking dictation from Mr. Brown and translating his grunts and moans into music for some of the finest musicians in the world to play.

The bands that Emile put together for me were fantastic. All great musicians. Some I knew of and some I had never heard of—every one of them excellent at their craft. That first session, where I did two of my originals and Dave did some songs that James had ordered, the band consisted of Jimmy Madison on drums, Bob Cranshaw on bass, Kenny Asher on Fender Rhodes piano, Charlie Brown on guitar, with Jerry Dodgion, Joe Farrell, and Seldon Powell on the saxes, and Lew Soloff and Marvin Stamm on trumpets. I played the trombone, of course.

I was so nervous and my mouth was so dry, I could hardly blow the horn, let alone talk and try to conduct the session. But Dave was there, constantly whispering in my ear and pulling my coat, while trying not to let everyone know that I didn't know what I was doing. It was big-time on-the-job training, and no matter how hard we tried to disguise it, my inexperience was obvious. The amazed look on my face when I heard played immediately and correctly what had taken me almost a week of painstaking writing and rewriting. Rhythms that I thought would take at least a minute to work out happened "right now" and just as had I imagined them. Chords that I had voiced and re-voiced to achieve a certain sound I heard so fast that I didn't realize I had heard them and would have to ask to hear them a second time. They were playing music that I had created faster than I could hear it. There was a spot in one of the tunes where I forgot to write flats on what were supposed to be E-flats for everyone. The entire band went up a half step in that bar. I almost stopped it but realized that it sounded kind of hip, then proceeded to take credit for a very creative and innovative move. I've never—until now—admitted that the half-step in "Wine Spot" was a mistake.

Through it all, the individual musicians were extremely cooperative. Jimmy Madison played the drum part that I had written so exactly that I had to tell him not to "adhere directly" to the music; I didn't realize how Shakespearean that sounded until the whole place burst into laughter. Joe Farrell played a solo that totally took me by surprise. I wrote the solo thinking I would get a funky solo like what Maceo or King Curtis would play. When I saw that the tenor player was Joe Farrell, I resigned myself to the fact that I was going to get a jazz solo, probably like Coltrane or Sonny Rollins. What I got was a funky yet jazzy Joe Farrell solo that has remained one of my all-time favorites. All of the musicians on that first session were top studio players back in 1971 and could have made it very difficult for a half-trained, young, road musician trying to break onto the New York recording scene as an arranger and producer. But they all were very patient with me, and the session was a tremendous success. That session yielded two of my tunes, "Blessed Blackness" and "Wine Spot," which became part of the JBs's *Food for Thought* album.

The next day I got an up-close critique of the session from Dave and Emile. The music was hardly criticized at all, but I got some very helpful tips about the logistics of recording and arranging. My scores were unnecessarily detailed, so I was shown shortcuts and abbreviations that saved me much time. I learned the value of good copyists, which Emile and the people on his staff were. We also decided that, in the future, we would use a system called multitrack recording. A system wherein you record sections of the music one at a time. The rhythm section is recorded first, and then horns, strings, vocals, and all other parts are stacked or overdubbed, one at a time. This gives the arranger and artist time, freedom, and control to do a perfect recording. Over the years, I have become a master at multitrack recording, and it started with the education I received from Dave Matthews and Emile Charlap, working with New York studio musicians, the power and financing of Polydor Records, and James Brown's backing and support all the way.

There were pros and cons to that on-the-job training. Yes, I was getting great experience at producing records and stage shows. I was getting paid, not nearly what I should have been, but I was also piling up future royalties from all the James Brown, JBs, Bobby Byrd, and Lyn Collins records, as well as all the other projects me and the Boss could come up with. On the other hand, I hardly had any time to myself. I was on call twenty-four hours a day. It seemed like, no matter where he was, James knew when I was about to eat, sleep, make love, or take a shit. The phone would ring. He would get an idea for a song, and I would have to stop what I was doing and write it down. If I was actually with him, I would write on napkins, shoe boxes, my hand, the wall, or anything else I could put my hands on. Often, if he was on the phone, I would keep on doing what I was doing but act like I was writing something down, then later on just make up a groove that sounded something like what I remembered him humming. He never knew the difference. If he could have remembered it, I would not have had to write it down in the first place. Still, all this was severe pressure. I would nearly jump out of my skin anytime I heard a phone ring.

More and more, we used the studio musicians in New York, which meant that, more and more, I would fly into New York on days that we didn't do shows. I was a busy musician. Mr. Brown was definitely into making a solo career for me, or so it seemed. I signed an artist contract with James Brown Productions, and Mr. Brown produced a solo album on me. He got Dave Matthews to contract some of the top musicians in New York to play with me on arrangements of tunes selected by, of course, Mr. Brown. We got Ron Carter on bass, Steve Gadd on drums, Hugh McCracken on guitar, Pat Rebillot on piano, Lew Soloff and Randy Brecker on trumpets, and Joe Farrell, Michael Brecker, Seldon Powell, and Eddie Daniels on woodwinds for the strictly jazz tunes. Gordon Edwards on bass and Cornell Dupree on guitar replaced Ron Carter and Hugh McCracken on the funkier stuff. We did such tunes as "Secret Love," "You've Got a Friend," "Alone Again, Naturally," and two originals by Dave entitled "Seulb"—a blues tune—and "Transmorgrapfication"—a funky-jazz, modal vamp. We also recorded, with the former rhythm section, my original ballad, "Sweet Loneliness," and, with the latter rhythm section, tunes such as "Use Me," "Everybody Plays the Fool," and "Get on the Good Foot."

The production was a complete success. (The album was never released in its entirety, although "Alone Again Naturally was the B side of the Fred Wesley and the JB's single "Watermelon Man," and "Transmorgrapfication" was part of the *Slaughter's Big Rip-Off* soundtrack.) I was thrilled to play with such great musicians, but I discovered that the dat-di-dat-dahs that I played regularly with the James Brown Show didn't prepare me to do the truly representative performance that I could have done had I been playing bebop everyday. I was forced to accept the fact that I was no longer a jazz trombone player, but an artist, a producer, and a music director. Not the path I had chosen for myself, but a respectable and profitable position to be in. I was happy, and I was proud.

About the middle of 1972 the band Maceo and All the King's Men was beginning to break up. These were my boys, and I always felt a little guilty for supporting James when I knew that the underlying reason for their departure was to bring him down. Bringing down James Brown would have been a good lesson for all stars who mistreat or underpay or deny proper respect to the people who support them. I had more or less come to Mr. Brown's rescue. Not that he would have fallen out of existence if I hadn't rejoined him and taken over the duties of music director. Mr. Brown would have survived—and survived big-time—one way or another. I had simply seen an opportunity to save myself from the oblivion I had been facing in L.A. I don't know for sure if James ever did anything overtly to cause their records to fail. I do know that he seemed pretty sure that they would not get any airplay, and they didn't. All I could do was wish them the best, and I did. It would have been great had they been successful. But I saw the handwriting on the wall when I heard that they had hooked up with Pete Tyler, the same man who had managed my band, the Mastersound, back in the late '60s. James had bet that they all would come crawling back, and he was right, I'm sorry to say. The first to return was the very pragmatic Jimmy Nolen, who had invested and lost a lot of his personal money in the group. James made him swallow *a lot of stuff* at first, but we both were glad to have that real, powerful, Jimmy Nolen chang-a-lang back in the band, although I hated to see such a great musician grovel his way back. I couldn't have done it. I think I would have eaten shit and drank muddy water rather than give Brown the satisfaction.

And it did give Brown great satisfaction to see Jimmy, then L. D. Williams, the tenor saxophone player, and Charles Sherrell (who had been fired for some silly reason before the others left as a unit) return, more or less begging for a gig. Charles was not only a great bass player, but he played keyboards, wrote and arranged music, and had a unique singing voice and style something akin to Marvin Gaye. When James brought Charles back to the gig, the first thing he did was to get me and Dave to produce an album on him. James gave him a new name right away. At first, Mr. Brown toyed with the idea of naming him Chuck Willis. Chuck Willis was a deceased singer who had two big hits in the early '60s: "C.C. Rider" and "What Am I Living For." Brown said that identifying Charles with a name that had already been famous would give him a head start on becoming famous himself. On further consideration, Brown finally agreed with us about the ridiculousness of that idea and dubbed him "Sweet Charles" instead, since Charles, for good reason, did fancy himself a ladies man. I think James might have said Sweet Charles as a joke, but Charles went for it because it flattered him and reinforced his belief that he was irresistible to women. I think James was a little jealous of Charles's tall, slim good looks and took every opportunity to rib him about his popularity with women.

In any case, the name stuck, and the album, which was completed in one week, was called *For Sweet People from Sweet Charles.* Dave and I wore a track in the sidewalk between the studio and Emile's office. We did rhythm, horns, strings, and background vocals on eight tunes. Dave wrote while I recorded. He recorded while I wrote. We were back and forth all day and half the night for almost a week. This project was a true testament to the organizational skills of Emile Charlap and our

Me and Bob Both. Photograph by Fred Wesley Jr.

staff engineer, Bob Both, and to the arranging and producing skills of Dave Matthews and myself. I came of age as a producer/arranger on this project.

I was ready to fly solo. A team was developing with me clearly in charge. My staff included Mr. Charles Bobbit, whose official title was president of James Brown Productions but whose duties included doing just about anything for James and making whatever legal, political, or diplomatic moves I needed made in order to expedite my recordings. (Bobbit went down on every music union contract as a trumpet player.) He made sure that I had all of the finances I needed. He oversaw the distribution of publishing credits and was general liaison between me, the Boss, and the record company. Together, Bobbit and I made everyone, including James, believe what we wanted them to believe in order to get things done. It was a real juggling act, but Mr. Bobbit was adept at it. I was learning.

Bob Both was the recording engineer hired by Polydor to take care of the studio operations. He moved the recording activity from A&R Studios, where Emile had us, to a new, state-of-the-art studio called Sound Ideas. Bob was only about twenty-one years old at the time, unusually excitable but a certified genius and very knowledgeable about the goings-on in the electronics field. Of course, Emile Charlap remained the copyist and the contractor for the musicians, as well as an advisor and mentor. Through him, I had access to all of the best musicians in the world. Dave continued as back-up arranger and consultant. The great tap dancer Mr. John T. McFee (who was kind of down on his luck in his waning years) served as my runner and general consultant about things pertaining to "the street." He was an invaluable member of the team and saved my life many times. Got me through many a sleepy night. Of course, everything I did was subject to the approval—or in most cases, disapproval—of Mr. James Brown. But I was having fun, having wonderful experiences, making good music, learning how to record, feeding my family, and almost being a star.

The star part was eluding me. I knew it, and Mr. Brown knew it too. We had released the *Food for Thought* album, and it was doing well. We did songs like "Pass the Peas" on the show, but if James wasn't on the stage, there was not a real spark to excite the audience. No matter how hard I tried, I just didn't feel right fronting the band by myself. If he was there going "Blow, Fred," I got down. The two of us back and forth on the mike I could handle. I felt funny, but he was still there. But me? By myself? My mouth got dry. My knees got wobbly. I broke out in a sweat. I never, during that part of my career, got comfortable being out in front of the band.

Mr. Brown was still pursuing his favorite pastime of playing games with peoples' lives. Bobby Byrd and Vickie Anderson had defied the Boss and bought a fabulous house in Houston, Texas. I guess you wonder why buying a house in Houston would be considered an act of defiance? Mr. Brown was dead-set on having everybody who worked for him live where he said and how he said. He was constantly after me to buy a house in Augusta, Georgia. Although I never for a second even thought of living in Augusta, I did lead him to believe that I *was* at least thinking about the move. I told you that I was getting good at making people believe what I wanted them to believe. I didn't want what happened to the Byrds to happen to me. As soon as Bobby and Vickie got settled in Houston, had bought a nice car, and had begun living the good life, James, for no good reason, fired them both. The Byrds, being totally dependent on their gig to support their affluent Texan lifestyle, were devastated. I guess they got too independent for J.B. He took every opportunity to demonstrate to us all that, without him, we were nothing and had nothing. Bobby was one of the original Famous Flames and had been with James from the beginning. If James could snatch the rug from under him like that, the rest of us knew that we could expect anything. It was a very insecure atmosphere that prevailed over the organization at all times, and I had to constantly guard against falling into one of those traps. My motto was: "Lay up for yourself treasures at the house for you know not the day or the hour when you might fall."

Firing the Byrds was bad enough, but the way he did it was really cold. He waited until we were to play Houston, which is Vickie's hometown, and just before the show, out of the blue, with all of her friends and relatives around, he told her that she couldn't go on. He said something about how her show wasn't happening anymore. The songs that she was singing weren't getting to the audience. The hurting part about it, the hard part about it for me was I had to agree with him. "Ain't that right Mr. Wesley?" Although I loved Momie-o, as she was affectionately known, and dearly and deeply respected her talent, I looked at it as part of my job to agree with the Boss. "Yes sir, Mr. Brown." "It's a new day." "We have to keep up with the times." I felt like a pile of doo-doo saying stuff like that right in front of Momie-o. She was like a big sister or even, at times, a mother to us younger guys. But what could I do except lose my job, too, by standing up for her? She was not only surprised but also hurt to the core. I know Bobby wanted to jump down the little nigger's throat, but for some reason he kept his cool and accepted the humiliation quietly. However, he did make it clear that if she was gone, so was he. This meant that I had to emcee the show, sing background on things like "Try Me" and "Please, Please, Please," do that "Git on Up" part on "Sex Machine," and play organ on "I Lost Someone." I was also into sucking it up and doing whatever had to be done.

We had all known to expect something because he had shown up in Houston with a new woman. Well, she wasn't exactly a new woman. She was Lyn Collins. We had seen her before down in Macon, Georgia, where we recorded her on two songs that she had written. I had wondered at the time who she was and why we were recording her. She was very beautiful but obviously not an experienced singer, although the recordings we had done of her songs had turned out very well. I dismissed her as some girl who the Boss was trying to get it on with. She did fit the general description of every woman I had ever seen him with. Light skin, pretty face, long hair, big ass.

J.B. always acted some-kinda-way funny when he was trying to impress someone, usually a woman, about how powerful he was and how he ruled with an iron hand. He raved about how good her songs were, now that we had recorded them, and said she could go onstage tonight and perform them. The only thing that topped the surprise on my face was the surprise on Lyn's face. She had thought that she had come to Houston for one thing and just now found out that she was about to go on-stage without ever having rehearsed at all. Sure, this was the same band that had recorded the songs, but that was weeks ago and in the studio. It was going to take some doing to get everyone to recall what was done a long time ago and do it right now. But, like I said, I was getting good, and my boys believed in me and I believed in them. Lyn turned out to be a real trooper, too. With only a few minutes of rehearsal, we felt that we could pull it off. And pull it off we did.

After Momie-o burst into tears, with embarrassment more than any-thing else, J.B. finally agreed to let her do one last song since it was her hometown. As if possessed, she showed James who she was and why they call her Momie-o. I've never seen her give a more fiery performance. She brought the house down. She left the stage and the show totally trium-phant. As if Lyn was not nervous enough, now she had to follow the most dynamic performance of Vickie Anderson's life. She handled it very well. The band handled it very well. I was very proud of how we all faced an impossible problem and overcame it with flying colors. We all kind of bonded with Lyn Collins that night, but at the end of the second song, she couldn't figure out how to get off the stage. As the emcee that night, I said "Lets have a big hand for Lyn Collins!" relieved that we had made it to the end. She backed up. I waited for her to take a bow and walk off the stage. The band was to keep playing the vamp of her tune until she got off stage, but we hadn't discussed exactly how she was to get off of the stage. I just assumed that she would know what to do. But she just kept slowly backing up, all the way until she backed into Jabo's drums. Again I said, "Lyn Collins." She just stood there, frozen with a strange kinda half smile on her face. The band continued the vamp, wondering what the hell was going on. Finally, I realized that she was in some kind of stupor and went over to her, wrested the mike from her hand, and led—almost dragged—her off the stage.

My title was music director for James Brown Productions. Mr. Brown had clearly explained to me that I was responsible for everything that happened on the stage or in the studio. What it really meant was that I was the fall guy. I took the final weight for whatever negative stuff went down. I couldn't hire anybody, or I didn't dare hire anybody. The one time I did, this drummer named Melvin Webb from Kansas City broke up his band, loaded his stuff onto the bus after the usual altercation with Ms. Sanders, rode to St. Louis, went straight onstage, played about four bars, and was waved out and sent right back home to Kansas City. I was really mad because he was a good drummer and I really needed his type of groove in the band, not to mention the fact that I had to hear him crying about how he had alienated himself from his band and had to go back and face them in disgrace. I remained cool, although I wondered why James had done that to me. He didn't even really hear the boy play. So I knew that it wasn't about that at all. He was just trying to teach me some kind of lesson. I sure did learn it. I never even suggested anyone for the band after that. I left that all up to him. Even if he asked me, I said, "I don't know anybody." But if anybody needed to be fired, I had to do it or take part in it, like what happened with Honey and the Bees, and Vickie.

I did the dirty work. I was the one who put the songs together in the studio, with both the studio bands and the road bands. When he showed up, the arrangements were already in place enough for him to praise or criticize. If he had the time, he would tear apart the music—and me, too—just to emphasize the point that he was in charge. If time didn't permit, he would simply do his vocals and take credit for the whole thing. I was the perfect little pawn in his little game. I took all the shots from the musicians, the record company, and anybody who had a beef with the show or the records. And when everything went right, I relinquished credit for my hard work to him without a fuss. When he trashed people, I helped him. When he praised people, I was there to reinforce whatever he said. "Yes sir, Mr. Brown." "You're right, Mr. Brown." "Anything you say, Mr. Brown." I said stuff like that so much that I made myself sick sometimes. However, I was convincing. James felt like I was the best thing since sliced bread. He grew to trust me as much as or more than anybody who had ever worked for him. And he never hesitated to tell people. He would hold me up to the band as an example of how to be a good employee. I was his trophy boy, and he showed me off to people in the industry. "Mr. Wesley here will go far in this business because he listens to what I tell him." "He does what I say." "He's a college man, but he listens to me, who only went to the sixth grade."

I didn't really believe in all the things that James said or did. I was simply being pragmatic. After my experience in California, I was convinced that a person has to have an edge to succeed in this business. I had missed my chance at a good education. I hadn't dedicated myself to mastering my instrument enough to be the great jazz player I wanted to be. The responsibility of marriage and kids had sidelined any thoughts I might have had about hanging out in New York and trying to hook up with the type of musicians I really wanted to get in with. My best alternative was clear. Get back with James Brown, who needed what I had to offer him, and be the kind of person who could deal with him and do for him what he needed done. It wasn't that I loved him or respected him so much—it was that I needed him to get what I wanted, which was to advance in the business. I had seen what happened to people who confronted James or tried to make sense out of what he did. I just went with the flow and, in a lot of cases, helped make the flow.

I was paying a heavy price, though. I was giving up all my moral and musical ethics. On the real side, I was ashamed to be associated with tunes like "Pass The Peas," "Gimme Some Mo'," and "Mo' Peas." Not only were the songs musically lightweight, but I thought the whole concept was, frankly, silly. I really didn't want musicians who I respected like Pratt, Noon, Coleman, or my Daddy to hear me playing stuff like that long slide thing at the beginning of my "Gimme Some More" solo. I thought that these things were a joke and that nobody would ever actually put it out, and if they did, that no radio station would dare play it. But I was wrong. For some reason, radio stations played it and people liked it. I really thought that I would die of embarrassment when I had to perform this silly shit on stage. But I was tough. I sucked it up and made a good show out of it every night.

I kept on putting together James's hums and grunts and groans, and making music out of them, no matter how stupid I thought it was. I began to take pride in my ability to make something out of anything or something out of nothing or something out of any combination of things. I gave James no trouble when he laid out formats to songs. I simply took the orders as he gave them, never questioning, and worried about how to make it happen later. But sometimes I had trouble getting the musicians to accept such unorthodox patterns as readily as I did. I had to argue, convince, trick, and manipulate guys into doing all kinds of unusual things. On one of the rare occasions when James was in the studio as I did a session with the studio guys, Gordon Edwards, the great bassist, was having trouble understanding what James was trying to get him to play. Finally Gordon, totally frustrated, got up, packed his bass, and told James to his face that he was crazy. He then faced me (I had been trying to help James explain what he wanted) and told me that I was crazy, too, for understanding what James was talking about, then stormed out of the studio. Another time James was trying to show Ralph McDonald, the great percussionist, a beat on his congas. McDonald had heard stories about James, including the Gordon Edwards story, and after only a few seconds simply walked out. After that, James hardly ever came to the studio when the session cats were there. He would wait until the basic tracks were done and they were gone, then would come in and terrorize me. He knew I could take it.

It was a different matter with the road band. He would want to be there as soon as I got the basics down. The road band was like a captive group. Their jobs, their livelihood, was based on doing anything that popped into the Boss's mind. He would really get creative with them. However, there is a thin line between creativity and tripping. My staff and I had to clean up a lot of his tripping, I mean, creativity after he had left the building. He knew who to terrorize and who not to terrorize. We, the people who were in close proximity to him on a regular basis, considered part of our pay to be an aggravation fee. We were, however, supposed to be paid extra, according to union scale, for all sessions and TV shows. The TV shows were not a problem. I simply turned in withholding forms to the TV show's union contractor and the checks came through sooner or later. Recording sessions were a different matter. We looked to the road manager, Freddy Holmes, or to Mr. Bobbit to give us our session money sooner and, in most cases, later.

James got this bright idea to record another song on Lyn. We were in Kansas, and somebody booked us a studio in a cave. The Boss said we should get a real good bass sound in a cave because it was already underground. The bus drove us right down into the cave. It was kind of weird, but there, underground, was a state-of-the-art recording studio. We waited for the Boss. Prior to the recording call, we had been enjoying some time away from James, who was with Lyn in Dallas, Texas. It was her turn to spend time with him and write songs, then bring them to me and the band.

While we waited, the guys in the band started to pin me down about getting paid for the sessions we had done earlier. I tried to explain to them that the session money didn't come from me, that it had to come from the Boss. They insisted that, since I was the bandleader, it was my job to get their money for them. I was owed money, too, but I wasn't as hard up for it as they were because I was getting paid regularly through the union for the sessions and the arrangements that I had been doing in

New York. Emile Charlap contracted all of those sessions, and Polydor had no problem paying them. I agreed that it was my place to see that we all got paid for the sessions, which we did all over the place in many different union jurisdictions. So we decided not to do this particular session until we got paid for the others. Being the bandleader, I was to ask the Boss about this matter as soon as he came in. I should have known that James would see this as a confrontation, but I had gotten a little too relaxed during my time off. And I really didn't mean it as an ultimatum. I simply planned to state the problem, which he would somehow resolve, and then everything would be all right.

Relaxed? I must have been sound asleep. When he came in, we exchanged our usual greetings.

"What's happening, Wes? You know we're hotter than we ever been."

"Yes sir, Mr. Brown, we the baddest in the world."

"Er, Mr. Brown, I'd like to talk to you about something before we get started."

"Sure, Wes. What is it?"

"The fellas and me want to get paid for the other sessions that we've done before we do this one."

He was facing me as I stood with my back to the other guys in the band.

"Who said it?" he asked me.

I said, "We all said it."

He walked around me and faced them and asked again, "Who said it?" looking them all in the face. They all were silent, kind of looking down and looking off. "Who said it?" Jimmy Parker started to mutter something when James cut him off and came around and got right in my face, yelling as he pointed his finger in my face.

"You said it! You said it! You're trying to pull that Maceo stuff on me again. I ain't going for it this time. You're fired!"

Now I'm awake. I realize what's happening to me. I stand up for someone else's money, and I get fired. I try to explain. "Mr. Brown, I didn't mean . . ."

"I don't wanna hear it. You're fired. Get your stuff and get out."

I was shocked and surprised that nobody stood up with me. After all, I was basically asking him for their money. It really wasn't that important to me. I got my stuff and left the studio. I didn't know how to get out. We were underground, for Christ's sake. And if I did find my way out of the cave, I still didn't know where I was. The last sign I had seen on the highway said Independence, Mo. Plus, all my stuff was on the bus. So I went to the bus and just sat there in the dark. I was hurt, disappointed with my brethren, and mad as hell. I didn't know what to do, so I just sat there fuming.

After about an hour, somebody came out and told me that he wanted me in the studio. At first, I said, "Fuck him. Fuck all y'all. Kiss my ass." But I had actually calmed down and had begun trying to figure out how to get back into everyone's good graces. I tried to remember that the reason I was here was to get as far in the music business as I could and to make as much money as possible. I guess James also was trying to figure a way to retract that "You're fired" without looking like he gave in. So I went back in and got right into my job, helping him with the chords and horn lines and things, just like nothing had happened. The band members still didn't get their money, and I sure as hell didn't ask for it again. In fact, that was the last time I ever asked for anyone's money other than mine. We continued business as usual, with me having learned another valuable lesson. When you're playing a game, be sure you know who is on your side and who is on their own side. In the James Brown game, everyone was forced to be on their own side. I learned that each person was there for his or her own reasons and dealt with the situation in his or her own way. Ironically, the song we recorded that night was Lyn Collins's "Think (About It)."

People in the James Brown organization were always getting fed-up and leaving. But there was said to be a mysterious force that always drew them back. Such a force must have caused Martha Harvin to return. Martha had been with the show years before I joined, the first time with a group called the Jewels. Mr. Brown said that she had returned just to sing background. I suspect it was also to keep Lyn off balance. Martha was a very good singer, older that Lyn but good-looking for her age and always well dressed and impeccably groomed. She was living in Washington, D.C., at the time and later sent for another singer from D.C. named Binkie. Although they didn't need a name other than the James Brown singers, James dubbed them the Soul Twins—not that they looked anything alike. The whole thing might have been a ploy to diminish the stardom of Lyn Collins. She had come from nothing to, overnight, become the featured female singer on the James Brown show. Mr. Brown was a firm believer in having everyone, no matter how good or important they were, pay some dues before taking center stage. So, in the beginning, Lyn went onstage with Martha and Binkie as Lyn Collins and the Soul Twins.

The Boss insisted that I dress in a suit and tie at all times. I didn't mind that. I kind of liked being dressed up. Keeping a wardrobe like that cleaned and pressed at all times was somewhat of a problem, but I dealt with it. The Man, however, was also always on my case about getting my hair fixed. This I didn't want to do. Too much trouble. People would think I was a pimp or something.

And let's talk about hair. Lets talk about Elvis, Patti LaBelle, Lyle Lovett, Michael Jackson, Dennis Rodman, Dolly Parton, Cyndi Lauper, Prince, Grace Jones, Bob Marley, and Lenny Kravitz, just to name a few. From James Brown to Coolio to Fabio, hair seems to be the single most important element of a star's attire. From weaves to Jheri Curls. From wigs to relaxers. Every star or would-be star spends an inordinate amount of time fussing with his or her hair. The most important piece of equipment on the James Brown tour, for instance, was the hairdryer. "Where's the hairdryer?" was a constant cry. When you see a band, you can easily tell what each member is about. The ones totally into the music and satisfied with being sidemen will have normal or indifferent haircuts. The would-be stars, usually singers and tenor players, will have some type of bizarre hairdo. Observing bands as I grew up, I noticed that most of the serious jazz players like Diz, J.J., Trane, and even Miles had normal hair. Whereas singers and what we called rock-and-roll and blues players always had some kind of thang done to their hair.

In the old days, it was the "process." It was just that. A process by which the hair was "burned" with a lye product until it was straight and then waved or styled into a pompadour or some other curly creation. In recent years, hair technology has progressed to include "the weave," "the Jheri Curl," "falls," various types of extensions, dreadlocks, braids, and all sorts of wigs. These hair phenomena can be applied to both men and women. I'm sure Nick Ashford, for instance, didn't grow his long curly locks naturally—it was probably a weave. In the early '80s almost everybody I knew had a Jheri Curl or some variant thereof. The cry of the era was "Where's my moisturizer?" I think Michael Jackson must have a combination of every hair thang known to man and something flammable that he made up himself. Many people think James Brown wears a wig or a weave, but I know for a fact that that is his real hair, conditioned daily, rolled up and dried, and regularly relaxed. It takes a lot of time out of your day, but it is beautiful. I know. I wore the same thing myself for two years. I would have to allow an extra two hours every day for my hair—that or look like something the cats drug in. If I took care of it religiously, it looked so good and grew so long that all my friends, even women friends, were envious. But if I missed a day, I would have to stay in the house or wear a hat or one of those "mammy rags."

I finally had to wear his hairstyle to convince Mr. Brown that I was on his side. You see, Mr. Brown has an innate mistrust of people who don't wear the hairdos. Wearing the do separated me from the regular guys in the band. It proved that I was trying to one day be like him and that I was therefore on the side of management. I looked like a star even though I was still a sideman inside. He was correct in saying that you are perceived differently when you pursue stardom. Your peers begin to watch what they say around you, because you're no longer into music for the sake of music—you're now reaching for something beyond doing a good show. Now you're trying to please the Boss and might do anything to anybody as long as he is all right with you. I also was getting perks from record-company executives, promoters, DJs, groupies, and anyone else who saw me as a way to get close to the Man. And the Man felt better about confiding in me and allowing me to represent him in important situations, because he felt that I had demonstrated a desire to climb farther up the ladder and so had a stake in properly doing his bidding.

Of course, I wouldn't say the hair was the only thing that got me the new respect that I was enjoying—I was also doing as well at the musical aspects my job as I was at the political and diplomatic aspects.

The first movie Mr. Brown scored, *Black Caesar,* was a political and diplomatic nightmare for me. Since I was music director of James Brown Productions, when it came down to actually doing the music, Mr. Brown gave the whole thing to me. I met with the producer-director. I met with the music coordinator, who gave me the theme song to arrange. After that, I met with Mr. Brown, and together we arranged the theme, "Down and Out in New York City." As per my meetings with the movie people, I reported to him that we needed music for a chase scene, a funeral scene, a love scene, and so on. He gave me basic outlines for the chase scene and a couple of other things, including "Paid the Cost to Be the Boss." I recorded the tracks, some with the road band and some with the New York studio players. Brown came in and did the vocals. This was clearly not enough music; the first sessions only provided about 30 percent of the music needed to complete the score.

So he instructed me to inform the movie people that we would use some of his old, previously recorded songs for the rest. "Try Me" for the love scene. "I Lost Someone" for the scene where his mother dies. That sort of thing. The music coordinator, Barry DeVorzon, totally freaked out. This was during the time when Isaac Hayes and Curtis Mayfield were doing all brand-new music for movies. I don't think that James understood that we all stood to make a killing on publishing with the release of the soundtrack. (It's a funny thing that nowadays using old music is a popular idea.)

Mr. Brown would not budge from his position of using old music, and Barry and producer Larry Cohen insisted on new music. Mr. Brown and the movie people refused to talk to each other, relaying messages only through me. Once again, I was on the spot because both sides were depending on me to get it done their way. So, along with Mr. Bobbit and Barry, I decided to go ahead and write the music that was needed to complete the score. I wrote a song called "Mama's Dead," a "Love Theme," and some other pieces that were needed to complete the score. The movie was finished without Mr. Brown actually seeing it or knowing about the extra music I had written. I felt terrible about deceiving the Boss, but I convinced myself that it was for his own good. It certainly was for my own good to get my name on a movie score, even if only as orchestrator. If we hadn't finished, we would almost certainly have lost the score to someone who was easier for them to deal with.

At the premiere, Mr. Brown and his entourage sat down front with Fred Williamson, the star, and Larry Cohen. Mr. Bobbit and I sat way in the back, so as to avoid the immediate and direct ire we knew would be coming when Mr. Brown heard "Sportin' Life" and "Love Theme" instead of "Maybe the Last Time" and "Try Me." When he heard "Love Theme," he turned around, looked directly at me, and mouthed the words, "You're fired." Although I did feel guilty about going behind his back, for some reason his firing me like that made me very angry. I couldn't wait to get to him and explain how I had saved the movie for him and what I had been through—flying back and forth from the gigs to New York, staying up all night writing and recording—to pull this off for him. I just generally wanted to give him a piece of my mind. After months of pressure— hiding what I was doing from him and dealing with these Hollywood people by myself—I was ready to explode.

When the movie was over, I tried unsuccessfully to get to him, as he was surrounded by people who were congratulating him on the wonderful score. He was even getting more attention than Fred Williamson. He saw me and made his way over just to say, "You stabbed me in my back" and to tell me to wait because he wanted to talk to me. Damn right, I'll wait. I wanted to talk to him, too. How dare he accuse me of stabbing him in the back? It was because of *me* that he was getting all these accolades for scoring a movie he had never even seen before. When he finally got away, I was ready to choke his little black ass. He approached me and Mr. Bobbit, who had waited with me, and said, "Good job, fellas." When he said that, all the anger drained out of me. The rest of the night, I had to hear about what a good team we were. How well we worked together. He was exactly right, but he had no idea about all I had had to do to make our collaborations come out looking good and sounding good.

At that point, that "come-back force" had failed to work its magic on Maceo. J.B. often mentioned Maceo. Have you seen him? Have you talked to him? Do you think he's ready to come back? We did need him, and I had talked to him. Maceo was really in a funny place, mentally, with regard to the whole music business. He was seriously bummed out about the failure of All the King's Men. Not only was he disillusioned by the people who controlled the business of music, he also was disappointed with his musicians and friends who, at the end, were unable to hang together and survive the turmoil. I think that he was through with the music business altogether. He had even sold his sax. Financially in trouble, he had taken a job with his father-in-law, collecting trash in Brooklyn.

I passed on to him that the job was available if he wanted it, although I didn't want to see him go through the humiliation that we both knew James was going to put him through. On the other hand, I knew that he needed the job, so I promised that I would protect and shield him from whatever I could. Maceo continued to resist. In a way, I was proud of him for taking a stance, but I knew that he was suffering. I didn't like to see that. So I didn't encourage him one way or another. But, while I wasn't looking, somebody was talking some other kind of talk to Maceo, because I looked up one day and there he was—in the studio as we were recording "Doing It to Death." Right away, he got to play a feature solo on flute as a welcome-back perk. I also managed to do a solo on that track. (Thanks loads.)

The next thing that we did was record an entire album on Maceo. This time it was all on me to produce. And Mr. Brown, of course. The songs were, as usual, selected by Mr. Brown. We did instrumental versions of the then-current hits "Show and Tell" by Al Wilson; "Drowning in the Sea of Love" by Joe Simon; "Just You and Me" by Chicago; and a dynamic version of "Man's World," which we re-titled "Soul of a Black Man" and which has become a Maceo trademark. There also were a few originals made up from some funky tracks that we already had in the can. We titled the album *Us* and released it immediately.

The Boss hadn't yet put Maceo through any of that proverbial shit that I had expected. Quite to the contrary, Mr. Brown was giving Maceo everything but a parade and a party. Maceo took his usual solos on "Cold Sweat" and "I Feel Good." And we didn't do any special rehearsing to find Maceo a part. Not that he needed it, but I did expect some concentrated, intense rehearsing designed to demonstrate to Maceo that everything was different and that he had to relearn the show, as had been the case when Jimmy Nolen returned. But no—Maceo went right onstage and just kind of found himself a place and a part. I was glad. I hate to rehearse the same thing over and over and was happy that my buddy didn't have to go through any unnecessary hassle. At least, not yet. You never know what's on the Man's mind.

I'm not an envious person, but it did occur to me that Maceo, who had caused a mutiny in the James Brown organization, was now back and reaping benefits from that organization, which I had been instrumental in restoring. This didn't seem fair to me. I had been promised a record deal in return for keeping the organization flourishing. I had recorded an album, but it hadn't been released yet. We did have a few tunes out there with prominent Fred Wesley solos on them, but there still weren't any records—either singles or albums—circulating with Fred Wesley as the artist. While I did have some writing credits, there was a single ("Soul of a Black Man") *and* a whole album by the prodigal Maceo. I didn't want to see Maceo punished for his attempt at revolution, but I did expect at least a comparable reward for my loyalty, however contrived it might have been.

When I brought this disparity to the attention of the Boss, he reminded me of the value of publishing residuals versus artist residuals. He also assured me that I would get the records he had promised me. To prove this, he was putting out *Doing It to Death* under the name Fred Wesley and the JBs. This made me happy. With Mr. Bobbit's help, I had my contract amended so that I received half of all artist royalties earned by Fred Wesley and the JBs. The JBs half went to Mr. Brown, of course.

This new agreement was made just in time. *Doing It to Death* was released in the summer of 1973 and took off like wildfire. "Doing It to Death (Gonna Have a Funky Good Time)" was an essential part of every party, picnic, and barbecue throughout the country that year and in the years that followed. That song also became one of the big production numbers on the show, with my big solo, me and James doing the down D, funky D thang, and the big flute solo that Maceo rejoined the band just in time to record. Talk about being in the right place at the right time. The *Us* album had not done very well but the single "Soul of a Black Man" got Maceo a lot of attention, especially as part of James's rendition of "Man's World" on the show. Maceo's solo was one of the highlights.

Early in 1974, Mr. Brown ordered me to take Maceo into the studio to do an instrumental version of "Soul Power." We simply removed the James Brown vocal and replaced it with a horn line played by me and Maceo. The rest was Maceo's solo. We released it as the single "Soul Power 74," which took off like a rocket, and Maceo was all the way back to the big-time. James, for the first time, had two hot soloists both on the show and on records. The Boss really enjoyed having the two of us to play against each other. On the road, we pretty much knew who would play which solo on what tune and where—but not necessarily. He would surprise or trick us anytime he could catch one or both of us off-guard. It got to be a game that kept everybody on their toes. It was fun for us, and the audiences enjoyed it tremendously. In the studio, James played the same game: Who would he call to play the solo? Would he say "Maceo, won't you blow?" or "Hit me, Fred"? Be ye ever so ready.

The period between 1973 and 1975 was action-packed for me as music director for James Brown. We recorded a lot of music that was used in albums for Fred Wesley and the JB's, Lyn Collins, Bobby Byrd, and James Brown. We never did another Maceo album or another Sweet Charles album. We never did another album on Fred Wesley the single artist, but we did release some inconsequential singles on me from that one jazz album. *Breakin' Bread, Damn Right I am Somebody,* and *Hustle with Speed* were subsequent Fred Wesley and the JBs albums. We also did two albums on Lyn Collins, *Check Me Out if You Don't Know Me By Now* and *Think (About It);* one on Bobby Byrd, *I Need Help;* and three on James Brown, *Reality, Hell,* and *The Payback.* We also used some cuts from the Fred Wesley jazz album in the second movie that we scored and on some selected Fred Wesley and the JBs albums. We also did some music on some artists outside of the "First Family of Soul," as people now referred to us. Johnny Scotton, Stan Holland, and a group called the Variations come to mind.

My old boss, Hank Ballard, had resurfaced, and Mr. Brown was supposed to be giving him one more chance at a recording career. But it seemed to me that Brown was using Hank to demonstrate how not to succeed in the music business: Here's a man who went to the top and blew it. Here's a man who wrote and recorded "The Twist," then lost it. He didn't take care of business—didn't know the business like I do. He would say things like that about Hank on TV and everywhere. Hank took the humiliation in stride and became part of the James Brown entourage. Hank, by the way, was the person who had introduced James to Ben Bart of Universal Attractions. Bart had become James's manager and was responsible for his early success. So it can be said that Hank gave James his first big break. Now, James was making it appear as though he were returning the favor. I didn't even try to understand the psychology behind this association. We never did another Hank Ballard album, after *You Can't Keep a Good Man Down* (1969), although we did try to put his voice on a couple of tracks that were lying around and released a single, but with no real success. All the artists except James Brown were released on the People label, which was owned by James and distributed by the Polydor conglomerate. The mainstays of the label were Fred Wesley and the JB's and Lyn Collins.

James Brown's second movie score was for *Slaughter's Big Rip-Off,* starring Jim Brown. Same music man, Barry DeVorzon. Although this movie proceeded more smoothly than the first one, the problem was that they wanted us to do the music in Hollywood so that Barry could keep closer tabs on what was going on. This was good for me in one sense and bad for me in another sense. My home and family were in L.A., so I would get to be home more and make some L.A. contacts. But my well-oiled recording machine was in New York. This meant that I had to hire another contractor and get used to new musicians and a new studio and engineer. The great trombonist Benny Powell and his wife, Petsy, took the contracting job and put me in touch with some very good musicians. Snooky Young, Cat Anderson, Ernie Watts, Harvey Mason, Chuck Rainey, Ndugu, and Joe Sample were just some of the great musicians that I was happy to meet and pleased to have work with me. Although we never settled on a studio or an engineer, moving around from place to place, I was better equipped to communicate with engineers and musicians than I had been when I first started in New York.

The California sessions went smoothly, as James, again, hardly saw the movie or got involved at all until I had finished the basic tracks. Lyn got involved more on this movie, helping me write some of the new songs and performing two of her own on the score. Everyone was pleased with the outcome of *Slaughter's Big Rip-Off,* both the movie score *and* the soundtrack. I was really pleased. I made a lot of money, as well as numerous friends and contacts in L.A.—something I hadn't had when I made L.A. my home. If I ever left James Brown again, I would fare better in L.A. than I had the first time.

The gig was getting to be routine. For some reason, the James Brown Show was not as popular as it had been in the late '60s. Since we only played on the weekends, for the most part, most of my work was in New York in the studio. I really hated to interrupt what I was doing to go somewhere like Milwaukee, where the crowd would be sparse at best. I was tolerating the show in order to record. And record I did. My team and I were having a good time, basically experimenting. With James's often ridiculous ideas—he would get wind of certain instruments and order me to use them in impossible situations—we were doing things that had never been done before. We did some very innovative things with strings, for instance. We put woodwind instruments like the oboe and the English horn to new uses. When James discovered the harp, he and I went harp crazy, trying to put harp on anything and everything, especially when I discovered that Corky Hale and Margaret Ross could play jazz on the instrument. The only constant was that it had to be funky.

It was a sweet time in my life, a time in which I gained an immeasurable amount of knowledge while earning a good living. Everything was totally financed, without question, by Polydor Records, for a long time anyway. The devil that I had to pay was spending time with James Brown. Most of the time, he went his way and I went mine. We would meet after the shows to evaluate the completed recordings and plan for the next ones. Often, James would come to New York with me to do vocals or to take care of some business in the New York office. This was expected, and I could deal with it. The hard part was when he "let" me fly with him to whatever central point he was working from—such as Dallas, Cincinnati, Miami, or Nashville. These trips were torture. It meant that I would have to be on the airplane with him and Lyn; watch them eat (he would not offer anybody else food: "You should have gotten yourself something before we left"); ride in a rented car with him to the hotel (he drove like he was on a race track—as fast as the car would go, passing every car any way he could on either side of the road or on the sidewalk, backing up on freeways if he missed an off-ramp, and just generally scaring the for real shit out of me and everybody else in the car, laughing and talking all the time); and deal with all kinds of other madness.

Once he got mad at a pilot at 30,000 feet. He accused the man of disrespecting him and cursed him out—calling him boy and talking about his mama—then pulled his gun and threatened to kick his ass and/or shoot him right there in the plane, reminding him all the time that he was James Brown and could buy and sell him and this plane. It was one of the scariest hours of my life. I was debating whether to knock James out or just hope that his reason would take over and that he would wait, at least until we landed, before he started shooting. Fortunately, he calmed down before anything serious happened. That was the last I saw of that pilot, and I started making plans to get the hell out of there myself.

When we would get to the hotel the real torture began. We—usually me, Lyn, and sometimes Mr. Bobbit—would have to sit and listen to him go on and on about how he was the only black person in the world doing anything. Everybody else was either controlled by "the man" or was "selling out." Nobody was selling records but us. Nobody was making money on shows but us. He was bigger than Sinatra and Elvis put together. We had to sit there and go, "Yes sir, Mr. Brown," "You're right, Mr. Brown." Then he would come up with some outlandish orders like "Mr. Bobbit, call the White House. Make an appointment with the president," or something else completely off the wall. "Fred, I want you to get the best Latin band in New York and record all my big hits like, 'Please, Please,' 'I Feel Good,' and 'Cold Sweat' in a Latin style."

• • •

What was it that kept people from confronting James Brown about the things he said and did? No matter how silly, no matter how stupid, no matter how totally untrue, no matter how brutal, he always got away with it. Once, he told me that he was going to run for president, and that I was going to be his running mate. This was after I had been away from the organization for years. Why didn't I say, "Go to hell and don't call me no more with this silly shit?" There was another time in a dressing room in Macon, Georgia, when James pulled a gun on Jimmy Nolen and slapped him repeatedly. We all just stood around and did nothing like a bunch of punks. Why didn't we jump on the little motherfucker, kick his ass, and dare him to say anything about it? There were numerous times when we saw evidence that he had blackened Lyn's eyes and bruised her body. We said nothing and just pretended that it hadn't happened. Pee Wee and I actually saw him beat up Marva Whitney one time and didn't say or do anything.

I don't think that it was fear. I don't believe that he ever could have whipped me physically. I know that he couldn't whip a group of us together. I think it was his aura of power that made everyone he came in contact with respect and fear him while in his presence. It was the same kind of dominance that slave owners exerted over their slaves. The same type of total power that abused women feel helpless against. There was plenty of after-the-fact rap about what you should or could have done, but as it was happening, you just went along with the tyranny—making up all kinds of excuses and reasons to justify your inaction. You would think that a show and recordings produced in this kind of atmosphere would be obvious to the audiences. But even when the band was totally pissed off or totally subjected to a reign of terror, people enjoyed the performances just as much as they did when everything was okay. So, no matter how poorly James treated the band, there were no consequences in the music. This was yet another testament to the entertainment power of James Brown. When he started singing and dancing, everything negative flew out the window for the band and for the audience.

Strong bonds formed among the people who worked for James Brown, especially the ones closest to him, including me, Mr. Bobbit, Lyn, Maceo, and Ms. Sanders, who was renowned for "running and telling it." Sure, we were all there for different reasons, were abused in different ways, and handled the abuse in different ways, but we were all united by our common disdain for the man. Our favorite pastime was to get together and laugh about the crazy things that he had done or said. We compared notes on what he had said to one about the other and on the different slants he put on the same issue, according to which one of us he was dealing with. For some reason, we didn't worry about any of us running and telling what went on within this exclusive little clique. Although a similar bond existed between everyone in the organization, most invested less and consequently had less at stake, so events and situations were less funny and less tragic. I think Lyn and I laughed the hardest and cried the longest. My heart really went out to Lyn because she had to be with him all the time, except when he had another woman or went home. Then she got to ride the bus with us and was like a young colt out of the barn. Most of her out-of-the-barn time was spent with me because I was the only one in the band that she had really gotten to know. We got to be really close friends.

I can't speak for everyone, but I had begun looking and planning for a way out. My yes-man posture was beginning to cause a real pain in my back—my lower back. I was less and less convincing as a yes-man as my justifications for being there got weaker and weaker. My reply to "Ain't that right, Mr. Wesley?" went from "Yes sir, Mr. Brown" to "Uh huh" to a very weak nod of the head. Every day I came closer and closer to telling the Boss exactly what I thought of him and his silly-ass music. But I was getting credit for a lot of the music, as most people were looking at the music as James's and mine together. While I admit that I did most of the implementation of the music, the concepts were practically all his. It didn't sit right with me to be getting credit for music, especially since, frankly, I didn't think it was all that great. Deep down, I wanted to do my own music. My music would be much cleaner, with better forms and more meaningful lyrics and better performances. I got this sick feeling when anyone told me how great "Pass the Peas" was. I would say, "Yeah, but listen to this," and play something like "Blessed Blackness" or "Wine Spot" from the same album. I would get a sympathetic "Oh yeah, that's good, too." I wanted so much to get away from James to go record my own album and show everyone what great music I could do on my own. But who would sign me? I was under contract to J.B. Productions, and no way was I ever going to do anything but a James Brown–sounding record as long as I was here. I would just have to bide my time and look for a way out.

I was kept too busy most of the time to think about leaving. The show had expanded to include three dancers. With Martha High and Binkie, the Soul Twins, Lyn Collins, Sweet Charles Sherrell, and a serious JBs set, we were now presenting a James Brown extravaganza. Before, I had been very happy just to play all the songs in the correct order with as few mistakes as possible and nobody dying or getting seriously injured. Now I had to choreograph, stage, and produce a pretty complicated show—complete with openings, segues, interludes, and introductions. Mr. Brown had made it clear to me that, as music director, everything and anything that happened on the stage was my responsibility. The music and show part was hard enough, but I had to deal with all these sensitive, star-type personalities. The guys in the band were familiar to me. Most of the time I had no problem dealing with them, as long as they got paid and had their fun with the girls and playing cards and such. Every now and then, I would have to use some homespun or street psychology on them to keep them loving me.

Integrating the dancers into the show presented a slight problem. There was Lola, who was an educated speech therapist, out with us as a

Ladies of the James Brown show: Lyn, Martha, Lola. Photograph by Fred Wesley Jr.

dancer for the sheer fun of it. She was a for real wild-child who reminded me of my daughters. She was so sexy and so fine that I was afraid she would cause trouble between guys in the band, but she was smarter than she appeared to be and knew how to handle such things. Then there was Gloria, a veteran dancer who, at times, gave me some ego and attitude problems, but I went to my diplomatic skills and kept her in line and on her toes. And David, who was a very sweet guy but also streetwise and not to be taken lightly. He grew up in Harlem and could take care of himself in any situation, no matter how rough.

Meshing all of these performers together onstage and offstage was a challenge. The offstage part sort of took care of itself naturally. Martha, Lyn, and Lola became good friends; Gloria and Ms. Sanders had similar backgrounds and friends in common; the guys in the band were arranged into groups of gamblers, whoremongers, and druggies; and I was everybody's friend. I was known as the wild card. Whatever came up or went down, I might or might not be involved in it. I was even known to spend time with the girls. I had no self. As always, I was whatever I needed to be in order to keep things running smoothly, but my main job, as always, was to be the buffer between the show and the Man. I had everybody

Surrounded by Africans. First on left: Ms. Sanders; kneeling in center (with glasses): me; standing, seventh from right, David Butts; fifth from right, Johnny Griggs; fourth from right (with mustache), Maceo. Courtesy of Photographie General, Dakar, Senegal.

thinking what I wanted them to think. The Boss thought that I was totally on his side, and the band thought I was totally on their side. The truth is that I was on the side of keeping peace and getting the job done.

It seemed that every time I really got fed up, something would come along that caught my interest. Going to Africa was certainly interesting to me. We went to Senegal—a democratic, French-speaking, West African nation—and played in a soccer stadium in the capital city of Dakar. The people loved us to the point of hysteria. The local police had anticipated the crowd rushing the stage, so they had set up a strong fence to keep the audience about twenty feet away. Still there were people who risked a serious ass-kicking to get as close to the stage as they could. One young man jumped the fence and eluded the police for quite a long time, much like Gale Sayers or Barry Sanders, until the police caught up with him and beat him with a pistol belt until he appeared to be dead. I remember thinking that Africans were still a bit primitive to stand by and watch a man be beaten to death and continue to focus their attention on the show. I was devastated and still wonder if the man lived or died. On the whole, though, I think that we were as entertained as the Africans were, watching the police chase people around the stadium. James demonstrated his endurance, to my amazement, by jumping off the ten-foot-high stage and running a lap around the stadium, wearing his "Please, Please, Please" robe, after singing and dancing for two hours. The audience loved it, and he lived to tell about it.

The next day we were taken on a tour of Gorée Island, which is where Africans had been taken, held, and loaded onto the slave ships to be transported to the "new world." We visited holding pens where slaves—men, women, and children—had been packed, one on top of the other. Although, these pens had been designed to hold ten to fifteen people, they had usually been forced to accommodate up to sixty. We saw the holes in the ship walls from which the sick and lame slaves had been thrown out into the Atlantic Ocean for the sharks to eat. Mr. Brown was so affected by these stories that he broke down and began to sob uncontrollably. We were all surprised to see such a cold-hearted person so moved by these sights. Although I did get an overpowering feeling of remorse and horror, I didn't cry and nobody else did, either. I figure it was some kind of act to get attention, because Brown stopped crying immediately after the tour guide whispered to him that a man should not cry in front of Africans, as they would take it as a sign of weakness.

The tour took us to two cities in Cameroon: Douala and Yaoundé. One of our most famous laughing sessions happened in Cameroon. The show time was delayed because Mr. Brown wouldn't go on until the promoter paid the balance of the fee, as required by the contract. The place was packed, and the promoter promised that all he needed was for James to hit. He could then collect the money, and the contract would be fulfilled. Mr. Brown said no—money first. The promoter said he could not pay the money until the people were sure that there would be a show. It was a standoff until the government police stepped in, insisted that the show begin, and guaranteed that they would collect the money. After the show, Mr. Bobbit went to see if the police had collected the money as promised. He discovered that they had collected it all right—and kept it, along with our return airline tickets. This left us stranded in the hotel for a week while Mr. Bobbit, James, and government diplomats from Cameroon and the United States tried to sort out the problem.

With nothing much to do since we had no money, we got involved in a pretty serious game of Acey-Deucey. We started playing in my room for pennies, and the game went on for two or three days with players in and out, and nobody really winning or losing any significant money until one pot kept growing until it got up to $1,200 dollars, on credit, of course. When the pot hit that figure, we all just walked away, left the cards on the table, and completely forgot who owed who what. With the game ended, we commenced our other favorite pastime, verbal Boss-bashing. We were way off into "James did this" and "the Boss said that" and laughing until it hurt when the phone rang. It was him. I motioned for everybody to be quiet. He said, "What's happening, Wes?" I said, "Oh nothing, Mr. Brown. We're just sitting here anxious to get back to the studio." He had always advised me to not associate with "the fellas" in the band. He said that I couldn't be their leader and hang out with them at the same time. I couldn't do the things that they did. I had to be above them. His motto was "You can't be big and little at the same time"—complete bullshit to me, but I always let him believe that I followed his suggestion. So I couldn't let him know that Maceo, Sweet Charles, Danny Ray, Cheese, Jasaan, Fred Thomas, and Russell Crimes were all in my room, along with two African girls.

Mr. Brown started into his usual boring talk about how big he was all over the world and how we needed to tighten up the show and how glad I should be to be with him. He mentioned that he had gotten some record by some African artists and that we should copy them for our own personal use. I was doing my usual agreeing thing, going "Yes, sir," "Uh huh," "You're right," "I am glad," "Okay," "I'll do it." The guys picked up on the fact that I was talking to the Boss and trying my best to be serious. So they got the idea, probably from Maceo, to try to make me laugh. First, they started making faces. Then tickling my feet. But nothing they could do made me break. I kept going "Yes, sir" "Uh huh." One of the African girls, who spoke very little English, realized what was happening. She went into the bathroom, got a roll of toilet paper, and started wrapping it around my ankle. I thought it was real strange, but I did not react. She then poured water on the paper. I didn't (and still don't) know what this was about—probably some African joke. Still I didn't break. I kept it up. Didn't break, didn't laugh. "Uh huh," "Right," "You know you right." Finally, Charles Sherrell came out of the bathroom with a sheet wrapped around him, stood right in front of me, flung it open, stood there buck naked, then did a little dance. I still didn't break, but I did almost laugh. After about an hour of this, everyone left the room one by one until I was there by myself, still going "Right," "Uh huh," "Okay." Finally, he hung up, and I sat there in the room by myself and laughed until I almost fainted, with nobody to witness it. I felt real silly. I should have told him that I was busy and to call back later. Much later.

A representative of the people of Gabon named Jimmy Ondo was at the Douala concert and invited us to his country to perform for their president and his family. We didn't have many open days in our schedule in which to return to Africa so soon. But they offered to pay an exorbitant amount of money and to send a private airplane anywhere in the world to pick us up and take us back. Somehow, a week got freed up, and, sure enough, an Air Gabon Boeing 747 came to Dallas, Texas, picked up the entire show and all of the equipment, and flew us to Paris, where we checked in to the Meridian Hotel at the foot of the Champs-Elysees to spend the night. The next afternoon, we reboarded the Air Gabon 747 and flew to Libreville, the capital of Gabon.

We were greeted like royalty and checked into the ultramodern International Hotel. We were given a tour of the city and the elaborately decorated palace of the president. We were introduced to the president, Mr. Albert Bernard Omar Bongo, and his wife, Madam Bongo, as well as their daughters, Pascaline and Albertine, and their son, Alain. The president was very gracious, but it was Madam and the children who seemed to be most interested in James Brown and us as entertainers. In fact, Alain was somewhat of a musician himself and had done some recording with his friend and our host, Jimmy Ondo. Jimmy was a singer and actor who had had some success in Germany with his own TV show. Alain, who was about sixteen at the time, played keyboards, sang, and wrote songs. He had a fairly well-equipped studio in his part of the palace. I spent a little time with him listening to his mediocre songs. I spent more time with Jimmy Ondo, who was an adult and had lived all over the world, including New York, so we had a few more things in common than I had with Alain. Ondo also was a pretty good guitar player and singer who had had some experience on stage. But he was definitely and foremost a hustler, and his main mission was to get with James Brown on some business scheme with President Bongo. I wanted no part of that. Jimmy realized that I would not be any help to him in that venture, so he turned his attentions to Mr. Bobbit, who handled James's money business.

The show went very well, even though the audience was not quite as exuberant as in the other parts of Africa. The crowd seemed to be limited to the more affluent citizens of the country. After the show, we all were treated to a reception and an elaborate dinner during which champagne flowed unceasingly and the food was prime everything—

from lobster to some elegantly prepared local dishes. Mr. Brown, who always traveled with a trunk full of American canned goods and nabs, had his man Leon Austin—a jack-of-all-trades friend of his from Augusta who did everything from singing to hairdressing to cooking—open up a couple cans of Dinty Moore beef stew for him and his immediate entourage. Mr. Bongo, who could have very well been insulted, took it as funny and graciously asked to taste the canned delicacy. He patronizingly said, with his French-African accent, "very good." The rest of us enjoyed the feast to the point of overeating and overdrinking, trying to sample everything on the amply endowed table and to ingest as much of the rarely available-to-us Dom Perignon as possible. It was truly a first-class state dinner attended by all of the local dignitaries. We were all treated just as any diplomats would have been treated. I brought us all back down to earth and gave the entire party a big laugh when I accidentally mooned the presidential table by ripping the seat of my pants when rising for a toast. It was one of my most embarrassing moments.

Our trip to the Zaire Music Festival was a little different. Fight promoter Don King and music festival producer Lloyd Price had teamed up with Zaire's then-president Mobutu to promote a fight between then-heavyweight champion, George Foreman, and his popular challenger and former champion, Muhammad Ali. I, along with the James Brown band, flew to Kinshasa, Zaire, on the same overloaded DC-8 as Muhammad Ali and his crew. The plane was dangerously overloaded because the organizers tried to get *everyone* who was to participate in the music festival on that same airplane. I don't think that they had properly anticipated the amount of equipment that performers carry with them. I'll bet the wardrobe for the Pointer Sisters alone took up an entire bin, and James, spoiled by our recent trip to Gabon, insisted on carrying all of his own equipment, although Stu Levine had a state-of-the-art sound and recording systems already installed in Zaire. The plane barely got off the ground. I was seated in the center of the plane, and I saw where the runway ran out. No kidding. We were barely off the ground.

Along with the Pointer Sisters and James Brown, the cast included B.B. King, the Fania All-Stars, the Spinners, Bill Withers, the Jazz Crusaders, Sister Sledge, some African bands and dancers, and many artists I'm sure I am forgetting. On the plane, I sat with Big Black, the great percussionist. I remember asking him how it felt to be returning home to Africa. He told me that, contrary to his persona and attire, he was from South Carolina and that this was his first trip to Africa.

A feeling of excitement prevailed throughout the plane, as we inter-
acted with each other, laughing and talking and anticipating each other's
performances in Africa. Johnny Pacheco of the Fania All-Stars provided
much of the entertainment with his flute and his comedy during the
long flight over. Already the fun had begun. Actually, the experience had
started even earlier for me, as I had been one of the emissaries for James
Brown in a planning-stage meeting with Don King and Lloyd Price. However, the enormity of the undertaking didn't hit me until I saw all these
great stars, the sound and camera crews, and the beautiful hostesses, who
also kept the long trip from becoming boring. One hostess in particular
I remember meeting was Veronica Porsche.

But the real fun began when we arrived in Kinshasa. I was personally greeted by Hugh Masekela. For some reason he had sought me out,
and we were frequent companions for the whole two weeks. We checked
into our hotels and were told to charge all food and drinks to our rooms.
This was hard to believe. Who in their right mind would let a bunch of
entertainers eat and drink free with no limit? I think maybe some of the
economic problems that the country of Zaire is experiencing today is a
residual effect of that 1974 music festival.

I, for one, went crazy. My drink of choice was immediately upgraded
from beer to cognac. Double cognacs at that. On the nights we didn't perform, we were treated to fabulous concerts by such great artists as Celia
Cruz backed by Ray Barretto, the Fania All-Stars (a favorite of the Africans), Sister Sledge, the Spinners, B.B. King, and my personal favorites,
the Pointer Sisters and the Jazz Crusaders. I had idolized the Crusaders
during my formative years, and I loved the Pointer Sisters just because
they were the Pointer Sisters.

The whole scene was one big party. Every night after the concert, we
were invited to the home of a different local dignitary, where we would
be treated to more drinks and fantastic and exotic food. Some of the food
was so exotic that it left us wondering what the hell it was. Stix Hooper
of the Crusaders dubbed one pasty substance cellulose. Since then, it has
become a private joke between Maceo and I to describe any food we don't
understand as "cellulose." This was the most legal fun I ever had. (I think
it was legal.) We were there for two weeks—eating, drinking, and generally enjoying each other's performances and company. I think Big Black's
solo performance on three giant drums was the highlight of the festival
for me—and for a lot of the Africans.

Every now and then we would run into Ali and Foreman. At different times, I got to shake both of their hands. The size of Foreman's hands compared to the relatively small hands of Ali led me to predict a victory for Foreman. I didn't see how any man, even Ali, could withstand a punch to any part of his body from this young, powerful, giant of a man and live to compose a poem about it. Plus, I had seen what Foreman had done to Frazier. Even so, I knew Ali would put up a good fight, and we all were eager to witness it.

As fate would have it, Foreman injured his eye during training and the fight was postponed for two weeks. Well, even the eloquence of Don King couldn't convince President Mobutu to house and feed all these musicians for another two weeks. I didn't care. I was satisfied. I had spent two weeks enjoying the performances and company of some of my favorite artists. I had made lifelong friends in Hugh Masekela, Stu Levine, and many others. Besides, I like music way better than I like fights. So we—the musicians, the performers, and the sound crew—were sent home. We had to hear about the famous "Rumble in the Jungle" fight via TV and radio like everyone else. The Zaire Music Festival was one of the greatest experiences of my career and is also filed in my brain, near the top of the list, under "Most Fun I Ever Had."

Returning from what had turned out to be a vacation in Zaire made it very difficult to continue the James Brown Show routine. James gave me some 45s by African musicians to copy. I went to work and copied them almost note for note, reorganizing where I deemed necessary. I thought that James would come in and do likewise with the vocals. But no. He went an entirely different direction with the lyrics, renamed the songs, and took all of the publishing and credit for the arrangements. This didn't seem right to me, and I told him so. He said that all he was doing was taking back from people who had taken from him. It was true that much of the music had been influenced by James Brown, but I couldn't understand why he thought it was necessary to go backward. We were, without a doubt, leading the way as far as black music was concerned. Plus, I didn't like stealing someone else's material. Along with the other compromises I'd made with my principles, I was now stealing other people's music.

I could not do this anymore. I made up my mind that I would refuse to copy anything else. In fact, I made up my mind to quit, because refusing to do what the Boss ordered was the same as quitting. When David Bowie came out with a record titled "Fame," James and I both thought that it sounded like a James Brown track. He ordered me to copy it. Here was my chance to take a stand and confront the man about how stupid I thought it was to copy people who were copying him. I didn't confront him, however. But I didn't copy the record, either. I just never did it. I didn't give any reason. I just didn't do it.

At that point, it wasn't like I didn't have anywhere to go. Parliament had just put out a tremendously successful album entitled *Chocolate City,* and Bootsy had had a major part in the production of this album. When Bootsy had left James, we had made a promise to each other that one day, somehow, someway, we would work together again. At the time, it was far-fetched, and neither of us knew how, when, or where. I had seen Bootsy a few times since then, and we had stayed in touch by telephone. I knew that he was with Funkadelic, but I didn't fully understand what that had to do with *Chocolate City.* I was just hoping and praying that he was all right, because I had heard scary stories about Funkadelic being this wild and crazy group.

Well, one night, when I was chilling in the Americana Hotel in New York, where nobody was supposed to know I was, a knock came on my door. All kinds of things went through my mind. Had the Boss found me? Was it the police come to get me for smoking weed? Was it this girl's husband come to shoot me? Please let it be one of the latter two, I prayed. I didn't feel like being bothered with the Boss tonight. Anything else I could handle. I looked through the peephole and saw sunglasses, funny hats, a lot of leather clothes, boots, and strange jewelry on about four or five people. I hoped that they were people. They looked like creatures from outer space. I continued to look, contemplating whether or not I should open the door. I finally recognized Bootsy. Still a little apprehensive, I opened the door and in walked Bootsy, George Clinton, Bernie Worrell, Garry Shider, and Cordell "Boogie" Mosson. The girl was terrified, and I would have been, too, had it not been for the fact that I knew Bootsy—or thought I did. Bootsy started talking, and the fact that he was somewhat speaking English calmed us down a little. He introduced me to George and the others, and they also spoke in a way that I kind of understood. After exchanging a few jokes and some small talk, they pulled out tapes and stuck one in my tape player.

What I heard scared me again. All rhythm tracks. Funk. Bass, guitars, drums. Musically simple, but with an attitude. A Sound. An aggressiveness like I'd never heard before. Bold. Overwhelming. Compelling. And real funky is the best way I can describe it. Bootsy, George, and the guys all said that it needed horns. This music was brand-new. It was what

I was doing with James but with an attitude that was fresh. It was the next step for funk, R&B, and all popular music. Off the top of my head, of course, I had no ideas for horns with this music. So, not being from outer space, which was obviously where the roots of this music were, I asked, "What do you want the horns to do?" Bernie said, "Whatever you come up with." Bootsy said, "Something different." George said, "Gimme something bad." I told them that I still worked for James Brown and that it would take some time to do this in between my duties with James. They said that it would be okay, to take my time. There was no real hurry.

What they really wanted and what was sort of urgent was that I join them in their new venture. They explained how they were Parliament of the *Chocolate City* recording, but had taken the name Funkadelic in order to keep recording until the contract to which they were signed expired. Right after the contract expired, they signed with Casablanca Records. *Chocolate City* was the first recording. Funkadelic was still a viable entity on Westbound Records but was about to sign a new contract with Warner Brothers Records. Bootsy also had signed with Warner Brothers. One of the tapes I heard was for Bootsy's first record. The other was for Parliament's second record on Casablanca. It was a sweet setup, and everyone stood to profit—in terms of both work and money. I was a bit confused about where exactly I could fit into this situation, but it sounded good, and it was a perfect next step after the James Brown organization.

Now I'm wrestling with my sense of loyalty and appreciation. After all the hard work, the boring conversation, the sleepless nights, and other unnecessary things Mr. Brown had put me through, I was feeling guilty about leaving him. I had seen him do many cold-blooded things to many people, but I myself had done very well with him and had no real personal beef. When I had rejoined the band five years earlier, I had been broke, with absolutely nothing to look forward to in the music business but returning to James Brown. By the time Parliament and Bootsy approached me, I had learned a profession, amassed a pretty good publishing catalog, gained recognition as the funkiest trombone player in the world, and earned a good living for my family. I owed a lot to James Brown. The question was whether or not I should exhaust what I had gained just to show appreciation, when I did feel like I was spinning my wheels, not making any progress.

Once I asked Mr. Brown for a raise, after he had fined me for a trumpet player dipping his horn on the finale. He had demanded that all horns be held straight up all the way to the end of the show so as not to show any fatigue. I—as bandleader—had to make sure this order was adhered to. When he fined me, I told him that $500 a week was not enough salary if I was to be responsible for what everyone did or didn't do onstage. If that was my job description, I had to have more money. He explained to me that I wasn't working for $500 a week, I was working for $500 a week plus the opportunity to make that arranging and producing and publishing money that I also made on the side. I told him that that had been all right when I was learning, but now that I knew what I was doing and was taking a lot of weight and flack off of him, I deserved to get paid for everything I did, on and off the stage. He didn't agree, didn't give me the raise, and accused me of getting too big for my britches. He felt that he had made me and that I now belonged to him, which would have been all right with me had I been getting paid adequately for the work I was doing. I didn't issue any ultimatums, but he knew that I didn't like it. I still hesitated to just walk away.

Then I got real busy again. The same people who had done *Black Caesar* were doing a sequel that they were calling *Revenge*. Naturally, they wanted to use James for the music. That meant James got to running his mouth again, and I got to work again. As usual, he mumbled a bunch of stuff to me, and I half listened and half wrote it down. By then, I was into maybe getting the grooves from him or just writing down titles, then making up things myself, especially after I realized that he generally didn't remember what he said. Sometimes he didn't even remember the titles. I wrote a song called "Revenge," and by the time he finished mutilating the words, it became "The Payback." I was creatively incensed that he couldn't even sing a song like I'd written it, although he did a little better with "Papa Don't Take No Mess."

We were getting pretty good at doing movie scores by now, so we finished the thematic stuff and timed out all the cues, wrapped it all up in a nice package, and I was off to Hollywood to deliver the goods to Larry Cohen and Barry DeVorzon. Although I lived in Los Angeles, I went straight to Larry's office in order to complete my business right away, then have a little time to spend with my family before heading back to the East Coast. I didn't anticipate any problems. Larry put the tape on and heard what was now titled "The Payback." He played about half of it, then skipped to the next track, played a little of that, then stopped listening altogether. He looked me straight in the face and said, "This isn't funky enough, Fred." I retorted, "Isn't funky enough? I don't know what kind of Hollywood game you're beginning to play, but I do know that this is extremely funky music." He began to try to explain something to me when I stopped him and asked to use the telephone. I figured that if we were going to play games I had better get the best game player I knew of to be on my team. I dialed the phone.

"Hello, Mr. Brown? This is Fred. Larry says that the music isn't funky enough." Brown said, "Let me speak to Larry." I passed the phone to Larry who, I now realize, would rather have dealt with me than with Mr. Brown. He got on the phone and said, "Hel–. . . Well, yeah . . . I mean . . . er . . . You see . . ." At the same time as he was trying to get a word in edgewise, he was turning different shades of red and breaking out in a sweat, flailing his arms. After about three or four minutes of this, he handed the phone back to me. James said to me, "Bring the music home, now." Bring it to Augusta. So, without ever going home, I drove to the airport and flew back to Augusta, Georgia, where we put the music together into an album after adding little things here and there. The album was titled *The Payback* and was an instant hit. The movie was renamed *Hell up in Harlem* and was scored by Fonce Mizell and Freddie Perren (with Edwin Starr). Neither the movie nor the soundtrack were nearly as successful as *The Payback* was for James. Although he had had many gold singles, *The Payback* was James Brown's first gold album.

Payback was such a big hit that attendance at the shows increased. Mr. Brown was so encouraged that he had the bright idea to self-promote a huge show at Madison Square Garden in New York City. As we traveled through the Midwest and the South, all he could talk about was his Madison Square Garden show. I had gotten so sick of hearing all the "We're bigger than we ever been" talk that most of my energy was spent trying to stay away from the Boss. After each show was over, I would haul ass out of the dressing room before he could send for me, sometimes still in my uniform. It was amusing to the guys in the band, because they were used to me going to the Boss's dressing room every night as a matter of routine. But it had gotten to the point that the worst thing that could happen to me was to see Danny Ray or Henry Stallings burst through the door of the dressing room, point at me, and say, "He wants you." Well, I had had enough. I could no longer stand being with him and bullshitting him, hiding the way I really felt about things. I rode the bus as much as possible. I got actually sick and angry if he trapped me into flying with him. I know that he must have known. Everyone else knew. My attitude was almost impossible to hide. I don't know why he continued to put up with my obvious discomfort when I was with him. He would always ask how I felt, if I needed anything, if everything was all right at home? The whole situation was getting more and more pathetic. I had to find a way to leave. I could not take it anymore.

The night before we were to play the big gig at Madison Square Garden, we performed in Fayetteville, North Carolina. In order to make it to New York in time, we had to leave Fayetteville right after the show. I had hoped that we would arrive in New York at about noon so I could get some sleep before having my hair done and getting ready to rehearse the augmented horns and strings that were scheduled to be with us on the show. Things didn't work out as planned. Mother Nature greeted us with a severe snowstorm at the Virginia border and slowed us down considerably. At the same time, something happened to the door of the bus. We stopped for a long time to try to have it fixed, but to no avail. We ended up tying the door up with some string. At noon, we were barely into Maryland and moving very slowly through snow and heavy traffic. It was cold. We were all bundled up, trying to keep warm. We were hungry and didn't have time to stop to eat. Everyone was in a bad mood.

At some point, we were forced to stop again, and Freddie Holmes, the road manager, called the Boss to tell him what was happening. Freddie came to me after talking to the Boss and told me to get off the bus in Washington and catch a flight into New York so that I would be there in time to rehearse the strings and horns. I said okay just give me the money for cab fare and the plane ticket. Freddie said that he didn't have any money—the Boss took all of the gig money with him the night before. I was to use my own money and be reimbursed when I got to New York. I knew that tune and had danced to that music before. Plus, I wasn't about to fly to New York, leaving all of my band to suffer on that raggedy-ass bus to try to pull yet another something out of the fire for James Brown. If it meant so much to him to have a good show in New York, let him fly the whole band in. This time I wouldn't do it. I had the money, but I just refused to leave everybody else out there on the bus. This was his band, his show, his promotion. It was reported that he had already spent $100,000 promoting this show, as it was. I saw no reason why he couldn't spend another three or four thousand dollars to make sure the band arrived in time.

I sat right there in the cold and rode all the way in with everybody else. We were in a real bad mood now. We didn't have time to go to the hotel. We went straight to Madison Square Garden, where the horn and string players were waiting for me. I was all tired and funky—hair a mess, cold and hungry. I was greeted by a friend of mine whom I hadn't seen for a long time. He saw the condition that I was in and offered me what I thought was some type of speed pill. He said it would perk me up and put me in a better mood. I had taken bennies and dexies before and really thought nothing of it. I did need a boost to get through this night. I rehearsed the horns and strings. No problem except that we had to pay them two hours overtime for waiting. Filiyau did a rush job on my hair, and I got dressed in my least favorite uniform, that red-cape suit, and headed for the stage, still not feeling the affect of that speed pill. I figured that it must have been something mild, that wouldn't really knock me out of the box.

With everything in place and all the adversity overcome, we headed for the stage. All of a sudden, just for a second, everything went @#$^&*()!@#$ t^&*—that's actually what I saw, only in broad, three-dimensional colors. I had no idea what it was at first, but when it started slowly coming on again, that pill came to my mind. By the time I reached the stage, I was zooming. My head was spinning, I was seeing things, my feet felt like they were not touching the floor. I knew that I had been given some acid or some kind of hallucinogenic drug. The whole show ended up seeming like a windstorm, with music being the wind that I could see in different colors swirling all around my head. I don't know how I got through it. Somehow, I played all my solos and sang all my parts and did all the dances as usual. I do remember Melvin Parker keeping me on track through most of the show. I think that he was the only one who knew that I was messed up. The show seemed to go on forever. When it was finally over, I made it to the dressing room and just sat there thinking about what I was going to do to my so-called friend when I got my hands on him. I thought about all that I had been through that day—trying to get to a gig that would not make me or the guys in the show much money, but would make a person who was already rich a lot more money, and how unfair this situation was and how people who work the hardest get the least reward. I was just generally feeling used and abused.

Just then, Henry Stallings came through the door and pointed to me and said those bone-chilling words that I dreaded so much, "He wants you." This, I didn't need. Was he going to say something to me about being so high onstage, or would it be the regular, "We killed 'em," or did he make up something to be wrong with the show in order to bug me about it? Whatever it was, I didn't want to hear it. Still in the hated red cape, I went down the hall to his dressing room. He was there with Buddy

Nolen, a man from Philly who had once worked as an advance man for James, but who now worked as manager for Harold Melvin and the Blue Notes. The Blue Notes had headlined a show the night before at the Nassau Coliseum on Long Island to a sold-out crowd. I hadn't noticed, but there had not been many people at Madison Square Garden that night. In fact, now that I had come down a little, I realized that James had lost his ass promoting this show. He was ranting and raving to Buddy Nolen about how they—I have no idea who they were—had given away tickets at the Nassau Coliseum just to keep him from having a good crowd at Madison Square Garden.

I heard him say that as I walked in. When he saw me, he said "Ain't that right, Fred?" I was caught off-guard and didn't have time to think. I paused a second and said "Haeyell naaw. And plus, I quit." I turned around and walked out, went back down to our dressing room, changed clothes, put all of those funny looking uniforms and the music in a hangup bag, dragged it back to his dressing room, and told him again that I was quitting. As I walked away, I heard him saying, "You're making a mistake. You'll be sorry. You better think about it." I didn't stop to talk to anyone. I walked to the bus, got my stuff, got a taxi, and checked into the Americana Hotel, my favorite hideout place. I had myself a private pity and celebration party that night. I didn't know whether or not I had really quit until the next day when I was all the way sober. I vacillated between going to the Boss and explaining that I had been high and apologizing, like Waymon had, or leaving it like it was and taking my ass home. Since I wanted to leave anyway, I decided to leave it like it was. This was not the way I wanted to do it, but it was as good a way as any. I went to my friend, the controller at Polydor Records, got a $25,000 advance against Fred Wesley and the JBs royalties, had myself another party—this time with St. Clair and some Kentucky Fried Chicken—and caught a plane to L.A.

I left James Brown, feeling like I had betrayed him. After all, I had nothing to dislike him for. He had seen in me a person who would take advantage of an opportunity, and he gave me that opportunity, to both of our benefits. The problem was that we saw the world from two different points of view. The world had taught him that if you wanted something, you had to get it yourself, to fight for it. He had never had a mother or father or anyone to provide for him, to guide him, to make a way for him. Everything he had he had to fight for, and he didn't understand giving anything to anyone or even letting anyone earn anything from him in an

James Brown and my daughters. Left to right: Shana, Lya, Joya. Photograph by Fred Wesley Jr.

easy way. I, on the other hand, grew up believing that if you treated everyone with respect and kindness, good things would happen for you. I was protected and led and taught and provided for until I was able to go for myself. Having been given breaks, I didn't mind giving a person a break here and there. James had been forced to be a tough man because he had never been given anything. He had had to overcome tremendous adversity just to live, let alone achieve greatness. Very few people in the world have experienced the kind of poverty that was his early in life. He had to work ten times as hard as anyone else just to have food and shelter. So he expected everyone to work ten times as hard to get what they got from him. You can't expect mercy from a man who has fought himself up from the depths of degradation to the pinnacle of the entertainment world. I cannot find it in my heart to dislike James Brown, even though I've seen him do cruel things to many people. And, although he did make my life a living hell sometimes, I'm a better man for it.

The fact is, he never did anything to anyone who didn't make him or herself available to the abuse by trying to get something free or cheap from him. I will always admire James Brown because he is a man true to his principles. His principles are not my principles, but he is as true to what he is as I am true to what I am. That's why I cannot work for or even be around him anymore, but I do love and appreciate the man for what he allowed me to do for myself. I will always believe that he respected me as a man. I certainly respect him for being an extraordinary man and for making himself the greatest entertainer who ever lived. I am privileged to have been in his company.

7

Bootsy's Rubber Band and

Parliament/Funkadelic

• • •

I did feel a tinge of remorse about leaving all of my boys and girls to deal with James without my intervention. But there was that unwritten rule that we all did our own thing when it came to the Boss. Everyone knew I was unhappy and ready to go, but I don't think anyone expected me to leave so suddenly—not even me. I just had to suck it up and deal with the animosity that was hurled at me, and they had to suck it up and deal with the Boss without me. I had been taking weight off of everybody, and it was about time for most of them to stand on their own two feet anyway. Plus, they still had jobs. I had the promise of a job.

I still had Bootsy on hold about what I was going to do with the projects we had discussed. I looked forward to doing the horns for the music that I had heard, but I didn't know if playing with Bootsy and/or Funkadelic was a good idea or not. Now that I was free of James Brown, my desire to play jazz began to creep back, and I didn't want to rule out the possibility of a jazz gig. To even dream of a jazz gig, of course, would mean starting immediately to woodshed seriously (that is, go in the woodshed and practice until I got it right), but it was questionable whether I had the time or the guts to make that kind of commitment. The advance I had gotten would not last very long in L.A. If I could keep money flowing by writing arrangements for Bootsy and devote all my spare time to getting my chops together, maybe I could prepare myself for a jazz future and still make money on the side. That sounded like the best plan, so I went for it.

I approached the arrangements with the directions that Bootsy,

Bernie, and George had given me in that New York hotel room: "Whatever you come up with." "Something different." "Something bad." With these directions, my only goal was to avoid doing anything ordinary or mediocre. I've always held the belief that funk and jazz are basically the same thing, with emphasis on different elements and playing with different attitudes. Jazz is cool and slick and subtle, emphasizing the melodic and harmonic side of the music, and appeals to the more cerebral listener. Funk is bold, arrogant, and aggressive, emphasizing the hard downbeats and tricky rhythms of the music, and tends to appeal more to the booty-shaking listener. I submit that there is a very thin line separating the two schools of music appreciation. Having been given the freedom to experiment, I went about using this project to prove my theory.

I made the horns add color by using every chord voicing possible on the home chord of the vamp, other voicings that I made up, and groups of notes that I put together just for the sound of it. In some cases, I would use melodies and counter-melodies against the rhythm track or even against the vocals or alternate horn tracks if the opportunity presented itself. Sometimes I used counter-rhythms to add what I termed "snap and jiggle" to an already funky groove. In most cases, you could say without contradiction that I was using jazz theories for the horns against funk rhythm tracks. What made it gel was the attitude with which the horn parts were played. More than once I have given the direction, "Play it like you mean it!" This injection of attitude made the difference between a part simply laying across the track with no consequence and a part locked in like a hand in a glove, adding punch, color, snap, and jiggle.

The first project was Bootsy's Rubber Band. We decided to use four horns. Two trumpets, sax, and trombone. Me, of course, on trombone. Maceo, of course, on sax, if I could get him away from James for the session. The trumpets were the question. Waymon Reed was my first choice, but he was now traveling regularly with the Count Basie band. We needed someone who had that bebop feel yet was open-minded enough to play bebop to a funk beat. I have had it happen that a jazz purist would just flatly refuse to even try to lock with a funk beat. When I had done the *Black Caesar* theme, for instance, I had gotten Buster Williams Jr. on upright bass. His part was very simple, and I had written it out for him note for note. This didn't sit right with Buster because he was used to reading mostly chord changes and basically making up his own part. But the *Black Caesar* score was a different case. We needed that upright sound, but the part was simply a redundant phrase that required some drive and force. Buster Williams Jr. was a bass player who could and would swing you into bad health on a jazz tune, but driving the same phrase over and over again was beyond his understanding. He saw it as stupid and said so right to my face.

He asked, "When does it start swinging?"

I told him, "It don't swing. It's not that kind of thing."

"Well, where are the changes?"

"Ain't no changes. This is it."

"Why did y'all call me? This ain't my thing. Why didn't you call an electric bass player?"

Finally, out of anger and disgust—and intent on making fun of that silly-ass part—he locked a heartstopping groove that made the whole song. Attitude. I needed trumpet players with that bebop feel who could give me that funk attitude.

Bootsy and George were using the United Sound studio in Detroit. I searched my memory for trumpet players who fit the jazz/funk profile and lived in Detroit. A very bright light came on in my brain and illuminated the name Marcus Belgrave. I had met Marcus when I was a kid back in Mobile and he was playing with Ray Charles. I can't say that we were friends, but I did greatly admire and idolize him both as a trumpet player and as a person. Since our first meeting, I had been in his company maybe two or three times and had actually played with him on one jam session. All of these encounters occurred in Mobile during his trips through town with the Ray Charles band. I rated him up there with Lee Morgan and Freddie Hubbard as my favorite trumpet players. What distinguished him from Lee and Freddie was the fact that he, like me, was a be-bopper who had R&B experience. His bebopability coupled with his funkability made him perfect for the gig. By the grace of God, he was available. Although I hadn't seen him in fifteen years, he convinced me— almost—that he remembered me. I don't think he really did, but it didn't matter. Our meeting was a joy for me, and he received me like an old friend. He put me in touch with another trumpet he said was cut from the same jazz/funk mold named Maurice Davis.

After I ran the deal down to Maceo, he somehow worked his way out of the James Brown thing, which had really begun to fall apart anyway, and I had my horn section. After we perfected the very first phrase, I knew that we had the right combination.

The studio was state-of-the-art and the engineer, Jim Vitti, was a

Maceo and Bootsy getting ready. Photograph by Fred Wesley Jr.

proficient yet open-minded and free-thinking technician who was the final, ultimately necessary, component of this crack recording team. He miked each horn and recorded each horn on a separate track. We then doubled each part on four additional tracks. Each pass was also recorded on another track from an overhead mike that picked up the ambience from the very large, high-ceilinged room. All ten of these tracks were balanced and mixed down to two left and right stereo tracks. The sound was awesome. We were breaking new ground musically and technically.

The atmosphere around the sessions in Detroit was vastly different from the James Brown sessions. Recording with James was a tense situation, as were all interactions with him. You never knew when he would go off and verbally attack somebody. Trying to be creative under those conditions was difficult to impossible. Whenever I had an idea that I thought was necessary for the recording, I either had to present it in a way that made it seem like it was his idea or be accused of trying to take over his session. "You don't know what you're doing, son. Just do like I tell you." I usually just let things go however they were going, giving a nudge here and there to help make sense out of the real crazy stuff without infringing on the boss's authority.

Work and life in general with the Funkadelic people was, literally, "nothing but a party." George was not only the boss but the partymaster as well. He was always laughing and joking, trying to keep everybody relaxed. It was clear that he was in charge, but he ruled with a soft, friendly, respectful approach that made everyone feel comfortable. Creativity was the order of the day. All day. Every day. Nothing that popped into anybody's mind was dismissed. Everything, no matter how crazy or unconventional, was considered. You had to be careful about what you said or played for fear that it would wind up on the record as a song or part of a song. The James Brown recording method was get a groove, lock a groove, record a groove. That was it. No matter what mistakes were made or what sounds were out of balance, when James said it was finished, it was finished. I remember when we cut "The Payback," the engineer said that it would be perfect as soon as we mixed it. James said that it was perfect now and that he had better not touch a thing. On the other hand, George, Bootsy, and Jim paid strict attention to details when it came to putting innovative ideas on tape. The groove was ultimately important, but using the multitrack recording technique allowed us to stretch it to and beyond its current limits.

In the studio, George was the boss and Bootsy was second in command. Faithful and dutiful lieutenants Bernie Worrell, Garry Shider, and Glenn Goins were always on hand to make suggestions and give advice. It took me a while to figure out who was who and what was what when it came to the Funkadelic and Parliament road show. The who turned out to be this: Garry Shider, Bernie Worrell, Glenn Goins, Cordell "Boogie" Mosson, and Jerome Brailey made up Funkadelic; Calvin Simon, Clarence "Fuzzy" Haskins, Ray Davis, Grady Thomas, and George Clinton were Parliament. The what turned out to be this: Funkadelic had originally been hired as the backup band for Parliament, a singing group in the Temptations/Four Tops mode that had been put on the shelf, so to speak, by the record company to which it was signed. Unwilling to stay dormant while their company decided what to do with them, George had made a deal with Westbound Records to record a group called Funkadelic. The actual recording was done by a combined crew that included people from both groups.

Once the old contract had expired, George was free to pursue another deal on the heels of his successes as a producer with Funkadelic. This

Clarence "Fuzzy" Haskins.
Photograph by Fred
Wesley Jr.

deal came from Casablanca Records. Parliament's first venture on Casablanca was the tremendously successful *Chocolate City*. With George's credibility as a producer exploding, he was able to make a mega multi-album deal with Casablanca. At the same time, he was able to land a deal with Warner Brothers Records to record Bootsy and Funkadelic under some kind of an arrangement with Westbound. It was all very complicated. I think I've gotten it right, but I'm not sure. I am sure that there seemed to be unlimited budgets, because we recorded as long and as much as we needed and wanted to. I had all my expenses paid and was getting $500 for every arrangement, double American Federation of Musicians scale for all sessions, and collecting regularly with no problems— at least in the beginning.

I don't know exactly how Bootsy got to be with the P-Funk organization, but he was an integral element of the team. The first project that I worked on, *Stretching Out in a Rubber Band,* was with his band, Bootsy's Rubber Band. In his band were some people I knew from the James Brown band. Catfish on guitar, and Frank Waddy, now known as Frankie "Kash," on drums. The keyboard player for the Rubber Band was a white guy from Baltimore named Frederick "Flintstone" Allen (Bootsy the nicknamer strikes again). He was a fine, classically trained, jazz-oriented musician. There were two singers, Gary "Mudbone" Cooper and Robert "Peanut" Johnson. I was not present when they recorded the rhythm tracks, but I understand that the tracks were not necessarily cut by the members of the Rubber Band. Bernie seemed to be somehow involved in just about every recording, as did Garry. Anybody, including Mudbone, might play drums on any track that they had the best feel for. I learned that Bootsy played drums on "Stretching Out" and that Boogie played drums on "Make My Funk the P-Funk." Many of the guitar parts were Bootsy's, but anybody might overdub anything on any track if a particular part was needed. The rule was: whatever, wherever, by whomever—as long as it worked. The studio vibe was like a musical laboratory staffed by many, on-call, funk scientists, each skilled in his particular field of endeavor.

Between sessions, the guys would play Funkadelic gigs. I was real anxious to see the Funkadelic show that I had heard so much about, but the opportunity didn't immediately present itself. I had heard about the wild outfits they wore. What they wore every day was wild enough. I couldn't imagine what their stage dress was like. It was rumored that they might get naked during the show, pee on stage, curse out the audience. I heard that George had once actually given a girl some head right onstage, or was it the reverse? I wondered what I had gotten myself into. What I had seen so far was some pretty bizarre behavior, but nothing I couldn't handle. I was not the most in-between-the-lines type of person myself. I had been known to stretch the envelope and skirt the perimeter and even lean heavily toward the outside at times. Not to worry, though. I had my ace buddy, Maceo, with me, watching my back at all times. In turn, I did my best to look out for him and keep him in line. That "free your mind" attitude that constantly prevailed made it easy for a person's ass to follow all kinds of temptation into all kinds of trouble if he wasn't careful.

The first show that I got to see, I got to see while I was onstage. It was at the Capital Center outside of Washington, D.C. In the dressing room before the show, there was macho posturing and trash talk about "kicking ass," "killing 'em," "turning it out," and "tearing the roof off of the mother-fucker." It was more like an army preparing for battle or a football team getting psyched for a big game than a band getting ready to do a show. In the center of the room, there was a very large trunk to which everybody went, each ritualistically choosing an outfit or piece of clothing or some strange accessory to wear onstage. The trunk had obviously collected bits of uniforms and other dressing-room trappings over the years. The odor that it emitted prompted me to name it "The Funk Trunk."

People's dress varied from Jerome Brailey's meticulous coordination of a pith helmet, a jumpsuit made out of some shiny metallic material, and matching knee-length silver boots to Fuzzy's tie-dyed long johns adorned by a large, jewel-encrusted, big-buckled belt. Michael Hampton—a young, Sunday-school-boy–looking guitar player whom I hadn't seen before—came out wearing a fencing mask and helmet and a long black cape. Calvin was kind of low-key, dressing up as an Indian, complete with moccasins and a feathered headdress. Grady was a purple-hazed, purple-hued, purple-everything Arab, down to his sandals and desert sunglasses. I saw Garry dig down in the trunk until he found a Holiday Inn towel that he simply wrapped around his naked ass like a diaper, before putting on some over-the-knee, extremely high platform boots and then getting on with applying his make-up. They all put on make-up, even if nothing but a ring around one eye. Most really went to extremes to create their own individual looks. Unusually high platforms boots were the style for those who weren't wearing sandals, moccasins, or going barefoot. George wore platform boots and a sheet. That's all. Boots and a white sheet. No drawers, no T-shirt. Boots, buck naked under a sheet. I showed up in a brown, big-lapeled, bell-bottom suit. To be real radical, I wore a bright green shirt with no tie. That was about as out-of-the-norm as I could do without some notice. That red cape I had worn on my last gig with James Brown probably would have looked right at home in this band.

They walked to the stage still threatening to funk up the stage, the building, the audience, and each other. They looked like a bunch of race-horses anxiously approaching the starting gates, wielding their instruments like weapons and slapping each other in the hands. The stage looked like an electronic warehouse. Keyboards, drums, and speakers were everywhere. Guitars, percussion instruments, wires, cables, and a wall of amplifiers. Lights, front, back, and all around. We never used a monitor system with James Brown, but the monitor system on the stage at the Capital Center was itself as big as and had as many pieces as did the whole James Brown sound system. All of this equipment was attended by a bevy of T-shirt-and-blue-jean-clad, long-haired white boys. A technician each for the drummer, keyboards, and guitars. This was a big-time rock-and-roll stage.

The people in the audience were mostly from D.C. and the surrounding area. This was a fitting venue for the band that had recorded a hit record about this city, with its high percentage of chocolate-colored people. There were over 20,000 mostly black people on hand that night. Most were new fans brought in by the hit *Chocolate City,* but there also were many loyal followers of the Funkadelic movement. There were a few older fans of Parliament and—I would like to think—maybe even one or two people who had heard that Maceo and I were performing. You could tell the Funkadelic crowd. They were dressed much like the people onstage. There was a fairly large contingency of hippie-looking white people, also. A few college types, but the overall majority were black kids from their late teens to late twenties. They were all joined together by one common purpose: to give up the funk

The stage went black. Everyone took their positions. Maceo and I stayed on the side of the stage, waiting to be called on. Our main job was to observe and find a spot in the show for ourselves. There weren't actually any horn parts yet. Our mission was to observe, plan for the future, and contribute solos or riffs wherever we found a good spot.

Out of the darkness came a sharp, popping rhythm from the snare drum—^..^..^ . . . ^.^^ // ^..^..^ . . . ^.^^ // for four bars—then every guitar, every keyboard, every instrument on stage hit and held a low E that was so loud and so imposing that it really made a start at fulfilling that promise to tear the roof off the Capital Center. With the low E came lights that flooded the stage, illuminating the players—who were staring menacingly at the audience. I don't know how it affected everyone else, but it sent a thrill through my body. It made me brace myself for whatever was coming next. I knew it could be anything. After holding that low E for four bars, they hit it again, further emphasizing that something serious was about to happen.

What happened was a slide into a simple yet ultimately compelling groove. Not the irregular, broken-up funk of a James Brown groove, but hard rock with a severe attitude. It was a tune that was recognized instantly by the Funkadelic devotees as "Cosmic Slop." But first, the stage lights were killed, leaving only the spots, all of which were focused center stage on Michael Hampton, the guitar player in the fencing outfit, in a rock-and-roll-guitar-player stance, screaming and wailing the melody of the song. He left the melody and went into a solo worthy of Van Halen or any of the great rock guitar players. After what seemed to be a five-minute, masterfully timed solo that gradually rose in intensity until the band, the audience, and I were in a complete frenzy, the bottom dropped out—leaving the groove quietly, yet still intensely, backing Fuzzy, who was suddenly singing the song.

The spots now highlighted Fuzzy, and the effect was mesmerizing. Fuzzy was singing like any other singer—Lou Rawls, Wilson Pickett— but standing there in some long johns and (did I mention this?) a mask that made him look like a creature from outer space? The lead vocal was passed back and forth between Fuzzy and Gary, who—you remember— was wearing the diaper. When the other singers came in, the sound was so full and so musically perfect that you could have been listening to the Mormon Tabernacle Choir. But what you were looking at could have been aliens from the moon. I was totally amazed. As the show progressed, the band went through every genre of music from James Brown–type funk to Jimi Hendrix–type rock, with extremely musical vocals—R&B vocals, gospel vocals—and even some classically inspired keyboard renderings from Bernie. They also made full use of the latest electronic effects. All were excellent musicians. All played with serious funk attitudes.

When George came on, things really got going. He was like the party-master. He didn't sing, didn't play an instrument, but he did direct the whole show, telling who to play, where and what, guiding the audience through all the sing-alongs and dances, and directing where and how to clap your hands. He was everywhere, wearing only a sheet, mind you, so you know that he flashed everybody at one time or another. At one point, he brought the guitar players together, and they all went to the edge of the stage and challenged the audience by making phallic gestures with the necks of their guitars. Only thing was, George didn't have a guitar. At another point in the show, all the people on stage gathered around George like a pride of hungry lions devouring a fresh kill, gyrating and hunching like they were engaging in a mass orgy. Throughout the show, the players and the singers made sexual gestures and suggestive moves and actually said and did things that I thought would get you arrested and put in jail if done in public. It was nothing to see Garry or Glen crawling across the stage while playing some funky lick or Grady sticking out his tongue at a lady in the audience. Grabbing a handful of your crotch was a regular and common part of the show. All of this went on while they were playing and singing some really good music. It literally drove the audience crazy. The only thing that I would have added was horns. Horns with that jazz attitude. That would have brought the music full circle and completed the overall picture of the show. I played a little, but mostly I watched and enjoyed the show. I should have bought a ticket.

The plan was to do a tour that was self-contained, with Bootsy's Rubber Band opening and with the combination group Parliament/Funkadelic closing. Maceo and I were to put a horn section together and play with both groups. But, for the time being, we were still recording and doing just selected gigs now and then. We were recording not only in Detroit but now in L.A. and New York as well. It was still just Maceo and me, and we were hiring trumpet players as we went along. Once, while in L.A., Bootsy asked me if I knew a trumpet player who could play real high notes. It just so happened that I had been talking to Melvin Webb, that short-lived drummer I had hired for James Brown out of Kansas City. He had since moved to L.A. and was doing very well playing with Johnny Nash and doing a lot of recording sessions. He had told me about another musician from Kansas City, Rick Gardner, a trumpet player who had just left Chase, a trumpet group renowned for playing high and fast. Rick had recently relocated in L.A. and was looking for a gig. I already knew of Chase. Bill Chase, the former lead trumpet with Maynard Ferguson's band, had formed his own group featuring himself and three other equally fantastically talented trumpet players, and they performed arrangements that seemed physically impossible for human beings to play. So Rick sounded perfect for what Bootsy wanted. We contacted him, and he showed up at a session we were doing at Hollywood Sound recording studio. Melvin hadn't told me that he was white. Not that it mattered. It was just that this made him the only white person in the P-Funk–Bootsy's Rubber Band clan. I did wonder if he could dance. Rick was not a jazzer, but all of that high-note playing, fast reading, and big sound that a trumpet player with a Chase background promised was fulfilled.

The recording was getting to be a little confusing, much like what I had experienced with the James Brown–People Records stable of artists. We were doing horns to many tracks in many different stages of development. It was hard to tell which tracks were Parliament, which were Bootsy, and which were just material to be named and used later. We were supposed to being doing songs for Bootsy's Rubber Band's *Stretching Out in a Rubber Band* and Parliament's *Mothership Connection*. Some tracks had titles, some didn't. Some had vocals, some didn't. Sometimes I would get a cassette with only a click track and guitar or click and bass. I approached it all as a challenge and really took liberties on the tracks that didn't have a clear direction. Our policy was to completely cover the tracks with horns and deal with how they were used during the mixing process. I didn't know it at the time, but with the horn arrangements I was inspiring the theme for many of the songs.

And I was having the time of my life. Doing some hellafied horn arrangements to some hellafied rhythm tracks. We didn't have to worry about how long it took. We didn't have to worry about how much it cost. We got paid on time most of the time. I got to continue to work, although in a much more relaxed atmosphere, with all the great musicians on both coasts whom I had befriended while working with James Brown. When George showed up in the studio, the only worry was "Did he bring the goodies?" He almost never disappointed us. The records came out and were climbing steadily up the charts. So far, J.B.'s prophecy that my move would be a mistake was being proven very, very wrong. This was the right place to be and the right time. The P-Funk movement was about to jump off big-time.

Up to that point, the guys in the Rubber Band had been just hanging around, showing up in the studio every now and then. They had been sort of auxiliary musicians, doing specialized things like a percussion overdub here and a vocal part there, things like handclaps and crowd noises. But now it was time to go to work. Maceo, Rick, and I were flown to Cincinnati to rehearse the Rubber Band Show. The rehearsal was held in the basement of Bootsy's mother's house. Ms. Nettie, as we called her, served as hostess, cook, and whatever else was needed, as did Bootsy's whole family. Everyone was excited about the upcoming tour and fully supported Bootsy in his quest for stardom. It seemed that everyone knew that his inevitable ascension to stardom was now at hand.

We toiled for days in that cramped little basement and put together an exciting yet complicated show. Everyone contributed, including Rick, who created the opening that eventually became the ending—a masterful little interlude that we still call "Hit Me, Band." After all the basics were laid out, we went to a large rehearsal studio and fine-tuned the production. Bootsy had outfitted the stage with custom-designed and -decorated equipment. The first thing that I noticed was that stars were on everything. This was before star glasses and star bass, but such items soon followed. Everything was in white, accented with red. Bootsy was creating an identity for himself and the Rubber Band. It was then that I realized that the record company, the tour company, and the management company were all serious about taking Bootsy to the top of the entertainment industry. I, apparently, had been selected to go along for the ride. Along for the ride is what I was in for, because I hadn't prepared for what was about to happen. I had no management, no contract with anybody, neither Bootsy nor George, no kind of agreement about publishing, and no kind of performance agreement. I was just out there, taking whatever I got, however and whenever I got it. I should have been more aware and more careful about what I was doing. After all, I was giving up an awful lot of music or creativity—as expressed in the P-Funk vernacular, "I was giving up the funk." And, as it turned out, giving it up was exactly what I was doing.

I was expecting to jump first-class right off, but my expectations were a little premature. We first did what is termed in tour-promoting vernacular "the pre-tour tour." This meant that everything was cut to the bare bone, including the salaries. The pre-tour tour was designed to test the waters, so to speak, performing in smaller venues in preparation for the real tour, which was to follow. We traveled on the Parliament bus. All of us. Parliament, Funkadelic, and Bootsy's Rubber Band. We were about twenty people on one bus. More, if anyone brought guests, usually girls who wanted more than just a one-night stand. They were called Clingons and stayed around for two or three nights—or more, depending on their skills or on how wide they had opened a band member's nose. The name Clingon was derived from the manner in which they got to be a part of the entourage. They simply clung on, either at their own insistence or at the insistence of the band member or members they had endeared themselves to. (That's another book.) This was a miserable situation. Two or three in a room. Hit-and-run gigs. General chitlin-circuit conditions. This pre-tour tour didn't last long, but it did serve its purpose. The Rubber Band show was perfected, and we determined that the next tour would operate with us, the horns, doing both sets.

The next tour was much better. I was making twice as much money per week as I had ever made with James. Bootsy's Rubber Band had gotten its own bus, and P-Funk had a new, mo-better bus. Accommodations were upgraded to single rooms in mo-better hotels. We added another trumpet to the horn section. Another act, usually the Brothers Johnson, opened the show, although a few shows were opened by Chaka Khan and Rufus, and one or two by Natalie Cole. The opening act was followed by Bootsy's Rubber Band, then finally Parliament/Funkadelic. The tour was truly fantastic. Every night was better than the night before, due to a spirit of competition that had developed among the three acts. The Brothers Johnson featured one of the most-recorded bassists on the Hollywood session scene, Louis Johnson, who was impressed with Bootsy, who of course was similarly impressed with Johnson and his reputation. The Brothers also had a great horn section, as did we. We had added our boy Richard "Kush" Griffith from the James Brown band and from Maceo and All the King's Men. Since we couldn't get Waymon, we got the man who replaced Waymon (again).

The Bootsy's Rubber Band act was doing okay, but there was still that element of total confidence missing from our performance. We managed to make it through all the songs, and the flash and glitter did excite the audience, but Bootsy didn't seem quite as relaxed as he should have been. He could get the audience on the ropes but was not yet able to take them out. His lack of sureness affected the whole band. None of us really got off. It wasn't any particular person's or section's fault, we just all seemed to be waiting for the other to lead the way.

Well, one night in Orlando, Florida, it all came together. It was Bootsy who led the way, with his electronically sensual, sexy, soulful solo on "I Got the Munchies for Your Love." He worked it like he was making love to the entire audience, slowly and methodically bringing himself, the bass, the band, and everybody in the audience to an explosive orgasm. After that, everything caught fire. The horns locked with the rhythm section as never before, instinctively doing new things like playing up an octave and, for the first time, joining in on Maceo's solo. It was wonderful. From then on, Bootsy's Rubber Band had arrived. It was and will always be the funkiest and most dynamic band that ever was. The vocals, the horns, the rhythm, and, of course, Bootsy have never been topped or even equaled before or since. I just knew that we would soon be the hottest band around—and this was during the time when Kool and the Gang, Maze, the Commodores, the Ohio Players, and War were making big noises all over the world. I had seen all of these bands, but we were head and shoulders above them all.

With the success of that second tour, I began to think about the future. My future with Bootsy's Rubber Band. My future with Parliament/Funkadelic. And the future of me getting paid from all of these entities that I was helping to build. As it stood, if the Rubber Band, of which I was an original member, sold a million records, all I would get was what I had already gotten from my tour salary and my arranging and recording fees. The same was true of Parliament/Funkadelic, although that was different because I had come on with an act that already was happening. I had invested too much in time and talent to be left out in the cold when the big payoff came. I confronted George and Bootsy about the problem,

Horny Horns. Left to right: Me and Maceo. Photograph courtesy of Fred
Wesley Jr.

but we never came to a real solution. No percentage of artist royalties or
publishing royalties were ever agreed on. The issue kept getting pushed
to the side and put off until later.

In the meantime, I raised my fee on the arrangements, and George
had his managers put together a deal for me and Maceo with Atlantic
Records. Between tours, we went to work on an album under the artist
name Fred Wesley and the Horny Horns, featuring Maceo Parker. The
name came from George's wife, Liz, who commented on a track during a
horn session, "That sure is horny," not intending any sexual connotation,
just referring to the preponderance of horns on the track. Well, the name
of the group itself should have indicated to us how many ways the proceeds from this group would be split up. A fairly large advance came with
the deal, so Maceo and I were kept quiet, for a while anyway. The shows
and the recordings were going well, and we were still having a whole lot
of fun. But I did have a constant and insidious feeling that I was getting
screwed.

The issue was further clouded and postponed by preparations for the
new show and the new tour we had all been waiting for: the Mothership

Connection tour. The album had done better than expected, and the stage was set to make this tour an unprecedented extravaganza. Never before had a black act produced a tour that employed such elaborate props and illusions. The premise was that the players onstage were all aliens who had come to earth to free Earthlings from their funklessness. These out-landers were lead by the all-powerful, all-funky Dr. Funkenstein, played by George Clinton. The rehearsals were held in a large warehouse in Newton, New York. I had never seen so many long-haired white boys scurrying around, carrying ropes and wires and the like. When I arrived, a bunch of them descended on me, telling me where to stand, when to go offstage, to look out for this piece of equipment, things like that. This wasn't just a show, it was a circus. For real. Most of the stage crew were, in fact, circus riggers, lighting engineers, and circus stagehands.

The props included a giant platform boot (at twelve feet high, a much bigger boot than the ones on George's feet); a silver car that the players would steal, piece by piece, as part of the show; and a baby spaceship that was suspended by wire over the audience (the baby ship was rigged to fly in from the back of the venue and join with the mothership). The gargan-tuan mothership hung, out of sight, over the stage and actually appeared to land on the stage at the appropriate moment, delivering Dr. Funken-stein, who wore a white fur coat, white fur hat, and long, blond wig. This spectacle—the show—was operated by complicated hydraulics and elec-tronics, and orchestrated and cued by the music. "Starchild," "Mother-ship Connection," "Make My Funk the P-Funk," and "Dr. Funkenstein" highlighted the thespian activity onstage. I basically did the same show as always, except that I had to be aware of where to be and where not to be at certain times. It was an ambitious and tremendous undertaking, but it was working. I was proud to be a part of this history-making tour.

The tour got rolling, and everything was first-class all the way. Not only did we have the two band buses, but there were also three addi-tional buses that transported the crews. The horn players had the option of riding a bus that carried only two stagehands. We had gotten so much into the game of poker with the Parliament guys, however, that we rode on whatever bus had a big enough table for all of us to play. The tour turned into one big long party.

I was now making three times the money I had been making with James Brown. Drugs and girls were easier to get than ever before. I had no real responsibilities except to show up for the gig. As long as I got a mini-mal amount of money home to take care of my family, I was footloose and fancy-free. We were still recording when time permitted. It took an entire day to set up for a show, so we had plenty of time between shows to record. I was making a lot of money, but I also was spending a lot of money. I was wild and crazy while on the road, but managed to appear sane and responsible whenever I went home or had to deal with business people. I completely lost sight of any goals that I might once have had about playing jazz or doing anything for myself. I was just drifting. Going anywhere the P-Funk movement took me.

I never thought about what would happen to me if this gig folded. Although the Horny Horns album turned out to be a joke, I guess I was counting on the deal with Atlantic to last and carry me through the rest of my career. The first album, except for two poorly recorded originals of mine, was just a collection of discarded George and Bootsy tracks with the horns up in the mix. Maceo and I had put in no real time, consideration, or input, but I was promised that the next one would be different. The Rubber Band was kicking, and I knew that if all else failed we all had a sure future with Bootsy. There was already talk of Bootsy headlining his own tour. For the time, though, the shows were going extremely well. I had more fun on- and offstage than I have ever had. Life was about sex, drugs, and whatever category you put the Mothership Connection tour in. Sex, Drugs, and Funk. I have to add poker into the equation because whenever I wasn't involved in the aforementioned activities, I was playing poker.

Officially called the P-Funk Earth Tour, it was truly a musical, visual, and sensory spectacle. Of course, the music was basically categorized as R&B, but the overtones of rock, gospel, and jazz were present throughout the show. The music included some old tunes by Parliament and Funkadelic like "Red Hot Mama" and "Maggot Brain," along with the new hits "Tear the Roof off the Sucker" and "Make My Funk the P-Funk." With the extremely large props, the lighting (including a laser light show), the updated costumes and stage sets, the performance was worth the money, even to a person who couldn't hear it.

The P-Funk players kept their same idiosyncratic costumes, although with some improvement in their quality. For example, Garry would use a *new* Holiday Inn towel every now and then, and there were new platform boots all around. Grady's faded purple-Arab outfit was given up for a brand-new, brightly colored, gold-trimmed purple outfit. Instead of the simple white sheet, George now had an array of outlandish costumes, including the fur thing I mentioned before, as well as an alien-looking creation complete with wings, fins, and a clown mask. I wore a floor-length, black velvet, gold-trimmed dashiki with white, alligator-skin platform boots.

The Earth Tour performers could have very well been space travelers who had observed the planet Earth and were making poor attempts at emulating the garments of Earthlings with materials that they had picked up from around the universe. I wondered myself if maybe these people were in fact aliens that had managed to fool even me. I was pretty sure about Maceo, Kush, and Rick. I just about knew exactly where they came from. I knew Bootsy, Catfish, and Frankie, but had they been captured or cloned or somehow been indoctrinated into some extraterrestrial cult? Was the plan to capture and brainwash all of us over a period of time? The show was definitely mesmerizing. As we traveled from place to place, we could see people beginning to adopt that P-Funk attitude and dress like P-Funk, act like P-Funk, and talk the P-Funk talk. It was scary how fast the P-Funk movement was spreading. It was like a religion.

Bootsy's Rubber Band was not quite as dogmatic but just as compelling. The Bootsy stage set had a more organized look. All of the amps and speakers were white with red stars on them. All of the band wore white, skin-tight uniforms made of stretch lamé and ornamented with little round mirrors. I was especially sexy in mine. Bootsy came onstage draped in a long cape that dragged the ground. With his very high platforms adding to his already-tall stature, with the famous star sunglasses and his form-fitting, star-studded jumpsuit, he appeared larger than life and had the audience in the palm of his hand before we played a note. He would appear out of a puff of smoke and just stand there for a while, allowing everyone to marvel at what they were seeing and what was about to happen.

When the music began, it was like an atomic explosion, the effects of which lasted for an hour and a half of very, very funky and very, very sexy music. The entire show was Bootsy firmly supported by the rhythms of Joel "Razor Sharp" Johnson, Frankie Kash, and Catfish Collins; the vocals of Mudbone and Peanut; and the Horny Horns. The Bootsy show was tight, yet loose at the same time. We were like a basketball team, all over the place and in exactly the right place, passing the ball when necessary, shooting the ball when necessary, and always complementing and blocking out and throwing it in to our great center to slam-dunk. From the opening "Stretching Out" to the closing "Hit Me, Band," the show didn't have a dead or even a down spot anywhere. The only difficult part of the show was: how do we end it? We solved that problem simply, by finishing "Hit Me, Band," then shouting in unison, "Okay, bye!" and disappearing from the stage.

The Earth Tour continued for about a year. It seemed like a year anyway. During that time I had approached George again about receiving residuals for the horn players. Again to no avail. He actually thought that it was funny that I had the audacity to think that something as menial as horns deserved royalties. The real slap in the face came when the first royalty checks for the *Mothership Connection* album came out. Everybody else was flashing nine- and ten-thousand dollar checks, while the horns had absolutely nothing. It didn't seem fair. I and the rest of the horn players felt that our contribution had been just as important as any of the other elements of the recording. It came down to a matter of opinion, and my opinion did not carry any weight now that the recording was complete. The work of the horn players was viewed by everyone in control as work for hire, and that's the way it remained. When they had first approached me to do this work for hire, it was like nobody else could do it like I could. I should immediately have made an agreement that took into consideration the kind of exclusive and unique "work for hire" that I was bringing to the project. But had I insisted on a royalty in the beginning, perhaps I wouldn't have gotten to be a part of the P-Funk movement at all. Anyway, it was too late. All I could do was to press for as much money as I could get and try to get some of my originals on the bandwagon as much as possible.

After George let me know that he didn't think that my horn work deserved residual remuneration, I never felt the same about him again. I did respect him for providing an arena in which I could practice my craft and expand my fame while earning a good living, but a cloud of resentment covered all the work I did for him from then on. I was given even more reason to wonder about the business practices of George and his managers when I found out, by accident, that the horns were earning three times as much per week as anyone else in the band. I never knew the exact details of anyone else's deal, but toward the end of the tour, I did notice a growing mood of dissatisfaction among the singers and the other members of the band. It didn't matter to me, because now the talk was about the Bootsy tour, which was to begin when the P-Funk Earth Tour ended. At that point, I wouldn't have to worry about the George Clinton organization again. Everybody's money was supposed to increase dramatically. We were to headline a tour with Kool and the Gang as the opening act. It was all set. We were finally going to get what we had been working so hard and so long for.

I don't remember exactly, but it seems like we went straight from the Earth Tour to the Bootsy tour. I do remember seeing a brand-new bus parked in front of the hotel next to a Winnebago-style mobile home. I was told that the new bus was for the Rubber Band and the mobile home was for Bootsy. I never saw the inside of the bus, but we were all called to a meeting in the Winnebago. I thought that the meeting was to announce the new salaries or pass out itineraries or something pleasant like that. But I was wrong. The meeting was to announce that the tour had been canceled. Bootsy, who had been in apparently perfect health the day before, had suddenly been stricken with a strange illness (shingles) and would need a undetermined amount of time to recuperate. I didn't know exactly what shingles was, but it was said to be a nerve disease that caused boils and sores to grow on different parts of the body. I didn't think that it was serious enough to cancel the whole tour. Maybe postpone it for a while. I always wondered to what extent Bootsy's business was intertwined with George's organization. Bootsy had not been able to help me with my royalty requests. Maybe he was also having trouble with George and was using this illness as a way to break free. That is what happened. After the Earth Tour, the whole thing did kind of fall apart. At least, it was not all lilacs and roses like it had been.

At first, I was really concerned for Bootsy's health. I never saw him. I was just sent messages that he was resting comfortably and was on his way home. Then it dawned on me that I was without a gig. My concern was suddenly shifted to my needs and my family's needs. It was like the rug had been snatched out from under me. Everyone was left to fend for himself. I had no idea what I was going to do. There was no word as to when or even if the Rubber Band was going to get back together. I just had to realize that that gig was over and that I had to look elsewhere for employment.

The party was over. My two-year vacation was over. Although the P-Funk experience hadn't gone as far as I had expected it to go, it certainly was not a loss. I had been part of a pivotal moment in the history of music. I had been part of the most extravagant and exciting road show ever put together by an R&B artist. I will be forever famous for my participation in the P-Funk's influence on the world society. I had the pleasure and privilege of working with some of the greatest musical innovators of my time. I had stretched my own creativity to its limits, and beyond, which gave me the nerve and the permission to go further with my own music—all thanks to my association with great freethinkers like George Clinton and Bootsy Collins. A confidence in my ability to make music had been awakened, and I felt that I could produce records. After watching George and Bootsy, not only did I know what to do, I also knew what never to do. However, I still lacked the knowledge and connections with which to make the deals that were ultimately necessary if I were to do my own producing. I needed a business partner, but I had no idea where to find one nor who I could trust. In the meantime, I needed a gig.

Count Basie

• • •

I put my producing aspirations to the side while I called every musician I could think of to announce that I needed a gig. I even called Ike Turner, as I had heard that he and Tina were doing well. I was in a desperate situation. But what happened was far different from anything I could have expected, even in my wildest dreams.

I got a call from Emile Charlap, who was contracting the Broadway show *Dancin'* and wanted to know if I would be interested in playing in the pit band. I wondered why Emile would call me. I had never played a Broadway show, he had never called me for any kind of gig ever, and there were really good trombone players in New York who did Broadway shows all the time. Well, it seems that there was a new rule being enforced by the New York Musicians Union that required every pit band to be 25 percent black. Emile simply did not know too many black musicians, and the other black trombonist he knew was already working. I was just happy that he remembered that I played trombone.

It would have been difficult for me to do the gig. It would have meant renting an apartment in New York, and the commute from L.A. would have negated the salary. But I had to consider the possibility. It would make it possible for me to hang in New York, do sessions and arrangements, and possibly hook up with that elusive jazz gig I had always wanted. This could be, I thought, what I had always dreamed of having. My friend Cecil Bridgewater, for instance, was doing a show and playing with Max Roach at the same time.

While I was thinking about the Broadway gig, I got yet another unlikely call. This one from Waymon Reed. He was playing with the Count Basie band and asked if I would be interested in filling the second trombone chair that had recently been vacated by Al Grey. Would I be interested?! Was he kidding? Of *course* I was interested. My first thought was, can I cut it? To me, it was the top big-band gig in the world, and I hadn't played in a big band since I had been in the Army. Waymon assured me that if I dedicated myself, I would be able to handle the gig in no time at all. It didn't pay as much as the New York gig, but I would not have to move and I would already be playing the jazz gig that I wanted so badly. Plus, this was Count Basie, and the Basie gig always led to bigger and better jazz opportunities. I was scared and apprehensive, but hopeful and eager. I took the Basie gig.

The first thing I had to do was get a haircut. In two years, that do that I had worn with the James Brown Show had deteriorated into sort of a freestyle Afro bush that I combed only every now and then.

I joined the band in Philadelphia, where I was sent to a suit wholesaler to pick up my navy-blue, three-piece, two-button polyester suit and a black tuxedo. These two suits, along with white shirts, a pair of black shoes, a string tie, and a black bow tie, were the extent of my Count Basie wardrobe. My street clothes were still sort of in the bizarre P-Funk mode. It took me a little while to assimilate back into wearing regular attire among normal people. My patched blue jeans, fur and knit sweaters, and high-top Dingo boots were especially difficult to give up. I hung on to my Playboy, mirrored-lens sunglasses for a long time.

I met the band at a hotel in downtown Philadelphia, where we boarded a chartered Greyhound bus for a short ride to the gig, which was somewhere nearby in New Jersey. Most of the guys reminded me of the gentlemen musicians I had grown up with. No one was exactly like anyone that I could put my finger on, but the overall vibe was similar to the feeling that I had when I was around the guys in my father's band. It was not as much an age thing as it was simply a comfortable, not-having-to-watch-your-back feeling. The band members all greeted me cordially but not too enthusiastically. Waymon made sure that I met all the key people, including a personal introduction to Basie, who he and everyone else called "Chief." It was like meeting a god. He was sitting there in the front seat of the bus, very relaxed. He hardly moved, but he did extend his hand readily and speak in a very friendly manner, although with a hope-you-make-it smile on his face. He might have actually said, "Hope you make it." Although I was welcomed, I got that "on-trial" vibe from

Backstage. Left to right: Sonny Cohn, Mel Wanzo, me. Courtesy of Greta Reed.

everyone. It was like, "We are glad to see you, but we don't want to fall in love with you until we find out if you can play in this band or not." Waymon had built me up, but it was still wait and see.

Then Waymon introduced me to Bill Hughes, the bass trombone player, and Melvin Wanzo, the lead trombone player. They had apparently heard of me from my solos on the James Brown records and, of course, from Waymon. I guess many of the guys had already heard of me, especially the younger ones like bass player John Clayton, third trombone player Dennis Wilson, and singer Dennis Rowland—they were the ones who kept up with what was happening on the popular music scene.

I was given a seat right behind Freddie Green, the band's famous guitar player. I was in the second to last seat on the bus. Across from me was Dennis and in front of him was John. That part of the bus was called "the ghetto," where card playing and other debaucherous activities took place. I guess I got a seat back there because there were no other seats available. Or maybe it was because I was younger than most of the guys up in front. It couldn't *possibly* have had anything to do with assumptions about my habits and/or character based on the reputation that attended musicians who had played for P-Funk and James Brown.

The gig in Jersey turned out to be in an old, twenties-style ballroom. No kidding. It looked straight out of the movie *The Cotton Club*. The people, too. I found out later that the format we followed in nightclubs was different from the usual concert format. But the Jersey gig was the perfect forum in which to get accustomed to the music—a relaxed situation in which nearly everyone was there to dance, as opposed to the concert mode, where the audience would simply sit and listen. A concert consisted of two 45-minute sets during which we would play twenty tunes at the most. In a dancehall, we might play as many as fifty tunes over a three- to four-hour period. That night, we also had a guest singer, a famous old lady vocalist whose name I can't recall.

It certainly was lucky for me that everyone was dancing. The music was not that hard, although I hadn't had to read music in a long time and I did miss a lot of notes. The problem was, first, my sound. Bear in mind that I had just come off of a gig in which the stage was filled with a six-foot-high wall of amplifiers and speakers to my rear. One very large, very loud bass speaker had been positioned directly behind me. Facing me had been monitors turned up as high as they would go, because each person wanted to make his monitor louder than everybody else's. To the right of the stage had been what we call a side-fill aimed directly into my right ear, so I could hear the mix of the whole band. This had caused me, for two years, to play extremely loud in order to hear myself and to match the attitude of guitar players who had their sound assisted by thousands of watts of electricity. Now, without a rehearsal, I was in a band setup in which the only mikes were at the piano, for Basie to talk into, and in front of the band, for solos. Although some of these guys had been doing this type of gig for thirty or forty years, I was expected to blend with the acoustic aggregation immediately. It didn't happen. No matter how hard I tried, I still sounded like an elephant in a bunny-rabbit parade. When I tried to play soft, either nothing came out of the horn or what did come out sounded like a duck calling its mama.

The second problem was that nobody played exactly what was in the score. When I read a part correctly, it would sound wrong because they had become accustomed to playing it a certain way. You would simply have to be around for a while to understand their unique phrasing style. For example, eighth-note passages were often played like triplets, but not always. You had to just know when and where and how to phrase what. I really appreciated the fact that Mel tried his best to keep me up on what was happening, but I still had to manage it as well as I could on my own. When that first gig ended, I felt like I had run a footrace and wondered if I would be fired. If so, I had no case. I had totally butchered the gig. But apparently I hadn't completely blown it, because on the way back to Philadelphia, Sonny Cohn—who played fourth trumpet usually, lead trumpet sometimes, and doubled as road manager—came up to me and gave me some money. He explained to me about my salary, when payday was, when draw day was, and so on.

About three nights later, as I was packing up my music after butchering yet another gig (only not quite as badly), Waymon, whose reputation as a judge of musicianship was in serious jeopardy, whispered in my ear, "You know that you can take that music to the room with you." It's funny but that had never crossed my mind. I don't know if I thought that everyone would think that I couldn't read well if they were to see me take the music home, but by now everyone knew for sure that I couldn't read well. Maybe I thought that there was some rule that forbade not putting the music in the case and passing it in to the band guy like I saw everyone else do. Whatever kept me from practicing on my own was dispelled by Waymon's words.

Over the next few days, I took my time and got all of the notes right, which was only half the battle. Learning to blend with and familiarize myself with the unique phrasings and dynamics of this band was something that only time and paying close attention would accomplish. Mel was constantly in my ear, alerting me to everything that he could while still playing his part. Getting used to managing the various mutes was another problem. After I started to get it, and I did get it after a short while, everyone began to help me more and more. It was like, "Okay, we see that you can hang and all you need is a nudge here and there and you'll be all right." I had definitely been correct about the feeling of being on trial, but as I progressed everybody loosened up and accepted me, little by little, as one of their own. This was, and still is, a special musical fraternity, and I was extremely proud and gratified to belong, especially since I knew that not just anybody could make it.

I became good friends with almost all the guys. Freddie Green, Dennis Rowland, John Clayton, and I played Tonk together. Bobby Plater and I shared an interest in the soap opera "The Young and the Restless." Of course, Waymon and I renewed our friendship. He was very close to Bill Hughes, so as we associated with each other I also grew to love and respect Bill like a big brother. Mel Wanzo was my first friend. It started out with him coaching me, but after a while I realized that he was helping me far beyond the normal "getting a new guy to fit into the band" type of help—he had literally taken me under his wing. We are still close friends.

Most mornings, you would find the older guys—Eric, Sonny, Poop-

Count Basie Band Dressing Room. Left to right: Sonny Cohn, Bobby Plater, Nolan "Shaeed" Smith. Photograph by Fred Wesley Jr.

sie, Danny, and Basie—sitting in the hotel lobbies, doing all the things that mature men do: drinking coffee, reading newspapers, smoking cigars, taking walks. Nolan Smith, who had replaced the lead trumpet player, Lin Biviano, soon after I had joined the band, was, and still is, a world-class runner and got me into jogging whenever we had the time. I was nowhere near his class, but I did become addicted to that positive endeavor for a long time because of him. Of course, all of the guys had their little funny ways, as we all do, but the Count Basie fraternity was stocked with a unique bunch of musicians who gelled, not only musically but also intellectually, philosophically, and socially, as well. We all found a way to get along.

The band traveled by airplane most of the time. A Greyhound bus was chartered in most cities to transport the band from airport to hotel, hotel to gig, gig back to hotel, and hotel back to airport. If the gigs were less than three-hundred miles apart, the bus was used. All Greyhound buses were identical, so it was like the same bus met us all the time. The band was very well organized, and its members were well mannered and wise in the ways of the road. Any one of them could have had a great career as a travel agent. If a plane were late, they had a routine that would automatically kick in. The road manager would make calls to the gig, bus, and hotel. Individuals would make calls to friends and loved ones in the city we were going to next. Guys would break out books, magazines, and crossword puzzles, according to how long the delay would be. With extra time, if space permitted, card games would start.

There was rarely a hassle about money—you got paid on payday and received a draw on draw day. Never late, sometimes early. Extra money was automatic when the band was overseas or anywhere that the cost of living was higher. There was hardly a situation that the guys hadn't had to deal with before, so there was no tripping or complaining. Everything just moved on in an orderly fashion. It was a joy for me to be in this relaxed atmosphere after the chaotic lack of logistical planning with the James Brown and P-Funk organizations. There was a genuine respect among everyone in the band. After all, everybody there really wanted to be there, and everybody really wanted everybody else to be there, too.

I was so busy trying to learn the parts and the phrasings in those first few weeks that I couldn't really enjoy the great music of the Count Basie Orchestra, the style of which, of course, I had grown up revering as one of the best ever created. When I settled down and realized that I, Fred Wesley Jr., from lowly Mobile, Alabama, was actually here playing second trombone in the Count Basie Orchestra, sitting in the chair formerly held by one of the all-time trombone greats, Al Grey—well, it was mind-boggling.

I had the best seat in the house. To my right front, at about two o'clock, I looked directly into the face of the Chief himself. At first, this had been a terrible place to be, because I could see the pain on his face every time I played a wrong note or played a note too loud or in the wrong place. Seeing his pain hurt me almost as much as it apparently hurt him. But now that I was playing the right notes in the right places, it was a pure pleasure to enjoy the music with him. He did, without a doubt, enjoy every minute of the band's performances. At about one o'clock sat, almost always with his legs crossed, Freddie Green. No way could I have ever imagined how wonderful it would feel to actually see his hands and fingers chunk out that relentless four-on-the-floor method of playing the chord changes. Just the sight of it made it even more dynamic. Once,

Freddie missed a gig for some reason, but his presence was still there in the hearts and minds of everybody in the band. I can't explain it, but he was there so hard when he was there that he was still there even when he wasn't there.

At about three o'clock stood the tall, young bass player, John Clayton. How a twenty-five year old found the maturity and wisdom to lock grooves like "Shiny Stockings" and "Corner Pocket" with perennial professionals like Freddie Green, Count Basie, and Butch Miles, I don't know. He must have grown up the same way I had, hanging out and playing with guys twenty years his senior.

As I looked around to my right, I had an unobstructed view of the entire rhythm section. I could almost reach out and touch the drum set of Butch Miles, who was set up just beyond and behind my outreached right hand. We shared many a mutual thrill, hand slap, and congratulations during my short time in the band.

Directly behind me was Waymon Reed, my good friend and mentor and hot man in the trumpet section. Next to him and behind me to my immediate left was Nolan Shaeed Smith. Although Nolan was from L.A., I had never met him. He had apparently been in the Count Basie band before, as everyone seemed to know him. I thought that he was an exceptionally good lead player for his age, but then I found out that he was way older that he looked. He still was a great player. Next to Nolan sat Sonny Cohn, a longtime member of the band. His main gig was fourth trumpet, but on special songs like "Lil' Darlin'" and other slow tunes, he played lead. He also was the road manager. On the end of the trumpet row, was Pete Minger, a quiet man who kept mostly to himself but who rivaled Waymon as a bebop soloist.

To my immediate left was my main man, Mel Wanzo, the consummate lead trombone player, expert in all the nuances of big-band playing. To his left was the third trombone player, Dennis Wilson, another youngster who was as good an arranger as he was a trombonist. On the end of the trombone row sat another veteran of the Count Basie band, Bill Hughes, the bass trombone player with a sound so big that it set the tone for most of the phrasing for which the Count Basie band is famous. I could always hear him over the whole band, subjecting everyone to his rhythmic and sonic will. It was necessary to play up to and down to whatever Bill Hughes was playing. If Basie led the band from the top, Bill led it from the bottom.

Directly in front of me to my right sat Kenny Hing, the second tenor player. A small, Asian American man who looked more like a doctor than he did a tenor player. He was heir to the solo spots of Eddie "Lockjaw" Davis and Jimmy Forrest and handled it like a champ. To my left front sat Danny Turner, the third alto player, a great soloist who had an outside way of playing inside stuff. In the center of the reed section sat the great Bobby Plater, who had successfully filled the chair vacated by the incomparable Marshall Royal. Bobby knew almost every chart in the book by heart. The only times I ever saw him get upset were when someone did something to Jill on "The Young and the Restless" and when Basie called a chart that was so obscure and so seldom played that he would have to get the music out of his case, which usually stayed under his seat unopened. He played so pretty that many times I had to restrain myself from jumping down there and kissing him.

The fourth tenor chair was occupied by Eric Dixon, to whom I still owe a hundred dollars for betting against the Dallas Cowboys in the 1978 Super Bowl. Eric was another of the twenty- or thirty-year veterans of the band. He also was a great soloist in style of Paul Gonsalves or Lucky Thompson and one of the many prolific arrangers in the band—Bobby Plater, Dennis Wilson, John Clayton, and Bill Hughes, to name a few.

Charles Fowlkes, affectionately known as "Poopsie," held down the baritone sax chair. And I do mean held down by a man who was not so much big as he was tall. He was at least 6'4." Somewhere in the world is a documentary of the Count Basie band filmed in eight millimeter by Charlie Fowlkes, whose avocation was motion-picture photography long before the videocamera was invented.

If I had had to pay for a ticket to see the band from the vantage point I had every night, it would have cost way too much to buy. Sometimes, I would sit there and think to myself, "This is the best thing that anyone can be doing. It don't get no better than this." I would drift off into a daze and forget that I was playing a gig. Once, I missed an entrance, and Chief yelled up to me, "If you want to watch the show, you have to buy a ticket." Tears would well up in my eyes every time I heard the reed chorus in "Lil' Darlin'." Another time, I tried to play the gig under the influence of marijuana—a terrible mistake. Between getting all enthused and thrilled and crying about the music, trying to remember where and what was going on with the music and the mutes, and finding the charts and everything, I completely messed up. At moments, I just sat there completely confused. I never tried that again.

There was a policy in the Basie band that nobody ever got fired. It

Count Basie Band at Disneyland. Left to right: Count Basie, John Clayton, Freddie Green, Butch Miles, Kenny Hing, Waymon Reed, me, Danny Turner, Nolan Smith, Mel Wanzo, Sonny Cohn, Bobby Plater, Dennis Wilson, Pete Minger, Eric Dixon, Bill Hughes, Charlie Fowlkes. Courtesy of Mel Wanzo.

was said that if you didn't fit the mold or didn't pick up the phrasings or didn't mesh socially with the other guys in the band, you would just fade away. One day, you would simply not be there anymore. I saw it happen to more than one really good player.

It was a little more of an event when Waymon left the band. It was rumored that he and the great song stylist Sarah Vaughan had a thing going on. I thought that it was highly unlikely because of their age difference, but, on the other hand, knowing what I knew about Waymon's unusual taste in women, I thought it was very possible. Sure enough, Waymon and Sarah were "courting." I got to see it firsthand, as Sarah was frequently making guest appearances with the band. In the summer of 1978, Waymon Reed and Sarah Vaughan did, indeed, get married. Waymon left the band to assume the position of manager and music director for his new wife. This left a gaping hole in the trumpet section and in the band as a whole.

To fill this hole, we had to find a trumpet player who could not only play the parts but who was also a good jazz player. This time I got to see for myself a guy come, not fit in, and go—all in the space of about a week and a half. He had the temerity to think that his clinical ability to play jazz gave him the right to have a jazz attitude. You know, aloof and distant, arrogant and cocky, like he was Miles Davis or somebody. I think that he really could play, but nobody liked him and he disappeared.

The next guy to try for the gig was a very young and extremely well trained trumpet player from Los Angeles, who I knew from the Brother's Johnson band—Ray Brown. (No relation to the great bass player of the same name.) Ray was very experienced for his tender years, and he went about sight-reading the parts instantly, with a humble attitude. His only shortcoming was his jazz playing. After Waymon, anybody would sound a little funny, but it was clear anyway that bebop was not Ray's strong suit. I had seen players struggle with bebop before, and in my mind it was something that you either got or didn't get. If you didn't get it right away, it usually took years of serious study and practice to get it. Although we all loved Ray right away, we were prepared to miss him fondly because of his inability to do the exciting jazz solos that the second trumpet chair required. He remained, however, because of his agreeable attitude and his likable persona, and because his sound was irreplaceable and most of the solos could be handled by Pete. And to everyone's surprise, little by little, and in a short period of time, Ray became a great soloist. I think that his commitment to conquering his shyness and the strength of everyone's vibe pulling for him simply enabled him to put what he knew in theory into action.

With the acquisition of Ray Brown, the edition of the Count Basie Orchestra that I, in my own, personal, humble opinion, consider to be the best that was ever assembled, was complete. It certainly was the most versatile. There was a perfect mix of old school and new school. Previously, there had been only old school players, and since, they have been mostly new school. When I was there, Basie was still alive, and all the players, young and old, were influenced and led by him personally. Now, all the band members are influenced by players who were influenced by Basie and the other originals who have since passed on. Second- and thirdhand influence. While the band still has its unique sound, the real power has been dissipated, with Bill Hughes, Mel Wanzo, and Johnny Williams (who replaced Poopsie) being the only original members still alive. They are simply outnumbered by well-meaning, very good young players. Together, nevertheless, they have succeeded in keeping the legend of Basie alive.

Most of my jazz resumé is a result of my playing with the Basie band and the many guests who appeared with or on the same bill with him. Technically, I have actually shared the stage with Joe Williams, Sarah Vaughan, Ella Fitzgerald, Tony Bennett, Jack Jones, Oscar Peterson, Milt Jackson, Dizzy Gillespie, Thad Jones, Cab Calloway, Della Reese, Peggy Lee, Billy Eckstine, Joe Pass, Mel Tormé, the Mills Brothers, and Buddy Rich. But my contribution to their performances was very small. Again, I really should have been buying some tickets.

The only drawback to the Basie gig was the low pay. Until the little money that I had saved from the Horny Horns advance and the publishing royalties from the J.B. tunes became inadequate to support my wife and daughters in the manner to which they had become accustomed, I didn't even think about the fact that I was only making $500 a week and paying my own rent out of that. On my own, I probably would have paid to be in the band, but the kids had to eat. I wondered if anybody else in the band was getting a salary that low. Of course not. I was the new boy. Guys like Bill Hughes and Sonny Cohn must have been doing far better than that. But I never asked, and I never found out. They all did seem to be very happy, even though some of them had kids in school and other personal responsibilities. It got to the point at which I would have to do something or my wife and kids were going to starve and get put out of our beautiful new house in affluent View Park in L.A. Even had I gotten paid twice as much, it still would not have been enough. I got a little relief by continuing to do sessions with George and Bootsy whenever I had days off.

Once, when the band was performing in Detroit, I got Waymon, Danny, and a few of the other guys to do a Bootsy session during the day before the gig that night. We must have done five tunes and barely made it to the gig on time. I was greeted by Basie with a "How you feeling, Fred?" I said, without thinking, "I'm tired. We have been recording all day." This was a concert, and I didn't expect to have to deal with any new music, but the first tune that Chief called was "Hey, Jim," a tune that he had never called since I had joined the band. I didn't have time to look it over, but I soon discovered that it was a fast blues in the key of G. Not a bad key for me, and thank goodness, because up popped a four-chorus second bone solo. After I scuffled through that one and before I could catch my breath, he called another unfamiliar tune with a second bone solo. The surprises continued throughout that first set. It was like the Count Basie band, featuring Fred Wesley. The only other times that Basie allowed me to play solos—even though he knew that was my best skill—were when we played dances in obscure places like Lanskrona, Scotland, and Leesburg, Florida. He reserved venues like Avery Fisher Hall in New York City and the Montreux Jazz Festival in Switzerland for featuring veterans like Bill Hughes and Sonny Cohn.

The second week that I was in the band, we played the Grammy Awards. We were scheduled to play a tune by the band that had been nominated for "Best Jazz Performance." The tune had a twenty-four-bar second trombone solo, on blues changes, in the key of F. I couldn't believe my good fortune. I was about to play a solo on changes that I could handle blowing out of my ear, with the Count Basie Orchestra, with everyone in the music industry in attendance, and everybody in the world watching and listening on TV. I was so calm and sure of myself that before we went on, I was backstage consoling Crystal Gale, who was very nervous about making a presentation. I expected that my part would be a piece of cake. We were to start playing behind a curtain, then, as the curtain opened, the stage would move up and forward to center stage. The rehearsal went great. My solo was very exciting, and I felt that I would perform even better on the actual show.

But as the band was being introduced, Basie changed the tune to "Sweet Georgia Brown," a Sammy Nestico arrangement that featured the second tenor player, Kenny Hing. I had expected to make a grand entrance, sitting calmly, smiling and enjoying a classic Count Basie piano intro. Instead, the curtains opened with me scrunched down in my music box, fumbling through the pages, trying to find number seventy-five in the book. It was one of my favorite charts in the book, but my part was so difficult that I didn't even have a chance to look up, let alone see who was in the audience or smile for the cameras. Kenny became a star that night. They must have had five different camera angles on him as he played LAMF (like a motherfucker) for what seemed like three minutes. Looking back, I guess that Basie realized, at the last minute, that a newcomer was about to get airplay that a player with more dues under his belt and more time on the gig deserved more. Maybe it wasn't a last-minute change for anyone but me. Nobody else was scrambling for their music when the curtain opened.

It seemed like Basie was always trying to teach lessons. I learned, on that night in Detroit for example, not to complain to your boss about

Basie at home. Photograph by Fred Wesley Jr.

outside work that you had been doing. Was he supposed to take it easy on me because I had worn myself out working on somebody else's job? From then on, I kept my outside activities to myself.

I certainly learned not to gamble with people I didn't know, especially at a game that I didn't know much about. I heard Basie and Eric Dixon talking about playing cards, and, of course, considering myself a pretty good card player, I asked if I could join them sometime. The opportunity came one day in Japan. We had a day off, and Basie, Eric, and a guy from the booking office who had joined the band for the Japanese tour were looking for a fourth person to play blackjack with. I didn't like blackjack and hardly ever played the game, but I did know the basics and thought that it would be a good chance for me to spend some time with the great Count Basie in a relaxed, personal, man-to-man situation. We gathered in Basie's room.

I should have known that I was in trouble when they announced what the bank was. The first bank was practically all the money that I had in my pocket. I didn't want to punk out right away, so I said that I would play a few hands. Who knows, I might get lucky and win some right away. I had been killing them in the Tonk game on the bus. Before the deal, everybody in the room lit up very large, very strong-smelling cigars. I don't know if the cigar smoke had anything to do with my decisions, but I didn't last one deal before I was completely broke. They were laughing and smoking. I felt like a real fool. I was now trying to find a graceful way out of the room before I was asphyxiated by the cigar smoke. Basie insisted that I stay a while longer and loaned me a hundred dollars. I continued to lose and choke. I finally had no choice but to just get up and leave. As I stumbled out of the room, broke and embarrassed and gasping for air, I could hear them laughing their asses off. In the end, I felt a little honored that I had given the great Count Basie and his boys a good laugh and a story to tell. But I never repaid his hundred dollars.

I have many fond memories of my short time with the Count Basie Orchestra. The best gig that I remember was at the Great American Music Hall in San Francisco. The band had just completed a two-week tour of Japan, during which we played almost every night. There followed about three days of not playing at all while we traveled from Japan, before the Great American Music Hall hit. With all that playing in Japan and the three days of rest, after a few minutes of warm-up, my chops and everybody else's chops were in tip-top condition. The audience was seated at tables, with everyone drinking and smoking and talking among themselves. I specifically remember the murmuring of the people and the smoke all over the hall. That murmuring stopped abruptly with the appearance of Basie and the band.

When the band was seated and settled, the concert opened with a very fast tune called "Wind Machine." As many of the Basie charts did, "Wind Machine" started with a quiet piano solo accompanied by only the bass, guitar, and drums. After about eight bars, all the horns entered at the same time, shocking the audience and blowing all of the smoke out of the hall. I was shocked, too. First, at seeing the hall completely cleared of smoke, then at realizing that the band seemed more powerful than its usual powerful self. At first, I thought that it was just the good acoustics of this famous music venue, but as the gig progressed I saw that the band was stronger, crisper, and cleaner than I'd ever heard it before. The solos were more creative, and the band was generally tighter. Everyone felt it. It was the physical strength we had gained from playing so much that made the difference. I learned that when an instrumentalist is strong, everything he does, from solos to blending with the sections, is better and far more enjoyable. That night, everybody was strong, and together we played the best concert that I ever witnessed with any Count Basie Orchestra.

I was especially proud when my father was able to see me in New Orleans with the Count Basie band. He had made the short drive over from Mobile with Mr. Charlie Smith, the trumpet player he had remained friends with since we all played together back in the late '50s while I was still in high school. I was very happy to finally gain his approval for a band I was playing with. He never quite got into the fact that his son, who he had had such high hopes for, used the talent that he had passed on to play with James Brown and, even worse, Parliament/Funkadelic. It was one of the few times that I ever saw him pleased with what I was doing.

As I traveled around the world with the Basie band, the issue of money kept creeping into the sheer ecstasy that I was experiencing, keeping me from being totally at ease. I finally had to face the fact that sooner or later I would have to give up the gig and pursue a more lucrative musical endeavor. I didn't have anything definite in mind. I really wanted to produce records, although I still didn't have any idea how I would land producing jobs. My chops were better than they had ever been, but it was still questionable as to whether or not I could break into the L.A. studio scene in time to keep the family from going under financially. I supposed I could return to the P-Funkers, but their business had gone the way of maybes and ifs. Plus, I really didn't want to step back into that situation, which had become a real mess since Bootsy had pulled out. I didn't know what to do, but I knew that I had to do something other than the Count Basie gig.

I finally decided to go directly after some producing jobs. My wife, Gertie, had the idea that we should write to all of the record companies and inform them of my credentials and of my availability to produce records for them. If I got work from any one or two of them, it would be worth the time and trouble. Sure enough, I heard from Dr. Don Mizell, who was with Electra-Asylum Records. He had a group called Chameleon that he wanted produced in the funk/jazz genre, and we agreed that I would be perfect for the job. I was both happy and sad. Happy that I was going to get a chance to try my hand at producing, and very sad that I was going to have to leave the Count Basie Orchestra.

It was the saddest severance of a gig that I had ever experienced. I left Ike and Tina disgruntled about not having enough solo playing to do. I left Hank Ballard and the Midnighters half dead. I left the Army very happy to form my own band. I left my own band disappointed at the members for not being able to understand and agree with my philosophy of music selection. I left James Brown the first time because I felt that he didn't respect me as a musician. I left Sam and the Goodtimers to keep from starving to death or resorting to a life of crime. I left James Brown the second time because I just couldn't take it no more. I left P-Funk and Bootsy because something happened with the business that I knew nothing about and had no control over. Now I was leaving Basie just because I couldn't figure out how to survive on the piddling salary that was paid to great jazz musicians. I thought it a shame that the music I loved the most paid the least.

9

Hollywood, Hollywood

• • •

The first time I had arrived in L.A, it had been by way of friends and family who already lived there. This time, although I was still technically a resident, it was like I was "brought in" to do a job for Electra-Asylum Records. Brought in not from New York or London but from "off the road." I was an enigma, filled with tales of adventures on the road with James Brown, P-Funk, and Count Basie. I was already a legend. Dr. Don Mizell, who was head of the jazz and R&B division at Electra-Asylum Records, got the bright idea to use this legend and my expertise in the studio to launch his new pet project: a group called Chameleon.

I spent my first meeting with Don answering questions about James Brown, Bootsy and George, and Count Basie. We agreed that my association with both funk and jazz music made me the best choice to produce Chameleon, because the group wanted to straddle the line between jazz and funk, which was becoming a trend at that time. Groups like Maze and War and artists like Grover Washington Jr. and Roy Ayers had been very successful following the jazz-funk theme. Having no agent and very little experience at solo producing, I was ready to take pretty much whatever deal Dr. Don offered me to do the job. It turned out to be very little more than a chance to prove myself as a producer, which I anxiously and eagerly accepted. I knew that I could do the best jazz-funk album in the history of modern music.

I anticipated certain problems. Bands consist of people. Creative people. Sensitive, creative, artistic people with egos and opinions. I felt that I could deal with such issues, since I had plenty of experience doing so with the James Brown Show. Chameleon had an array of highly skilled, very intelligent, well-mannered, good-looking young men who, right off, took me in as a friend and as someone they were willing to take directions from. Also in my favor was the fact that they all loved and respected each other. There were no visible rifts between the guys in the band— they all had the same goal, which was to do whatever was necessary to make a good record. I didn't foresee any personal or ego problems in working with Delbert Taylor, the lead vocalist and trumpet player; Azar Lawrence, the saxophone player; Michael Stanton, the keyboard player; Jerold Brown, the bass player; Earl Alexander, guitarist and singer; and Ron Bruner, the drummer.

Together, we uneventfully selected the best of their original songs and went about recording at the trendy Indigo Ranch recording studio, nestled in the mountains of Malibu, California. The studio was state-of-the-art, complete with an imported English engineer and a very sweet guy who cooked us different vegetarian delights every night. Although my pay was small, this project was regarded by the Hollywood community as one of the top productions in progress. I allowed a relaxed atmosphere. I would seldom have a closed session, having learned that visitors and drop-ins caused the artists to perform beyond their normal abilities. Consequently, we had girlfriends, wives, buddies, record company executives, groupies, drug dealers, and other people who had heard about what was going on. (Olivia Newton-John came by one night.) However, we continued to make steady progress amid the constant party that was going on. I had a capacity for garnering good work out of chaos by making every aspect of the confusion seem like part of the performance. I made myself the center of attention, because I had to completely control what was going on in order to keep things from getting out of hand. I was the partymaster, but I had to keep myself centered and focused while everyone else had fun. This way the atmosphere stayed light and relaxed. The performers would "show out" for whatever audience was on hand, and they really did deliver much better performances than would have been possible in the usual tense and structured scene of the recording studio. It was like a controlled live performance. I simply organized the fun into the making of a record.

We were having a good time and making a good record, until one day a report came out that KISS-FM had become the number one station in the country by programming, almost exclusively, disco music! Dr. Don called me into his office and told me that he had decided to change the jazz-funk approach for our project to a disco approach. It never occurred to me to argue the jazz-funk position. Instead, I proudly used my ability to do whatever he and the record company thought was necessary to sell a million records. What we ended up with was a record that was almost completely unsellable. It wasn't jazz. It wasn't disco. It wasn't funk. It wasn't R&B. It wasn't anything that you could put your finger on. It was good, but good what? My first solo production job ended up on the Electra-Asylum shelf somewhere. The band that started out so compatible ended up going their separate ways, and I ended up as yet another unemployed producer on the streets of Hollywood.

But there was not, ultimately, a sad ending to my producing story. It was the first chapter of what I hoped would be a long career in the studio. I now knew how much I loved doing it. I found that I was very good at it. I knew what I had done wrong. I would not let a record company executive change my direction mid-stride again without coming up with a fresh budget and a fresh deal. Trying to make a disco record out of an almost finished jazz-funk record was a terrible mistake—although I nearly pulled it off. I could hardly wait for an opportunity to do it again.

That opportunity came very soon. Apparently, Dr. Don had not lost trust in my abilities. We were set to do another Chameleon album, but the band had begun having internal problems, so that project was put on hold until they could figure out who was who and what was what in their organization. I remembered having had similar problems with my own band, the Mastersound, back in the late '60s. While the leadership and direction of Chameleon was being resolved, Don turned me on to another project by another self-contained band, Trussell, a group from Virginia. This situation was slightly different and presented a different set of problems. Trussell had a manager, and the manager had the production deal, which credited him as co-producer. This time I had to deal with the sensitive, creative, artistic personalities of the guys in the band, as well as the tyrannical, demanding personality of Al Richardson, their manager. The deal was further complicated by the fact that Al had made the deal directly with Joe Smith, the president of Electra-Asylum Records. So I had to please Al; two executives from the record company; Michael Spratley, the lead vocalist; Bill McGhee, the trumpet player; Ron Smith, the drummer; Larry, keyboard player and vocalist; Chicken, the guitarist; Juicy, trombonist and guitarist; and Blue, the bass player.

The profile of this band was a little different from Chameleon. None of the players were professional musicians, unless you consider the fact that Bill was a music teacher. They all were either currently enrolled at Virginia State College or had recently graduated from that school. Most were not even music majors but students of pre-law, engineering, history, and the like. The band had been formed as a sideline for making a little extra money while in school but had mushroomed into a very popular unit with a promising future as a recording band. Their original songs were reflective of the post–Civil Rights Movement attitudes of black college campuses during the late '70s.

Although Al Richardson had heard the band and secured a deal for them at Electra-Asylum, he didn't seem to be their type of guy. He was a slick, fast-talking, high-rolling, big-city-hustler type who didn't really seem to match the low-key, country college kids in the band. But they had found common ground in the pursuit of a hit record. I came in as the ultimate catalyst for the project, and it took all of my diplomatic and political skills to complete the record. Focusing the various points of views into one direction was one of my greatest achievements. But I had to use the various expertise of a hustler, intelligent college students, and myself—a producer who would say anything to anybody and be everything to any and everybody—to pull it off. Together we labored through problem after problem, mind-game after mind-game, and ultimately created a great album and a Top Ten single, "Love Injection." We were set to do a second record, but the tour that followed the hit record took its toll on the band. On the tour, the differences between the band and their manager widened. Without me to moderate, the band fell apart. So the second album never happened. Nor did I become the next big R&B producer with a string of hits.

I was encouraged by the success of "Love Injection," although disappointed at not being able to follow up with another hit. Again, I assessed what had gone wrong. Things over which I had no control had caused the failures. If I had been the manager, if I had gotten the deal, picked the songs, had the final say, the results would have been different. What I needed was someone who knew the inner workings and how to manipulate the political structure of the music business.

In the meantime, I still had to earn a living. When I had gotten back to L.A., I had contacted my old buddies from Sam and the Goodtimers and had found that they were all into much different things by then. Mack Johnson was recording on his own, so I helped him out with little things when I could. Clifford was bandleader for Ray Charles and invited me to join that band. Although I remembered a time when I would have jumped at a chance to play with Ray Charles, this was the wrong time and the wrong place. During the Ray Charles band's yearly vacation, Clifford called me to do some horn overdubs for Andre Fischer, the Rufus drummer-turned-producer. Andre was producing a band from Oklahoma City called the Gap Band. Their horn section was being augmented with Clifford, myself, and a bari-sax player named David Ii. I asked, "David who?" I didn't want to carry on too much about the man's name, especially since he was a very large, unpleasant-looking fellow, but the name did strike me as strange. It turned out that he had renamed himself Ii, the "big I, little i" being a statement of his self-esteem. Rather than embrace yet another ethnicity to protest an imposed ethnic name, he simply named himself himself. It could have come out as David Me, but to be grammatically correct, he went with David Ii. David remained true to his name throughout our friendship. He was a very self-centered, self-promoting, proud, extremely talented person. He was not only a great musician but a great motivator and deep-thinking philosopher.

David invited me to join his big band, the Love Eye Orchestra, which rehearsed weekly at the musician's union rehearsal facility and to which he devoted much of his time when he wasn't traveling with Ricky Lee Jones or Little Richard. The band gave him the means to express his unique way of performing and a forum for his philosophical renderings. "Be good to yourself before you end up by yourself" was his usual theme. It was interesting how he could blend music with philosophy and make it entertaining. He was a dynamic speaker and a compelling performer, both on the saxes and on a homemade percussion instrument.

I learned from David. I learned from him the importance of self-confidence. David said, "You can't convince the audience to believe in your solo unless you believe it yourself." I retorted, "I believe my solos." He came back, "Okay, you can't convince the audience to believe in your solos unless you look and act like you believe it yourself." David had no patience with humbleness when it came to performing, and his band reflected his cocky attitude. "Its just like making love," he'd say. "If you perform like you know what you're doing, it frees the person you're making love to or the audience you're performing for to relax and enjoy what's happening to them. They know that you're in charge, and they don't have to do anything more than simply enjoy." Those few words—along with David persistently instructing and worrying me about the subject—transformed me from a so-so, timid, tentative soloist into the take-charge, confident, dynamic soloist that I am today.

I became the lead trombone player in the band. Nolan Shaeed Smith from the Count Basie Orchestra was back in town and played lead trumpet with David's band. Ed Pleasant played lead alto, Benny Parks was the drummer, and Bill Carter was the baritone sax player. The rest of the band varied from week to week, with some guys sticking around longer than others. David demanded a certain loyalty to the band and to himself personally, so if a player wasn't able to commit to the unique music and/or deal with the unusual personality of David Ii, he didn't last long. You had to be really self-confident or you would be intimidated by David Ii. David would say, "You have to train people how to treat you."

David had numerous Basie charts in his book, but most of the band's material he either wrote himself or confiscated by hook or crook from many different sources. I became one of those sources. Besides the rehearsal, the band had one regular gig on Sunday afternoons at the Take Five Club, located deep in the neighborhood. It didn't pay much, but the rehearsal kept my chops up and the gig was a whole lot of fun. No matter what else I was doing, the Love Eye Orchestra remained an important part of my weekly routine.

During the last few years with James Brown and the two years with P-Funk, I had managed to get my family into one of the most affluent neighborhoods in the Los Angeles area. The house was big and spacious, just right for parties. While I had been on the road, I had never had time to enjoy the benefits of living the high life in L.A., but my wife had done so in my stead. She had befriended many of the Hollywood in-crowd. No big stars, but a number of Hollywood hopefuls, as I call them, were her friends and regular visitors at my house. My wife, Gertie, had become quite the socialite, and parties would break out at the house at any time, especially on holidays.

One of her best friends was Miss Vonny Sweeny. Vonny was a very nice lady who was interested in discovering and managing people who were talented and had an obvious future in the entertainment business. She thought of me as one of these people. Although she had not made the big score yet, she was connected with a lot of people who could make things happen in "the business." Always in my corner, Vonny got me arranging and producing jobs whenever she could. We never managed to hook up the big producing or recording deal for me, but she did introduce me to Chip Donelson, who was at the time managing the small but successful Pizazz record label.

Chip and I hit it off right away. He, too, had had successes in the business, promoting records and generally managing record releases and recording artists. He, too, was looking for that big score that would put him over the top. As we got to know one another, we became aware that we each had what the other needed. We developed a close friendship and set about planning a partnership to make some music and some money.

The first thing we had to do was find an artist. We decided it had to be someone really good, with a temperament we could deal with. We considered all the musicians Vonny was managing and the Pizazz artists Chip was working with. They included the unbelievably beautiful Kellee Patterson and the veteran jazz singer O.C. Smith, who was still working off the big hit "Little Green Apples." Vonny had a girl group called Crystal and a male singer, Michael Wycoff, who all ended up commiting to a record deal or some other producer. We finally settled on Delbert Taylor.

Delbert was the featured singer with Chameleon. Although the guys in Chameleon were all extremely talented, Delbert stood out as the most visible, the most versatile, and the easiest to deal with. Delbert was an imposing presence. He was a 6'5," 230-pound, light-skinned black guy who was the first man I ever saw who wore his long curly hair in a ponytail. Delbert's vocal style was unique. He was a classically trained baritone who used his powerful, melodious voice to sing jazz and soul like Lou Rawls and Wilson Pickett. A natural showman on stage, he could dance way better than you would expect for a man his size. The effect was thrilling, and we were sure that with the right songs he could be the next great soul or pop or R&B or jazz singer. One of our challenges would be to channel the music in a specific direction—the most lucrative direction. Chip assured us that he had that covered. In addition to Delbert's extraordinary vocal talent, he also was a decent trumpet player, an exciting pianist, and he wrote beautiful love ballads and other original music. Plus, he was a regular guy who got along with Chip and me very well. We had our artist. Now we needed money to make some demos.

I was still in pretty good shape financially and was making a good living by arranging and playing horn and string sessions around town. Since I was completely convinced that we had put together the proper team to make a big smash in the business, I didn't hesitate to take out a second mortgage on my house to finance the Delbert Taylor project.

We wanted to make the demo as representative of all of Delbert's talents as possible, so we did two of his love ballads and two up-tempo R&B tunes. We took our time and did basic production—rhythm section, vocals and background vocals on all four tunes. The demos came out really well, so we put together a package and sent Chip out to shop for a deal. We didn't anticipate a long period of waiting. With the quality of material that we had put together and the big names that Chip had lined up to listen, we were sure that a bidding war was the only long thing that we might have to deal with. Chip knew and had personal relationships with people like LeBaron Taylor and Larkin Arnold. Plus, most of these people had at least heard of me due to my James Brown and P-Funk associations.

Apparently our music and our track records didn't mean a whole lot to the business biggies. After many weeks of beating on doors and ringing telephones off the hook, we barely got anyone to listen, let alone sign us to a deal. I learned that no matter who you knew and how many times they might tell you to "let me hear something" at a party or in a barber shop or at somebody else's session, when that real deal goes down, who gets it is dependent on who has his politics in place. Not only did we not have our politics in order, we didn't have any politics at all. All we had was music. Good music, but only music. We didn't have any favors to collect on, no Greek fraternity affiliation, no wife who was somebody's sister, no law degree, no hidden sexual preference, nothing that could get us in that magic door. It's a sad day when you realize that good music alone won't help you make it in the music business.

Undaunted, I decided to do some demos on some of my own stuff. I was still earning a living by doing horn and string arrangements for whoever Vonny or Chip or I could turn up. I had just finished a big job for Sigidi Abdallah, a copyist-turned-producer I had met at the music preparation office, run by Marion Sherrell, that I used. Sigidi had hooked up with Clarence Avant of Tabu Records and was producing a new, young band from Atlanta. I guess Sigidi must have liked the arrangements that he had copied for me, because he hired me to do the horns and strings for the S.O.S. Band. It was a big payday for me, and Sigidi got a monster hit out of the production. I also was working off and on with Bunny Sigler, a producer-songwriter from Philadelphia. He was producing a singer I rated up there with Delbert named Dutch Robinson. I arranged horns and strings for Dutch Robinson, Patti Brooks, and a Curtis Mayfield album—all produced by Bunny Sigler. There were other little projects that kept me going. One or two tunes here, a horn session there, a string arrangement every now and then.

But I wanted to do my own record. I was watching all of these other producers as I worked for them and thinking to myself that I could do

S.O.S. Band.
Left to right: Skin,
Billy, Jason, Mary,
Bruno, James Earl
Jones, Sonny,
Abdul Ra'oof.
Courtesy of First
Class PR files.

this just as well as they were doing it. I felt that I could do as well as some of the artists, too. Even though I wasn't a songwriter, I was hearing some marginal material getting over like a fat rat, which led me to believe that I could write songs. So, between jobs, I worked on writing my own songs, and when I got the chance I went into a studio and recorded demos, with me doing the vocals.

True to my personality, I wrote humorous songs about things that I observed in everyday life. Unplanned parties broke out at my house all the time, so I wrote a song called "House Party." I saw my bachelor friends falling in love for a while, then finding something wrong with the girl and moving on to the next one—over and over again—so I wrote the tune "I'm Still on the Loose." As I recorded these demos, I passed them on to Chip, who was still doing his thing, promoting records. He let Marv Stuart, who was managing Curtis Mayfield's Curtom Record label, hear my demo. Marv liked "House Party" and signed me to do a single with the understanding that an album deal would follow if the single did well.

The single did do well. "House Party" got into the Top Forty on the R&B charts and stayed there for five or six weeks. We followed with what I considered to be a very good album. I reinvented myself as Fred Wesley, the artist; Fred Wesley, the songwriter; and Fred Wesley, the singer.

I pictured myself as a musician who also sang and entertained, like the great Louis Jordan. There was not an artist doing that type of show on the scene at that time, and the format had been tremendously successful for Louis Jordan. I sang well enough and danced well enough and certainly played the trombone well enough to pull it off. As Louis Jordan did comedic songs like "Caldonia" and "Open the Door, Richard!" I wrote songs like "Bop to the Boogie" and "Let's Go Dancing." I sought to add a serious, philosophical element to the concept by including songs with subtle messages like "Life Is Wonderful" and "Are You Guilty?" Bootsy calls these "silly-serious" songs. I also wrote a self-promoting song called "I Make the Music" and a musical masterpiece of a love ballad entitled "If This Be a Dream." I was completely satisfied with the entire production. I was—and remain—very proud of every aspect of my first venture as a vocalist, songwriter, solo artist, and solo producer.

I put together a small but formidable band that included Melvin Webb, the drummer from Kansas City whom I had hired for James Brown. He lasted only minutes on the J.B. gig, but he was the heart and soul of my band. Melvin also brought to us the most unique, most energetic, and funkiest musician who ever lived—Lewis DuPriest—to play bass. The sightless yet all-hearing, all-knowing, all-feeling, most insightful keyboard player I ever worked with, Rudy Copeland, co-wrote "Bop to the Boogie" and also did lead vocals. The melodically sensitive, harmonically eloquent, and rhythmically aggressive Spencer Bean did the guitar work. The great percussionist Razz Abo Guinea, the son of my homeboy, pianist Ben Baker Jr., did all the hand-drumming, shaking, clip-ti-clopping, and pinging for the band. I performed most of the lead vocals and was the only horn. Rudy was the only real vocalist, but we all sang background when necessary. I was just as proud of this band as I was of the Mastersound. The difference was that these guys were all practicing professionals, as well as good friends.

For the album, we added a group of professional singers put together by Delbert, which included Carl Anderson of *Jesus Christ Superstar* fame. We also used one of Vonny Sweeny's girl groups, Alton McClain and Destiny, for background on "Are You Guilty?" David Ii added the special percussion instrument he invented to "If This Be a Dream," and Butch Bonner overdubbed a blues guitar on "Are You Guilty?"

The record company staged a real party at my house and hired a photographer to take pictures of the gala for the album cover. The party pictures, along with a beautiful picture of me as the partymaster, made an album cover that literally jumped out at you. The mix and mastering process went without a hitch. The product was delivered to Curtom and was approved and accepted by the company and its distributor, RSO Records. The release date was set for November 10, 1980.

I continued to do sessions here and there to support myself while I waited for the album to drop. I also rehearsed the band as much as possible in preparation for a tour that was being planned for after the album came out. All of the band members had agreed to do the tour but continued to do their own sessions and gigs until the big tour took place. We even turned down gigs because I didn't want to do anything for less than what we could get after the album had made some noise. We just waited and prepared for what we all were sure would be a new and very long, lucrative, and fun career. I even had regular physical and dance training to prepare for fronting my own show for the first time.

I didn't see it, but my wife said that I had developed an air about myself. She said that I had become cocky, argumentative, and selfish. I was very happy about the completion of the album and the success of the single, but I didn't detect any change in myself. I was just happy and confident to be getting attention from people who hadn't had time for me before. I dismissed what she said as her own negative reaction to seeing me less needy and less dependent on her support. I tried to pay more attention to her, thinking that maybe I had been neglecting our marriage by being so involved with the record. I was disappointed that she didn't seem to share my happiness and enthusiasm about the album. But I felt that after the money started to roll in, all of this dissension would disappear, and everything would be all right.

When that fateful day arrived, I headed up to Hollywood in my Cadillac, full of hope and joy. This was the day on which everything would come together for me. All the work, all the disappointments, all the years of doing other people's bidding was about to pay off. When I parked the car and went up to the RSO office, I was greeted by Chip and Marv. I noticed, right away, the funny looks on both of their faces. It turned out that, for some reason, RSO had, just that morning, dropped Curtom from its distribution roster. Marv assured me that this would only mean a little more time to wait for him to find another distributor for *House Party* and the music of all the other Curtom artists, who included Linda Clifford, Ava Cherry, and Jimmy Ruffin. I was mortified but still kept a positive thought. If Curtom and RSO thought that *House Party* was a good record, then it should not be difficult to find another major label that agreed. I remained hopeful until, after a month of beating the bushes for another distributor, all of the other Curtom records had been picked up except mine.

I couldn't believe it. The other records were all right, but clearly nothing special like *House Party*. The others were ordinary. There must have been a thousand records on the market at that time that sounded just like them. *House Party* was then and still is now a one-of-a-kind creation. To this day, I am baffled about why none of the geniuses in the music business ever heard what a unique and special piece of work *House Party* was and still is.

I was completely deflated. I listened to the album from beginning to end, over and over again and could find not one thing wrong. Even the sequencing was perfect. (Twenty some years later, I listen to it, and it still sounds just as enjoyable, just as entertaining, just as funny, just as skillfully produced as it sounded in 1980.) I couldn't imagine what the industry was looking for. I was angry. I was demoralized. I was disillusioned. And I was bitter. Bitter with myself for putting so much trust in the power of good music. Bitter with my wife for knowing that I was tripping all the time. Especially bitter with any and everyone in positions of authority in the entertainment business. I'm sure that I showed it with the cynical attitude I began to display anytime I was in contact with the Hollywood crowd.

I just could not accept the fact that my music wasn't good enough. I came up with all kinds of rationalizations. Maybe people thought that I belonged to James Brown and was unapproachable, or that I was wild and crazy and difficult to deal with like the P-Funk crowd. Maybe I had offended someone without knowing it and had been secretly blackballed or something like that. Maybe I did come off cocky and arrogant and people just did not like me. I didn't know what to think. I went into a shell and never wrote another song or tried to sing or do another record on myself again. I joined the large contingency of people in Hollywood who spend a lot of time—too much time—sitting around getting high and trashing the successful artists, producers, and executives in the music business.

The industry's rejection of my album didn't stop the calls for me to do horn and string overdubs. I didn't have a staff in place in L.A. as I had had in New York. Benny Powell had moved to New York, so I didn't have him to depend on as I had when I had worked on the movie scores. Instead, I would write at home and usually get Marion Sherrell or whoever was available to copy the charts. Either the client hired the horns or the band had their own horns or I made the calls myself. As long as I was working like that, I had no problems.

Much of my work was with self-contained bands. Once, I got an out-of-the-ordinary call from James Gadson of the Watts 103rd Street Band. I knew Gadson from when we played a short time together with Hank Ballard and the Midnighters. I had not seen him since that time, but I had heard that he had become the first-call studio drummer in Los Angeles and was singing and drumming with the Watts 103rd Street Band. They had had a big hit with "Love Land," on which he sang. The call was for me to arrange the horns and strings for an album he was producing on the singer Vernon Burch.

The players were all booked. The copyist was already engaged. All I had to do was to turn in the music and show up for the session. Benjamin Wright also did a couple of charts. I knew Benjamin from Montgomery, Alabama, where he was stationed in the Air Force during the time in which my band, the Mastersound, had played the Montgomery Elk's Club every Sunday night. His organ trio had played a matinee at the same club on Sunday evenings before us.

I was, however, the only second trombone player. Garnett Brown played first trombone. It was a rather large horn section. Two bones, three trumpets, and three saxes—alto tenor and baritone. I had been using my friends or horn players already in the bands that were being recorded. This was the first time that I got to do a session with "the cats." Even the players that Benny Powell had booked for me were of the upper-echelon persuasion, the players who were on call for top-notch movie and commercial dates that these not-so-well-hooked-up but still just-as-good musicians were not called for. These were, however, the top black cats. On trumpet we had Bobby Bryant, who was considered the best session man in town. He was a fine bebop player, but he could never nail to my satisfaction the funky licks that I wrote, and he got an attitude if I said anything to him about it. My friend Nolan Smith from the Basie band surfaced again on that session, along with Harry Kim, the only nonblack on this particular gig.

There are three Fred Jacksons that I have known during my musical career. The first one was a great jazz player I met in Chattanooga while I was playing with the Hi Fi's, the band from Huntsville, Alabama. The second one traveled with Smokey Robinson for years. The one on this session was distinguished as the one who drove the BMW, because they

Ernie Fields.
Photograph by
Fred Wesley Jr.

all played saxophone, and nearly everybody knew them all. This Hollywood yuppie was a fine session player, usually on alto.

The bari-sax player Bill Green was the first-call reed man in L.A. Mr. Green was first-call on a variety of reed and double-reed instruments. It was reported to me that he was a favorite with most of the great Hollywood arrangers, from Nelson Riddle to the guy who wrote "Moon River," Henry Mancini. He was a black-belt martial artist and a private reed teacher whose students included some of the best be-boppers in the world. It was a pleasure and a privilege to meet him, as he was also a very helpful and caring man.

The tenor player, who was also the contractor, was Ernie Fields. The name sounded familiar to me. I had heard it many times in connection with road shows and circuses. Old-timers would tell stories about when they had traveled with the Claxton Circus or the Ernie Fields Road Show, usually in the same breath. I wondered if this could be the same Ernie Fields. Naw, he was too young to be the same Ernie Fields. Maybe he was related in some way.

Ernie turned out to be the son of the famous owner of the famous Ernie Fields Revue. He was the epitome of what you would expect a Hollywood musician to look like. Tall, not too dark, and very handsome, drove a big Cadillac, had a white secretary, and dressed in the latest clothes. He and Harry Kim were the only ones who understood exactly how to phrase my music. I had to force everyone else. I realized why he was so adept after I got to know him better. Besides the big Cadillacs, we had many other things in common. We both were sons of bandleader fathers. We both grew up knowing that we would be just like our fathers. We both played with our fathers from a young age. We both went to black colleges. (He went to Howard University, a more highly respected black college than Alabama State, but he did experience the same kind of tutoring from the same kinds of hip teachers and older students as I did with Andre "Fats" Ford and Willie Gresham.) Fields was from the South. (Or, the Southwest anyway—Tulsa, Oklahoma.) He had played and traveled with Bobby Bland as his bandleader. And, like me, he had made a conscious decision to move to L.A. Although he was a little older than I was, we related on many levels.

I had a little more trouble getting my arrangements down than Benjamin did, for the simple reason that he knew not only what he was writing for but also who the players would be. I had learned previously that in order to get what you want from your music, you have to consider the musicians who will play your music. There are certain things that Bobby Bryant wouldn't play as well as Nolan Smith would, and vice-versa. I was writing material that Maceo, Kush, Rick, and I would take all day to get perfect for people who were used to throwing down three and four tracks in one session. I had to adjust my writing to fit the situation. Benjamin had the Hollywood session routine down to a science, and his horn parts were very effective and efficient. I learned from his example.

I also noticed how smoothly the session went by having an experienced contractor on hand to manage the musicians. I didn't have to think about anything but the music. This was the kind of luxury that I had had in New York with Emile Charlap in control of the sessions. I hadn't seen the need for a real contractor in L.A., until one time I had let Rick Gardner from the P-Funk and the Horny Horns talk me into letting him contract a session for me. He had assured me that he could make all of the calls, take care of the union paperwork business, and generally relieve me of everything but the actual writing of the music and conducting the session.

The session was a horn and string overdub on four tunes for an album that Bunny Sigler was producing on Patti Brooks. It was a relatively big-budget album. Bunny had done the rhythm tracks in Philadelphia on some absolutely beautiful songs that he had written. Having completed some of his best work, he kind of relaxed and gave me free rein to do a big horn session and a big string session. I was challenged to create arrangements that would be worthy of the outstanding foundation he had laid down. I guess we all got a little excited. Bunny booked the newest, most expensive studio in Hollywood. In Burbank anyway. It was Kendon's Studio D, a new, highly computerized facility still in the experimental stages. To operate that cutting-edge technology, we hired the much-sought-after Barney Perkins, the most expensive engineer in Hollywood. Rick hired the top-name horn players he always idolized and paid a lot of them double scale, out of respect for their reputations.

I scheduled two three-hour sessions for the horn overdub, to be followed by a one-hour break, after which I had scheduled two more three-hour sessions to do the strings. I figured that if we started at four o'clock in the afternoon, we could be finished and back at the hotel celebrating by one o'clock in the morning.

At four o'clock, I swaggered into the studio, confident that I had matched Bunny's composing and rhythm-track efforts with some fabulous horn and string sweetening of my own. Rick and all of the horn players were in place, the music had been passed out, and everything was ready to go. Or so we thought. The studio was not quite ready. I carried on an impromptu comedy performance for the horn players while the erudite technicians scurried back and forth in the control room, trying to jerry-rig that electronic marvel so we could do some simple horn overdubs. After about an hour, I ran out of comedy material and gave everybody a break. For another hour the studio crew struggled to get the electronics going. Bunny finally arrived with somewhat of an entourage: a beautiful lady and a kid. He apparently had started celebrating a little early. I explained the situation to him, and he told me to handle it any way I saw fit. He went about interacting with his lady friend and the kid.

After about two and a half hours, we started getting sounds and managed to finish one tune before the start of the second session. During the break (there was a mandatory break between sessions or overtime would be charged to the first session), the engineer lost the horns that we had just recorded. Somehow the track just disappeared from the tape. Another two hours were spent trying to find out what had happened to the music.

By that time, the string players were beginning to arrive. I was about out of my mind, and Bunny had fallen asleep. I still held out hope that we could complete the sessions by doing the horns and strings at the same time. It would be a tremendous undertaking and would cost a lot of overtime for the horns, but it was the only way I saw to salvage this session. So, for another two hours, I paced back and forth from the studio to the control room, trying to keep about thirty very impatient, very expensive musicians from freaking out, at the same time that I was continuing to admonish the distraught electronic geniuses without pissing them off. We finally got going at about ten o'clock and labored straight through until we finished—at about two in the morning.

The music turned out surprisingly well, considering the mess that had to be overcome. When Bunny woke up from his nap, he was very satisfied. At least I thought so, until I got a call a week later from a lawyer who said that he was Bunny's manager. He was all bent out of shape about the bill he had just received from the L.A. musician's union. It seems that the fiasco that was the Patti Brooks horn and string overdub had cost about $18,000, way over what was budgeted for the entire project. I explained what had happened and asked if he had spoken to Bunny about the situation. Then I remembered that Bunny had been asleep and really didn't know exactly what had gone on. I guess Bunny had just passed all of the responsibility of the studio breakdown and the musician's overtime on to me. I did get the full force of this lawyer's ire and was assured that I would never work for Bunny or anyone else in the music business again. But I finally got paid, and very well, too. The overtime was tremendous. I realize now that an experienced contractor could have worked it out so that even that thwarted session didn't have to cost so much. And at least I would not had to have taken the entire brunt of the blame. I needed help for next time. I went looking for Ernie Fields.

I found Ernie just in time. He had his office in a high-rise at the corner of Hollywood and Vine in the heart of Hollywood. I was impressed. I found him just in time, because I had just been contacted by Mr. Bobbit, who now was in the employ of Mr. Albert Bernard Bongo, the president of Gabon, the African nation we had visited with James. The Bongo family's oldest son, Alain, whom I had befriended while there, wanted to do a serious production of some of his original songs. He and his friend Jimmy Ondo were coming to New York on a visit and wanted me to come and help with the production of two of his songs. Jimmy was the one who had first taken us to Gabon, and I was happy to reacquaint myself with him.

No matter how hard I tried, I couldn't get them to come to L.A. for the recording. They had their hearts set on doing the recordings in Nashville. Mr. Bobbit had taken the Bobby Byrd show back to Gabon since the James Brown concert, and the people in the Byrd band had hooked up with Alain and Jimmy and decided to record the original tunes in Nashville, where Bobby, Momie-o, their two sons, and most of the band lived. After Bobby and Vickie had left James, they had put together a very good

Studio. Left to right: Jimmy Ondo, me, old friend Charles Lott, Jim Shifflett.
Courtesy of Fred Wesley Jr.

show of their own, backed by a killer band. The band was anchored by
their sons Tony on drums and Bart on the Hammond organ and other
keyboards. The rest of the band included the great studio bassist of Nashville, Jesse Boyce, and a wonderful horn section led by Sanchez Harley
and Lloyd Barry.

In addition to the two originals by Alain was a song by Patience
Dabany, a wealthy family member who had written it to be used as a
theme for the Organization of African Unity (OAU), which had a big conference pending and wanted the song fully produced in time. The OAU
was a big and respected organization. Mr. Bongo, Alain's father and president of Gabon, was a high official in the organization and happened to
be hosting that particular conference in Libreville. The song was to add
to the stature of the proceedings. I was both honored and apprehensive
about being given such a prestigious assignment. The first problem was
that the song was, so far, only words—no melody, no chords, and no
rhythm that I could discern. To further complicate the assignment, the
words were in French. This meant that I would first have to find somebody to translate the words into English in order for them to make sense

to me, then I would have to rearrange the words back into French in some usable form, with verses and choruses and other such musical elements.

True to his do-the-impossible form, Mr. Bobbit somehow managed to book the personal studio of Johnny Cash. The studio was brand-new, and Mr. Cash seemed just as happy to see us there as we were to be there. He was a true Southern gentleman and extended every courtesy to the native Nashvillians, to me, and to the visiting Africans. No Washington diplomat could have made the visitors from Gabon feel more welcome.

The project was quite a challenge, but with the help of Sanchez, Lloyd, Bobby Byrd's rhythm section, and many great Nashville horn players, string players, singers—as well as a young lady named Iran, who was from Iran and attending Tennessee State University and who spent hours helping me translate poetic French to plain English and plain English back to poetic and musical French—with the help of all these people, I took the beautiful and sensitive words of Patience Dabany and produced an extravagantly beautiful and inspiring piece entitled "Enfant D'Afrique" ("Children of Africa"). I don't know for sure if it ever made it to the OAU, but it was a great collaborative work of art, certainly worthy of any international organization. The two tunes by the youthful Mr. Bongo came out very well, too.

Back in L.A., after having to hear a lot of guff from Ernie about how I should have brought the African project back to L.A., I began getting calls for gigs—both playing the trombone and arranging—from Ernie, Benjamin Wright, and other producers and arrangers in the circle of musicians centered around Ernie's Jade Sound office. Benjamin did most of the horn and string arranging for Solar Records, whose artists included the Sylvers, Dynasty, Shalamar, and the Whispers. I often worked through Benjamin with these groups and Chicago producer Chuck Jackson, who produced a singer named Ren Woods, among others. Not the Chuck Jackson of "Any Day Now" fame, but the Chuck Jackson of the Independents, the group that had the hit "Leaving Me." (He was also Jesse Jackson's half brother.)

Ernie had the corner on the spin-off market of the Hollywood music scene. We did everything from the funk things that I brought in to gospel music arranged by Billy Bickelhaupt for the producer Kent Washburn, whose recordings on Nicholas were twice nominated for Grammys in the mid-eighties. We even had an arranger/composer/bass player, Greg Middleton, who did music for porn movies. We looked forward to spending the day watching sex films and, at times, actually, doing some music.

The great conductor/arranger/composer/pianist/saxophonist H.B. Barnum also was a frequent client of the Jade Sound musical services. H.B. did everything from dances and banquets to award shows and R&B stage shows. H.B. was the best at any- and everything musical of anyone I have ever been associated with. Although doing award shows and stage shows that required heavy sight-reading wasn't my strong suit, Ernie managed to get me on many gigs of that nature that he contracted and H.B. conducted. I remember doing the NAACP Image Awards when the show was in its infant stages. Before it was even televised. When it was still being held at the Hollywood Palladium.

I was there in the band when Jayne Kennedy won the Best Actress award for her horrible performance in the Leon Isaac Kennedy production of *Body and Soul.* She was nominated along with Rosalind Cash, and everybody just knew that the Jayne Kennedy nomination was only a courtesy gesture. There was not a doubt in anybody's mind that Ms. Cash would win. When he presenter announced, "The winner is . . . Jayne Kennedy," instead of the usual burst of applause, a deafening hush fell over the audience. H.B. even forgot, for a minute, to bring the band in with the customary fanfare as Kennedy took her walk to the stage. Finally, a smattering of applause wafted through the room as she timidly made her way to the stage. She muttered some words of acceptance, with an obviously embarrassed look on her face.

That same night Aretha Franklin won about four awards and was not there to accept them, so they were accepted by her then-husband, Glynn Turman, who was apparently full of something and made a real spectacle of himself every time he made his way to the podium. At the end of the night, I saw Aretha's statuettes just lying on the piano backstage. I had to restrain myself from swiping at least one and keeping it for a souvenir. They were completely unguarded. I could have, but I didn't. It was a funny night.

The NAACP Image Awards show has progressed from that dubious beginning to the big, televised production that it is today. I was privileged to do it for a number of years. The last one that I did was memorable to me for two reasons. Number one, I saw Mike Tyson and Robin Givens meet for the first time. It was love, or something, at first sight. They were, right away, taken with each other and played like children throughout the rehearsals and the actual show. The next thing I heard was that they were married. I don't know what all happened later, but it started out like a fairy tale.

Number two, my most humiliating moment occurred on the set of that particular show. During a break, in front of the whole band, the audience, and all of the performers, I was having a conversation with one of the usherettes, a tall, beautiful, brown-skinned young lady. We weren't talking about anything in particular, but it was a pleasant interchange with a lovely woman. We were face to face, although I was looking slightly upward because she was taller than me. Suddenly, Magic Johnson walked up and positioned himself directly between us. He didn't say excuse me or hello or anything to me. He just began talking to the girl. I was completely blocked from her view and she from mine. I stood there for what seemed like five minutes, waiting for one of them to acknowledge my being a person or, at least, being alive. That never happened. They finally just walked away, leaving me standing there looking like a real fool. I was embarrassed and angry. Not so much at the girl but at Magic for completely disrespecting another person like that. I'm sure that the girl was so enamored of the idea of speaking to Magic Johnson that she forgot all about me, but for a brother to treat another brother like that was inexcusable, and I have never forgiven Magic for it.

Ernie booked all kinds of shows like that with H.B. and with other conductors. I mention H.B. specifically because he was my favorite and undoubtedly the best. I was amazed at the things he did and the ease with which he did them. I saw him write the cues and fill-ins for a whole show in about an hour. And the material was beautiful and interesting. He was the best at running the show down to the musicians so that they understood what was happening and remembered what and when to play without a whole lot of hassle.

Ernie would also call me for the Lou Rawls Parade of Stars, the telethon for the United Negro College Fund. The first year I was called for the entire twenty-four-hour affair and got a seat next to a ramp that gave me a clear view of each performer as he or she walked onto the stage and a complete view of the whole stage as they performed. I was amazed by New Edition and enjoyed very much chatting to Jack Jones as he waited to be introduced. I was struck deaf, dumb, and nearly dead when Lola Falana was escorted to the edge of the ramp, wearing a trench coat draped around her shoulders. She was positioned right in front of me, no more than a foot from my music stand. I nearly dropped dead when her assistant removed the trench coat and revealed that more-than-perfect body clad in a white, form-fitting gown. The gown was a simple piece of white cloth that began beneath her armpits and followed her treacherous curves all the way down to the floor. She had on absolutely nothing else. I know for sure, because when she walked to the stage, the spotlight shone directly through her long, fabulous legs. Needless to say, I saw everything. I didn't play many correct notes, if I played any notes at all, and I have no idea what she was singing.

I didn't get the call to do that show too often after that. I really didn't pay much attention to the music. I was so hung up on watching the stars, the music became secondary to me. This drove H.B. crazy. It was suggested that, if I wanted to watch the show, I should buy a ticket. I'd heard that before somewhere. I don't count myself a groupie, but I did enjoy seeing and, whenever I could, interacting with the stars.

I got many calls for scab gigs, dances, unimportant banquets, and sessions if all other trombone players were busy. I was also often busy doing other things like arranging, producing, and conducting, and was periodically unavailable for trombone calls. Once, when I was available, I got a call to do two acts on the Lou Rawls Parade of Stars. The band was already booked, but two of the artists, Pia Zadora and Frank Sinatra, required a fifth trombone for their charts. I got the call for the fifth chair. After Sinatra did his songs with the band, he suggested that he and Lou do one together. They chose Sammy Cahn's "All the Way." No orchestra. Just piano, Frank and Lou, voice to voice. I don't think anyone, not even Frank or Lou, realized what a glaring difference we were about to witness. Not only was Lou's voice an obviously stronger instrument, his execution and delivery was much more musical and artistic than Frank's. I saw Lou trying to hold back, but without thinking he went from his deep, rich low tones to his velvety falsetto, leaving Frank kind of hovering there in the middle, trying to make something happen with the melody. Needless to say, that little duet never made it to the TV screen.

The life of a Hollywood studio musician was very exciting, infinitely diverse, and adequately lucrative if you could string all the gigs together in a consistent schedule. Most of my gigs were union scale and scab scale. But because of my special reputation as a horn and string arranger, I would frequently get calls to do sweetening for R&B albums. This would periodically take me out of the regular big-band, small-session, club gig loop. Consequently, I had to depend heavily on Ernie Fields and the Jade Sound office to keep me involved with as much work as possible. In turn, I would bring as much of my arranging and producing business to and through the office as I could.

It was a good life. It was an interesting life. Everybody paid their bills.

Everybody was happy. The people in our little circle were ultimately talented, although we weren't doing the top sessions or the top gigs in Hollywood. We weren't connected to the top TV shows, although we knew all of the people who were doing the top stuff. We weren't making the top money, although we were constantly aiming for the big record, the call for the big TV show, the connection to the next big thing. We all made a good living. Things got tough at times but at other times were very good. We would all get shots at the really big-time every now and then.

I had a chance at a big TV show called the "Fun Zone" starring Howie Mandel. I got the call to do the pilot, in a band led by Ira Newman. Ernie Watts played the saxes, Walt Johnson was the trumpet player, Weird Al Yankovich played guitar, and I was the trombone player. I forget who the other players were. I held my breath for weeks, waiting to see if the show would be picked up regularly by NBC. It didn't happen, but it was a good payday. I remember expressing my boredom and restlessness to Ernie Watts as we went into overtime. Ernie Watts, a veteran of Hollywood TV music, said "Man, don't you know that we just went into what is called golden, premium time in the TV music business? That means that we're making triple scale. I'll sit here, very patiently, until I own NBC. If we keep going long enough, I'll call the wife and kid to come down and bring the dog, dinner—I'll help with homework and generally set up housekeeping right here in the studio." After that, I never complained about TV overtime.

Everything was going along fine, until one day I went into the office and Ernie was doing a union contract for an album by a new artist named Prince. There was nothing strange about doing a contract for a band that we did not actually play with. We did a lot of work documenting and legalizing projects for bands that did their own producing, arranging, and recording and paid themselves however they saw fit. But even self-contained bands had to file union contracts to properly document the project and make it legal. The odd thing about this particular contract was that all the instruments were played by the same person: Prince. We kind of chuckled at the time, not knowing that this particular contract marked the beginning of the end of the recording business as we knew it. Every instrument that was not a synthesizer was also played by Prince. Synthesized horns, synthesized strings, and percussion. The real bad thing about the album was that it was very funky and sounded very good.

I went from making a comfortable living doing horn and string arrangements and other odd assignments to scuffling, trying to make it on just the odd assignments. Horns and strings became obsolete in less than one year. Everyone who ever thought that they could do music was piecing together decent albums by using synthesized sounds for almost all the instruments. Not only strings and horns, but drums, bass, and a plethora of keyboard sounds. Guitar players were the only real musicians who still got calls to do sessions. And there was a marked decrease in guitar calls, because many of the producers were themselves guitar players and jumped at the chance to do their own drums, bass, keyboards, horns, and strings. Like Prince, most of the new producers were also singers. Music that would formerly have required a large studio, a competent engineer, a small army of great musicians, and lots of money was now being produced in people's bedrooms by would-be musicians who worked at the post office during the day. That was the real hurting part of the whole situation: most of these new producers didn't really have a musical background. What they had was a love for music and the ability to read and understand a manual. As the price of synthesizers and sequencers went down, more and more people with less and less real musical knowledge or talent became geniuses in the music business. The situation left us real musicians floundering around, trying to convince record-company executives and ourselves that this was just a passing fad and that the public would demand real music again soon.

Deep down in our old-school hearts, we knew that this was it. I personally remember when my father used to tell me that bebop was just a passing fad, that big band was the perennial jazz music, and that swing would last forever. I remember when my peers and I thought that rock and roll was just a little crazy thing that would fade out with Little Richard's make-up. I had no idea that forty years later I would still be hearing "wop bop a loo bop ba lop bam boom." History has dictated that trends move forward, never backward, although present-day music, with its samples and rare grooves and '70s and '80s nostalgia, would somewhat dispute that theory.

The next thing you knew, trumpet players, bass players, drummers, and trombone players had their own studios. Arrangers learned to do arrangements on computers. Everyone began to adjust. I was one of the last to get into buying equipment, mainly because I had a friend, Gary Bell, who was leader of Group Kilowatt, a band that I had produced when I first moved to L.A. Gary was early into the sequencing and drum machines and such. Together, we developed a system whereby we would write songs using the latest technology together. I would give him the parts, he would do the button pushing, and we would both play what needed to be played. We produced many projects together. Everything from reggae on a singer named Onike to some modern R&B on Delbert Taylor. I never saw the need to spend money on equipment, as I didn't produce and write songs all the time. Whenever I needed to do that kind of work, Gary was there.

Many of my friends did get very heavily into the electronics. The talk among musicians went from what type of horn you played and what type of mouthpiece you used to what is the best sequencer and what is the latest, most versatile, most cost-efficient synthesizer. Nearly every piano player bought his or her own keyboard. Every drummer owned his own drum machine. Instead of the conversations being about Olds, Selmer, Gretsch, Fender, and Olympic, everyone was talking about Yamaha, IBM, Mac, Fostec, Linn, Oberheim, and Emulator. Most of the busiest producers who were still working started to use the digital format.

When I finally stopped resisting the inevitable and evaluated my personal situation, I realized that all of the skills that I had spent the past fifteen years developing were practically obsolete. This was a rude awakening. I didn't know what to do. I felt like the rug had been snatched out from under me and I was left suspended in mid-air. Life was a question. I knew that I was still a good musician and a good producer, the question was how did I use what I knew in this new atmosphere of digital music?

My alliance with Gary Bell kept me in the mix to a certain extent, but I had to face the fact that he was bringing more to me than I was bringing to him. There was a new crop of young, digital-minded producers on the scene, and I had hardly any connection to any of them. There were some who experimented with live horns. For example, there was this producer who had had some success with New Edition. He had been given the job of producing some tracks on Debbie Allen. He had four tracks ready to overdub horns on, so he hired Ernie, Harry Kim, and myself for the job.

The studio turned out to be in someone's house in Tuluca Lake. We arrived and proceeded to set up in a recording area that had formerly been a living room. The engineer, who was also the owner of the house and the studio, set up chairs, music stands, and headphones. As we got our horns out and warmed them up, he set up the tape, aligned the machine, and sat back and waited for us to let him know when we were ready to record. We finished warming up, and for a while everything went still and silent. The engineer started playing the tape, then stopped

Rudy Copeland.
Photograph by Fred
Wesley Jr.

it, and asked why we weren't playing. We pointed out to him that he hadn't put up any microphones. He said "Oh, yeah! Mikes!" He was so accustomed to recording electronic instruments that he took directly to the tape that he had forgotten all about the mikes. Things had really changed.

Since horn and string arranging was my main source of income, I began thinking of another way to earn a living. Ever since the *House Party* album, I had a band sort of on call in case I got a gig—and if they were available. Those two things hardly ever happened at the same time, but every now and then I would get Melvin Webb on drums, Lewis DuPriest on bass, Spencer Bean on guitar, and Rudy Copeland on keyboards and do a gig somewhere. I thought that with all of my new free time I could seek out some gigs, maybe hire an agent, do some arrangements, have some rehearsals, and really pursue gigging for a living. The only thing was, by then Melvin was playing with Marvin Gaye, Spencer was with Gladys Knight and the Pips, and Rudy was regular with Johnny "Guitar" Watson. I even thought of taking a road gig myself. I could always go back with James Brown or George Clinton. For me, that would have been the very last resort. Things hadn't gotten that bad yet. I did, for a while, take a gig with Vernon Garrett. But that turned out to be one of those "join the family" things like James or George Clinton, but on a smaller, more local scale. I didn't want to go back to that way of life.

As things go with my life, the totally unexpected happened. I got a call from Mr. Bobbit telling me that the Africans were back in town and wanted to do some recording. I expected that young Mr. Ali Bongo

Dr. Theodric Hendrix and
Patience Dabany. Photograph
by Fred Wesley Jr.

had written some more songs and wanted to record them in the American style, using American musicians, as we had done in Nashville. This time, I would do it right. The first thing I did was call Ernie Fields to alert him that we had work and to clear his calendar as best he could. I knew that this would be a big payday for all of us if the Nashville experience was any indication. But to my surprise, it was not Ali Bongo this time, it was Patience Dabany. She wanted to record her dance group, which was called Kunabeli. Now, I'm good, but even I was going to have trouble recording a dance group. As it turned out, she had brought some two-track tapes of music to which the group danced, recorded in her studio in Gabon by the band that always accompanied the dance group.

The music, to my ear, was raw Latin. A drum trap played, but not in the way Americans play traps with the ride cymbal, bass drum, snare drum, hi-hat, and three tom toms. This trap emphasized the snare carrying the constant rhythm, with the bass drum usually punctuating, sometimes anchoring, four on the floor. The hi-hat was used with the snare to make up the basic beat of a particular song or groove. The ride cymbal and toms were used mostly for accents. The one drummer was the whole percussion section, and the individual parts of the trap were used any way the drummer worked it out to make a groove. The only rule was to get it together and hold it steady for what usually turned out to be at least fifteen minutes per song. I marveled at the drummer's stamina. The bass was always terribly out of tune, and its parts were always very simple— sometimes complicated rhythmically but never difficult to play—and, again, slightly Latin. There were two guitars. One rhythm guitar, which stayed with the groove of the bass and drums, and the lead guitar, which played a ringing, high-pitched, more melodic part that vamped throughout the groove.

The music was like a funk vamp in that it didn't have changes and each instrument played his part to make up the basic rhythm. It was a vamp in another language. With another sound. With another attitude. I say that it sounded Latin for lack of a better way to describe it, but it might actually have reflected African rhythms that had been exported to Latin America, then back to Africa and electrified. The guitars were playing what would be the cora (an African string instrument) parts and the traps were playing what a plethora of percussion instruments would play in the wild, so to speak. On top of all this rhythm were the vocals of Patience. Her voice was sort of a whine. Not a weak whine, but a strong, definite, always-on-the-rhythm, warm, wanting, almost melancholy vocal, sung in her native language. The dance group sang background and sounded like a choir of sopranos. Call and response was a big part of the vocals. I had no idea what the songs were about, but some made me laugh, some made me cry, and all compelled me to dance.

What turned out to be very interesting was that Patience Dabany wanted to Americanize this African music. It was a challenge that I embraced seriously and anxiously. I would listen to the tracks and get the basic idea, then write similar rhythms and let Patience and her girls do the singing. I looked forward to getting the bass and guitar parts in tune. I felt that I would have trouble duplicating the rhythms, but I had people like Benny Parks, a native of Panama, and Paulinho DaCosta from Brazil to help me work that out. I was sure that this project would be not only challenging but educational, very lucrative. Mr. Bobbit made it clear to me that whatever I needed in terms of money would not be a problem.

Attempts to duplicate the Gabonese musicians' recordings were complete failures. Even Panamanian and Brazilian musicians were too far away from the root to achieve the true African feel. I first had to understand that Ms. Dabany wanted to keep the native feel, but embellish it with Western sounds and technology. When I finally got it, I assembled a recording team to accomplish a sound that had never been recorded before.

I recruited Steve Williams as chief engineer. I had worked with Steve on some projects produced by Larry Williams (no relation). Specifically, a Rudy Copeland album and some tracks on Johnny "Guitar" Watson.

Left to right: me, Steve Williams, Ernie Fields. Courtesy of Fred Wesley Jr.

I was impressed with how flexible Steve was and how he didn't mind doing things that had never been done before. Steve would see a problem and go about solving it without giving you a whole lot of flack. I remember one night we were doing vocals on Johnny "Guitar" Watson, and we kept hearing a sssss sound coming from the booth. It seems that Johnny had his blowtorch running so he could get hits off of his freebase pipe between takes. Larry asked Johnny to turn it off until we finished the vocal. Johnny refused, saying, "Deal widit, baby. Deal widit." Without hesitating, Steve went about EQing the hiss out as well as he could and finished what turned out to be that unique Johnny "Guitar" Watson sound that has since become famous. I needed an engineer who could deal with unusual situations. Steve was my man.

We decided to transfer the quarter-inch, two-track recordings to two-inch, twenty-four-track tape, with plans to overdub horns, strings, synthesizers, vocals, and anything else that was needed to Americanize the African feel. It was an ambitious undertaking, but I was sure that with Steve we could pull it off.

I did most of the horn and string arrangements myself. At first anyway. A basic procedure had to be established, because the music didn't adhere to the forms with which we were accustomed to working. Finding the right procedure was a constant problem. Establishing the home key was a matter of opinion. Finally, I had to set the parameters of the key, the downbeat, intonation, and so on, so that everyone else who worked on a particular song would have a guide to play by.

When the groundwork was complete, I brought in Gary Bell to do the synthesizer work. Sound effects, keyboard sounds, and the like were his responsibility. I brought in my good friend Delbert Taylor to help with the vocals and to do some of the arranging. He ended up being my general assistant, doing whatever came up to take pressure off of me. Harry Kim, David Ii, Nolan Smith, and Bill Henderson were always on-call to do horns and strings. We got bass work from Gerald Albright, Greg Middleton, and Henry Thomas. Guitar work from John Hara, Wes Blackmon, and the unforgettable Clarence Taylor. And, of course, Ernie Fields was always on hand to keep everything in line and on schedule.

The first project was very successful. Madam had enough music for two albums. The finished product was unique and very interesting, although there was nothing to compare it to—it didn't fit any of the accepted categories of the Billboard or Cashbox charts. However, Madam was very happy and proud simply to hear her music fully produced and embellished. She didn't seem interested in a record deal or worldwide distribution, so we pressed about 500 copies of each record, which she sent to Gabon, being satisfied to have her music heard only in her own country. She certainly had the resources to promote and distribute the product if she had wanted to, but in the end we did all of this work just for her own personal pleasure. Which was fine with me. Only a small percentage of the work I was doing ever got out anyway. Only thing, this time we all made money. We all stretched our abilities, and we formed a bond among us that has lasted forever.

Over the next few years, we worked for Ms. Patience Dabany off and on. I can't speak for the other guys, but I was thankful for the intermittent work. It made it possible for me to survive in L.A. a while longer. She got more and more ambitious as we went along. We began doing some of her songs from scratch. She had begun writing songs in French, Swahili, and English, as well as in her native tongue. The English songs were relatively easy. I simply took her words, put them into poetic form, married the words to a melody, and then recorded them in the usual manner. Rhythm section, overdub horns, strings, sweetening with synthesizer tracks. Then, add lead and background vocals. The French and

Swahili songs required the extra steps of being translated and formed into English melodies. Dabney presented challenge after challenge, and every time we measured up to the test, so she remained very pleased with our work.

Once, she became enamored with a local singer named Grady Harrell and ordered me to do an album on him. Not an African album but an up-to-date R&B/pop album. The material was mostly his, but Madam contributed a few songs. We got Gary Bell involved very heavily on this project. As we wanted to compete with the other young artists and producers of that day—artists like Prince, Shalamar, even Michael Jackson —we went for the electronic sound that had become popular. Grady's cronies programmed a few of his songs, and Gary Bell programmed the others, while I basically supervised the whole thing. Madam served as executive producer, making sure that her protégé got what he wanted. For me, it turned out to be an education in electronic music, sequencing, programming, and the like, as well as an exercise in diplomacy. I was certainly the liaison among all of the other producers, writers, and artists who eventually got involved. After much politicking and negotiating, coordinating and refereeing on my part, we finally put together a very good state-of-the-art product that was ultimately released by Solar Records. The record got some positive attention and made the R&B charts.

Patience was a very talented musician and an extremely intelligent woman. She learned our recording techniques very quickly by simply watching and listening to what my staff and I were doing. She soon realized that whatever she envisioned musically could be accomplished, so she got more and more demanding, more and more creative, and more and more complicated. It was like working for an exotic yet reasonable James Brown. Before we knew it, we were creating monumental masterpieces from ideas she dreamed up. We got away from trying to stay with the African sound and even ignored conventional Western sounds and just went for creating works of art that didn't fit any musical classification. All rules went out the window. Fulfilling Madam's fantasy was our only goal. Once, as we were putting a synthesizer track on tape, someone suggested that we should all wear white smocks to the studio because what we were doing was truly experimental. And with everyone so organized into playing their own roles, no scientific laboratory could have been run more smoothly.

During my time working for the Africans, I reacquainted myself and fell madly in love with a treacherous white lady by the name of cocaine.

I use the word *reacquaint* because I had known about cocaine for years. We had first been introduced in 1968, backstage at the Apollo Theater, by one of the many fans who hung around during and between shows. During that time I had hardly ever bought any, just accepted a sniff every now and then from an admiring fan. Weed was what I was guilty of. Throughout my career, I had always had a supply of weed. To me, it was simply a harmless diversion. I never even thought of becoming addicted or neglecting important business because of it. And those occasional uses of cocaine had never made me afraid of becoming an addict. I would never have dreamed of shooting heroin. I had seen too many junkies to even chance getting involved with that. And my brief experience with the codeine cough syrup had let me know not to ever fool with that again. Even when I had started buying and sniffing cocaine somewhat regularly during my time with the P-Funk, I had never thought that I could become addicted to cocaine. I had even seen people smoke cocaine, and I had smoked some with them, only to walk away and not even think about it until it came around again. I was just fooling around. Smoking cocaine did give me a wonderful feeling, but only for a few seconds. I could just walk away. I never understood why people would lock up in a room for hours at a time, unable to leave it alone.

After about two years of working with Patience Dabney, I would leave the studio at about one or two in the morning and not feel like going home. The only people that I knew still up at that time of night were people who were smoking cocaine. So I would stop by every now and then, just for an hour or so at first. Without realizing it, I got to the point where I couldn't wait to leave the studio and would stay with the dopers through the rest of the night. I was always welcomed, because I was a lot of fun when I was high and I always had lots of money. I realized that I was addicted when I learned to cook the drug myself and bought my own pipe. I soon began smoking all the time, even at home. My entire personality changed, to the degree that I had to leave my home. I didn't want my kids and wife to know how badly I was addicted. I moved in with a dealer and amassed a whole new circle of friends. It was difficult trying to keep Madam's recordings going and satisfy my drug habit at the same time, but with the help of my staff, who finally realized what my problem was, I managed to complete all of the projects without blowing the gig. We even made a couple of trips to Gabon—once to record in her studio and once to play for her son's wedding reception. The trips to Africa gave me a break from the drugs, but I got right back into them when I returned.

I was able to keep things looking all right as long as I was making money. But when Madam suddenly stopped recording, I was left broke, unable to work at anything else, and with a very expensive monkey on my back. I would call Madam periodically to ask when were we going back to the studio. Her reply, with a French-Swahili-Bantu accent, was always, "Soon." But soon never came. I found out that the unforgettable guitar player with whom I had not been pleased had made himself available to Madam in a romantic way. Clarence Taylor was now the owner of a brand-new state-of-the-art studio in Hollywood where he was now supervising whatever recording Madam did.

I was a mess. My personal life was a mess. My friends got together and, with the help of my wife's insurance, forced me to do a month of rehab, during which I sort of got myself together. I had completely lost the ability to play trombone, but I did get my chops back enough to do some sessions and a few gigs when I got out. But rehab had introduced me to a new group of friends who turned me on to some cocaine that was twice as good and cost one-third less. In less than two months after getting out of rehab, I was back at it again. This time sex had been added to the addiction. At my age, I thought that I had experienced everything there was to experience when it came to sex. I was wrong. In the world of cocaine, unimaginable sex is performed by some fantastically talented women to get drugs. The drug made the experiences that much more fantastic. I was hooked and hooked in two ways. The next two years I spent my time chasing the drug feeling and the sex feeling. I lived from one drug dealer to another, one sex freak to another. I shied away from my friends, my family, and everybody who couldn't give me drugs and/or sex.

As long as I could gather up enough money to keep me in drugs, I was all right. Although I couldn't really play the trombone, Ernie still called me on whatever gigs he felt I could bullshit my way through. Maceo kept me in touch with George and Bootsy, and I did some sessions with them when they came to L.A. I bugged all the people who owed me money to the point of being ridiculous. This kind of spin-off stuff from my past and an occasional royalty check kept me with enough money to keep a roof over my head while I nursed my drug and sex habit. In between gigs and royalty checks I managed to stay high and housed by way of friends, usually girlfriends whom I lived with until I ran out of money or they ran out of money, depending on who was supporting whom. I went from living with a nice lady with a good job and a drug and sex habit to living

Bad Days. Photograph by unknown drug associate.

with a guy who was a professional burglar with a sex and drug habit, with various scenarios and similar associations in between. (No, I didn't have sex with the burglar or any other man, but life in the drug culture did stretch my ethics and morals to the limit and was filled with danger-ous adventures.) This sex and drug period of my life is really material for another book.

I am sure that all of the prayers of my friends and loved ones were all that kept me alive, out of jail, and somewhat sane during that time. Whenever I thought of knocking somebody in the head or robbing some-body or betraying the trust of a true friend or ending my pain by ending my life, I would hear a small voice in the back of my mind saying, "What will my kids think? How will they deal with it? What about all the people who enjoy my music? What kind of legacy will this leave for the Wes-ley name? My father didn't pass all of this talent on for me to waste it like this. My mother shouldn't have to think that she was wrong to let me leave school at such an early age to follow a music career. I couldn't leave that guilt on her. What about my brother, Ronald, and sister Janice, who are so proud of my accomplishments? I can't let them down because of stupid pleasures like sex and drugs. There is still a lot of music to be created. People still only think of me as a funky trombone player."

I had so many reasons to stay alive and continue my career. But cocaine is a powerful demon. I have never known anyone who could overcome it alone, and I had systematically closed off all of the doors to anyone who loved me enough to help me. I was too ashamed to let any of my loved ones see the horrible mess that I had become.

10

Mile High in Denver

• • •

It seemed that everyone just gave up on me, hoping and praying that the inner strength that they knew I had would someday bring me back to them. I don't blame them at all. All attempts by my wife and children to bring me home I met with anger, hate, and threatened violence. My friends did what they could, but in the end their own agendas made it necessary to leave me alone. Ernie went as far as letting me and one of my nasty girls live in his home for a while, but I knew and he knew that sooner or later this would lead to disaster. The only person who went the extra mile to save me was my brother, Ron.

He sent me a written proposal for us to produce a straight-ahead, bebop album on me. We had spoken of doing an album of this type many times in the past, but we had never gotten the chance to put it together. Ron was and still is a jazz aficionado and had always thought that it was a shame that I was only recognized as a funk player. He had been my biggest jazz fan since high school and had always had a problem with my playing only funky music. For years, his dream had been to produce a jazz album on me to help me assume my rightful position as a great jazz trombone player.

But Ron and I had not been real close through the years. After leaving Mobile with James Brown, I had never really returned for any length of time. Ron had finished college and spent time in the Army. Like many Americans who worried about their loved ones during the war, I agonized over Ron's stay in Vietnam. And, unlike the many Americans who never had the chance to see their loved ones again, I was totally relieved

Ron Wesley.
Photograph by
Fred Wesley Jr.

and thankful when he returned safely. After leaving the military, Ron had taken a job as an accountant for the University of Colorado in Denver, a good job, but he often spoke of how he felt unfulfilled, because his dream always was to produce music.

This time, though, Ron was serious. He had been at his accounting job for fifteen years. The proposal he sent me, which actually was a business plan, called for him to take early retirement from his job, use the money to first rehabilitate me, then record an album and self-distribute that album throughout the world. Rehabilitating me was the first and biggest problem. Getting me out of L.A. was a challenge in itself. At the time, I was living with a woman who felt totally dependent on me. The thought of being without the drugs and the sex that she provided had me totally dependent on her in the same way. I can't explain it, but we could not be out of each other's sight without feeling lost, fearful, and abandoned. So Ron basically tricked me.

The Slaton family—my mother's people in Georgia—was planning a reunion, and Ron wanted me to go with him. I knew that I could stand leaving L.A. for short periods of time. I had done it before. I had gone to my grandmother's funeral, but I scurried back into my safe hole in L.A. before anyone detected that I was strung out or before I died from deprivation of the drug and the woman. I had also once dragged myself away to spend some time helping my mother sell her house and get resettled. I had really been hoping to get some money from her, knowing that she would have an abundance of cash from selling the house. As it happened, before I got any money from Mom, my woman in L.A. got a big check from an accident settlement. On learning this, I broke out of Mobile like it was on fire, making a lame excuse about a big gig. In reality, it was "dope and sex time," and I couldn't stop myself from needing to get back to L.A. before my woman went through all the money herself, did all the dope up by herself, or found a new friend.

Ron's plan was for me to meet him in New Orleans and help him drive to Blakley, Georgia, spend three days with the family, help him drive back to Denver, then fly back to L.A. He sent me a ticket for the flight to New Orleans. Leaving the woman was more traumatic than I had expected. It was like I was leaving forever. The trip must have been divinely guided, as my flight from L.A. and Ron's road trip from Denver put us in New Orleans at exactly the same time. He went to sleep, exhausted from his thirteen-hour drive, and I drove straight through to Blakley without stopping for anything but gas and to pee.

I actually had a wonderful time at the reunion. I reunited with uncles, aunts, cousin, and many other relatives from whom I had been disconnected for years. I'm sure that they all knew of my addiction, but nobody mentioned it directly. I was constantly assured that the whole family was behind me and would support me in whatever I needed to do. It made me feel terrible to realize that I had distanced myself from so many people who loved me so much, no matter what. We all vowed not to let the disconnection happen again.

The drive back to Denver was made to seem short, as Ron and I spent the entire time talking about his plan for the album. He never said so directly, but he addressed the fact that I would have to spend a fair amount of time getting myself physically and musically in shape—he has been a fitness buff for as long as I can remember—so, written into the business plan was financial support for me while I got myself back together. When we arrived in Denver, I was somewhat, although not totally surprised to discover that he didn't have a return ticket to L.A. He said he wanted me to stay a few days to meet some of his friends and just relax a while.

Ron lived in a really beautiful, two-bedroom townhouse. The main bedroom was upstairs on a level with the kitchen, dining room, and a living room with a very high, atrium-type ceiling. The other bedroom was downstairs with the garage, storage room, and laundry room. It was a lovely design and just perfect for the bachelor life that he was living at the time. The place was very well kept. In fact, he was surprised at how spotless we found it when we arrived. A note from a person named Patrish explained the pristine condition of the abode. I found out later that Patrish was his friend, part-time housekeeper, fitness-training partner, and, I suspected, lover, as she sometimes spent the night. She had thoroughly cleaned and rearranged the house to accommodate a new tenant. Ron assured me that we were the only permanent residents, although we did have Patrish and our homeboy Eldridge Williams as periodic longtime guests. After it became clear that I was going to stay, Ron insisted that I use the upstairs main bedroom. Each bedroom had its own bath, so it was a very comfortable arrangement that he had obviously set up for my rehabilitation.

The townhouse complex was located in a very pleasant area outside of Denver, next to a canal along which a one-mile jogging path had been paved. Along the path were trees and horses and lots of ducks, birds, and other wonders of nature to enjoy as you jogged or, in my case, loped. Around the way was a complete gym, with exercise equipment, hot tub, and sauna. I was gently urged to use these facilities regularly. In fact, Ron suggested a program of jogging and calisthenics to help me regain my strength and endurance. I started each day by jogging to the end of the trail and back—a distance of three miles. After a slow walking start that took almost two hours, I worked my way up to being able to jog it in about an hour and fifteen minutes. I followed the jog with about two hours in the gym, sauna, and whirlpool. By the time I finished my fitness routine, it was about nine or ten in the morning, depending on how early I got started.

My bedroom was adjacent to the living room, where I had access to the stereo system and all of Ron's jazz records. He let me know that it would not bother him or the neighbors if I felt the urge to blow the trombone at any time of the day or night. Patrish was on hand most of the time to prepare healthy meals and help keep the place in order. She was a very positive-thinking and supportive person, and the three of us had many soul-searching, philosophical, spiritually motivating rap sessions. Sort of like group therapy. Within a week or so, my little brother had eased me into a full-blown drug detox and rehabilitation program. It was never addressed directly, but he spent every day guiding his big brother back to a normal, drug-free life.

As I began to regain my physical strength, my mind began to clear. I began to hear what Ron was saying in his business plan. The plan was already in motion. I was in Denver. He had quit his job and taken the retirement money. The next step was to record the album. But, before that could happen, I had to develop some decent chops on the trombone. I knew that I had slipped back, but I didn't realize how far. When I picked up the horn for the first time in almost a year, I could not even get a sound out of the thing. The horn itself was in serious disrepair. I had to clean the slide with a Brillo pad. The famous black lacquer was peeling off the bell. The whole horn, including the mouthpiece, was corroded, and the inside was lined with some kind of horrible-smelling green stuff. I restored the horn to an acceptable condition and began trying to put myself back together as a player.

It must have been the cocaine that had messed up the nerves and muscles in my face that control and support my embouchure. For days, I tried to hold a note to no avail. I could go dat-de-dot-dot and ba-doo-bee-di-bee-bop for short periods, but my lip would completely fail me after a few seconds and any sustained note was impossible. Ron, having played baritone horn and flute in school, assured me that if I just took my time and was patient, the nerves and muscles would respond sooner or later. Well, it wasn't sooner. I got scared. I thought that maybe they would never come back. After about three weeks of little or no progress, I began to feel guilty for wasting my talent and abilities on drugs and other debaucheries. I knew that my inability to play was the direct result of having neglected my God-given gift. I would sit in the dark at night and actually cry, as I wondered what would happen to me. What would I do? The fate that I was trying to avoid by leaving L.A. was catching up to me here in Denver. I was thinking, "Why should I clean up my life? If I can't play, I might as well continue to get high." But, with support and counseling from Ron and Patrish, these thoughts were not allowed to remain in my mind. They kept me interested in my physical training and in other positive things.

Ron pointed out that if I didn't get my chops back, I could always compose, produce, and arrange. I envisioned myself doing what Quincy Jones did, but he was a different case. The way I play is unique. Nobody came close to the exciting way I could spit notes out of a trombone. Quincy had never been a great trumpet player — that he no longer played the trumpet was no great loss to the music world. I, on the other hand, would be guilty of destroying a special gift, and I just could not reconcile myself to that. I cried like a baby, and I think that what I also did was pray and repent. I didn't specifically ask God to forgive me, but I consciously recognized the fact that I had done a terrible thing — or, in religious terms, sinned—and was truly sorry and wanted desperately to make amends. It seemed that this period of repentance had a cleansing effect on me. I began to practice more diligently and started to see small progress. When I realized that my reconciliation would not come fast or easy, I settled into a slow but relentless, often painful routine. After many nights of praying, crying, and making promises, I finally felt that I was forgiven and was sure that recovery was possible. I cried again. This time giving thanks for the opportunity to recover my gift, a second chance. I didn't mind the physical pain. I was so happy that the mental pain was subsiding. I didn't mind the long hours of playing the same notes and phrases over and over again. I was just thankful to know, in advance, that all of this would not be in vain.

I also thanked God, and I continue to thank God for my brother, Ron, and my friend Patrish who would not let me give up. I was their special project. Ron left me alone most nights. He was a disc jockey and did the midnight-to-four-in-the-morning jazz show on a radio station in nearby Castle Rock, Colorado. He was my total support. His money from the radio station and an occasional, only if necessary, withdrawal from the recording fund paid the rent and fed us. Patrish was a freelance house-keeper and would get us work cleaning or painting houses, moving fur-niture, and other little odd jobs as they came up. Ron made it clear that he didn't expect me to do anything but practice and train to get ready for the album. But I couldn't let him do all of the work. I helped out as much as I could, but he did many things that I could not physically handle, like cleaning the coliseum after the rodeos and working on the loading docks at warehouses. He really went the extra mile to keep us living and look-ing good as I worked my way back to health. He even considered taking a job cleaning the windows of skyscrapers. The pay was great—$25 an hour—but it required hanging along the sides of thirty-story buildings for hours at a time. Neither he nor I could handle that.

Our friend and homeboy Eldridge Williams—younger brother of Thaddeus Williams, my friend from the old Toulminville neighborhood who had been killed in the Vietnam War—introduced us to a poet, the Reverend David Nelson. David turned out to be the founder of the '70s revolutionary group the Last Poets. Although the group's message of in-surrection and revolution had frightened me, I had always admired their work. Their poem-to-music "Die Nigger" had caught my attention, al-though I didn't really get into it. I was happy and proud to meet Reverend Nelson, who was a culturally minded person. In addition to his minis-

Left to right: me and David Nelson. Courtesy of Roscoe Crenshaw.

tering of the gospel—which caused many heated discussions between him, Ron, and Eldridge (okay, I got involved, too, sometimes)—he was leading an improv group at the Eulipion Cultural Center, a place where local artisans, actors, dancers, and other creative personalities met and performed. The center was located above a storefront in the Five Points area of Denver. Five Points was quiet then, in the late '80s, but Mr. Homer Brown, one of the first musicians that I met in Denver, told me that in the late '50s and '60s "there was so much action in this part of Denver that whores were giving damn fools money." The Rossonian Hotel, in the center of the Point, had been in its glory days. Four or five clubs had bands playing on a regular basis. All of the big jazz and R&B stars from around the world had come to perform at the Five Points in Denver.

David invited us to come and join his improv group. The group was about dramatizing poems. We worked for weeks on David's production based on the Langston Hughes poem "Dream Explosion." The presentation featured dramatization of that Hughes poem as well as poems by David and other local poets. Ms. Isetta Crawford-Rawls's "Wanna Be" and Mr. Wardell Montgomery's "Do I Have to Live Like This?" were highlights of the show. David and I did a couple of poems together. "Women and Cars" and "Soweto." He recited the poem, and I accompanied him with jazz on the trombone. We connected and it worked out really well, so we talked about doing more poetry and jazz trombone projects together at some point. The whole ensemble acted out one of David's poems about his grandmother's passage into heaven. I played the part of Gabriel, of course. It was a fun endeavor, and we all enjoyed it very much during the four weeks it ran. Acting out was especially good for me. It got me out of the house and gave me a chance to interact with some normal, non–drug-using people for a change. My creative spirit was being challenged, and I responded positively. I was coming back to who I was, who God intended me to be. I was feeling proud of myself again.

After my religious awakening and my reconciliation with God, my progress took off. I devised a routine wherein I did long tones and lip slurs for about an hour, then spent another hour on scales and exercises from the Arban method book. After that, I would take maybe an hour break, then spend the rest of the afternoon working on tunes. Even though I had somewhat of a jazz repertoire from my early days of jamming in Mobile, there were many tunes that I didn't really know. So I got myself a fake book. A book that had the melodies and chord changes to most songs that were played by jazz musicians. I had always played by ear, and even though I knew how to read music, there were very few tunes that I actually knew from the inside out with the exact changes and the exact melody. I had studied changes seriously only during the short time I had spent with Willie Gresham at Alabama State, when Bobby Sharpe had taught me three or four songs in Mobile, and the time John Brown had meticulously taught me "All the Things You Are" when I was stranded in Washington, D.C. Everything else that I knew, I had learned by ear. I could fake most standards pretty well because I am gifted with an amazing ear. But real jazz tunes like "Whisper Not," "Nica's Dream," and "Joy Spring" are impossible for even me to fake. I knew that if I were going to pursue jazz as a livelihood, I would have to really study, really learn what it was these songs and chord changes were all about.

It was about six months before I got up the nerve to go out and play with anybody. Ron had mentioned that players like pianist Joe Bonner and the great drummer Bruno Carr were living in Denver at this time. I had once met Bruno with Larry Gale in L.A. when they played a gig at Marla's Memory Lane. I was thrilled by his playing then, and I had since heard him on records with Ray Charles and Herbie Mann. I was looking forward to experiencing his powerful groove myself. The opportunity presented itself at a gig Bruno was playing at a club called the Champa Bar and Grill. It was a little, tight place in a basement. The band was set

Bruno Carr.
Photograph by
Fred Wesley Jr.

up in a corner next to a post that was holding the building up. The band consisted of Bruno Carr on drums, Keith Oxman on tenor sax, and Mark Diamond on bass. That was it. Three cats jamming their asses off.

The feeling excited me and scared me at the same time. It was like trying to be cool before you made love to an extremely beautiful woman. You don't want your excitement to cause you to blow your program, lose control, and not do a good job. I couldn't wait to get into it, but I wasn't absolutely sure that I was ready to do justice to the strong groove that they were laying down. I was actually trembling with excitement as I introduced myself to the guys. They were all very cordial and welcomed me to the set. Making love to this woman would be a special challenge in that she was missing an important part. No brain, or in this case, no piano. I was going to have to make technical sense all by myself.

The first tune we played was "The Days of Wine and Roses"—not one of the tunes that I had been working on, but one that I knew and could fake very well. It was done to a bossa nova beat and I felt very comfortable with it. I did really well. Having passed the initial test, or the foreplay, if you will, I was now confident that I could do my thing. I called my favorite thing, a medium up-tempo blues in F, or said, "Let's stick it way up in there and fuck." She was ready and I was ready. And that was just what we did. The tune was Miles's "Walkin'." Out of the head, Bruno and Mark jumped on me, and we took each other for a ride that none of us will ever forget. When it was over, I had to restrain myself from cuddling

Andy Weyl and me. Courtesy of Ron Wesley.

with them, for I was truly in love, especially with Bruno. It was he who turned me every which way but loose. Trying his best to throw me off. I stuck to him like glue. He'd hit me, I'd hit him back. He would push, I would pull. It was really wonderful. Exactly what jazz and lovemaking are supposed to be about—interaction. I had it back! I could play again. The magic, the fire, everything was still there. I know that it wasn't these particular musicians who gave it back to me, but it was they who brought it out of me at that critical moment, and I was grateful to them in the same way I was grateful to Pratt, Noon, Leonard, and Booker, with whom I first lost my cherry. Now that I had it all the way back, I was planning to be very promiscuous with it.

The opportunity to spread it around came right away. There was a piano player in the house named Andy Weyl. He introduced himself to me and invited me to play a gig with him in Boulder. He and Mark did a duo every Wednesday and had a different guest horn player every week. I accepted the invitation and all other paid or unpaid chances to play around Denver. Making money was not my main concern. I was still in training for the album that Ron and I were planning. We foresaw the album taking off and selling a lot of units, thus causing us to have to travel around the world performing in jazz clubs. In the meantime, I played around town for whatever I could get. I became a regular at the jazz showcase, which is what Andy's gig was called. It was fun and helpful in that I had to play without drums. It was like jogging with weights or making love wearing a rubber. Good training for the real thing. Plus, Andy was an excellent pianist and helped me to really learn many new tunes from the inside out. There wasn't any room to fake on that gig.

I was contacted by a trumpet player named Lynn Watkins who had a band formed in the likeness of the Dave Pell Octet. Lynn was an adequate player whose chops had seen their best days. But what Lynn had was a book. He must have had a thousand arrangements of standards and originals for rhythm section and four to five horns. The band was mostly of local cats who played music on the side. Bobby Green, the piano player, seemed to be the only player who was always in the band. I rotated with a trombone player named Nelson Hinds. Keith Oxman did the gig sometimes. Other times the tenor was played by a guy named Dave Cannon, who looked like Bob Steel and played like Bob Berg. He must have been a cowboy during the day. The band rehearsed regularly on Wednesday nights and played mostly private parties and school and college functions. I agreed to do it when I could. Watkins only worked every now and then, but usually for very good money.

I made myself available to him off and on, until he asked me to do some funk charts for the band. I knew he could not pay much, so I said I would do it for $50 a chart. He thought that the price was outrageous. So did I. I was used to getting at least $500 for any chart that I did just for horns. But I thought, "What the hell. I'll sketch out some James Brown and some Ray Charles material for him and only charge $25 a chart." I did, and we actually played "I Feel Good" and "Hallelujah, I Just Love Her So" on a few gigs. Then I heard that he had told somebody that I had ripped him off for some arrangements. I confronted him, and he said that he didn't like the fact that I hadn't completely written out the arrangements. So I gave him his $50 back and took my two sketches out of the book. I felt I had done a pretty good job for $25. He didn't. We didn't work together again after that.

I finally got to play with Joe Bonner at a little place in the Baywolf shopping center in the affluent Cherry Creek neighborhood of Denver. Bonner's gig was kind of strange. Then Joe himself turned out to be kind of strange. He drank too much and acted a complete fool when he got drunk, which was nearly all the time. But he could really play—especially for me. I could tell just from sitting in with him that he was very sensitive to the person he was playing with. He would lead when nec-

(left) Joe Bonner (right) Ken Walker. Photographs by Fred Wesley Jr.

essary, follow when necessary, play with you when it was appropriate. Sort of like a thoughtful lover—there to satisfy your needs. I loved his playing.

The only real, all-the-time jazz club in Denver was a place called El Chapultepec. It was a well-known jazz venue and boasted a long, storied history of frequent appearances by many famous jazz musicians. This club had a house band led by a local tenor player named Freddy Rodriquez. It also boasted a fine rhythm section that included Billy Wallace on piano, Nat Yarboro on drums, and a fantastic young bass player named Ken Walker. The house band played every night except Mondays and featured a jazz great on Fridays, Saturdays, and Sundays. I hadn't yet been to the club, but I had heard of appearances by Harold Land, Eddie Harris, Bill Watrous, and Slide Hampton. The set was open every night to any musician who wanted to stop by and sit in.

One night Ron and I ended up at "the Pec," as it was called by the hipsters in town. I sat in and played, but I could never get comfortable. The players were all world-class, but the place was small and there was nowhere for the slide. There was not really a bandstand, just a space on the floor between the bathrooms and the back door. I could not believe that so many great musicians had actually played in this place, which amounted to no more than a dump. I guess the clientele viewed it as funky and down-to-earth. Most of the customers were yuppies letting their hair down among the common neighborhood people. I personally saw it as disrespectful to the music and to the fine musicians making the music. I got a sick feeling every time I went in the place and saw great drummers like Bruno and Nat jammed up in the corner next to the back door. It was convenient to step outside and smoke a doobie, but it looked like the management should, at least, build a comfortable bandstand. A beer was two dollars and fifty cents, for Christ's sake. And the place was always packed. I tried to get it on at the Pec a few times, but in the end I simply could not bring myself to go there, even though I longed to play with the guys, especially Ken Walker. He was something special. I see now why Ron had included the ownership of a state-of-the-art, respectable jazz nightclub as part of the long-range business plan.

The good part about going to the Pec was it that it completed my rhythm section. I couldn't think of any drummer, pianist, or bass player in the world that I would rather have than Bruno Carr, Joe Bonner, and Ken Walker to record with me. After making the rounds and playing as many jam sessions as possible at night and working very hard on my practice schedule during the day for a couple of months, I felt really strong and confident enough to start thinking about the album. We wanted to make a jazz statement. I chose not to use other horns, although it was a great temptation to do a combo-type thing featuring some hip arrangements. But we decided to present Fred Wesley Jr., the jazz trombonist. Not the arranger. Not the producer. Not the versatile musician. Only the jazz trombonist.

Tune selection was important. We selected my favorite vehicle as the opening tune. That medium up-tempo blues in F. (I found out later that Clifford Brown originally wrote "Sandu" in E-flat.) I had been playing an original arrangement of "Sandu" by Andy Weyl with Andy Weyl for a number of months, so I used that same arrangement on the album. The second tune was a new bossa nova arrangement of my original "Sweet Loneliness," renamed "La Bossa." We also wanted to introduce the world to probably its greatest composer, someone whom nobody had ever heard of outside of Mobile, Alabama. He was Ron's and my first horn teacher, Mr. E. B. Coleman. We chose one of his beautiful ballads, "To Someone," which I had been listening to Fortune play for years but had never gotten the chance to lead myself. Number four was a rather difficult tune by Coleman called "Minor Coated," a blues in E-flat minor. I had also been very impressed by a Jazztet arrangement of "It's Alright with Me" that featured Curtis Fuller and had viewed it as a trombone tune ever since. We did Joe Bonner's arrangement of the tune. We also recorded a Joe Bonner original called "The North Star." Two standards that I had been playing since my days at the Pratt jam sessions—"Autumn Leaves" and "The Way You Look Tonight"—were also added. The closest thing to funk on the album was the familiar Cannonball Adderly tune "Work Song." We closed the album with "Tippin'," an up-tempo, rhythm-changes tune by Horace Silver. Fast tempos are not my strong suit, but with that great and supportive rhythm section, I made it through with no problem.

Once the album was recorded, selling it was the next step. We sent it out to every jazz record company that we could find out about. We waited for what seemed like years for someone to hear what we heard—a great bebop album. But, once again, our timing was a little off. It seemed that all the record companies were moving away from straight-ahead bebop and embracing the new, electronic, cool jazz sound or the funky jazz sound. No company would take the album. We were very disappointed, but we didn't give up. We took what little money we had left and printed up some flyers advertising a cassette of the album for sale. We made as many cassettes as our limited income would allow, took orders over the phone, and sold a few around town. We mailed flyers all over the country, but the landslide of orders we expected never happened. The selling part of the plan had failed, mainly because neither of us really understood how to promote and market a product. Plus, we were out of money, and it was time to think about basic survival for ourselves and our families. We would get back to the plan when and if we could.

Ron took a job driving a taxi. I looked around for a gig in town. I hooked up with the local music guru, Mr. Joe Keel. Joe was doing the music for a production put on by his ex-wife, who actually ran the Eulipion Cultural Center. She was a dancer and a very nice lady I had met briefly while doing the poetry thing with David Nelson. Oddly enough, her name was Joe Keel, too. So, for purposes of identification, we included her maiden name, and she became known as Joe Bunten Keel. I call Joe Keel the local music guru because he is *the* homegrown, badass piano player in Denver. There are many good musicians in Denver, but they are either from somewhere else or were taught by Joe. There are legendary Joe Keel bands, but when I met him he wasn't leading a band. He was earning a very good living playing cocktail piano in hotel lobbies and piano bars and the like. I had met him at a jam session at a location where all the musicians in town had come to raise money for the local public radio station. He was very good, but I hadn't seen him since. However, his name came up whenever musicians from Denver were mentioned. He was, and probably still is, "the Man" in Denver.

I was flattered that Joe chose me to be in the handpicked band he put together for a production called *The Cotton Club*. It was a show with singers and dancers like the ones presented in the famous Harlem Cotton Club of the '40s. All of the best local performers were in the show. Some surprisingly good dancers and very good singers, including Ed Battle, a regular at the Pec, and Wendy Harelston, a singer-actress I had worked with in Lynn Watkin's band. The band—conducted by Mr. Joe Keel, of course—consisted of Joe on piano; Jo Jo Williams, an excellent swing drummer in the style of Sonny Payne; Dee Minor, a bass player named for his favorite key; Mr. Homer Brown, an older gentleman who would have been the music guru of Denver except for the fact that he was from Chicago, on sax; Hugh Ragin, a college professor whose professional credits include playing with Maynard Ferguson's big band, the Houston Symphony, and David Murray's Avant Garde Jazz Ensemble, on trumpet; and me on trombone.

The music was swing from the '40s. I copied and condensed, for example, big arrangements of Glen Miller's "In the Mood" and Gene Krupa's "Rhythm Dance." Joe Keel arranged the rest of the music, tunes like "God Bless the Child" and "Give Me a Pig Foot and a Bottle of Beer." The show turned out to be a lot of fun and helped my chops a great deal because it ran six nights a week for eight weeks. The highlights of the show were a dance that a woman named Janice did in a skin-tight body stocking to the tune "Harlem Nocturne" and an eight-bar solo that Hugh Ragin played on "Caravan." Both of these performances brought the house down each and every night. Janice's dance is a memory that has helped me through many a lonely night, and I decided then and there that Hugh Ragin was a trumpet player that I would surely use when and if I ever put my own band together.

After the show closed, Joe approached me about playing in a band that he was about to assemble. I hesitated. First of all because Joe was insecure and felt that all the musicians he had helped start in the business had failed to give him the credit he deserved for their success. He was constantly reassuring everybody and himself that he was so much better than all the other pianists in town. He was paranoid, believing that people were always trying to steal his music and his ideas. But he was a wonderful composer of music in every genre. Jazz, blues, funk, reggae,

(above left)
Joe Keel. Photograph
by Fred Wesley Jr.

(above right)
Mr. Homer Brown.
Photograph by Fred
Wesley Jr.

(right) Teresa
Carroll and me.
Courtesy of Ron Wesley.

pop, gospel, and classical music were all within his range. Plus, he could play all styles with equal dexterity and sensitivity. There was no doubt that he was one of the best in town at least, if not in the world. I wanted very much to play with him, but I wondered whether I could bear all the complaining and bragging that would surely be a part of a regular gig with Joe Keel. On the other hand, Joe was a very decent person. He was loyal and caring to his friends and family, hard-working, and serious about his music. He also was a survivor of many personal trials and tribulations that I could certainly identify with. I couldn't help but care very much for the guy, no matter how much he got on my nerves at times. So I agreed to do the gig.

The band members varied, as did most of the local Denver bands. The drummers were Christopher Lee and Tony Black. Chris was more jazzy, and Tony was more funky, but they were both very good and fit in well with the jazz-funk theme of the band. Most of the time the bass player was Dwight Killian, a fine and versatile musician. At other times, Colin Gee and a guy named Scott filled in on bass. We had a singer named Teresa Carroll, who was classically trained but way off into singing and writing jazz. Her specialty was putting words to bebop tunes. Therefore, she was used like a horn in most of Joe's arrangements. It was a very interesting and challenging gig that we all ended up enjoying very much. We were booked on the weekends at the York Street Café, where we had the hip-yet-yuppie jazz element of Denver, as opposed to the traditional, down-and-dirty clientele of the Pec. But we all ended up at the Pec after-hours on certain occasions, like when musicians like Eddie Harris or Slide Hampton came to town to appear there.

Our repertoire consisted mainly of Joe Keel originals or Joe Keel original arrangements. I would ordinarily have had an ego problem playing somebody else's music all night long, but in this case I didn't mind. Joe wrote so beautifully that it was an honor and a pleasure, as well as an education, to play his music. Our egos clashed only when he began to try to enforce band rules and band policies. These weren't the usual professional rules like being on time, not getting drunk, and not hogging solos. I had no problem with that kind of thing. This was stupid Ray Charles shit, like not talking to and laughing with each other onstage. (I think that Teresa and I kind of distracted attention from his solo one time by interacting with each other after our solos. I told you before that Joe was paranoid.) And it was Joe's policy not to pay the band on Sunday night after the last gig of the weekend like any sane bandleader would have.

Instead, he would have each member drop by his house on Monday to get paid. Well, I thought that this was ridiculous, that he just wanted to exercise his leadership and authority by having us go out of our way and listen to his criticisms and critiques of the previous weekend. That and other insecure, paranoid behavior made it difficult for me to enjoy the otherwise great gig. I loved playing with the guys in the band, especially Teresa and Joe himself, but the schizoid bullshit got the best of me, and I found it more and more difficult to make the gig. I did remember Teresa Carroll along with Hugh Ragin as people I definitely wanted to work with in the future.

I didn't want to just walk away. It was the kind of gig where all of the pieces fit or none of the pieces fit. If I left, the gig was over. So I stuck it out, hoping it would run its natural course and I wouldn't have to be the one who broke it up. And that's exactly what happened. The club cut us down to one night, then to no nights. Without the gig at the York Street, I saw no reason to keep the band going. Although Joe tried to get other gigs, it didn't work out. I think we all were glad that it was over. We had gotten all the good out of it. Joe struggled, but it was time to move on, so we went our separate ways.

I had been in Denver about two years at this point and had pretty much separated from my friends in the real world, except for an occasional phone call from Ernie or Maceo. A few others had stayed in contact, but Denver was my safe haven in an otherwise stormy world, and I had gotten used to it.

In August of 1988, Maceo called me to do one gig in Phoenix with James Brown. I thought that I would do it for the simple reason that I needed the money, which was purported to be really good. Plus, it would be good to see Maceo, St. Clair, Sweet Charles, all the other guys, and Martha again. I was also sort of anxious to show off my newly revived chops and to see how they fared on a real gig.

When I arrived at the hotel, I noticed a crowd of people hovering around what looked like a dead body. I paid it little attention because I was really looking for somebody I knew to help me check in. I finally got up with Maceo, and as we were checking in I mentioned the commotion outside. He took a look and said, "Don't worry about that. It's just the bass player." I wasn't sure what that meant, but he seemed sure that everything would be okay.

The gig turned out to be a private party for some big corporation from France. The James Brown Show was the entertainment for the end of the weeklong convention/party, which explained why I was getting $800 for the one gig. The hotel was a swanky golf resort. A stage had been set up way out on the back of a golf course. We were all loaded on a van and led to the backstage area by a man on horseback. A weird beginning to what would be a very weird gig.

The equipment was grossly inadequate. When the band hit, it sounded like a bunch of high-school kids on their first gig. I wondered where J.B. had gotten these strange musicians and why he kept them after he heard them play. Maceo was clearly in charge, and thank goodness, because it seemed that he and I were the only ones who were even re-motely into the gig. Somehow we got through the band set, which was nothing but the Maceo Parker Show. Then James came on. He was defi-nitely not the same James Brown that I had known. He was dressed in his usual style, and his hair was somewhat the same, but his performance was all screwed up. He never really sang any songs but basically just fumbled around on the stage, screaming every now and then and kind of jumping around and acting crazy.

Only Maceo seemed to know what the problem was, and he some-how guided me, James, and the whole show through to the end. The thing is, all the French people were drunk and/or high on something, too, so when the gig was over, everybody seemed to be happy. Except me. I didn't know what to think. Had it come to this? Was the great Mr. Brown going down all high and pitiful like this? I was amazed and saddened at the same time. Maceo assured me that it was not like this all the time, but some good and abundant cocaine had come around, so J.B. and a number of the others were into it a little heavier than usual. I hoped that Maceo was correct. Still, I got my money and locked myself in my room until morning, then got the hell out of there as fast as I could. I never really got a chance to talk to James. He kind of mumbled something to me as he was stumbling off the stage, but we didn't have a real conversation. Not that we had ever had a real conversation. But I expected him to at least tell me how good he was doing and how I was not going anywhere without him. I was certain that the James Brown legend had come to a sad end and that it was just a matter of time before the whole world found out. I almost cried.

I had really resigned myself to the fact that the James Brown thing was over. I had agreed to the Phoenix gig because it was available and because I needed the money, not because I had thoughts about perma-nently rejoining the band. It was a matter of convenience. And just like convenient sex, convenient gigs with James Brown eventually got me into trouble. On the advice of Maceo, I took another one-time gig with J.B.—a week at the Fairmont Hotel in San Francisco. I hesitated because I didn't want any part of the show that I had seen in Phoenix—not even for the money, which I still needed. But, as it turned out, the horrible show that I had witnessed in Phoenix was nowhere to be seen in San Francisco, just as Maceo had promised. He assured me that the situation in Phoenix had merely been the result of a terrible set of circumstances, which were not present at the Fairmont gig. This time the band was hitting. Not nearly as hard as when Pee Wee was there or even when I was the bandleader, but the old James Brown thing was there, and it was strong and good. I was glad that my doomsday prediction had not come true.

The week at the Fairmont was so good that I agreed to do another short stint with the band, since there hadn't been any talk about me coming back permanently. Plus, the gig was in Rio De Janeiro, Brazil. I couldn't resist the chance to see the "Girl from Ipanema" one more time. The Brazil gig was a bust from the beginning. First of all, there was not even one sighting of the "Girl from Ipanema." It rained from the time we got there until the time we left. Although the gig was supposed to be for three days and I was to be paid a total of $1,200, the first gig was canceled because of the rain, and, of course, you know that Mr. Brown was not going to pay me for a day that I didn't work, even though by rights I should have gotten the whole payment. I acceded to the reduced pay, mainly because I had known who I was going working for when I took the gig. Plus, I'd be safely back in Denver in a minute, and it all would be over.

But not quite. On the way back, the plane had to make a long stop in Venezuela, which gave J.B. a chance to corner me for one of those dreaded one-on-one conversations about how he was the only one in the business doing anything and how I needed to be with him if I was going to have any success. I don't know why, but I did my regular "Yes, sir, Mr. Brown. You're right, Mr. Brown" thing that I had always done in the past. I certainly didn't have to do it. It wasn't like he was going to fire me, although it was true that I hadn't been paid yet. I think I just didn't want to go through a long, drawn-out, unwinnable argument with him. Anyway, I'd be home in a minute, and it just didn't matter. Naturally, the fact that I still hadn't been paid concerned me a bit, and it should have, because when we got to Miami, where we were supposed to get paid, I got instead a proposal from Mr. Glenn, the road manager at the time.

Mr. Glenn told me that he couldn't pay me because it would take a few days for him to change the money. As if he hadn't known that he would have to change the money. The proposal was for me to ride the bus back to Augusta, then, instead of taking my scheduled flight to Denver, remain there for a week and rehearse with the band, ride the bus to New Orleans, play one gig at the New Orleans Jazz and Heritage Festival, and get paid double the $900 he owed me for the Brazil gig. I thought about it. I thought about how nice it would be to play the festival in New Orleans. I also thought about who the proposal actually came from and the chances of it being fulfilled exactly as it was proposed. My Daddy once told me that if you don't act on what you know, you might as well not know it.

In order to get the flight to Denver, I would have to walk, with all of my luggage, clear over to the domestic terminal. I did just that. I saw it coming. Me being trapped into having to keep doing one more gig with James Brown, then one more, until it would make more sense for me to stay with the show permanently. I took that walk across the Miami airport. I had just enough money in my pocket to buy a one-way ticket to Denver. I didn't mind leaving my pay because I knew that I was already falling into one of J.B.'s carefully laid traps. Plus, I wasn't about to spend a week in Augusta, Georgia—James Brown's hometown, where he would have had total access to me for seven days, probably rehearsing or listening to more of his bullshit.

It wasn't long after that that I heard that J.B. had gotten into trouble with the law and had subsequently been sent to jail. A feeding frenzy of sorts erupted in the music world, a frenzy that revolved around trying to either help get J.B. out of jail or capitalize on the fact that he was in jail. I got calls from many different sources wanting me to help organize benefit concerts or reunite the band for tours so that his suddenly unemployed people could earn some money. The idea was to capitalize on the J.B. name without having to pay or charge the J.B. money. It sounded like a good plan, but I didn't feel right taking advantage of J.B.'s downfall. I did, however, do a record with Maceo entitled *Let Him Out,* as well as another kind of a joke record making fun of J.B.'s situation, which I now wish I hadn't done. It was funny but in poor taste. I was glad when it went nowhere. Unfortunately, Maceo's record didn't do well, either, although it was one of the best things that Maceo ever wrote.

After the Brazil gig, I got a call from Bobby Byrd asking me if I would like to do a two-week tour in Europe with his band. It seems that, for whatever reason, there was a resurgence of R&B music in Europe—especially the music of James Brown. I don't know if J.B.'s unfortunate incarceration had anything to do with it, but records like *Sex Machine, Pass the Peas,* and *The Payback,* and even my song "House Party" were being played regularly in the discos and on the pirate radio stations. The music that we had created in the '70s was being brought back big time by the underground dee jays in London. This "rare groove" movement had spread throughout mainland Europe like wildfire.

JB Horns

• • •

I didn't want to leave Denver. I was safe from all of the things that had run me out of L.A. I didn't care that there was a demand for the music that I had a hand in creating with James Brown. I just wanted to continue to study my jazz and form a little quartet and play gigs around the jazz clubs and jazz festivals. Ron's plan had not been completely realized— we still had to figure out how to sell our recordings in order to make it happen—and I wasn't ready to give it up altogether. But Byrd insisted, and then Maceo and Pee Wee called to add to the hype, saying how we'd be able to make some good money in Europe.

Byrd had put together a show that included his band, which was working around Nashville and Atlanta. Along with Lyn Collins, Marva Whitney, Vickie Anderson, and Miss Martha High—who had been put out of work when Mr. Brown had gone to jail—Pee Wee, Maceo, and I would complete the perfect James Brown nostalgia show. Byrd and his sons, Tony on drums and Bart on the Hammond B-3 organ, formed the nucleus of a band that included Jerry Preston on bass and Bruno Speight from the S.O.S. band on guitar. Bobby, Vickie, and their daughter Carleen were the featured singers on the show, which had been presented around the states. So the basic show was already in place. We just had to add some familiar hits like "Mamma Feelgood" by Lyn Collins and "It's My Thang" from Marva Whitney. The London dee jays also insisted that we do "Pass the Peas," "Gimme Some Mo'," as well as "Doing It to Death" from the JBs, "Foreplay" from the Horny Horns, and my own "House Party."

I definitely needed the money, with three daughters about to or already entering college. I had sadly neglected them during my rehab period and could hardly continue to leave their support to my estranged wife. It was certainly time to face reality and make some money by any means available. The Bobby Byrd tour was a means available. So I decided to do one tour, which was only for a few weeks, after which I could return to the plan that Ron and I had laid out, with a little more money to help distribute our record and do some public relations at the same time. Jazz also was going good in Europe. I thought that perhaps I could hook up with some record company over there.

It was good fun doing all the old James Brown stuff again. It was like stepping back into history, but without the duress and stress that had come with having James Brown as the boss. On top of that, we actually made more money per person than any of us ever had ever made with the Godfather of Soul. The European audiences were amazing. Just like the London dee jays had predicted, they reacted to "Pass the Peas" and the other old songs like they were hearing brand-new music. For our first gig, which was at the Town and Country Concert Hall in London, we played to a packed house of over 1,500 screaming people of all ages. There were fans from the old days who remembered the music, fans from the discos who knew the music from the records, and fans who specialized in the collection and preservation of what they called "rare grooves." We performed for three weeks to similar audiences, although of varying sizes, in cities throughout Great Britain, Holland, France, Germany, and Switzerland. The London crowd was the largest and a 300-person, standing-room-only disco in France was the smallest.

Although we made good money, it was made clear to us that we, the ones not in the Byrd family, were employees and not privy to the management and distribution of the money. The concert in London was recorded by a company co-owned by a German, Mr. Stephan Meyner, and an Italian, Mr. Gian Carlo Duilio. We never found out how the business of that project went down. This didn't sit well, of course, with those of us who felt like we were the real draw and who had made the records that the majority of the audiences wanted to hear. We did manage to finish that first tour on an amicable note, but Maceo, Pee Wee, and I thought about doing another tour with a different distribution of the proceeds.

Pee Wee, Maceo, and I were deluged with one offer after another. At one point, we went to Florida with Pee Wee's friend Jim Payne and did an album for the King Snake label. We didn't get any money up front but

(left) Jim Payne (right) Bob Greenlee. Photographs by Fred Wesley Jr.

shared equally in the production and publishing points. The album was a put-together bunch of grooves that we basically made up on the spot. Jim played drums and label-owner Bob Greenlee played the bass. Along with local guitar player Ernie Lancaster and piano player Marc Puricelli, a friend of Jim's from up east, we did a pretty good recording that took a total of one week to complete. The rhythm section was used to recording blues tracks together, and we had our James Brown training in common, so many things just fell into place. Still, it was amazing how easily the whole thing came together.

The album was released and did a fair amount of international business, as the King Snake label had a good worldwide distribution network. That network was usually set in motion to distribute their blues recordings, but with our James Brown affiliation, the name Maceo, and the group name JB Horns, our record did very well. The record did so well in Japan, in fact, that Jim organized a tour there. We used Jim's rhythm section. Mark Helias on bass, Allen Jaffe on guitar, and Jim on drums. We took along one of King Snake's recording artists, Miss Yvonne Jackson, as the featured vocalist. The gig went very well. Maceo, Pee Wee, and I were as automatic onstage as we were in the studio. The audiences loved every minute of our performances, and so did we. On top of it all, we made more money than any of us had ever made on one gig in our entire careers. We did a video and a live recording during the tour and, to this day, continue to receive residuals from those recordings.

The JB Horns. Left to right: Pee Wee, me, Maceo. Courtesy of Fred Wesley Jr.

Hadji Akbar, who had played with James Brown until the incarceration, was using the name JB Horns for his band, which was based in London. He had hit on Maceo and Pee Wee to join him for a tour and a recording. The tour and recording part appealed to Maceo and Pee Wee, but Hadji replacing me as the third horn part was not acceptable at all. Hadji was a fair trumpet player of whom it was said, "He can almost play." But this was a time when money was dictating our moves, and we had to at least consider his offer.

The recording was to be produced by Englishman Richard Mazda. They had already cut a funk single and another jazz tune of Pee Wee's before I got called into the project. At that point, I was back in Denver and really didn't have time to go to London. I had just sold my house in L.A. and moved my family to Denver and was very busy trying to put my life back together. I had a little money left from the sale of the house and really didn't need the meager advance that the producer was putting up. But they really wanted me to do the album with them, so we worked it out such that Richard, Maceo, and Pee Wee, but not Hadji, traveled to Denver to record the album. Before they arrived, I received the track of the singles on which to add horn parts and solos. It was a very funky track in the style of "Funky President" and featured vocals by one of Richard's artists, Miss J. Ella Ruth. The single was to be released in London immediately.

When the guys arrived in Denver, we put together tunes in pretty much the same way we had for the King Snake project. The difference was that instead of using a real rhythm section, we went the electronic route and used Richard's sequencer. And we played most of the parts ourselves. Richard was skilled at using the Fostec sequencer and had some drum and bass tracks already down. We made up horn and vocal parts and wrote some more tunes as we went along. Richard was a decent producer and worked with us respectfully and efficiently. We had a really good time and put together a really good album called *I Like It Like That,* which was also the title of the single. The album had a truly unique sound that effectively combined our talents with Richard's directions. I liked the way we worked and hoped that we could use the same system to do more albums.

While Richard mixed the CD and prepared for a release, we started to talk to Hadji's people about a tour of Great Britain. Hadji's people turned out to be Mrs. Cecilia Whitten. A novice entertainment manager whose only credential was that she had once taken a bunch of Boy Scouts to camp for a summer. Somehow she had taken control of Hadji's career and convinced her wealthy husband to finance a tour for the JB Horns. I don't know how she and Hadji had originally gotten together, but they seemed to be very close friends. He lived in their home in the suburbs of London and was treated like a part of the family.

We used Hadji's band for the tour. The band consisted of local London musicians, most of whom were of West Indian descent. We performed all of the JBs and James Brown hits, with Maceo doing most of the lead singing. The tour was poorly organized, but due to the reluctant backing of Mr. Mike Whitten, we did manage to make the money that we had been promised. We didn't, however, plan to ever do another tour with Hadji or his people again.

I hauled ass back to Denver. Maceo and Pee Wee stayed in London, playing with some local blues bands and doing whatever they could to make a living.

Back in Denver with a little money, I was still thinking of working my jazz quartet. Nothing was happening, though, so I was wide open for the invitation that I got from Maceo, which was to help him with an album that he was going to do for Stephan Meyner, who was one half of the partnership that had produced the live Bobby Byrd album that we had recorded in London. Stephan had his own label based in Koln, Germany, and had plans to do an album on Maceo. And planned it was. From the selection of tunes to the musicians who would play on the album. The album would be called *Roots Revisited*. The great Don Pullen would play the Hammond B-3 organ. This in itself was strange to me, because I knew Don Pullen as an avant-garde jazz piano player. Then there was Rodney Jones, whom I didn't know. He turned out to be the guitarist on the *Live at the Apollo* TV show. He also was regular with Ruth Brown and Jimmy McGriff. The drummer, Bill Stewart, was a fine young man from Iowa who was well educated in all the modern drum styles and was in New York honing his skills and making a name for himself.

The tunes were strange, too. We did R&B tunes like Curtis Mayfield's "People Get Ready" and Ray Charles's "Them That Got"; jazz tunes like Mingus's "Got to Get Hip to Your Soul"; an arrangement on the standard "Over the Rainbow"; Maceo's original jump shuffle "Up and Down E Street"; and a Maceo spin-off of James Brown's "Man's World," which he had renamed "Children's World." Although the collection was odd, it was held together by the prevailing jazz-organ trio sound. At first Pee Wee and I struggled with the album's format, but in the end Stephan paid us enough money to shut up and play what we were told to play. We didn't expect it to go nearly as far as it did. We were very surprised when it rose to number 1 on the jazz charts.

The record did so well that Stephan put us together with a Mr. Gert Pfankuch, who operated a booking agency out of Hofhiem, Germany. I didn't know what to expect. At that point, all of the business was coming and going through Maceo. If the first gig was any indication of what was to come, we had a bright future with the Musikburo booking agency. Pfankuch flew me, Maceo, Pee Wee, Don Pullen, Rodney Jones, and Bill Stewart to Munich, where we were picked up in brand-new BMWs and rushed to a little town in the Bavarian countryside where tents and all the facilities necessary for a jazz festival were set up. We did our sound check and moved into a typical European hotel that reminded me of the French hotel in which the ghost had attacked me. The only difference was that the German hotel had a real friendly vibe and the food was outstanding.

The only problem that we had was with the organ, which was not the standard Hammond B-3 that Don was used to playing and that we were used to listening to. It was supposed to be a sound-alike by Yamaha. It was smaller and more portable and was supposed to have computerized sounds in it just like the Hammond. We spent more than an hour trying to figure the thing out, to no avail. Finally, we decided to just make do with the funny sounds that we did manage to get and just make the gig. We had a good bass sound and, with Rodney exaggerating the guitar parts, we could make the gig. But Don went off into a prima donna bag on us and said that he refused to play on an inadequate instrument. His exact words were, "I wouldn't disgrace myself or you all by playing on this organ." Well how about that? Up until then, we had been putting up with the kinda strange-acting and funny attitudes that we had been getting from Don, but his funny-style ways hadn't mattered that much. This was a little different. I was about to make $800 for one gig. It wasn't going to be perfect, but it certainly was not going to be a disgrace. Right then and there, we knew that if we did anything long-term, Don would not be the organ player. Stephan seemed to have some influence over him, and between us all we managed to talk him into doing the gig, however reluctantly and halfheartedly.

I guess this first booking by Mr. Pfankuch was sort of a test by which he could see how we operated and by which we could see what kinds of gigs he could book and how he operated. He boasted that there were hundreds of similar music festivals in Europe and that he knew and could book most of them for us. We must have passed the test. He certainly passed with us. The next thing we knew, he had booked us a four-week tour in Europe.

Mr. Pfankuch was a no-nonsense person, and that's the way he booked his tours. He didn't ask us how did we want to do, he told us how it was going to be. We could have had a tour-bus, but he pointed out that if we rode in style, we would go home with very little money. So we rode the train. First-class, mind you. We also didn't have a lot of extra people around to carry our luggage. He had gotten all of us Euro-rail passes that allowed us to go anywhere in Europe for one low price. It was beautiful. Sometimes we had close calls trying to make train changes with short time and so much luggage. Once, Maceo almost hurt himself trying to get my bag on the train. It was like that. Everybody did their part, and we all made money, and we all had fun. It was the best situation anyone could ask for. Hell, we were working for and with our best friends. The really unbelievable part about it was that we didn't have any of that boss bullshit to deal with.

We replaced Don Pullen with a friend of Bill Stewart's, Larry Goldings. Bill and Larry were doing a duo gig at a local New York club. When Maceo went to check out Bill for the recording, he came back raving about a young man playing some kind of small keyboard that sounded like organ, bass and all. It was just talk then, because Don Pullen had already been booked. But after Don had funny-acted himself away from us,

Larry and his highly portable keyboard (which Don probably would not have disgraced himself by playing) were perfect for the gig. Plus, Larry could play. I first saw him on a gig that we did at a club in New York, standing next to a real Hammond B-3 organ that was rented for the gig. He looked so young and unassuming that I said to him, "Hey, kid, get away from that organ. It's not a plaything. Don't be fooling around with it. Where's your father?" He proceeded to whip out some outlandish funk, bass and all, for about five minutes and then looked me in my astonished face and said, "Hi. I'm Larry Goldings, the new organ player."

So, the whole show was me, Maceo and Pee Wee, Larry, Rodney, and Bill. A big German guy named Deithart Meyer served as production manager, road manager, interpreter, and generally anything we needed. He spoke English, French, Italian, and was learning pretty good Alabama. He once called me a black motherfucker. I've felt really close to him ever since. He could even play the drums in a pinch. He had had experience road managing for people like Eddie Harris and a few other American artists and bands, so he knew how to deal with all kinds of situations. We ended up giving him the affectionate nickname D.D.

This compact little show toured all over Europe for four years, playing clubs and discos to mostly young, beer-drinking people. There were also the some older R&B aficionados, who came to get a nostalgic look at the music they had partied to when they were young. And then there was a smattering of jazz fans who simply came to hear us blow, both individually and collectively. We didn't disappoint any of them. A high-paying festival was thrown in whenever possible to help the budget equal out. Mr. Pfankuch's system was to work as much as possible. He would say that you make money when you play and spend money on days off; therefore, we had as few days off as possible. Most of the time, we each had a single room in a nice hotel—great hotels, sometimes. Occasionally, we were forced to stay in what seemed to be nothing more than a room in "somebody's house," as my son Fredric put it. Overall, Gert booked fast-moving, somewhat comfortable, hardworking, and always lucrative tours.

The shows that we did consisted of music from the *Roots* album and some of my music like "House Party," which was and still is a standard in the European discos. We performed some of Pee Wee's songs, like "The Chicken" and "Inarticulate Speech of the Heart." We ended up having tunes by which we were individually recognized, like my "Doing It to Death," Maceo's "Soul Power 74," and Pee Wee's arrangement and co-

composition with James Brown of "Cold Sweat." It was a very enjoyable show that spotlighted equally the talents of Pee Wee, Maceo, and myself. It also satisfied the complex mix of the audiences. The show was billed as "Maceo Parker, featuring Fred Wesley and Pee Wee Ellis." And that's exactly how it was presented. Maceo handled the lead mike because he was best at manipulating the audiences. But we all had our features, and everybody was happy—in the band and in the audiences.

As time passed, the management or lack of management of the band changed. A foiled attempt to secure management with Englishman Vanya Hackle's Favored Nations management company yielded Maceo a personal manager, Miss Natasha Maddison. After many of Mr. Hackle's suspect, ill-advised, and badly managed projects—including an HBO special with James Brown and MC Hammer for which we were paid very poorly—after many of these were saved or straightened out by Vanya's then-partner Natasha Maddison, it was clear to Maceo that Vanya should go but Natasha should stay. Thank goodness for Maceo, because I was so disenchanted with Favored Nations that I wanted everyone involved to go away and stay away. However, Natasha proved to be of immeasurable value to Maceo and the rest of us. It was one of many times in which the ability of Maceo to see the big, long-term picture had saved me from making a serious mistake.

We had gotten involved with a booking agent in New York to book our state-side tours, but I didn't like the way he handled his business. He emitted the attitude that we were working for him, and I didn't feel he gave the musicians, especially the three of us, the respect and concessions properly due to the people who made it possible for him to do his job. His previous job had been road managing for Buddy Rich. Our situation with him came to a head one day in New York after we had played the Beacon Theater. It was the end of that particular week, and he had promised to pay off after that show. Instead, he told us to come to his office the next day to collect our salary for the week. Although I didn't think that was all right, I didn't make a fuss at the time.

But overnight I began to think about how he was thinking about his convenience rather than ours. As I got up the next morning, I continued to stew. As I waited for a cab to take me downtown, I asked myself, "WHY am I out here fixing to spend MY money to go downtown to collect MY salary that I should have gotten LAST night right here at the theater, which is NEXT DOOR to the motherfucking hotel?!" By the time I found his office, I was steaming. I was going to give this motherfucker a piece of my mind, and anybody who didn't like it could kiss my ass. When I got to his office his secretary gave me a check. The check was SHORT of what I had expected. I went crazy. He had probably known that I was gonna go crazy, because he was nowhere to be found. I ranted and raved all up and down the hall cussing out anyone and everyone I came across. The secretary tried to give me the itinerary for the next tour, and I threw it back at her. That made her mad and it was on. I'm yelling. "Where is this mother-fucker? I gonna kill him. Take this itinerary and stick it up his ass. I quit. You know me. I'll go to Denver in a minute!"

That's exactly where I was headed as I was leaving the office going to try to cash that motherfucking check. I knew that the first thing the cashier was going to ask me was, "Do you have an account here?" I met Maceo coming in to the office as I stormed out, still cussing. He asked what the problem was. I told him, and I told him to call me in Denver sometime because that's where I'll be as soon as I cash this motherfucking check. He literally pulled my coat and whispered in my ear, "Don't let this guy break us up. We'll get rid of him." He reminded me about how well we were doing in Europe and how we were making more money than we had ever made in our lives. I calmed down immediately and said, "Oh. I didn't think about that." And before long that particular New York agent disappeared and became a standing joke with the band as we continued to prosper. I'll always thank Maceo for not letting me make that terrible hot-headed, half-cocked mistake.

The personnel of the band began to evolve, as well. Rodney Jones left us to continue his freelance recording and other studio work in New York. I'm sure that he had enjoyed the gig as much as we had enjoyed having him, but we had spent so much time away from New York that his musical work had been becoming one-dimensional. He was replaced by Bruno Speight. Not as jazzy as Rodney, but jazzy enough, and a funk and R&B specialist. It was good for the band, because the music had also begun to evolve. We were doing more and more grooving and vamping, and fewer and fewer actual songs to accommodate the audience, which anyway was becoming more and more dancers, and fewer and fewer listeners. It wasn't as much fun musically, but the audiences were getting larger, we were playing larger venues, and our money was increasing.

Bill Stewart was next to leave. He had filled the funk requirement toward becoming the first-call drummer in New York, and he had filled it real good. The next thing we heard from him was that he was doing big-time sessions and had landed the gig with John Scofield. We missed him, but we all knew that he was bound to end up doing bigger and more varied things.

We searched around for a while, trying out many drummers, searching for the one who could play the music to everyone's satisfaction and whose personality would gel with all of ours. It was not an easy task. Rodney sent us Kenwood Dennard, very enthusiastic and very funky, but he couldn't fit the straight, no-frills groove that Maceo required to do his thing comfortably. I thought the interplay between them was beautiful and interesting and took the funk to another level, but Maceo was not interested in elevating or innovating. He wanted to stay safe in the groove that had gotten him to where he was and where he was sure the people were. Maceo has always been real careful about not surprising his audience. Kenwood did manage to stay around long enough to do the biggest album we ever did with Maceo, the live recording *Life on Planet Groove,* which remains Maceo's biggest seller and my personal favorite.

With remaining safe in mind, we got Maceo's brother Melvin. Melvin should have been the perfect answer. He would surely satisfy Maceo. They had developed their styles together and both had polished their skills with James Brown. Plus, Pee Wee and I have always loved Melvin's playing, even though he was not a prolific jazz drummer. But he was one of the best funk drummers in the world, and his jazz was far more than adequate.

Melvin had quit the road after the Maceo and All the King's Men had broken up. He had returned to college, where he obtained his master's degree in elementary education, after which had taken a teaching position at a school in Maryland, just outside of Washington, D.C. It took some prodding, but he finally agreed to come out for at least the summer. We thought that after he got a taste of the gig and how easy and free of bullshit it was, he just might stay permanently. He stayed the summer and, I'm sure, enjoyed the gig very much, but after the gleam wore off, it got to be a real pressure to play a three-hour gig, even without the bullshit, so Melvin decided not to let the years he had spent finishing his education go to waste, and he returned to his less physically taxing job of teaching kids.

We tried James Gadson, whom I had known since 1962, when we had played a few gigs together with Hank Ballard and the Midnighters. We had remained friends through his brilliant career as first-call drummer in Hollywood, through his recordings with the Watts 103rd Street Band, to his work as a producer. (It was his Vernon Burch project on which

I had done the horn arrangements that had broken me onto the Hollywood arranging scene.) But he didn't seem to have the will to work as
hard as this gig demanded of a drummer, so he didn't last long. We tried
Jimmy Madison, the drummer I had used on most of the James Brown
studio recordings I had produced in New York, but he also didn't have
the wherewithal to handle the demands of the gig. We tried Tony Cooke
from the James Brown band and found out that he was so locked into the
James Brown Show style of playing that we couldn't break him into doing
it any other way. We even tried a guy, whose name I've forgotten, who
was the son of the guy whose band Maceo had first played in. He had a
good attitude and would one day surely be great, but he didn't yet have
the chops to play a big-time, hard-hitting show like ours. These were all
good drummers, and they played the gig very well for as long as they were
there, but we needed a drummer we could depend on to be there and be
strong all the time, even when Maceo decided to hold a vamp for half an
hour or more, without complaining or losing the groove. Bruno Speight
said he knew of such a drummer.

His name was Jamal Thomas, and he was from Macon, Georgia. He
had played with many R&B artists, including Millie Jackson and Joe
Simon. He had grown up admiring John Morgan, also from Macon, who
had played and recorded with me and Maceo during the Fred Wesley
and the JBs days. He and Bruno had worked together in the S.O.S. band.
Bruno's recommendation and Jamal's history proved to be correct. He
was the right man for the job and is on the gig to this day.

Larry was the last of the New Yorkers to leave. We had all pretty much
forgotten about the jazz part of the gig anyway, so his departure was not
exactly devastating, but he did leave a big gap in that we had all gotten used to his particular flavor of funk. Larry had taken his jazz chops
and knowledge and created a style of playing funk on the Hammond B-3
organ that was completely fresh and unique. We had all grown from the
association. Larry went on about his career as a complete, well-rounded
musician, and we were left feeling more certain of our contributions to
the music world.

Once again, the great discoverer of talent, Stephan Meyner, came to
our rescue. He brought us yet another great organ player, Will Boulware,
who had jazz chops and jazz knowledge like Larry Goldings. He wasn't
Larry, but he was as unique and as funky. Even safe, nonadventurous
Maceo quickly came to love Will and his playing, especially after he performed so beautifully on the new *Mo' Roots* album. He did not do the

Maceo Parker Band, November 1994. Left to right: Maceo, me, Jerry Preston, Bruno Speight, Will Boulware, Jamal Thomas. Courtesy of Fred Wesley Jr.

bass thing quite as well as Larry, but we had decided to use a real bass player anyway. Enter Jerry Preston.

Or maybe I should say, re-enter Jerry Preston. Jerry had been the bass player with the Bobby Byrd family band that put us all together in the first place. He was an unbelievably funky player with the musical savvy of an old man and the energy of a frisky child. You always thought that he was playing too much but then you realized that he was playing right on the top edge of "just enough," and he managed to stay there all night long. I often just watched and listened to him and felt obligated to buy a ticket. It was a pleasure to watch him play with so much ease and perfection and not miss a note or a beat.

With the addition of Jerry, the new band was complete. Within a few weeks, it had become the tightest band I have ever played in, with the possible exception of Sam and the Goodtimers. Maceo always found some flaws and some reasons to rehearse, probably just to nail down his position as leader and to keep everybody on their toes, but everything was perfectly cool with me. This was one of the reasons I stopped going to sound checks.

In the first place, sound checks, although sacred to touring bands, are to me a joke. It has been my experience that even after the most extensive and successful, well-planned sound check, where you have gotten every possible thing just right, the actual gig will be either perfect or completely fucked up or somewhere in between. If you don't have a sound check at all, the actual gig will be perfect, totally fucked up, or somewhere in between. Sound checks were usually in the late afternoon—perfectly timed to end too early to stay until the start of the gig without spending three or four hours with nothing to do but rehearse or try to sleep in a dank, dingy dressing room in a chair or on the floor, assuming that there even was a dressing room. To make sound check, you had to get off the bus, check into the hotel, get settled in your room, have something to eat. Then it was time to go to sound check. Sound checks went for about an hour or so, depending on the mood of the boss, in this case Maceo, who had taken over as boss, since we had less employable, more dependent musicians who were less likely to express how they really felt about conditions. Maceo was more likely to rehearse Jerry, Bruno, Jamal, and Will up until gig time than he would have been to rehearse Rodney, Larry, and Bill Stewart in the same way. We knew that Rodney and the New York crew would be working in the city as soon as people knew that they were back. Bruno and the southern crew would have to look long and hard to find another gig that paid as much and as regular as this one did. So they were more willing to take with a grain of salt unreasonable requirements like long, meaningless rehearsals.

I refused to go to sound checks unless I deemed it absolutely necessary. I wasn't about to stand there while Maceo did a James Brown impersonation, trying to get somebody to play "ying" not "yang," when I could be having a nice, long nap. I would tell Pee Wee, "Check my mike for me. I'll be on later." Pee Wee soon got hip and followed my lead, and we both told Maceo to check our mikes. "We know our parts." I guess this was cool with Maceo, as he never said or indicated anything to the contrary.

With Pee Wee and I avoiding sound check, Maceo gained total control over the rhythm section and therefore over the band. Pee Wee and I just kinda showed up and did our parts. We would find, from time to time, that little changes had been made. We just fit ourselves into them, and things went on. The crowds were increasing, the gigs were getting longer and longer, and Pee Wee and I had less and less of a hand in what was going on. It was like watching the Maceo show and sitting in from time to time. It was still fun, and the money was getting better and better, but the gig was getting more and more boring. What had started out as an exciting musical venture between the three of us had deteriorated into one long vamp after another. What had started out as a very musical gig had been reduced to a dance party attended by young, beer-drinking, pot-smoking, ecstasy-dropping white teenagers and young adults. The fact that I had the best chops of my life didn't make any difference at all to me or to the audience. They really only needed to see the guys who had once played with James Brown and hear any semblance of the beat and they were satisfied. This made my pockets fat, but I felt like I was shooting sparrows with a bazooka—totally wasting my skills and talent. I could have played "Mary Had a Little Lamb," and the fact that it was Fred Wesley playing was good enough for these drunk, high-out-of-their-minds kids.

One day I noticed that the posters that had once read "Maceo Parker and Roots Revisited, featuring Fred Wesley and Pee Wee Ellis" now read "Maceo Parker." So now I know that not only did my performance not make a difference, my name made no difference either. I began to ask myself, "What am I doing here? I'm not playing anything. If I don't show up, it won't affect the crowd. So I'm here just for the money. And what about the money? What good is it doing me? The money was used mostly for appeasing my loved ones for me being in Europe all the time." I could do without the money. Plus, since leaving Denver, I had reunited with and married Gwendolyn Oliver, the wonderful young lady with whom I had a 22-year affair and two sons. My new home with Gwen and my sons Fredric III and Victor in Manning, South Carolina, was not only peaceful and happy but also very inexpensive compared to Los Angeles and Denver. I discussed it with my new wife, who is a devout, born-again Christian, and she said that if I was so unhappy with the gig, she was willing to endure whatever life changes that came about. Gwen's exact words were "the Lord will provide." So, on faith, I gave up the gig that had started out so happy but ended up so sad.

Pee Wee had seen the light, or the dark, before I had. He had gotten so bored that he would actually sometimes fall asleep onstage. He left a year before I did for a new life with his new wife in London. I had understood how he felt, but after he left, I had gotten still another raise and felt that if I left at the same time I would mess up the gig for everyone, and I surely didn't want to do that. I just wanted out as smoothly and as painlessly as possible. So I gave about a five-month notice, which gave Maceo time to pull together whatever little gap I was leaving. And so it went. The Maceo gig didn't miss a step, and I went about seeking a new, more productive life.

It seemed that everyone assumed that I was going to front my own band and the thought did cross my mind. I did do one more Gert Pfankuch tour with my own band. But when I realized that I made far less as a leader than I had as a sideman with Maceo, touring with Gert became a non-option. Plus, he was booking me in the same funky places in which he booked Maceo, and that had been one of the main reasons that I had quit. So I put touring on the side until I could find someone to book me in places and on gigs that I could enjoy playing. And I really wanted to be at home more. Continuing to tour, even with my own band, would put me back in the same predicament I had been in with Maceo, riding the same trains and little dinky vans but for less money. I had no desire to start over.

The eight years that I spent with Maceo and Pee Wee saved me from the drug death that my career had experienced in L.A. After my rehabilitation in Denver, I was ready to move forward, and the JB Horns was the vehicle that carried me on. I got my first straight-ahead bebop album out by associating with Richard Mazda. I was featured on three JB Horns albums, one produced by Richard Mazda and two by Jim Payne. This gave me, Maceo, and Pee Wee credit on music other than James Brown's. I was featured on four Maceo albums produced by Stephan Meyner. The association with Stephan Meyner and Minor Music also spawned four albums for Fred Wesley as leader. I have now been recorded with such jazz greats as Geri Allen, Steve Turre, Robin Eubanks, Anthony Cox, Tim Green, and Stanton Davis. Mr. Meyner also was responsible for putting together my present band. He brought me Dwayne Dolphin, Bruce Cox, Peter Madsen, and Karl Denson, who, along with Hugh Ragin—to whom I kept a promise to have in my band one day—played on the last three of my Minor Music albums. This is the same band I took on the few tours that I did between the Maceo tours.

So, here I am. Still alive and still well and famous for things other than my time spent with James Brown. Although my James Brown credit is still the most obvious, I have established myself as someone other than just a funky trombone player who once played with James Brown—not really a star but a very important music icon and probably the world's most famous sideman.

12

Star Time

• • •

The dictionary defines "star" as a celestial body visible as a point of light, or as a leading performer. When you see a band, it doesn't take long to figure out who is the star. He or she will shine, stick out, be most visible. The star will not necessarily sing the best or play the best or even look the best, but it will seem that way simply because you give the star more attention. Stardom is an essence that, I believe, is God-given. If this essence is recognized and if whatever talent it's attached to is developed fully, you have what is called a "superstar."

This star quality is not only a look, it also—and maybe most importantly—is an attitude. A star is confident, self-assured, even cocky and arrogant. Stars have the ability to focus on themselves and refuse to take no for an answer. They believe in themselves and make others believe that they're right no matter how ridiculous they sound or may actually be. The most prevalent aspect of a star's psyche is a desire for attention and a willingness to do anything to get it. A star will wear clothes that attract attention. They will wear things that the average person wouldn't think of wearing and act as if it's nothing when their clothes are complimented, criticized, or even mentioned. Plus, as I've said before, you have to have a crazy, attention-getting hairstyle to be a star. I've seen a star walk into a roomful of people, not get instant recognition, and just yell out, "Hey! I'm here. Get to making over me."

Compare Michael Jordan to Clyde Drexler. I would say that they are equally talented basketball players. The difference is that Jordan is a natural-born star as well as a great athlete. Therefore he has the edge. Shining matters to him more than it matters to Drexler. Tell Drexler he's second best and you'd likely get an "oh well." But Jordan couldn't sleep with a number two ranking. In sports it's called the "killer instinct." I guess it's a killer instinct in entertainment, too. I saw Patti LaBelle, Linda Hopkins, and Brenda Lee Eager try to out-sing each other one night to the point that I was afraid they were going to hurt themselves. The only thing that stopped them was the fact that it was Aretha Franklin's show and she could care less. You see Aretha is not a born star. Because of her extreme talent, stardom has been thrust upon her. Without even trying or caring, Aretha Franklin is—without a doubt—the best. Therefore, she gets over—big time—on talent alone.

A lot of entertainers, however, get over on stardom alone. It was a long time before I realized that Hank Ballard couldn't sing, and I was right up there on stage with him. His showmanship, stage presence, and personality were so compelling that no one noticed that he actually could not sing. Frank Sinatra is another example. He, at best, is an average singer with an average voice and below-average looks—who was not very nice. But he was revered as one of the greatest entertainers in the world. Maybe it was the blue eyes. He definitely was a star. I think deep down Sinatra knew the truth, because he always surrounded himself with the best musicians or sidemen, as did many other stars, in my opinion, including the following:

— Miles Davis. On his playing alone, Miles Davis could not have made it as a trumpet player with contemporaries like Art Farmer, Clifford Brown, and Freddie Hubbard, or even guys I grew up with like Jimmy Seals, Bobby Sharp, or Robert Agnew—all of whom worshiped Miles. But Miles had a certain mystical attractiveness and a confidence that drew great musicians to him.

— Thelonious Monk. Monk did things that no other musician would dare try with so much confidence that his playing became a style subscribed to by many musical artists with much more talent. I heard Monk play a wrong chord so long and so hard that it became right—anyone who played the correct chord against it sounded wrong.

— James Brown. Do you think you could have accepted a tune as radical as "Cold Sweat" from a less bizarre artist?

— George Clinton. George made himself and a lot of us believe that he could dance under water, but the truth is that he's one of the few black people who can't dance at all.

Another thing all stars have in common is energy. A star will out-last you talking, performing, scheming, rehearsing, and doing everything else you can think of. Being seen as the best means everything to a star. That's what makes them stars. Unless you're willing to do anything—and do it all day long—to get attention and that number one spot in everyone's mind, you're not a star and you'll never be a real star.

Some stars take unfair advantage of their special blessing and charac-terize themselves as prophets who have seen something or have knowl-edge of things the ordinary person isn't aware of. They justify their right to be followed, no matter what sacrifices have to be endured, by claim-ing some special anointing by a higher power that speaks only to them. Much like preachers and other ministers of whatever gospel lead with the claim, "The Lord said to me," entertainers also lead by elevating them-selves to the rank of savior.

For years, James Brown claimed to be working, despite a bad heart, because of his people's need to feed their families. The truth was that he was making millions, while his people struggled along on $225-a-week salaries. "Do this for me now and in the future we will all get rich," he often said. In my forty years in the music business, I have never seen this promise fulfilled—even when I made the promise. The real truth is and has always been, "Whatever you do for me now, I will benefit from, and in the future I will ask you to do the same thing for me again, so that I can benefit from it, again." This will go on until the star doesn't need you any-more or until you get hip to who is actually benefiting from your work and your talent. The star will never remember to let you benefit. He will remember, however, that you fell for his game once and probably will go for it again.

Another important aspect of many stars' personalities is the need to hold rehearsals. Most of these rehearsals turn out to be no more than forums for the star to exert his or her authority over his or her employ-ees, affectionately known as their people. Almost always there is a time when the star goes into a rage and questions the loyalty or commitment of one or all of his subjects. "I do all of this work so that you people can have a good job and a better life, and you can't even concentrate enough to remember when to go to the bridge!" Could it be that the people I've heard make statements like this actually believe that they are ordained to help us poor, unenlightened, minimally talented, unambitious musicians earn a living and feed our families? Since I've seen this behavior from so many different stars, it's more likely that this savior thing is another intrinsic element in the make-up of the star mentality. It's part of a mind-game designed to make us, the sidemen, grateful for our jobs and satisfied with our meager percentages.

I have suffered through these sermons by James Brown, Ray Charles, David Ii, Willie Bobo, and many other great and famous (and not so great, not so famous) people designed to aggrandize themselves and belittle the sideman. In the name of "keeping the gig," my fellow sidemen and I have feigned attentive listening, then grumbled behind the star's back after the ordeal ended. Having learned how to recognize these time-wasting events, I avoid them whenever possible, but I paid a price for avoiding one such rehearsal.

Whenever Lena Horne came to L.A., she would put together a band of her favorite L.A. players. Thurman Green was one of her (and my) favorite trombonists. Thurman also was a regular in Willie Bobo's band. Willie had a great band and I considered myself fortunate when Thurman asked me to sub for him for two weeks while Lena was appearing around the L.A. area. Thurman gave me a cassette tape and music to all of the tunes that Willie would probably play on the six gigs on which I would sub for him. There were two weekends. The first was at the Playboy Club in Century City and the other was at a club in Fullerton in the Orange County, California area. The rehearsal and the first weekend at the Playboy Club went very well, although I did detect that savior thing in Willie Bobo's attitude toward his band. I didn't pay it any attention, mainly because I knew that I was only there for a short time and didn't think I would be affected. It usually takes time for a star to gain control and work his program on a new player. Plus, I saw it coming and carried myself in a way that prevented any such program to even get started on me. Although I was very respectful to Willie, I never related to him in any way but as his equal. I made sure that he knew that I had been as many places as he had been, and had played with as many big-time people as he. He seemed to be all right with this and we got along very well, on and off the stage, throughout the two weekends. I really enjoyed the gig and got great ovations from all of the audiences we faced. I also felt that Willie enjoyed having me. The interplay between us was especially thrilling for us, the other guys in the band, and the audiences. We were having a good time.

After the first weekend, I was paid the agreed-upon $100 a night for the three nights. $300. No problem. At the end of the second weekend, however, the road manager told me that he would have to bring the money to me on Monday morning after the bank opened. I didn't foresee any problem since everything had been okay so far. When Monday morning came, the road manager showed up at my door, as promised, with an envelope. We exchanged pleasantries for a few minutes and he left me holding the yet-unopened envelope. When I finally opened it, I discovered that the money was short. Very short. Too short to be a simple mistake. Along with the short money was a hand-scribbled note from Willie saying that I had been fired because of unsatisfactory performance and paid only the required union scale for the three nights. Orange County scale is notoriously low—$34 a night. So I ended up with $102. To top it all off, the note said that a copy of the unsatisfactory performance notice had been sent to the American Federation of Musicians, Local 47 (the Hollywood Local)—probably to cover Willie's ass if I tried to bring him up on charges. I was comprehensively screwed. I had no out but to appeal to Willie himself.

For weeks after the incident he refused to answer my calls or speak to me at all. I eventually let it go, but I will forever wonder why he led me to believe that everything was fine between us, and then stabbed me in the back like that. All I can figure is that Willie had been insulted when he had a rehearsal on a Wednesday between the first and second weekends, and I couldn't make it because of a recording session. I remembered that he had a funny look on his face when I told him that I had listened to all the tapes and looked at all of the music and knew all of the tunes. Maybe he didn't think I took his music seriously enough. Maybe I got too much attention from the audiences in Fullerton. I don't know to this day what the problem was. I know that my performance was satisfactory to everyone but him. I didn't see him again until years later when it was announced that he had terminal cancer, and we did a benefit concert for him at the Hollywood union hall. I walked up to him, shook his hand, and told him that I hoped he got better soon. He was so weak and so sick looking. I couldn't bring myself to confront a dying man.

• • •

Although I may carry myself in a way that makes me appear to be humble, in my heart I believe that I am the best or at least very good at all the things that I do as a musician. It might be my ego talking, but I have always felt that I could have been the boss in all of the situations in which I have participated. After I got over the shock of seeing Tina and the Ikettes and learned my part in the Ike Turner show, I felt like I could have done what Ike did, as well or better—not the dancing and singing, but the overall managing of the band and the music. I also know that I could have restrained myself in the face of all the sexual attention and available drugs and done a better job of running the Hank Ballard and the Midnighters show. Maybe. Even when James Brown was showing me how to direct his band, giving me bass lines and teaching me how to handle the men, I felt that he didn't really know what he was talking about. He was only able to instruct me because he was the star and the boss. In my heart, I knew that I knew better. Once I figured out what producing records was all about, I knew—even though I greatly admired the work of Bootsy and George—that I could do it more efficiently and just as well or better musically and conceptually. After their first successes, it sounds to me like they've done the same thing over and over again. Maybe I'm wrong, but I feel that if I had been given the same opportunities, I could have been a bigger success in the music business than Quincy Jones. Easy to say. If I hadda, then I woudda.

So what is it that has kept Fred Wesley Jr. from becoming a star? Should I have stayed in school at Alabama State and gotten a degree? Should I have stayed with Ike and Tina Turner and become bandleader? Was it Pete Tyler who failed to advance the career of The Mastersound or was it my insistence on sticking to our original format that prohibited the band from progressing and expanding its territory? Could I have gotten more from my James Brown experience if I had made a more strategic exit instead of running off angry and disgusted? I know that I should have made a deal in writing with the P-Funk crew from the beginning. I had the opportunity in my hands when instead I simply took what was offered and enjoyed the quick money and the ever-present fun. Is my desire to be recognized as a jazz player preventing me from getting the most from my fame today?

There are a plethora of excuses to explain why it never happened, but the main thing is that I have always lacked those star attributes. For example, I was in the house band for one of the first Soul Train Awards shows. One of the performers, a rapper, ended his act by dropping his

pants and doing the last few minutes in his jockeys. My fellow trombonist on the gig turned to me and said, "Fred, lets me and you do a two-
trombone thing where we perform in our underwear." I told him that it
sounded like a good idea, but I knew and he knew that neither one of us
was about to do anything in public in our drawers. It takes a certain kind
of person to do such a thing. I think the rapper was L.L. Cool J, who's now
an international star. The trombone player was Slide Hiede, a respected
L.A. studio musician who, like me, lacks the buffoon quality it takes to
make a star. Plus, we don't have the wardrobe or hairstyles for it.

It's hard to get your good ideas across without having the power that
comes with being rich and/or famous. When you're rich and/or famous,
your mediocre ideas are perceived as inspired creations. I've actually
seen so-called great musical geniuses like Miles Davis, Quincy Jones,
Ray Charles, and James Brown throw out the most mundane, simple,
thoughtless piece of music and inject it into the brain of a truly great, so-
called sideman like Herbie Hancock, Greg Phillinganes, Hank Crawford,
or Jimmy Nolen. What results is an everlasting work of art for which the
more visible star gets the credit. On the other hand, a true piece of musical innovation from a musician with no fame, no money, and no track
record—me, for instance—has to be fought for, proven, and re-proven
just to get a chance to be heard.

There is a thin line between creativity and tripping. The power that
comes with fame and money makes it easy to accept incoherent bab-
blings that clearly belong on the tripping side of the line as works of
art. Thank goodness for good sidemen who direct this tripping, I mean,
this creativity, into acceptable music. And thank God for my intellect,
which makes me sure of my creativity—and immune to both criticism
and praise. I have had the unique opportunity in my life to experience
both deserved and undeserved criticism, and deserved and undeserved
praise. I have been perplexed by receiving praise for things that I knew
weren't good. I also have been hurt by being criticized for things that I
knew were very good. I have grown to understand how things like hype,
fame, politics, and money greatly influence people's perception. I judge
my own work and try not to be affected by what other people think of it,
or say they think of it.

When dealing with the rich and famous, you have to remember to remain true to yourself. You have to be careful not to give the star too much
credit. Fortune and fame does not make a person smarter or more knowledgeable. It does not make a person more spiritual or more sensitive to

the world around them. In fact, all money does for a person is give them the ability to live better—wear better clothes, drive better cars, eat better food. I have had to be careful over the years not to let the impression that someone is doing better than I am influence my opinion about his or her character. I have learned that, without fame and fortune, some of these people would not have the confidence even to be in my presence. Some stars really need all the money that they can get to simply feel and/or look worthy enough to associate with normal people. Imagine Michael Jackson working at the post office, making civil-service wages, interacting with other civil-service employees. Imagine Lyle Lovett or James Brown trying to get a girl without their fame, fortune, wardrobe, and make-up.

I admit to being a jazz snob. A bebop snob, specifically. To me, the best that music can be is a medium up-tempo twelve-bar blues in F. I rate all other music according to how close it comes to that. That's why I find it hard to understand how some of our biggest artists ever got on stage in the first place.

Let's imagine that I had been the boss at King Records when James Brown came to audition. I would have said something like, "Well James, that fast-dancing thing you do with your feet is kind of interesting in a funny sort of a way, but all that loud screaming is just annoying. Did you say that you could box and play baseball? Maybe you should try one of those. I don't think you'll ever make it as a singer."

Or suppose I was the one to audition Little Richard. It would have gone like this: "Mr. Richard, or may I call you Little? First of all, I love your outfit, and your hair and make-up are simply marvelous. But I don't think that it's enough to just look good on stage. At some point you have to actually sing a song. 'Wop bop a loo bop' is not a real song. Lucille is a good title, but the lyrics don't make much sense. With your flair and those clothes, maybe you should try the ministry. You certainly have the voice for that."

How about Otis Redding: "No, Mr. Redding. You certainly have the energy, but you can't dance and you can't sing. Plus you're big and ugly—you look more like an auto mechanic than a singer."

Or Mick Jagger: "I see what you're trying to do, but you are nowhere close to singing and performing like a black person. Plus, you're so skinny and funny looking and jittery. You make me nervous just looking at you. I don't think even Tina Turner could teach you how to dance. And that guitar player you've got with you, he's on something isn't he?"

. . .

Although I don't see myself as a star, I do see myself as the best at what I do. The lack of recognition and lack of money has not weakened my belief that were it not for certain circumstances—some attributed to luck, some due to lack of knowledge, some due to laziness, some put upon me by others, some of which are part of my make-up and some of which were self-inflicted—I would be recognized as the best. I've had to put into proper perspective all the Grammys, big royalty checks, big movie deals, and big recording contracts that I didn't get, in order to arrive at the understanding that these things only measure how others view me. In my heart, I know that I am the best at all the things I do.

The point that I am trying to make is that where you head out for isn't necessarily where you end up. You can't expect to have the good fortune or blessings of a Michael Jordan or a Julio Iglesias. Even if you work tirelessly at what it is that you strive to be or do, it may not happen. And if it does happen, it may not happen the way you planned. What makes life happy and satisfying is the knowledge that life is not fair and that the circumstances that befall you may take you up or take you down. You must not be arrogant about the things that take you up. If it was in your plan, then you're lucky it turned out the way you planned it. If it was not in your plan, it's obviously lucky that it turned out in your favor.

By the same token, if circumstances take you down, you cannot become totally distraught and abandon your ethics to follow a path that seems to work for others. You must remain true to your ethics and morals and try to make the best of whatever it is that you now view as a setback. What might seem to be a setback at the moment may simply be a change of direction leading to a better plan. What may be seen as a downfall might simply be a valuable lesson that you will benefit from throughout your life.

Attempts to control life can be very depressing and lead to serious mental fatigue. All that you can be sure of is that you are not in control. Your energy is better spent moving in a positive direction. Weeping and moaning over tragedies can waste much valuable time, as does celebrating good fortune too soon and too much. Time is better spent repaying helpful loved ones and giving thanks.

If you remain true to your beliefs, your morals, your convictions, and your ethics—no matter how good or how bad it gets—in the end you will be happy, as I am, knowing that I did what I believed to be the right thing at the time, and also recognizing the reality of the times when I willfully turned away from my righteous path. I'm happy and thankful that I had the courage and the love of good people around me to pull me back onto the right path.

I believe that in the end we all get exactly what we deserve, exactly what we have worked hard enough for. To try to measure our accomplishments by another person's is an exercise in futility. Every man has to live his own life as honorably and ethically as he knows how. The way you feel about yourself is the true reward in the end.

Today I draw from the experiences of my life in the popular music world to continue to create new music. I am constantly striving to establish a sound and a style of music that is uniquely my own. This is very difficult because so much of my creativity has been incorporated into many other artists' music. One thing, for sure, nobody plays the trombone like I do. The FRED WESLEY trombone sound has yet to be successfully copied or even imitated. But convincing record companies of the marketability of that sound has been a problem. I am still hopeful that one day I'll have that big, hit CD without "AND THE" tacked on to my name.

I also am called upon regularly to counsel young people who seek to pursue music for a living. My associations with so many famous entertainers has made me somewhat of a celebrity and an expert on things pertaining specifically to the trombone and to the history of creating popular music in general. I have overcome my fear of speaking directly to people, especially kids looking for magic, and I have become adept at conducting clinics and workshops for schools, colleges, and universities around the world. I am comfortable in front of ten thousand people playing "House Party" with my band behind me but trying to explain circular breathing to ten or twelve high-school trombone players took a little getting used to. Most of my living, these days, is derived from royalties accumulated from the work I have done with and for other artists. These residuals make it possible to pick and choose when, how much, and with whom I work.

My father always told that if I kept learning from my many mistakes, I would be a wise man one day, if I lived long enough. I have learned a lot of what to do and a whole lot of what never to do by making mistakes and watching other people make mistakes. I have lived a long, interesting, and eventful life following the road down which my God-given talent has led me. I feel that the mistakes and the triumphs along the way have made me the learned, if not the wise, man that I am today. I know now that I am not a star, not a celebrity, but a musician who understands and

I can't go no further. Courtesy of Jon Mided.

supports stars. A musician who contributes to the creativity of great artists. A musician who is the necessary organizing element of the creative process. A musician who stabilizes and coordinates volatile talents into a wonderful and entertaining show. I understand my purpose, and I am proud of my role. And, in the words of a great songwriter, "I Feel Good!"

Selected Discography

With James Brown

Say It Loud, I'm Black and I'm Proud (King, 1969)
Sex Machine (King, 1970)
Hot Pants (Polydor, 1971)
Revolution of the Mind (Polydor, 1971)
There It Is (Polydor, 1972)
Get on the Good Foot (Polydor, 1972)
Black Caesar (Polydor, 1973)
Slaughter's Big Rip-Off (Polydor, 1973)
Payback (Polydor, 1974)
Hell (Polydor, 1974)
Reality (Polydor, 1975)

Also with James Brown on these generally excellent compilations and later issues (many with new material)

Doing it to Death 1970–1973 (Polydor, 1984)
In the Jungle Groove (Polydor, 1986)
Motherlode (Polydor, 1988)
Messing with the Blues (Polydor, 1991)
Star Time (Polydor, 1991)
Love Power Peace: Live at the Olympia, Paris, 1971 (Polydor, 1992)
Soul Pride: The Instrumentals (1960–69) (Polydor, 1993)
Foundations of Funk: A Brand New Bag, 1964–1969 (Polydor, 1996)
Funk Power 1970: A Brand New Thang (Polydor, 1996)
Make It Funky—The Big Payback: 1971–1975 (Polydor, 1996)

Dead on the Heavy Funk, 1975–1983 (Polydor, 1998)

Say It Live & Loud: Live in Dallas 1968 (Polygram, 1998)

Fred Wesley and the JBs

Food for Thought (People, 1972)

Doing it to Death (People, 1973)

"Damn Right I am Somebody" (People, 1974)

Breakin' Bread (as Fred & the New J.B.'s, People, 1974)

Hustle with Speed (People, 1975)

Funky Good Time: The Anthology (Polydor, 1995) collects many single-only
releases as well as key album tracks.

Other James Brown productions

Marva Whitney, *Live and Lowdown at the Apollo* (King, 1970)

Bobby Byrd, *I Need Help* (King, 1970)

Lyn Collins, *Think (About It)* (People, 1972)

Sweet Charles (Sherrill), *For Sweet People* (People, 1974)

Lyn Collins, *Check Me out If You Don't Know Me by Now* (People, 1975)

Maceo, *US!!* (People, 1974)

> ### These collections compile some of the best funky material of the period released under different artists' names often as singles or cuts of rare albums
>
> *James Brown's Funky People* (Polydor, 1986)
>
> *James Brown's Funky People, Pt. 2* (Polydor, 1988)
>
> *James Brown's Original Funky Divas* (Polydor, 1998)
>
> *James Brown's Funky People, Pt. 3* (Polygram, 2000)
>
> *. . . King Funk* (BGP, 2000)

Parliament

Mothership Connection (Casablanca, 1976)

Clones of Dr. Funkenstein (Casablanca, 1976)

Live: P-Funk Earth Tour (Casablanca, 1977)

Funkentelechy vs. the Placebo Syndrome (Casablanca, 1977)

Motor Booty Affair (Casablanca, 1978)

Trombipulation (Casablanca, 1980)

> ### Parlet
>
> *Pleasure Principle* (Casablanca, 1978)

Bootsy's Rubber Band

Stretchin' Out in Bootsy's Rubber Band (Warner Brothers, 1976)
Ahh . . . The Name Is Bootsy, Baby! (Warner Brothers, 1977)
Bootsy? Player of the Year (Warner Brothers, 1978)
This Boot Is Made for Fonk-N (Warner Brothers, 1979)
Ultra Wave (Warner Brothers, 1980)

Later Bootsy Collins albums

What's Bootsy Doin'? (Columbia, 1988)
Blasters of the Universe (Rykodisc, 1994)
Fresh Outta "P" University (WEA, 1997)

Fred Wesley and the Horny Horns

A Blow for Me, a Toot for You (Atlantic, 1977)
Say Blow by Blow Backwards (Atlantic, 1979)
The Final Blow (AEM, 1994)

George Clinton

Computer Games (Capitol, 1982)
You Shouldn't-Nuf Bit Fish (Capitol, 1983)

Bernie Worrell

All the Woo in the World (Arista, 1978)
Blacktronic Science (Gramavision, 1993)

P-Funk All Stars

Urban Dancefloor Guerillas (Uncle Jam, 1983)
Hydraulic Funk (Westbound, 1995)
Dope Dogs (Hot Hands, 1995)

With Count Basie

Milt Jackson, Count Basie & The Big Band, Volume 1 (Pablo, 1978)
Milt Jackson, Count Basie & The Big Band, Volume 2 (Pablo, 1978)

As solo artist

House Party (Curtom, 1980)
New Friends (Polygram, 1990)
Comme Ci Comme Ca (Polygram, 1991)
Swing & Be Funky (Minor Music, 1992)
Amalgamation (Minor Music, 1994)
To Someone (Good Hope, 1995)
Full Circle: From Be Bop to Hip-Hop (Cleopatra, 1999)

With Maceo Parker and Pee Wee Ellis (as the J.B. Horns)

The J.B. Horns (Mesa Blue Moon/Gramavision, 1991)

Funky Good Time/Live (Gramavision/Rhino, 1993)

I Like It Like That (Instinct, 1994)

Maceo Parker

Roots Revisited (Verve, 1990)

Mo' Roots (Verve, 1991)

Life on Planet Groove (Verve, 1992)

Southern Exposure (Verve, 1993)

Funk Overload (1998)

Without Maceo, but from the current revival

The J.B.'s Reunion, *Bring the Funk on Down* (Instinct, 1992)

**Other productions and guest appearances
(there are many more)**

Axiom Funk, *Funkcronomicon* (Axiom, 1995)

George Benson, *Good King Bad* (CTI, 1976)

Deee-Lite, *World Clique* (Elektra, 1990)

Deee-Lite, *Infinity Within* (Elektra, 1992)

Dr. John, *Creole Moon* (Blue Note, 2001)

Cecil Parker, *Chirpin'* (Hot Productions, 1994)

Soulive, *Doin' Something* (Blue Note, 2001)

James Taylor Quartet, *Creation* (Acid Jazz, 1996)

Bobby Womack, *Poet 2* (Beverly Glen, 1984)

Index

A

Abdallah, Sigidi, 235
Africa trip, 174
Akbar, Hadji, 288
Alabama State College, 36
Alexander, Earl, 229
Ali, Muhammad, 178, 180
Allen, Frederick "Flintstone," 195
Allen, Jonelle, 123
All the King's Men, 151
Al Stringer Band, 36
Amvets gig, 74
Anderson, Carl, 237
Anderson, Cat, 168
Anderson, Vickie, 154–55, 156, 285
Apollo Theater: James Brown Band, 132, 145; new James Brown Band, 142
"Are You Guilty?," 237
Armed Forces School of Music, 56–59
U.S. Army, 55–83; FW decision to join, 54; FW decision to leave, 78; gigs outside of, 66–67
Arthur, Theodore, 27, 52
Ashburn, Bennie, 82
Asher, Kenny, 149
Ashima, Rashi, 38, 41
Attitude, 191, 192; and stardom, 301

B

Baby James, 89
Ballard, Hank, 167–68, 302
Baritone horn, 11
Barnum, H. P., 247, 248
Barry, Lloyd, 245
Basie legend, 221. *See also* Count Basie Orchestra
Bass, Mickey, 48
Bass playing experience, 28
B.B. King Band, 35
Bean, Spencer, 237, 253
Bebop: first hearing, 18–19; training at Redstone, 68
Belgrave, Marcus, 192
Bell, Gary, 251, 257
Big Black, 178
Bird, Charlie, 17
Birdland, 50–51
Biviano, Lin, 216
Black, Tony, 279
Black Ceasar: music for, 163–64
Blackmon, Wes, 257
Black pride, 109
Blakey, Art, 50–51, 116
Blue Diamond Cafe, 15
Blues: FW early experimentation, 22

Bluiett, Hamiet, 58
Blunt, Dee, 123
Bobbitt, Charles, 153
Bobby Byrd tour, 286
Bobo, Willie, 304–5
Bogosh, Al (Fred Wesley Sr. band), 6
Bohemian Caverns, 48
Bongo family, 244, 253; first meeting, 177
Bonner, Butch, 237
Bonner, Joe, 270, 273, 274
Booker, 18
Booker T. Washington Junior High, 10
Bootsy's Rubber Band, 191, 201–2; Orlando gig, 203
"Bop to the Boogie," 237
Both, Bob, 152, 153
Bouchelion, Conrad, 12
Bouchelion, Fortune, 12
Bouchelion, Horace (Toby), 13
Bouchelion, Toby, 22
Boulware, Will, 296, 297
Boyce, Jesse, 245
Bradley, Kathleen, 123
Brecker, Michael, 151
Brecker, Randy, 151
Bridgewater, Cecil, 57
Brisco, 49
Broadus, Harold, 10; in Fred Wesley Sr. band, 7
Brookley Air Force Base, 4
Brooks, Patti, 234, 242
Brothers Johnson, 202
Brown, Charlie, 149
Brown, Garnett, 240
Brown, Homer, 277, 278
Brown, James, 48–49, 188, 302, 304; Brazil gig, 282; control of musicians, 154, 157–59, 161; creeds of, 102; difficulty traveling with, 169–70; effect on bands, 145; first period with, 84–114; FW decision to leave, 187; and FW's career, 150; and FW's contract, 166–67; and hair image, 162–63; and horror rehearsals, 96–101; music vs. personality, 170–71; on-stage, Orlando, 90, 91, 92–93; Phoenix gig, 280–81; second period with, 132–89; studio stops with, 110. *See also* James Brown Band
Brown, Jerold, 229
Brown, Johnny, 48
Brown, Ray, 221
Bruner, Ron, 229
Brunette, Willie, 58
Bryant, Bobby, 240
Bumpers, Alice, 36
Bunn, Jimmy, 124
Burke, Solomon, 128
Burns, Joe. *See* Poonanny and the Stormers
Butler, Frank, 124
Byrd, Bart, 285
Byrd, Bobbie, 154–55
Byrd, Bobby, 167, 283
Byrd, Carleen, 285
Byrd, Tony, 285
Byrd band, 285; tour in Europe, 286

C
Caldwell, Teddy, 74
California Club gig (Goodtimers), 128
Cameroon gig (JB Band), 175
Cannon, Dave, 273
Canyon Records: FW job with, 122
Capital Center gig (Funkadelic), 196–99
Carn, Doug, 128
Carr, Bruno, 270
Carroll, Teresa, 278, 279
Carter, Bill, 233
Carter, Ron, 151
Casablanca Records deal, 195
Caste, Nicky, 61
Castiglia, Nick, 63
Cecil Hotel jam session, 50
Central High School, 1

Chameleon, 228

Charlap, Emile, 147, 152, 211

Charles, Ray, 304. *See also* Ray Charles Band

Charles Lott Allstars, 20–21

Cheese stroke, 144

Childhood music lessons, 3

"Chocolate City," 181, 182

Chord changes, 12, 17; jazz, 270

Christianity: changing role for FW, 23–25

Cincinnati studio: James Brown Band in, 111

Clark, Brisco, 88

Clayton, John, 213, 215, 218

Clinton, George, 181, 194, 303

Club La Rue gig (Goodtimers), 127, 128

Cohen, Larry: and *Revenge*, 183

Cohn, Sonny, 215, 218

"Cold Sweat" rift, 80–81

Cole, Natalie, 202

Coleman, E.B., 10–11

Coleman, Robert, 142

Coleman Orchestra, 12; influence of, 14

College days, 28

Collins, Bootsy, 181; JB Band, 133; and Funkadelic, 194; and Parliament, 193

Collins, Lyn, 155, 173, 285; albums, 167; dancer, JB Band, 172

Collins, Phelps "Catfish," 133, 134, 195

Commodores, 80

Cooke, Don, 57

Cooke, Tony, 296

Cooper, Gary "Mudbone," 196

Copeland, Rudy, 237, 253

Cotton, Floyd, 63

"The Cotton Club" production, 277

Count Basie Orchestra, 211–27, 216, 220; Broadway gig, 211; guest artists with, 221; legend of, 221

Cranshaw, Bob, 149

Crimes, Russell, 143

Cybren, Clarence, 57

D

Dabany, Patience, 245, 254–59

Dakar, Senegal performance, 174

Dance production: JB Band, 172

Daniels, Eddie, 151

Davis, Maxwell, 121

Davis, Miles, 5, 302

Davis, Sam, 69

Dennard, Kenwood, 295

Denver trip, 265

Departures, 226–27

Destiny, 237

DeVorzon, Barry, 168

Diamond, Mark, 270

Digital music, 251–52

Disco music, 229

Dixieland: early experimentation, 22

Dixon, Al, 79

Dixon, Eric, 219

Dodgion, Jerry, 149

"Doing It to Death" album, 166, 167

Dollar, Bo, 71

Donelson, Chip, 233

Drama group (Denver), 269

Drugs, 102–4; cocaine period, 258–59; Madison Square Garden gig, 186

Drumming experience, 28; FW's Army, 56; FW's with Midnighters, 47

Drummond, Tim, 111

Duilio, Gian Carlo, 286

Dupars, Joe, 100

Dupree, Cornell, 151

Du Priest, Lewis, 237, 253

E

Earth Tour, 206–8; cancellation, 209

Edwards, Gordon, 151, 158

El Chapultepec (Denver), 274

Electra-Asylum Records, 228, 230–31

Electronic revolution, 252

The Elks Club gig, 75

Ellis, Pee Wee, 84, 111–12, 285, 288; FW assistant to, 105–6

"Enfant D'Afrique," 246
England: with James Brown Band, 139
Erie, Pennsylvania: with Ballard band, 48–49
Esquires, 34
European tour: James Brown Band, 138–41; Musikburo, 291–93
Excelsior Marching Band, 21
Ezell, Marshall, 12, 22

F
Fairmont Hotel gig (JB Band), 282
Falana, Lola, 248
Fania All-Stars, 178, 179
"Farmer's Market," 18
Farrell, Joe, 149, 151
Favored Nations management, 293
Fields, Ernie, 241–42, 244, 256, 257
Fields, Vanetta, 39
Fifty-fifth Army Band, 64
"First Family of Soul," 167
Five Points (Denver), 269
Five Royals gig, 35
"Food for Thought" album, 154
Foreman, George, 180
Foreman-Ali fight, 178
"For Sweet People from Sweet Charles" album, 152
Fortune, Eugene: in Fred Wesley Sr. band, 4
Fowlkes, Charles "Poopsie," 219
Fox, Roy, 63
Franklin, Aretha, 302
Fred Wesley and the JBs albums, 167
Freeman, Henry, 84
Fuller, Curtis, 17, 50–51
Funkadelic gigs, 196–99
Funk: and jazz, 191
"Fun Zone" TV show, 250

G
Gabon: music, 255; trip, 177, 259
Gadd, Steve, 151
Gadson, James, 240, 295

Gales, Larry, 124
Gales, Rose, 116
Gardner, June, 35
Gardner, Rick, 200
Garnell Cooper and the Kinfolk, 50
Garner, Erroll, 48
Gee, Colin, 279
Gerry Mulligan Orchestra: Birdland, 51
Gholston, Carl, 73
Ginyard, Joe, 86
Gloria, 173
Goins, Glenn, 194
Goldings, Larry, 291, 296
Gorée Island, 175
Grammy Awards performance (Basie), 223
Gray, Betty, 48
Great American Music Hall gig (Basie), 225
Green, Bill, 241
Green, Bobby, 273
Green, Freddie, 213–14, 215, 217
Green, Thurman, 116, 304
Greenlee, Bob, 287
Greer, Cortez, 69
Gresham, Willie, 36, 45
Griffith, Richard "Kush," 100, 203
Griggs, Johnny, 134
Guinea, Razz Abo, 237
Gunther, Junior, 86

H
Hampton, Michael, 197, 198
Hank Ballard gigs, 49, 51
Hank Ballard jam sessions, 44–46
Hara, John, 257
Harlem (Ballard band), 50
Harlye, Sanchez, 245
Harrell, Grady, 258
Harrell, Vern, 43
Harris, Buggs, 43
Harris, Gene, 116
Harvin, Martha, 161, 173
Haskins, Clarence "Fuzzy," 195, 199

Haywood, Leon, 116
Hedman, Bob, 63
Heinz, Charles Everett, 63
Helias, Mark, 287
Henderson, Bill, 257
The Hi Fi's, 69, 72
High, Martha, 172, 285
High school days, 17, 20, 23, 28
Hinds, Nelson, 273
Hing, Kenny, 218
Holland, Stan, 167
Holloway, Red, 116
Hollywood, 228–62
Holmes, Billy: in Fred Wesley Sr. band, 7
Holmes, Stinson, 79
"Honey and the Bees," 137
Hope Chapel AME Zion Church, 10
Horn, Shirley, 48
Horne, Lena, 304
Horton, Leonard, 18, 25
Hotpants craze, 138
"House Party" album, 236; distribution failure of, 238–39
Howard Theater, 48
Hubbard, Freddie, 50–51
Hughes, Bill, 213, 215, 218
Hull, Kenny, 88
Humphrey, Paul, 124
Hurricane Alice, 69–70, 70, 81–82

I
"If This Be a Dream," 237
Ii, David, 232, 237, 257, 304
Ike and Tina Turner Band: at The Elks, 76; FW as band director of, 42–43; gig with, 38–46
Image, 162
"I Make the Music," 237
"I'm Still on the Loose," 236
Indigo Ranch recording studio, 229
Integration, 13
Irons, "Chief" John, 17
Italy (JB Band), 141

J
Jackson, Carl, 69
Jackson, Fred, 240
Jackson, Yvonne, 287
Jaffe, Allen, 287
James Brown Band, 84–114, 87; California, 105–9; FW bandleader for, 113, 135, 145–46; horns in, 144; JB control over, 159; Orlando stage set-up, 89; second job with, 132–89
Japan tour, 287
Jazz album: marketing, 276; proposal for, 263; tunes for, 275
Jazz: and funk, 191
Jazz band gig: and Basie Orchestra period, 226; and career as music director, 151; as life goal, 12, 44, 49, 190; Mastersounds as, 80; and music snobbery, 308
The Jazz Crusaders, 178
Jazz Messengers: Birdland, 50–51
Jazztet, 17
JB Horns, 285–300, 288
Jheri Curl, 162
Joe Lewis band, 22–23
John, Bobby, 39, 117
Johnson, J.J., 15–17
Johnson, Louis, 203
Johnson, Mack, 39, 40, 231; and Ike and Tina Turner Band, 38; with JB Band, 48; Sam and the Goodtimers Band, 117
Johnson, Magic, 248
Johnson, Robert "Peanut," 196
Johnson, Walt, 250
Jones, Lloyd, 69
Jones, Richard, 85
Jordan, Louis, 237
Junior high school band, 10, 12

K
Khan, Chaka, 202
Keel, Joe, 276, 277, 278
Kellum, Alphonso "Country," 86

Kelly, Wynton, 18
Kennedy, Jayne, 247
Killian, Dwight, 279
Kim, Harry, 240, 257
King, B. B., 178
King Snake album, 286–87
Klink, John, 63
Knight, Jesse, 39
Koch, Tom, 53

L

Lamier, Ray, 63
Lancaster, Ernie, 287
Lane, Ernest, 39, 117, 128
Last Poets, 268
Latin Casino gig: James Brown Band, 137
Lawrence, Azar, 229
Lee, Christopher, 279
Lena Horne gig, 304–5
Lenhoff, Ron, 111
Levine, Stu, 180
"Let's Go Dancing," 237
"Life is Wonderful," 237
"Life on Planet Groove" album, 295
Lincoln, Abbey, 125
Liston, Melba, 125
London tour, 289
Los Angeles period, 115–31; "Slaughter's Big Rip-Off," 168
Lott, Charles, 12, 245; in Fred Wesley Sr. band, 4
Lou, Pete, 74
Lou Rawls Parade of Stars, 248
Love, Lola, 172, 173
Love, Preston, 108, 117
Love Eye Orchestra, 232–33
Lyon, France: with James Brown Band, 139

M

McGhee, Bill, 230
Maddison, Natasha, 293
Madison, Jimmy, 149, 296

Madison Square Garden gig (JB Band), 185
Marching band, 17, 31
Mardi Gras, 21
Marla's Memory Lane (Denver), 270
Marshall, Burley, 74
Marshall, Curtis, 74
Marshall Space Flight Center, 64
Martin, Hearlon, 133
Masekela, Hugh, 179
Mason, Harvey, 168
Mastersounds, 75–77
Matthews, Dave, 133, 136, 137; recording session with, 147–49
Matthews, James "Noon," 18, 22
Mayfield, Curtis, 234
Mazda, Richard, 288
McCall, James, 11
McClain, Alton, 237
McCord, Mrs. Clayton, 35
McCracken, Hugh, 151
McCray, Frank, 69
McDonald, Ralph, 159
McFee, John T., 154
Metropolitan AME Church, 2
Meyer, Deithart, 292
Meyner, Stephan, 286, 289; influence of, 300
Middleton, Greg, 246, 257
Midnighters, 47
Miles, Butch, 218
Miller, Frank, 33
Minger, Pete, 218
Minor, Dee, 277
Minton's Playhouse, 51
Mizell, Dr. Don, 228
"Moanin'," 22
Mobile, Alabama, 1
Mobile County Training School, 1, 5, 9
Modern jazz, 51
The Moderns, 20
Momie-O. *See* Anderson, Vickie
Monk, Thelonius, 302
Monkees tour, 123

Montgomery, Robbie, 39
Morgan, John, 142
Morris, Joe, 12, 22; in Fred Wesley Sr.
  band, 5
Morris, Leo, 48
Mosson, Cordell "Boogie," 181
Mothership Connection tour, 205
Muhammad, Idris, 48
Multiple-drummer concept: James
  Brown Band, 89
Multitrack recording, 150
Munich gig (JB Horns), 290
Music, 109, 141; business and politics,
  235; trends and changes, 250–51
Musikburo booking agency, 290

N
NAACP Image Awards ceremony, 247
Nashville studio: "Enfant D'Afrique,"
  246
Navy SEALS, 56
Ndugu, 168
Nelson, Rev. David, 268, 269
New Jersey gig (Basie), 213
Newman, Ira, 250
New Orleans gig (Basie), 226
New York City gig (Ballard), 49
Nobles, Willie, 23
Nolen, Jimmy, 86, 152
Norman, Ann, 85
Norwood, Thomas "Nose," 39, 117

O
Oakley, Ike, 142
Odom, Randolph, 53
Odum, Bernard (Buddy), 53, 86–94
Odum, Jabo, 86–94
Okstel, Henry, 63
Ondo, Jimmy, 177, 245
Orange, Walter "Clyde," 82
Organization of African Unity (OAU),
  245
Orlando, Florida: James Brown band
  gig, 86–94

Owens, Ann, 10
Oxman, Keith, 270

P
Pacheco, Johnny, 179
Page, La Wanda, 127
Panting, Janie, 1–3, 3, 4; FW at home
  with, 52
Parker, Jimmy, 143
Parker, Maceo, 192, 294; All the King's
  Men Band, 151; and Bootsy's Rubber
  Band, 191; Europe tour, 285, 288; and
  JB Band, 87, 280; and rehearsals, 297;
  returns to JB Band, 165–67
Parker, Melvin, 295
Parks, Benny, 233, 255
Parks, Perry, 62
Parliament/Funkadelic, 182, 194; horn
  arrangements for, 191
Patterson, Pat, 45
Payne, Artee "Duke," 18, 19, 20
Payne, Jim, 286, 287
Payne, Marion "Mole Man," 53
Pedersen, Alf, 64
People label, 168
Pfankuch, Gert, 290
P-Funk, 196–99
P-Funk Earth Tour, 206–8
Phillips, Joe, 57
Phoenix gig (James Brown), 280–81
Phrasing (Basie), 214, 215
Piano study: childhood, 9
Pinckney, St. Clair, 86, 108
Pitts, Trudy, 51
Pizazz Records: FW producing for,
  233–35
Plater, Bobby, 215, 219
Playing by ear, 270
Pleasant, Ed, 233
Pointer Sisters, 178
Pollock, Danny, 69
Polydor Records, 168, 169
Poonanny and the Stormers, 69–72
Porsche, Veronica, 179

Portis, Ozzie, 53
Powell, Benny and Petsy, 168
Powell, Seldon, 149, 151
Pratt, Edward, 22, 115
Pratt Band, 18; early jam sessions with, 26–27
Preston, Jerry, 285, 297
Prince, 250
"Process" hair, 162
Producing (Hollywood), 228–31
Prysock, Red, 5
Pullen, Don, 290
Puricelli, Marc, 287

R

Racial tension, 68, 69
Ragin, Hugh, 277
Rainey, Chuck, 168
Ranson, James, 67
"Rare groove" movement (Europe), 283
Rasbury, Levi, 84
Rauk, Dyron, 63
Rawls-Sinatra duet, 249
Ray, Charlie, 74
Ray, Danny, 86
Ray Charles Band, 35, 36, 48, 232
Rebillot, Pat, 151
Recording sessions: Dabany dance group, 254–59; Denver (JB Horns), 288; Hollywood-style, 242–44; James Brown Band, 106–8, 147; James Brown style of, 133; Kansas cave, 159; Maceo Parker, 165; Parliament/Funkadelic, 200–201; payment for, 159–60; preeminence of, 169; "Roots Revisited" album, 290; "Soul Power," 137; Sun Recording Studio, 42; "Sweet Charles," 152
Recovery from addiction, 264–84
Redstone Arsenal, Alabama, 59–82
Reed, Waymon, 84, 100, 103–5, 108, 215, 218; and Bootsy's Rubber Band, 191; leaves Basie orchestra, 220

Revenge, 183
Rhodes, Sam, 39, 117
The Rhythmic Sensations, 8; end of, 12
Rice, Robert, 78
Richardson, Al, 230
Richardson, Maurice, 67
Robinson, Dutch, 234
Robinson, Marvin, 28
Rodriquez, Freddy, 274
Romero-Sepulveda, Esteban, 62, 63
"Roots Revisited" album, 290
Rowland, Dennis, 213, 215
Rubber Band. *See* Bootsy's Rubber Band

S

Sam and the Goodtimers, 117, 120
Sam Cooke Band, 35
Sample, Joe, 168
Sanders, Gertrude, 85, 86
Scoring music, 148, 149, 150
Scotton, Johnny, 167
Seals, James: in Fred Wesley Sr. band, 5
Seals, Jimmy, 13
Segregation: in '50s bands, 6
Seiler, Clyde, 64
Senegal trip, 174
Sharpe, Bobby, 27
Sheldon, Jim, 116
Sherrell, Sweet Charles, 152, 172
Shider, Garry, 181, 194
Shrine Auditorium gig (L.A.), 108
Sideman: ordeal of, 304, 306
Sightreading, 31, 57
Sigler, Bunny, 234, 242
Silver, Horace, 17
Silvers, Leon, Sr., 123
Sinatra, Frank, 302
Sir Lady Java, 127
Sister Sledge, 178
Skillet and Leroy, 127
Slaughter's Big Rip-Off, 168
Smith, Charlie, 226
Smith, Joe, 230

Smith, Louis "Smitty," 31

Smith, Nolan, 218; Count Basie Orchestra, 216; Love Eye Orchestra, 233; recording session with, 257; V. Burch recording session, 240

Smith, Ron, 230

Soloff, Lew, 149, 151

Solomon, Clifford, 117, 118, 121

S.O.S. Band, 236; FW arrangements for, 235

Soul'd Out Club gig, 117–21, 123

"Soul of a Black Man" single, 167

"Soul Power" instrumental, 167

Soul Twins, 172

Sound checks, 297–98

Sound Ideas studio, 153; producing and arranging gigs from, 246

The Sounds, 12

Speight, Bruno, 285, 294, 297

The Spinners, 178

Spratley, Michael, 230

Stallings, Henry, 88

Stamm, Marvin, 149

Stanfield, Edwin, 12; in Fred Wesley Sr. band, 5

Stanfield, Hubert "Hawk": in Fred Wesley Sr. band, 5

Stanton, Michael, 229

Star attributes, 301–12

Staton, Dakota, 124

Stewart, Bill, 290, 294

Stitt, Sonny, 17

Stubblefield, Clyde, 86

Swanson, Earl, 58

Sweeny, Vonny, 233

"Sweet Charles," 152

"Sweet Loneliness," 151

The Sweet Souls, 126

Synthesized instrumentation, 250

T

Taylor, Clarence, 257, 260

Taylor, Delbert, 229, 234, 257

Technique training, 31, 57

Tennessee State University, 29–30

Tha Do, 27, 28, 29

"The Payback" album, 184

Thomas, Henry, 257

Thomas, Jamal, 296, 297

Thomas, Jimmy, 39

Thompson, Tommy, 11, 13

Top Men's Store, 5

Touring, 101–101, 103, 145, 216

Trends in music, 250–51

Trombone: Armed Forces School of Music, 57; early band experience, 11, 13; first impressions, 6, 7, 9; recovery period, 267

Trombone players: Henry Freeman, 6; Robert Petty, 6

Trumpet playing, 10

Trumpets (JB Band), 144

Trussell: production for, 230–31

Tuluca Lake studio gig, 252

Turner, Danny, 219

Turner, Ike. See Ike and Tina Turner Band

TV opportunity, 250

Tyler, Pete, 82

Tyson-Givens meeting, 247

U

United Sound studio (Detroit), 192–93

"Us" album, 166

V

Vantrees, Earnest, 68

The Variations, 167

Vaughan, Sarah, 220

W

Waddy, Frank "Kash," 195

Walker, Ken, 274

Wallace, Billy, 274

Wally Roker's Showcase gig, 124–27

Walton, Ted, 69

Wanzo, Melvin, 213, 215, 218

Warrick, Marvin, 41

Washington, D.C. gig (Funkadelic), 196–99
Washington, Dinah, 18
"Watermelon Man," 22
Waters, Richard, 50
Watkins, Lynn, 273
Watts, Ernie, 168, 250
Watts 103rd Street Band, 240
Weaver, George, 22
Weaver, Jerry, 122
Webb, Melvin, 156, 200, 237, 253
Webb, Willie "Jitterbug," 117
Wesley, Fred, Jr., 16, 108, 121, 153, 256, 261, 269, 272, 288, 297; addiction period, 258–62; as arranger and producer, 147–49; Basie solos, 222; effects of industry rejection on, 239; and electronic revolution, 251–52; fired by JB, 160; first James Brown meeting, 94; fronting the band, 154; Funky Fred, 28; illness, after Ballard gig, 52; and JB's control, 157–58; leads Mastersounds, 75–77, 79–82; leaves James Brown, 187–89; leaves JB Horns, 298–99; marriage to Gertie Lee Young, 73; move to L.A., 115; as music director, 1973–75, 167; non-music job-hunting, 83; P-Funk era closes, 209–10; philosophy of life, 306–12; recovery period, 265–84; restarts producing career, 226; Rubber Band contract, 204, 208; solo career, Hollywood, 232, 236–37; temptation to leave JB Band, 171–75, 180, 182, 184
Wesley, Fred, Sr., 1, 2, 12; big-band rehearsals, 4; marriage, 3; as piano player, 8
Wesley, Ron (brother), 3, 264; engineers FW recovery, 263–84

West Coast gigs, 109
Weyl, Andy, 272
White, Costello, 15
Whitney, Marva, 88, 91, 285
Whitten family, 289
Williams, Buster, Jr., 191–92
Williams, Earl, 69
Williams, Eddie, 125
Williams, Jo Jo, 277
Williams, L.D., 152
Williams, Meza "Chappie," 13; in Fred Wesley Sr. band, 5
Williams, Rev. and Mrs. T.E., Sr., 14
Williams, Steve, 255, 256
Williams, Thaddeus E., 16
Wilson, Dennis, 213, 218
Winding, Kai, 17
Withers, Bill, 178
Worrell, Bernie, 181, 194
Wright, Benjamin, 240
Writing music, 148, 149; for *Black Ceasar*, 164–65

X
Xylophone, 28

Y
Yankovich, Wierd Al, 250
Yarboro, Nat, 274
York, Marshall, 35
York Street Cafe gig (Denver), 279–80
Young, Gertie Lee, 73
Young, Snooky, 168

Z
Zaire Music Festival trip, 178
Zale, Tom, 62, 63
Zimmerman, Jim, 57

Fred Wesley Jr. is a legendary soul, funk, and jazz trombone player and arranger. Best known for his work as the arranger for the JBs—James Brown's band of the late '60s and early '70s—Wesley also organized the horn sections for the funk groups led by George Clinton and Bootsy Collins: Parliament, Funkadelic, and Bootsy's Rubber Band. In addition to his major role in records by James Brown and Parliament/Funkadelic, Wesley recorded albums as Fred Wesley and the JBs, Fred Wesley and the Horny Horns, and under his own name.

Rickey Vincent is the author of *Funk: The Music, the People, and the Rhythm of The One* (St. Martin's, 1996). He could see *Hit Me, Fred* coming when Fred Wesley and the JBs played "Soul Train" in 1973.

• • •

Library of Congress has cataloged the hardcover as follows:
Wesley, Fred, Jr.
Hit me, Fred : recollections of a sideman / Fred Wesley Jr.
p. cm.
Includes discography and index.
ISBN 0-8223-2909-3 (cloth : alk. paper)
1. Wesley, Fred.   2. Trombonists—United States—Biography.
3. Funk musicians—United States—Biography.   I. Title.
ML419.W455 A3   2002
781.643'092—dc21   2001008259